# LEISURE SERVICES MANAGEMENT

## SECOND EDITION

Amy R. Hurd, PhD
Illinois State University

Robert J. Barcelona, PhD
University of New Hampshire

Jo An M. Zimmermann, PhD
Texas State University

Janet Ready, MA
Langara College

HUMAN KINETICS

**Library of Congress Cataloging-in-Publication Data**

Names: Hurd, Amy R., author.
Title: Leisure services management / Amy R. Hurd, Robert J. Barcelona, JoAn
M. Zimmermann, Janet Ready.
Description: Second Edition. | Champaign, Illinois : Human Kinetics, [2020] |
 Previous edition: 2008. | Includes bibliographical references and index. |
 Identifiers: LCCN 2018017726 (print) | LCCN 2018026005 (ebook) | ISBN
 9781492557128 (e-book) | ISBN 9781492557111 (print)
Subjects: LCSH: Recreation—Management. | Public relations.
Classification: LCC GV181.5 (ebook) | LCC GV181.5 H87 2019 (print) | DDC
 790.06/9—dc23
LC record available at https://lccn.loc.gov/2018017726

ISBN: 978-1-4925-5711-1 (print)

The web addresses cited in this text were current as of August 2018, unless otherwise noted.

Acquisitions Editor: Amy N. Tocco
Developmental Editor: Melissa J. Zavala
Indexer: Nan N. Badgett
Permissions Manager: Dalene Reeder
Graphic Designer: Joe Buck
Cover Designer: Keri Evans
Cover Design Associate: Susan Rothermel Allen
Photographs (interior): ©Human Kinetics, unless otherwise noted
Photo Asset Manager: Laura Fitch
Photo Production Manager: Jason Allen
Senior Art Manager: Kelly Hendren
Illustrations: ©Human Kinetics, unless otherwise noted
Production: Westchester Publishing Services
Printer: Sheridan Books

Printed in the United States of America

10 9 8 7 6 5 4 3 2 1

The paper in this book is certified under a sustainable forestry program.

**Human Kinetics**
P.O. Box 5076
Champaign, IL 61825-5076
Website: www.HumanKinetics.com

In the United States, email info@hkusa.com or call 800-747-4457.
In Canada, email info@hkcanada.com.
In the United Kingdom/Europe, email hk@hkeurope.com.

For information about Human Kinetics' coverage in other areas of the world,
please visit our website: **www.HumanKinetics.com**                    E7120

# Contents

Preface   vii

Acknowledgments   xi

Photo Credits   xiii

## 1  Competency-Based Management and Leadership   1

What Is Management? . . . . . . . . . . . . . . . . . . . . . . . . . . . . . . . . 3
Leadership Theories . . . . . . . . . . . . . . . . . . . . . . . . . . . . . . . . . 6
Management Theories. . . . . . . . . . . . . . . . . . . . . . . . . . . . . . . 11
Management Trends . . . . . . . . . . . . . . . . . . . . . . . . . . . . . . . . 20
Our Competency-Based Approach. . . . . . . . . . . . . . . . . . . . . . 25
Conclusion . . . . . . . . . . . . . . . . . . . . . . . . . . . . . . . . . . . . . . . 29

## 2  Leisure Services Managers   31

Levels and Functions of Managers. . . . . . . . . . . . . . . . . . . . . . 33
Resources to Manage . . . . . . . . . . . . . . . . . . . . . . . . . . . . . . . 37
Career Progression of Managers . . . . . . . . . . . . . . . . . . . . . . . 38
Management Drivers. . . . . . . . . . . . . . . . . . . . . . . . . . . . . . . . 39
Efficiency and Effectiveness . . . . . . . . . . . . . . . . . . . . . . . . . . 46
Critical Management Issues. . . . . . . . . . . . . . . . . . . . . . . . . . . 48
Conclusion . . . . . . . . . . . . . . . . . . . . . . . . . . . . . . . . . . . . . . . 51

## 3  Legal Foundations for Managers   53

Current Legal Issues and Trends . . . . . . . . . . . . . . . . . . . . . . . 55
Civil and Criminal Law . . . . . . . . . . . . . . . . . . . . . . . . . . . . . . 56
Legislation . . . . . . . . . . . . . . . . . . . . . . . . . . . . . . . . . . . . . . . 64
Risk Management . . . . . . . . . . . . . . . . . . . . . . . . . . . . . . . . . . 65
Legal Issues in Employment . . . . . . . . . . . . . . . . . . . . . . . . . . 67
Conclusion . . . . . . . . . . . . . . . . . . . . . . . . . . . . . . . . . . . . . . . 74

## 4  Organizational Structure   77

Three Sectors . . . . . . . . . . . . . . . . . . . . . . . . . . . . . . . . . . . . . 79
Organizational Structure, Design, and Culture. . . . . . . . . . . . . 88
Working with Boards. . . . . . . . . . . . . . . . . . . . . . . . . . . . . . . . 96
Form of Government and Organizational Structure and Design . . . . . . . . 103
Conclusion . . . . . . . . . . . . . . . . . . . . . . . . . . . . . . . . . . . . . . 104

## 5   Coordination of Resources, Programs, and Services   107

Internal Organizational Coordination . . . . . . . . . . . . . . . . . . . . . . . . . . . . . . . 109
External Organizational Coordination . . . . . . . . . . . . . . . . . . . . . . . . . . . . . . 120
Conclusion . . . . . . . . . . . . . . . . . . . . . . . . . . . . . . . . . . . . . . . . . . . . . . . . . 126

## 6   Planning and Decision Making   129

Planning . . . . . . . . . . . . . . . . . . . . . . . . . . . . . . . . . . . . . . . . . . . . . . . . . . .131
Problem Solving and Decision Making. . . . . . . . . . . . . . . . . . . . . . . . . . . . . 147
Ethical Decision Making . . . . . . . . . . . . . . . . . . . . . . . . . . . . . . . . . . . . . . . 150
Conclusion . . . . . . . . . . . . . . . . . . . . . . . . . . . . . . . . . . . . . . . . . . . . . . . . . 152

## 7   Marketing and Public Relations   155

Definition and History of Marketing . . . . . . . . . . . . . . . . . . . . . . . . . . . . . . 157
Market Segmentation and Target Marketing . . . . . . . . . . . . . . . . . . . . . . . . 158
Marketing Mix. . . . . . . . . . . . . . . . . . . . . . . . . . . . . . . . . . . . . . . . . . . . . . . 164
Social Media . . . . . . . . . . . . . . . . . . . . . . . . . . . . . . . . . . . . . . . . . . . . . . . . 181
Conclusion . . . . . . . . . . . . . . . . . . . . . . . . . . . . . . . . . . . . . . . . . . . . . . . . . 183

## 8   Communication and Customers   185

Functions of Communication. . . . . . . . . . . . . . . . . . . . . . . . . . . . . . . . . . . . 187
Communication Process . . . . . . . . . . . . . . . . . . . . . . . . . . . . . . . . . . . . . . . 188
Communication Breakdowns. . . . . . . . . . . . . . . . . . . . . . . . . . . . . . . . . . . . 189
Strategic Approach to Communication . . . . . . . . . . . . . . . . . . . . . . . . . . . . 190
Internal Communication . . . . . . . . . . . . . . . . . . . . . . . . . . . . . . . . . . . . . . . 193
External Communication. . . . . . . . . . . . . . . . . . . . . . . . . . . . . . . . . . . . . . . 196
Conclusion . . . . . . . . . . . . . . . . . . . . . . . . . . . . . . . . . . . . . . . . . . . . . . . . . 206

## 9   Personnel Procedures and Practices   209

Human Resources Perspectives. . . . . . . . . . . . . . . . . . . . . . . . . . . . . . . . . . .211
Personnel Planning . . . . . . . . . . . . . . . . . . . . . . . . . . . . . . . . . . . . . . . . . . .213
Personnel Processes . . . . . . . . . . . . . . . . . . . . . . . . . . . . . . . . . . . . . . . . . . 220
Managing Volunteers . . . . . . . . . . . . . . . . . . . . . . . . . . . . . . . . . . . . . . . . . 243
Conclusion . . . . . . . . . . . . . . . . . . . . . . . . . . . . . . . . . . . . . . . . . . . . . . . . . 246

## 10   Motivation, Rewards, and Discipline   249

Employee Engagement and Development . . . . . . . . . . . . . . . . . . . . . . . . . . 251
Motivation . . . . . . . . . . . . . . . . . . . . . . . . . . . . . . . . . . . . . . . . . . . . . . . . . 255
Employee Recognition. . . . . . . . . . . . . . . . . . . . . . . . . . . . . . . . . . . . . . . . . 258
Rewarding Volunteers. . . . . . . . . . . . . . . . . . . . . . . . . . . . . . . . . . . . . . . . . 265
Rewarding Yourself. . . . . . . . . . . . . . . . . . . . . . . . . . . . . . . . . . . . . . . . . . . 265
Discipline . . . . . . . . . . . . . . . . . . . . . . . . . . . . . . . . . . . . . . . . . . . . . . . . . . 267
Conclusion . . . . . . . . . . . . . . . . . . . . . . . . . . . . . . . . . . . . . . . . . . . . . . . . . 271

## 11 Sources and Methods of Financing — 273

Sources of Revenue. . . . . . . . . . . . . . . . . . . . . . . . . . . . . . . . . . . . . . . . 275
Expenditures . . . . . . . . . . . . . . . . . . . . . . . . . . . . . . . . . . . . . . . . . . . . 286
Pricing . . . . . . . . . . . . . . . . . . . . . . . . . . . . . . . . . . . . . . . . . . . . . . . . . 289
Pricing Trends and Issues . . . . . . . . . . . . . . . . . . . . . . . . . . . . . . . . . . . 296
Conclusion . . . . . . . . . . . . . . . . . . . . . . . . . . . . . . . . . . . . . . . . . . . . . . 299

## 12 Budgets and Financial Cost Analysis — 301

Defining Budgets . . . . . . . . . . . . . . . . . . . . . . . . . . . . . . . . . . . . . . . . . 303
Budget Cycle. . . . . . . . . . . . . . . . . . . . . . . . . . . . . . . . . . . . . . . . . . . . . 304
Cutback Management . . . . . . . . . . . . . . . . . . . . . . . . . . . . . . . . . . . . . . 306
Types of Budgets . . . . . . . . . . . . . . . . . . . . . . . . . . . . . . . . . . . . . . . . . 308
Approaches to Budgeting . . . . . . . . . . . . . . . . . . . . . . . . . . . . . . . . . . . 316
Budget Implementation. . . . . . . . . . . . . . . . . . . . . . . . . . . . . . . . . . . . . 319
Financial Analysis and Reporting. . . . . . . . . . . . . . . . . . . . . . . . . . . . . . 322
Conclusion . . . . . . . . . . . . . . . . . . . . . . . . . . . . . . . . . . . . . . . . . . . . . . 328

## 13 Evaluation — 331

Why Evaluate?. . . . . . . . . . . . . . . . . . . . . . . . . . . . . . . . . . . . . . . . . . . . 333
Performance Measurement . . . . . . . . . . . . . . . . . . . . . . . . . . . . . . . . . . 335
How to Evaluate . . . . . . . . . . . . . . . . . . . . . . . . . . . . . . . . . . . . . . . . . . 338
Selecting Evaluation Participants. . . . . . . . . . . . . . . . . . . . . . . . . . . . . . 349
Best Practices and Benchmarking . . . . . . . . . . . . . . . . . . . . . . . . . . . . . 354
Conclusion . . . . . . . . . . . . . . . . . . . . . . . . . . . . . . . . . . . . . . . . . . . . . . 356

Appendix A  Certified Park and Recreation Professional (CPRP) Competencies   357
Appendix B  One-Page Strategic Plan, City of Fairfax, Virginia   361
References and Resources   362
Index   371
About the Authors   377

# Preface

The leisure services profession is a dynamic and ever-changing field. It is an exciting time to pursue a degree in this service-oriented industry. The first edition of this text came out in 2008. Since then, we have seen a lot of changes in the field. The changes include such things as increased fiscal accountability and entrepreneurship, staff development and succession planning to prepare staff for higher level positions with more challenges and responsibilities, and more creative partnerships that enhance the recreation opportunities and decrease duplication of services. All of these and the many other changes in the profession require managers who are highly skilled. The purpose of this textbook is to prepare you to be a manager in the field. Whether you plan to pursue a career in commercial recreation, work in a public agency, or be a part of the nonprofit sector, you will need management skills to be successful.

We hope you will look at each chapter as a building block to your educational foundation. We will provide real-life examples of concepts so that readers make the connection to the profession. It is our desire that by the end of the book you will understand what a manager does and how this work affects the agency, customer, and profession. We hope you will feel more ready to accept the challenges you will face as a manager and have some foresight into what to expect in your first job. To help with this, we showcase young professionals who were in your shoes as students just a few years ago. They will talk about their jobs—both the challenges and what makes them want to come to work every day.

## SCOPE OF THE TEXT

The contents of the book are competency driven. Research has determined what knowledge, skills, and abilities entry-level practitioners need in order to be successful on the job. This text presents those competencies in such a way that an effective manager can emerge. The book has two primary audiences. First, the book is aimed at junior and senior level undergraduates who have some experience in the field. It is our hope that you will read each chapter and apply your own experiences to the content and activities to better understand management in this dynamic profession. Second, graduate students will gain an understanding of management, and the ancillary materials include research in the field so that these students can study theory to practice more in depth. You will be able to see where our current knowledge of management lies and what the future holds.

*Leisure Services Management* begins by building a foundation of what management is and where it has been historically and conceptually. It then builds on this knowledge by providing a legal foundation for managers. Next, it moves to the framework of the organization from staff structure to coordination of resources and planning. The remainder of the text focus on specific skill areas managers need, such as marketing, communication, human resources management, financial management, and evaluation.

# FEATURES AND BENEFITS

There are several beneficial features of the second edition. They include:

- This text centers on a competency-based approach to management. It identifies the competencies needed for entry-level professionals, and you can measure your own skills against these competencies.
- Many of the chapters have a new author to broaden the perspectives of each chapter.
- Throughout the book there are updated snapshots of professionals in the field giving early career advice on management.
- A concerted effort is made to provide new examples from all three sectors—public, nonprofit, and commercial. This will give readers a broad perspective of parks and recreation and encompass tourism, sport, recreation therapy, outdoor recreation, and more.
- Leisure is an international concept and one in which employees need to think globally. Chapters will feature international examples, especially from Canada and Australia.

# STUDENT RESOURCES

*Leisure Services Management* also includes a web study guide. A unique feature about the *Leisure Services Management* second edition is that the web study guide was designed to provide both undergraduate and graduate students with learning experiences to facilitate learning. It will help you build your knowledge of the content area, apply the information learned to your current work environment or your future internship, and help prepare you for future certifications such as the Certified Park and Recreation Professional.

This resource includes:

- An electronic version of the competency scorecard, allowing you to print a copy and fill it in.
- An overview of the key concepts covered by each chapter.
- New graduate and undergraduate case studies where you can apply chapter concepts.
- New learning activities to promote student involvement and application of concepts presented in the book.
- Learning resources such as glossary terms, keywords, learning outcomes, and web links for more information on a topic.

# INSTRUCTOR RESOURCES

The second edition includes several fully updated instructor resources. An instructor guide offers a sample syllabus and chapter outlines. The case studies found in the web study guide are included, as well as additional case studies the instructor may use to supplement class discussion. Ideas for assignments, research projects, and class discussion topics are included for each chapter. The test package offers over 270 questions. A set of chapter quizzes containing over 100 questions is new to the edition. Instructors may use these test and quiz questions as they appear or choose specific questions to create customized tests. The presentation package provides PowerPoint slides covering the most important concepts in the chapters.

All student and instructor resources can be found at www.HumanKinetics.com /LeisureServicesManagement.

It is hoped that by the end of the journey through *Leisure Services Management*, you will feel prepared to enter the workforce and understand the intricacies of management, be able to build on your existing skills, and understand what additional experiences you need to close that competency gap.

# Acknowledgments

A textbook is quite an undertaking and one that is challenging, frustrating, rewarding, and time consuming, but the end result is worth it. We would like to thank our institutions: Illinois State University, University of New Hampshire, Texas State University, and Langara College.

This text would not be possible without the tireless efforts of the Human Kinetics staff. They were a terrific group to work with, and we appreciate them immensely: Gayle Kassing, Amy Tocco, Melissa Zavala, and many others.

Each of us had our own support system, inspiration, and mentors.

Thank you to my family: Dr. Deb Garrahy and Mike and Linda Hurd. You have walked this parks and recreation journey with me and never faltered in your support. My appreciation to you is immeasurable.

Thank you to the managers who have had to wrangle me, inspired me, taught me, and mentored me through their own actions, advice, and patience: Sara Hensley, Robert F. Toalson, Dr. Alan Lacy, Dr. John Baur, Dr. Jonathan Rosenthal, and Dr. Jan Murphy. You each have positively influenced my career along the way, whether you knew it or not. Thank you!

–Amy Hurd

To my wife Heather and to my five awesome children—Madeline, Nathan, Emily, Dominic, and Lucy.

To all of the park, recreation, event, and sport managers in New Hampshire, Vermont, Maine, Massachusetts, North Carolina, and South Carolina—I've always been a "reluctant academic" and my work with all of you over the years has kept me grounded in reality.

Finally, to all of my students at UNH—you are the future of the field. My contributions to this book are for all of you.

–Bob Barcelona

Thank you to all the people who helped teach and inspire me to keep learning: Dad, Carol, Dr. Frank Lupton, Dr. Nick DiGrino, Jamie Sabbach, and too many others to list. A special thanks to Eduardo Somoza for his unwavering support as I pursue my dreams!

–Jo An Zimmermann

To the managers and directors of recreation organizations who met with me, emailed me, had spontaneous conversations, and coordinated working groups to generously share their knowledge and experience—thank you. You helped the theory in these chapters come alive. I am inspired by your commitment to growing people. I am grateful for my colleagues in the recreation studies department at Langara College who walk the talk. And a very special thank you to my family—Craig, Claire, Kate, and Murphy—for supporting my work and keeping it real.

–Janet Ready

# Photo Credits

Photo on page xiv: ©SolStock/Getty Images

Photo on page 2: ©Alexis Moreno

Photo on page 30: ©Hero Images/Getty Images

Photo on page 32: Courtesy of Margaret Donnelly

Photo on page 52: © Wavebreakmedia/Getty Images

Photo on page 54: Courtesy of Aly Truesdale. Special Olympics Virginia.

Photo on page 76: ©Sean M. Haffey/Getty Images

Photo on page 78: Courtesy of USA Rugby

Photo on page 106: ©Claus Andersen/Getty Images for the Invictus Games Foundation

Photo on page 108: Courtesy of Jill Gravink, MS., CRTS/L

Photo on page 128: ©Darryl Leniuk/The Image Bank/Getty Images

Photo on page 130: Courtesy of Stacie Anaya

Photo on page 154: ©Getty Images/Mikolette

Photo on page 156: Courtesy of David Genty

Photo on page 184: ©Lance King/Getty Images

Photo on page 186: Courtesy of Kate McAfee

Photo on page 208: ©Greg Vaughn/VW PICS/UIG via Getty Images

Photo on page 210: Courtesy of Sarah Moore

Photo on page 248: ©Human Kinetics

Photo on page 250: Courtesy of Heather Nivison

Photo on page 272: © Witold Skrypczak/Lonely Planet Images/Getty Images

Photo on page 274: Courtesy of Joshua Chikuse

Photo on page 300: ©Kali9/iStock/Getty Images

Photo on page 302: Taken by Mary Connell in her employment capacity at the Woodlands Township

Photo on page 330: ©James + Courtney Forte/Getty Images

Photo on page 332: Courtesy of Jaimie Brown

Photo on page 377: Courtesy of Illinois State University

Photo on page 377: Courtesy of University of New Hampshire

Photo on page 378: ©Jo An Zimmermann

Photo on page 378: Courtesy of Langara College

# Competency-Based Management and Leadership

## Learning Outcomes

- Summarize the model for effective performance.
- Understand competency-based management.
- Describe competencies needed by entry-level parks and recreation managers.
- Compare and contrast leadership and management.
- Develop knowledge of how management theory has evolved since the Industrial Revolution.

## Key Terms

management, competencies, leadership, empirical, learning organizations, outcomes-based management, strategic management, competency-based management, characteristics

## Competency Check

Refer to table 1.6 to see how you assessed these related competencies.

3. Possess knowledge of management principles.

29. Have leadership skills and abilities.

30. Be able to work in a team.

## A Day in the Life

No day in parks and recreation is ever ordinary. I usually start my day by checking emails from home—this gives me an idea of where my day might be headed. On any given day, I am working on such things as preparing the sailing camp for inclement weather approaching in the afternoon, providing recreation programming through local partnerships and community organizations, supervising the Youth Service Initiative program, and reviewing survey feedback from parents about our new partnership with the local school district's summer school program. In order to be a successful instructor, coordinator, or supervisor within the field of parks and recreation, you must be adaptable, flexible, have great communication skills, and the ability to problem-solve within any setting. From weather concerns to engagements with parents or public officials, you never know what's going to come up!

Alexis Moreno, MSL, CPRP
Supervisor, Youth and Families
Boulder Parks and Recreation
Boulder, Colorado

The nature of the leisure services profession has changed since its inception many years ago. In the past, it had a simple, yet important, social service function, with a focus on activities, playgrounds, and public good. Today, agencies provide these things and more, including a wide breadth of services, a multitude of facilities, and revenue-generating entities. Many leisure services agencies have grown in the number of staff needed to deliver services and the required budget size. These changes and the evolution of the leisure services profession require a solid foundation in management principles for staff and agencies to be successful.

## WHAT IS MANAGEMENT?

The term **management** has many uses. It has been defined in a number of ways because it is a broad area and an integral part of all organizations. Management can be a group of people who direct employees and resources in an organization, such as the arts and culture management team. Management can refer to the level in the organization that an employee falls within, such as middle or frontline management. It can be the process of reaching organizational goals by working with others. It can also be a discipline with its own body of knowledge, principles, concepts, and theories. Management is the critical centerpiece of any agency regardless of whether it is a public park and recreation department, a facility on a military base, a nonprofit agency such as the Boys and Girls Clubs, or a commercial agency such as Hilton Head Resort. Management is the driving force that ensures tasks get done correctly.

**management—** Process of coordinating and integrating resources in order to effectively and efficiently achieve organizational goals and objectives.

For the purpose of this text, *management* is defined as the process of coordinating and integrating resources in order to effectively and efficiently achieve organizational goals and objectives (figure 1.1). These resources include human, financial, physical, and information and technology resources, which are discussed in detail throughout the text.

Given this definition of management, logic tells us that managers are people who manage—they motivate others to get things done. Imagine a company that has no managers. No one is organizing the tasks to be done, and no one is accountable to anyone else in the organization. The result is chaos, which does not lead to success. Thus, good managers are a necessity in any organization. Furthermore, learning to be a good manager takes time and skill building to be effective in that role.

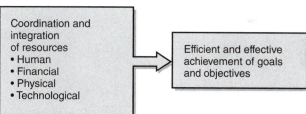

**Figure 1.1** Management defined.

Over the following chapters, you will put yourself in the shoes of a manager. You will explore many aspects of management, including human resource management, marketing management, planning, and communication. You will encounter exercises, case studies, and scenarios drawn from real situations in the field to help you start to think like a manager. It is our hope that by the end of this book you will understand what being a manager is about and have the skills to work in an entry-level position in this field.

## Universality and Multisector Approach

Before going any further, it is important to talk about the universality of management. Students have many different interests in the field of parks and recreation. They may be interested in tourism, sport, arts, recreation therapy, military recreation, fitness, outdoor education, or public parks and recreation. This text does not focus on any one of these areas; given the nature of management, such specification is not necessary. Management has a universality that makes it applicable to all fields: all managers have to coordinate and integrate their resources. The difference lies in what those resources are. National parks have park rangers, hotels have sales staff, and Boy Scouts and Girl Scouts have troop leaders. These human resources all have different jobs, but there is still a need to coordinate them. A student could realistically take a management course in a business college and learn what is necessary for his or her career. The examples would come from business, but the underlying skills would be the same.

The unique aspect of learning about management within a parks and recreation curriculum is gaining the multisector perspective. In addition to creating effective managers, this book examines management from the perspective of the public, nonprofit, and commercial sectors in both the United States and Canada. It looks at the similarities and differences among various jobs in the recreation field. Examples are provided that cover outdoor recreation, the hospitality industry, sport, the arts, special events, and municipal, state, and provincial recreation. Throughout the text, the term *parks and recreation* or *leisure services* is used to cover the gamut of the profession from tourism and recreation therapy to military recreation and public parks. Many times the sector will not matter in terms of management, but when it does, it will be brought to the forefront. The chapters that follow are meant to provide a well-rounded glimpse of management in the professions, not just management in public, nonprofit, or commercial recreation alone.

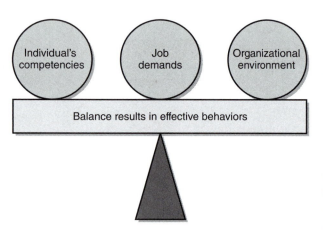

**Figure 1.2** Model for effective performance.

**competencies**—
Skills, knowledge, and characteristics needed to be successful in a job.

## Being an Effective Manager

Being an effective manager means meeting the goals, objectives, and expectations of the agency you work in. Although effectiveness is discussed in chapter 2, the model of effectiveness is discussed here to show you where this text is headed and what you can expect to learn.

To be an effective manager, there are three components to consider. Effectiveness results when there is a balance between a person's competencies, the job demands, and the organizational environment (figure 1.2) (Boyatzis 1982).

First, individual **competencies** are skills, knowledge, and characteristics that a person needs to be successful in a job. In the model of effectiveness, individual competencies encompass not only what people do on the job but what they are capable of doing as well (figure 1.3). In order for an agency to be effective, the staff has to be highly skilled. Later in the chapter, you will learn what competencies are needed to be successful as an entry-level manager in the field. These competencies are the foundation for this text. Individual skills will be built in planning and decision making (chapter 6), marketing (chapter 7), human resource management (chapters 9 and 10), finance and budgeting (chapters 11 and 12), and evaluation (chapter 13).

The second component of effectiveness is job demands. Job demands are the functions of management—planning, organizing, leading, and controlling—that are discussed throughout the text.

- *Planning.* Developing the future direction of the organization through such things as strategic planning and establishing goals and objectives

- *Organizing.* Managing resources to ensure the plans are implemented; creating an organizational structure where the right people are in the right places

| Skills | Knowledge |
|---|---|
| Physical or psychomotor aptitudes required to perform particular tasks and actions of a job | Understanding of information required for the position |

| Characteristics | Abilities |
|---|---|
| Distinguishing qualities, attributes, or traits | Aptitudes for a position, or what and how well a person is able to perform certain tasks or behaviors |

**Figure 1.3** Elements of competencies.

- *Leading.* Managing and motivating staff; training and developing staff; managing staff performance

- *Controlling.* Directing the work to be done; ensuring performance standards are being met; controlling financial resources, among others; evaluating the efforts of the organization

Such job demands or functions include tasks performed, roles of the manager, and the manager's function within the organization. The job functions aspect of effectiveness will be learned through topics such as theory and current issues in management and leadership (this chapter), the roles and functions of managers (chapter 2), and legal concerns and risk management in recreation (chapter 3), among others.

Finally, the organizational environment includes the climate and culture of the organization. It can include the structure of the organization (chapter 4), policies, procedures, and coordination of resources (chapter 5), and communication methods (chapter 8). A manager is only effective when the three components are balanced. An incompetent manager, an organization with poor organizational structure and policies, or a misalignment of job demands will not be effective on a consistent basis. Agencies and the managers within them may have to adapt one of these three elements for effectiveness to be consistent. For example, training an employee who lacks skills, changing the job description to meet the demands of the customers, or improving communication to help different departments work better together are all means to becoming more effective as an agency. As you can see, each chapter in *Leisure Services Management* is a building block to becoming an effective manager. By the end of this book, you should have a solid understanding of the dimensions of management and how the skills you have learned can be applied in the field.

## Role of Leadership in Management

Although the purpose of this text is to outline management principles, management cannot be addressed without discussing leadership. The topic of leadership could more than fill an entire textbook; it is as vast and deep as management.

Because leadership and management are so interconnected, a brief discussion of leadership is warranted.

Having the skills of a manager—planning a budget, hiring staff, or delegating responsibilities—is necessary, but a manager without leadership skills will often not be effective in the eyes of the staff. **Leadership** can be defined as interpersonal influence over others that is aimed at achieving organizational goals, objectives, and strategies. Management is the technical side of the job, and leadership is the human side. As we review management and leadership theories later in this chapter, you will see how the two start to merge, especially as management theories take on aspects of leadership.

The main difference between leadership and management is the interpersonal influence of leadership and the planning, organizing, leading, and controlling aspects of management. Both leadership and management are directed at achieving goals, but they require different processes to do so. People in administrative positions in an organization are often called managers, yet they are required to use both management and leadership skills. Management skills are more task oriented, whereas leadership skills are more people oriented. A task orientation focuses on things that need to get done, such as event planning, writing a news release, or screening job applications, whereas a people orientation focuses more on relationships with supervisors and coworkers, encouraging staff to do a good job, or enabling them to make decisions and solve problems on their own. People can demonstrate both sets of skills and different degrees of management and leadership as the situation dictates.

**leadership**—
Interpersonal influence over others aimed at achieving organizational goals, objectives, and strategies.

# LEADERSHIP THEORIES

When students hear the term *theory*, it is often accompanied by yawns, eye rolling, and disinterest. However, management and leadership theories—and the historical aspects of each—are the roots of management today. With most disciplines, theories are the building blocks of practice. Management and leadership are no exception. Leadership theories have evolved through four generations: trait theories, behavioral theories, contingency and situational theories, and modern theories.

## Trait Theories

This group of theories posits that certain traits are inherent in leaders and people who are born with these traits will be good leaders. The focus was originally on physical traits such as height or eye color and later moved to interpersonal characteristics such as being decisive, diplomatic, creative, and assertive (Stogdill 1974). Research has discredited this theory over time, showing that situational factors dictate needed traits and skills more than any genetic traits or personality characteristics do. Furthermore, leadership as a learned process is not a part of the trait theories. According to trait theory, a person must be a born leader and cannot learn to be a leader.

## Behavioral Theories

Behavioral theories focus on the behaviors leaders exhibit rather than the traits they possess. These theories claim that leadership is learned rather than inborn and that followers learn from leaders by watching what they do. There are many behavioral theories, but three popular examples include Lewin's leadership styles, the Ohio State and University of Michigan studies, and the Leadership Grid.

## Lewin's Leadership Styles

Kurt Lewin's work at the University of Iowa pioneered the notion of leadership behavior. His studies explored three broad leadership styles: autocratic leadership, democratic leadership, and laissez-faire leadership. Autocratic leadership reflects a leader who limits employee participation, dictates work methods, makes unilateral decisions, and centralizes authority. Democratic leaders, on the other hand, involve employees in making decisions, delegate authority, encourage participation in creating work methods and goals, and use a coaching style to provide employee feedback. The third style, laissez-faire leadership, reflects a hands-off leader who gives employees complete freedom to make decisions and determine work methods.

Lewin and his associates wondered if one behavioral style might be more effective than the others. From their studies of actual leader behavior, they concluded that a laissez-faire leader was not effective on any of the performance indicators of leadership (quantity and quality of work as well as group satisfaction) compared with the other two styles. When examining the quantity of work done, the studies suggested that democratic and autocratic leaders performed equally well. However, the quality of work completed and group satisfaction were higher in the democratic group. There are situations when each of the three styles may be an excellent choice for leaders. For example, an autocratic style may be a good choice when a quick response is needed, when the group does not have the skill to deal with the situation, or when safety is an issue. Lewin's work raised the idea that it may be important to differentiate between getting work done and focusing on employees. This dual nature of leader behavior is the central feature of the Ohio State and University of Michigan studies.

## The Ohio State and University of Michigan Studies

The Ohio State studies sought different dimensions of leader behavior and narrowed more than 1,000 behavioral dimensions to two main dimensions they called *initiating structure* and *consideration*. Initiating structure refers to focusing on the work; it is the degree to which leaders define and structure their role and the roles of employees in order to achieve organizational goals. Consideration, on the other hand, is the degree to which leaders develop mutual trust and workplace relationships based on respect for employees' ideas and feelings.

The Ohio State model suggests that a leader can fall into one of four quadrants. The leader who scores high in both consideration and initiating structure gets both high employee performance and satisfaction scores. However, high ratings on these dimensions are not always positive. For example, leaders who are high on initiating structure have shown higher rates of employee turnover, more grievances, higher absenteeism, and lower job satisfaction for employees undertaking routine tasks (e.g., staff members taking tickets or checking passes at a facility).

At around the same time, leadership studies at the University of Michigan found similar results. They came up with two dimensions as well: *employee orientation* and *production orientation*. Employee-oriented leaders take a personal interest in their employees, whereas production-oriented leaders are more focused on technical approaches to getting the job done. Both the Michigan and Ohio State studies were instrumental in furthering our understanding of leadership by examining behaviors in more depth (e.g., Leadership Grids) as well as taking the context or setting into account (e.g., situational and contingency theories).

### Leadership Grid

Built on the people and task orientation of the Ohio State and University of Michigan studies, the management grid was first developed by Blake and Mouton (1964) and later revised and renamed the *Leadership Grid* by Blake and McCanse (1991). The grid (figure 1.4) shows varying degrees of people and task orientation with labels for each quadrant. Although this theory is considered a leadership theory, it has strong elements of management theory with the task variable. It combines leadership and management theories and measures a person's tendencies on both aspects, which is a more realistic assessment of what a manager does.

The five different types of managers or leaders from the Leadership Grid include:

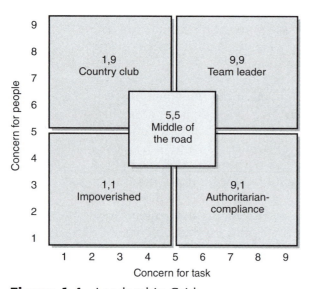

**Figure 1.4** Leadership Grid.

Adapted with permission from Grid International, Inc.

1. *Impoverished management* has little concern for people or task and tries to do as little as possible on the job. This person does not want to be held responsible for anything.

2. *Country club management* is concerned with the leader's relationship with people and has little concern for task. This leader hopes that by building good relationships with people, productivity will result.

3. *Authoritarian-compliance management* focuses on arranging work environments and people to maximize productivity and minimize the human elements.

4. *Middle-of-the-road management* satisfactorily balances the needs of people and the need for production.

5. *Team leaders* rely on teamwork to get things done. They want employees to know that they are important, and they help employees achieve company goals. This is the ideal leader for most organizations.

This leadership theory has been widely used in research. It is a solid mix of management and leadership, as can be seen from the five dimensions.

## Contingency and Situational Theories

After the behavior theories, it was clear that no single set of traits or leadership styles could adequately describe leadership effectiveness, so researchers began to look at context and how leadership changes as the situation changes. The result was a group of theories labeled as *contingency* and *situational theories*. These theories take into account the leader, the follower, and the situation.

These streams of theories have four common threads (Peretomode 2012, 14):

1) They are both an extension of behavioral leadership theories.

2) There is no one best way to successfully lead a group because there is no one best leadership style.

**3)** Successful leaders in one situation may fail in another when factors around the situation change.

**4)** Leadership effectiveness is determined by internal and external organizational factors as it relates to the leaders and followers.

The differences between the two streams of theories lie in the flexibility of leadership styles. Situational leadership theories assume that leadership styles are relatively flexible and allow leaders to change their style to meet the needs of the group within a situation. Contingency theories assume leadership styles are far more inflexible. So, rather than the leader changing his/her style to meet the needs of the group, a different leader with the right leadership style is placed in the situation (Peretomode 2012).

Probably the most well-known situational theory is Hersey and Blanchard's tridimensional leader effectiveness model. They developed four leadership dimensions that change based on the situation—the leader assesses the situation and selects the best leadership style for that situation. The dimensions (task behavior and relationship behavior) are dictated by the direction given to staff in terms of tasks, processes, and patterns of organization, as well as how supportive the leader's relationship is with the staff in terms of being sensitive to their needs, listening to them and respecting their ideas, and establishing trust (Hersey, Blanchard, and Johnson 2012). The following describes the four leadership dimensions:

1. *High relationship behavior/low task behavior.* Highly supportive leader with followers who control how they do things; joint decision making, values harmony first, and will not risk relationships; appears to totally trust staff

2. *Low relationship behavior/low task behavior.* Control is with the follower; no structure or socioemotional support; considerable delegation of tasks to staff

3. *High relationship behavior/high task behavior.* High socioemotional support; often appears ungenuine in relationships; meets goals of organization and workers

4. *Low relationship behavior/high task behavior.* Well-defined methods for completing tasks; directs, guides, and makes decisions; imposes processes on others

The relationship and task behaviors make the model two-dimensional, and adding the effectiveness dimension completes the tridimensional model. When a leader's style is appropriate for the situation based on the task and relationship behaviors exhibited, the leader is effective. When the leadership style is inappropriate for the situation, the leader is ineffective (Hersey, Blanchard, and Johnson 2012).

Contingency theories focus on how the situation dictates what individual with a specific leadership style will be successful. Fiedler (1971) presented a contingency model asserting that group performance depends on the leader's style. This style is determined by (1) leader–member relations, or how well the leader is accepted, trusted, and respected by the followers; (2) task structure, or how well the goals and objectives of the task are defined; and (3) position power, or the leader's level of control over rewards and punishments. High or low levels of these factors create a favorable situation for leaders who are more task oriented, whereas relationship-oriented leaders work best when levels are more in the middle. Fiedler suggested that it is difficult for people to change their leadership style, so the situation needs to change rather than the style for the leader to be effective. Thus, people who consider themselves to be good leaders overall will not always be good leaders in all organizations. They have to be in the right situation where their strengths complement the organization.

# Modern Theories

Four current theories have received a great deal of attention and deserve mentioning: charismatic leadership, transactional leadership, transformational leadership, and Kouzes and Posner's five practices of exemplary leadership (2017).

## Charismatic Leadership

Charismatic leaders use personality and charm, or charisma, to draw followers to them. They speak and behave in ways that reach people's emotional levels and inspire them to act. Conger and Kanungo (1998) describe charismatic leaders as having a vision for where the organization is going, being able to articulate that vision, being sensitive to the environment and to the needs of the people in it, being willing to take risks, and engaging in unconventional behaviors.

## Transactional Leadership

Transactional leadership looks at the behaviors leaders use to influence their staff. Leadership is seen as a transaction between leaders and followers where followers are motivated to work by receiving rewards. Leaders use rewards to recognize quality work, and they use punishment to correct followers so that standards are met. Although it has received a great deal of attention, this theory of leadership pays little attention to the needs of workers, and some consider it to be more similar to management than to leadership.

## Transformational Leadership

Transformational leaders have a passion to achieve great things. They create a vision for the organization and get their followers to understand and accept this vision. Transformational leaders want their followers to succeed, and they work to motivate them to do so. These types of leaders build trust, work with integrity, and set an example for their staff. Transformational leadership was a forerunner to Kouzes and Posner's five practices of exemplary leadership.

## Kouzes and Posner's Five Practices of Exemplary Leadership

Kouzes and Posner (2017) interviewed thousands of workers and managers to find out what characteristics were desirable in leaders. The interviewees responded that they wanted leaders to be honest, forward looking (have vision), competent, and inspiring. These are the same characteristics Kouzes and Posner found in 1987, 1995, 2002, and 2010, showing that even as business and the world have changed, people still look for the same characteristics in their leaders.

Kouzes and Posner used the results of their interviews to develop five practices that exemplary leaders need to implement as part of their leadership abilities:

1. *Model the way.* Leaders and followers should work side by side, leaders should not ask followers to do things they themselves would not do, and leaders should set an example through their own behavior.

2. *Inspire a shared vision.* Leaders should have a vision for what could be, help followers understand and embrace that vision, communicate their own passion, and try to ignite that passion in their followers.

3. *Challenge the process.* Leaders should be risk takers, be innovative and creative, recognize good ideas, and challenge the system and the staff to get them done.

4. *Enable others to act.* Leaders should empower their staff to accomplish tasks, goals, and objectives; they should build a team atmosphere; and they should foster collaboration among the team.

5. *Encourage the heart.* Leaders should recognize the skills, abilities, and accomplishments of their staff, and they should celebrate achievements.

## Summary of Leadership Theories

The five practices of exemplary leadership define what leadership has become. It embraces the interpersonal elements that leaders use to achieve goals. However, without the management elements, an organization and its employees are unable to accomplish all that they should. It is leadership and management working together that makes effective employees, whether they are in upper-level, mid-level, or entry-level positions. The next section looks at several management theories that guide practice today.

# MANAGEMENT THEORIES

The history of management and its accompanying theories help explain how management works, help us predict behaviors, and allow us to see the big picture of management. You will find that although many of these management practices came into being during the Industrial Revolution, they still influence modern management today.

Management can be roughly categorized into four eras: classic, behavioral, human relations, and modern. These eras are not a timeline through the history of management but a continuum of management practices that have evolved within organizations. As you read these theories, keep in mind that although a particular management theory may have come into being decades ago, there are still elements that exist today.

## Classic Era of Management

The classic era of management, occurring approximately from 1880 to the early 1930s, has also been labeled *traditional management* and *machine models*. Traditional management styles were prompted by the Industrial Revolution and the resulting rapid economic growth. Although the Industrial Revolution began around 1810, its impact on management practices was not seen until the late 1800s. Work moved from agrarian to industrial, and people moved from working in their homes to working in factories. These jobs were low paying, had long hours and poor working conditions, and resulted in less leisure time despite improvements in transportation. The result of this important time in history was a set of management theories and practices that established rational principles for making an organization more efficient.

The classic era can be subdivided into two approaches: scientific management and general administrative. Proponents of scientific management believed that there was one best way to complete tasks that resulted in efficiency. This approach focused more on individual workers, whereas the general administrative approach looked at the organization as a whole and good management practices. Scientific management is most defined by the work of Frederick Taylor and Frank and Lillian Gilbreth. General administrative approaches are reflected by Henri Fayol and Max Weber, among others.

### Frederick Taylor

It could be said that Frederick Taylor started modern management with the publication of his instant bestseller, *The Principles of Scientific Management*, in 1911. Working in a Pennsylvania steel company, Taylor observed workers who were purposefully not working to their full potential, which he labeled *soldiering*. Many workers soldiered for fear of losing their jobs if productivity increased too much, since wages were not incentive based and there were no standardized methods of completing tasks.

Seeking to increase productivity, Taylor engaged in time and motion studies where workers performed tasks in different ways while he timed them on each method. From the results, he developed the most efficient means of performing tasks, both with the motion of the workers and the time it took them to complete the task. Taylor ultimately arrived at four principles of scientific management:

1. Replace existing work methods with methods based on a scientific study of the tasks.

2. Scientifically select and train workers rather than passively leaving them to train themselves.

3. Cooperate with workers to ensure that they follow the scientifically developed methods.

4. Divide work and responsibility almost equally between managers and workers so that the managers apply scientific management principles to planning the work and the workers perform the tasks.

By 1908, Harvard Business School declared Taylor's approach the standard for modern management.

### Frank and Lillian Gilbreth

Frank and Lillian Gilbreth (1916) were disciples of Taylor. Frank started out as a construction worker and Lillian as a psychologist. They studied work environments, especially in bricklaying, to eliminate wasted hand motions and body movements. They also looked at the design and use of tools in performing these tasks, and their research was the first to use motion-picture film to study these movements. Land was inexpensive at the time and most homes and business buildings were made of brick. The largest cost of building was labor, so by reducing wasted motions, labor costs substantially decreased.

### Henri Fayol

Henri Fayol (1949) was one of the first to deal with the administrative side of management; he looked at the entire organization, not just motions and methods. Fayol is best known for creating the 5 functions of managers and the 14 principles of management (see table 1.1). He posited that managers do five things:

1. *Planning.* Look at the future and develop plans to meet future challenges.

2. *Organizing.* Examine how employee duties will be planned and structured.

3. *Commanding.* Maintain activity among personnel in terms of motivation, communication, and use of power.

**Table 1.1** Fayol's 14 Principles of Management

| Principle | What the Manager and Employees Do |
|---|---|
| **1.** Division of labor | Jobs are divided by specialization of tasks by employees. |
| **2.** Authority | Managers have the power to give orders. |
| **3.** Discipline | Employees must respect and follow the rules of the organization as directed by the manager. |
| **4.** Unity of command | Employees report to only one supervisor. |
| **5.** Unity of direction | All employees should move the organization toward common goals. |
| **6.** Subordination of individual interests | Personal interests are put aside for the good of the organization. |
| **7.** Remuneration | Fair pay is given for work done. |
| **8.** Centralization | Decision making is relegated to different levels of the organization. |
| **9.** Scalar chain | Employees must follow the chain of command from the lowest level to the CEO of the organization. |
| **10.** Order | Employees and materials should be in their proper places to operate in an orderly fashion. |
| **11.** Equity | Managers are to be kind and fair to employees. |
| **12.** Stability of personnel tenure | It should be a priority to retain quality employees. |
| **13.** Initiative | Managers should encourage employees to take initiative. |
| **14.** Esprit de corps | Managers should encourage harmony and unity within the organization. |

4. *Coordinating.* Bring together and harmonize efforts of people, ensuring proper direction and teamwork.

5. *Controlling.* Ensure that activity conforms with policy and practice; establish performance principles.

Although Fayol was prominent in the early 1900s, in looking at the definitions of management you will see that many of these same principles define management today.

## Max Weber

Max Weber was a German sociologist who described an ideal organization that he called a *bureaucracy.* Bureaucracies are driven by clear rules, defined hierarchy, and impersonal relationships. Weber felt that a bureaucracy is a dominant institution because it is most efficient in terms of precision, speed, continuity, unity, and strict subordination. Bureaucracies have six key characteristics (Robbins, Decenzo, and Coulter 2013):

1. *Division of labor.* Jobs are broken down into well-defined, routine tasks.

2. *Authority hierarchy.* Roles in the organization are positioned so that each lower job is supervised by a higher one.

3. *Formal selection.* All employees are selected based on qualifications, skills, training, education, or formal examination.

4. *Formal rules and regulations.* Formal rules and regulations are strictly relied upon to ensure uniformity and regulate the actions of employees.

5. *Impersonality.* Rules and regulations are applied to all employees uniformly so as to avoid the personal preferences of employees.

6. *Career orientation.* Managers are professional officials who work for a salary and pursue a career in the organization.

The term *bureaucracy* is often seen as being negative and associated with government, but careful examination shows that those same practices are used in many organizations that are nongovernmental.

## Summary of the Classic Era

The classic era of management originated as a means to make management a scientific discipline of study. It is responsible for defining management and the role of managers, as well as improving efficiency and productivity. Many of the management functions found today in parks and recreation are derived from the classic era of management, including work simplification, production schedules, estimates of how much product can be made in a day, development of more efficient tools and products, and qualifications-based hiring practices. Many of these principles can be seen in chapter 4 when organizational structure and design are discussed.

The shortcoming of these theories is their oversimplification of management and jobs. The main criticism of this era is its lack of concern for the human element in management, including communication, conflict management, motivation, and interpersonal relations. The behavioral theories of management came next and addressed some of these shortcomings.

# Behavioral Era of Management

The behavioral era came into being in the 1930s and 1940s. There was not any one defining movement such as the Industrial Revolution that shaped management at the time. However, there were some milestones that had a major impact on how management was perceived and carried out, including the Great Depression (1930s), the Fair Labor Standards Act establishing the 40-hour work week and banning child labor (1938), World War II (1939-1945), the introduction of the first computer (1944), the establishment of Wal-Mart (1945), passage of the Taft-Hartley Act restricting union practices (1947), and Peter Drucker becoming professor of management at New York University (1950), the first person to hold that title (Crainer 2000).

The behavioral era of management focused on why people do things rather than how they do them. Psychology and sociology became important disciplines in management as theorists attempted to understand employee behavior. Although there are a number of behavioral management theorists, a few of the most influential at the time were Elton Mayo, Mary Parker Follett, and Chester Barnard.

## Elton Mayo and the Hawthorne Studies

What began as a scientific management study at the Western Electric Hawthorne Works plant in Cicero, Illinois, became an important study that sparked the behavioral era of management (Mayo 1933). Elton Mayo's study initially focused on the impact of illumination levels on productivity in controlled and experimental groups. The lighting levels for the experimental group were manipulated whereas those for the control group did not change, and the results showed that the productivity of both groups increased regardless of the change in lighting levels. Only when the lighting dropped to the level of moonlight did productivity drop. These results led to additional experiments where small groups of workers were isolated and studied. Productivity increases in these groups were attributed to the workers liking the recognition and attention paid by the researchers. Mayo concluded several things:

- Financial incentives did not increase productivity; being singled out and given attention was far more motivating to the workers.
- Workers would work harder if they felt managers were concerned about their well-being.
- Work norms drove productivity by establishing standards for a fair day's work.
- The social environment, or informal organization, influenced productivity; relationships with bosses and coworkers made the work more palatable.

The Hawthorne studies sparked the merging of management and leadership practices to increase worker productivity.

### Mary Parker Follett

Mary Parker Follett was seen as a management prophet by Peter Drucker and as the mother of management by many others. Follett's work was groundbreaking in that she saw the organization as a group of people and not just as a means to production. She argued that managers should use their skill and knowledge to lead workers rather than rely on a strict line of authority. Furthermore, she suggested that workers should be given more responsibility and managers should receive training in management, which was unheard of at the time. Follett strongly influenced how managers approach decision making, motivation, leadership, teams, power, and authority today (Robbins and Coulter 2016). Follett's work was virtually ignored at the time, yet today her views on management are seen as cutting edge.

### Chester Barnard

Chester Barnard, once the president of the New Jersey Bell Telephone Company, believed that an organization is a behavioral system consisting of people with interacting social networks. He suggested that there are three functions of managers: to motivate personnel, to maintain effective communication with personnel, and to hire and retain quality personnel. In addition, the success of an organization is based on common goals, but to achieve these goals, the individual needs of employees must be met. Barnard focused on leadership, communication, and motivation.

### Summary of the Behavioral Era of Management

The behavioral era of management and the resulting human relations era have many commonalities. What began with an examination of behaviors led to an even more pronounced focus on human relations.

## Human Relations Era of Management

Sparked by the Hawthorne studies, the human relations era was characterized by a people-oriented approach to management. Management scholars looked at the interaction of people and its impact on the organization. In this era, the ultimate goal within the organization was to enhance success by building appropriate relationships among employees (Certo 2003). The human relations era occurred approximately from 1950 to 1980 and saw such historical influences as the employment of women reaching the highest point to date in history in 1951, the New York Stock

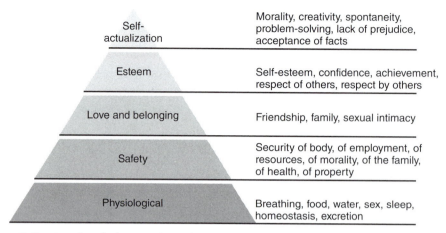

**Figure 1.5** Maslow's hierarchy of needs.

Exchange prices reaching the highest point since 1929, IBM introducing the first business computer in 1955, the Civil Rights Act of 1964 making workplace discrimination illegal, and Apple introducing the first personal computer in 1977 (Crainer 2000). As with the other eras, there were a number of significant contributors, but the most recognized are Abraham Maslow, Douglas McGregor, Frederick Herzberg, and systems theory.

### Abraham Maslow

Abraham Maslow was a humanist psychologist who developed what is known as Maslow's hierarchy of needs (figure 1.5). There are five needs that must be met according to their order on the hierarchy before the next level may be achieved. Once a need is met, it no longer serves as a motivator for behaviors (Maslow 1954). On the basis of this theory of motivation, countless managers reexamined their policies and practices to further aid people in reaching the self-actualization level in the hierarchy (Robbins and Coulter 2016). Although there is no **empirical** research to substantiate or discredit this theory, it is still respected and used in management today.

**empirical**—Relying on observation or experimentation to verify or disprove an assumption.

### Douglas McGregor

In *The Human Side of Enterprise* (1960), Douglas McGregor formulated two sets of assumptions about workers. He labeled these as theory X and theory Y (table 1.2).

These two theories appear to be polar opposites and difficult to attain. McGregor understood this and argued that people will be more productive if they are valued and given responsibility. He suggested that theory Y is the true nature of workers and should guide management practices.

### Frederick Herzberg

Wanting to find out what motivates employees, Frederick Herzberg (1966) developed the motivation-hygiene theory to explain employee attitudes and motivation (table 1.3). He found that there were satisfiers (motivators) and dissatisfiers (hygiene factors) that influenced feelings toward the work environment (Herzberg, Mausner, and Snyderman 1959).

Hygiene factors are environment related and do not provide satisfaction, but if they are absent, dissatisfaction occurs. In essence, hygiene factors will not motivate

**Table 1.2** McGregor's Theory X and Theory Y

| Theory X: Negative View of People | Theory Y: Positive View of People |
|---|---|
| People dislike work and have little ambition. | Work can be enjoyable and is as natural as rest and play. |
| People avoid responsibility. | People accept and seek responsibility. |
| People need to be closely supervised. | People can be self-directed. |
| People need to be controlled and threatened to get them to perform. | People want rewards that satisfy self-actualization. |

Created from text in D. McGregor, 1960, *The Human Side of Enterprise* (New York: McGraw-Hill).

**Table 1.3** Herzberg's Motivation-Hygiene Theory

| Hygiene Factors | Motivators |
|---|---|
| Can lead to dissatisfaction: | Lead to satisfaction: |
| Policies | Recognition |
| Working conditions | Growth on the job |
| Relationship with supervisors | Advancement |
| Supervision received on the job | Interesting work |
| Salary | Responsibility |

Created from text in F. Herzberg, B. Mausner, and B.B. Snyderman, 1959, *The Motivation to Work* (New York: Wiley).

an employee, but without them, the employee is not happy. Motivation factors, on the other hand, focus on what people do at work, and these factors lead to motivated employees who will perform well for the organization. Motivation factors need to be present because they lead to satisfaction in the workplace.

## Systems Theory

Systems theory began as a biological theory and has since been adapted into management and organizational theories. The premise of systems theory is that an organization is a system with interrelated parts, such as skilled people and departments. These individuals and groups rely on each other to get their jobs done. Not only is there a connection between internal parts, but there are external influences as well. For example, a special events management company is holding a major event that will attract 100,000 people to the community in a weekend. It will take a large number of employees in different departments working together to plan the event. In addition, a multitude of organizations outside of the agency are required, such as hotels, beverage distributors, security organizations, sanitation providers, and sponsors. Key to a systems approach is the idea of stability in the organization. The more stable the organization, the more effectively it will respond to problems. Stable and skilled staff working on this event will be better prepared to handle difficulties such as rain, sponsors pulling out, or entertainment acts canceling at the last minute.

Also within systems theory are the concepts of inputs, processes, and outputs. An organization has various inputs such as resources, time, money, and program ideas. These inputs go through processes such as program planning and event management, resulting in outputs such as programs, trips, and other products

**Figure 1.6** Systems theory example from the Fort Dix Morale, Welfare, and Recreation Program.

(figure 1.6). A systems approach is an underlying premise of team-based organizations, which are discussed later in this text. It also is a part of the outcomes-based management approach discussed later.

### Summary of the Human Relations Era of Management

During the human relations era, management saw many transformations, from a scientific perspective in the classic era to the human relations era where the relations among and between workers and managers was studied. Many prominent principles in each era carried over into the modern era of management.

# Modern Era of Management

The modern era of management has taken a slightly different twist since it began in the 1980s. Productivity in North America was falling and there was a growing distrust of major corporations and their commitment to their communities. However, the Japanese economy was flourishing at the time and expected to have the largest gross national product in the world by 2000 (Pascale and Athos 1981). What resulted were Deming's theory of total quality management and a plethora of other management scholars presenting best practices.

### Total Quality Management

W. Edwards Deming played an important role in the growth of the Japanese business market in the 1970s and 1980s, yet he was unknown in North America. Deming convinced the National Broadcasting Company (NBC) of his abilities and respect from the business world in Japan, and on June 26, 1980, NBC featured Deming in a broadcast titled *If Japan Can, Why Can't We?* This show changed the face of management in North America. Deming introduced total quality management (TQM) with the premise that managers must focus on quality from the customer perspective and make it the basis of everything the organization does. TQM has 14 points (Crainer 2000):

1. Create constancy of purpose toward improving products and services.
2. Adopt a philosophy of improving products and services so it is ingrained in the company.
3. Reduce variation in products so that dependence on inspection is not needed. Fix defects before the product is made rather than finding them during inspection.
4. Work with only one supplier to minimize variation in supplies. This may mean not going with the cheapest items.

5. Improve constantly and forever.

6. Institute training on the job.

7. Institute leadership where managers lead rather than supervise.

8. Drive out fear so workers will ask questions and give input.

9. Break down barriers between departments so teams will improve productivity.

10. Eliminate slogans, exhortations, targets, and posters because they generate frustration and resentment.

11. Eliminate quotas because they encourage the delivery of lesser goods.

12. Remove barriers to pride of workmanship, including annual employee evaluations and rating systems.

13. Institute education and self-improvement.

14. The transformation to TQM is everyone's job and all employees should be involved in its implementation.

TQM is not without its critics; some perceive it as inflexible and unable to quickly adapt to change. However, many principles are still in use today. Many of the principles work in the service industry, but TQM is better suited for companies that manufacture goods. A service industry like parks and recreation would find it difficult to embrace some TQM principles, such as eliminating variability in products.

## Best Practices

TQM sparked a new wave of management scholars who looked to present ideas on best practices within management. The leader in this wave was Peter Drucker, who wrote 38 books and countless papers on management. His last book was published in 2005, the year he died at the age of 95. Not only did Drucker study commercial business, he also worked with nonprofit groups, focusing on the specific needs of the sector. Drucker influenced many of the management practices that are considered the foundation of the field today.

Modern management has focused on reworking past theories and practices and includes such names as Mintzberg, Peters, Blanchard, Waterman, and Covey, in addition to Deming and Drucker. Eight key best practices emerge from their writings that contribute to management today:

1. Organizations must be driven by clearly defined values.

2. Organizations must have a known vision for where they are headed.

3. Organizations should be customer driven.

4. Managers must recognize the contributions of employees to the organization.

5. Managers must foster collaboration among staff, encourage cooperation, and treat employees as valuable assets.

6. Organizations must continually train and invest in employees, who are their greatest asset.

7. Managers must give employees the freedom to take risks so they may learn from mistakes and foster innovation and change.

8. Organizations must create a culture of trust among all employees that precipitates honesty, integrity, and ethical behavior.

### Summary of the Modern Era of Management

The focus of this era can best be described as quality and best practices. This approach to management combines the three previous eras to depict how a manager should both manage and lead.

## Summary of Management Theories

Walk into any bookstore and you will find shelves of books on management practices. Managers today could read a book a week throughout their entire career and never scratch the surface of all the publications that are out there. The practices outlined by great management thinkers have come a long way since the classic era. Some of the original practices are still evident in management, but where the focus was once on productivity, it is now on people. The behavioral and human relations eras laid the groundwork for management today, which is people focused and where leadership becomes intertwined with management. As stated earlier, it is difficult to differentiate between management and leadership since they each hold principles of the other as their foundation. As these two areas have come closer together, a few management trends have emerged in parks and recreation that deserve mention.

# MANAGEMENT TRENDS

The theoretical history of leadership and management demonstrates the interaction and progression of the disciplines. It explains behaviors and helps us understand the bigger picture of both management and leadership. This foundation has led to several current trends in management. Many of these trends are philosophies adopted by the public, nonprofit, and commercial sectors. The more popular ones right now include learning organizations, outcomes-based management, strategic management and leadership, and competency-based management.

## Learning Organizations

**learning organizations—** Agencies that instill the value of learning and education as means to developing individual staff members and the organization as a whole.

Peter Senge developed the concept of **learning organizations**, which emphasizes continual learning in order to get better. In a learning organization, learning and education are encouraged among staff because increasing one person's competence strengthens the organization so that it is better able to respond to changes. Senge (2006) outlines five disciplines that are required for learning organizations:

1. Systems thinking
2. Personal mastery
3. Mental models
4. Shared vision
5. Team learning

### Systems Thinking

The most important discipline, systems thinking, stems from systems theory. Remember, in this theory, all the parts in a system are interdependent. Personal development means organizational development, and when one part of the system is weak, such as an employee, it weakens the entire organization. This idea of systems ties the other four disciplines together and makes them work so that the organization is stronger.

### Personal Mastery

Workers must commit to personal mastery and have a personal vision for where they want to be and what they want to accomplish. Employees seek a special level of proficiency by committing to lifelong learning and developing the full potential of others and themselves.

### Mental Models

Everyone has deeply entrenched images, assumptions, and generalizations of how things are in the world. These mental models influence our thinking and decision making, and many of them are subconsciously ingrained. In terms of management, mental models define what we can and cannot do. Learning organizations force people to scrutinize their mental models to see how the models impede progress. This scrutiny increases the capacity of workers to see beyond their mental models and think outside the box.

### Shared Vision

The organization must have a unified vision for where it is going and how it is going to get there. People thrive on lofty goals and dedicate themselves to improving their intellectual capacity to help reach those goals.

### Team Learning

Workers must have positive group interaction involving open dialogue and skillful discussion. The members of the team learn from each other, and the intelligence of the team is superior to the intelligence of its individual members.

Many organizations today are learning organizations. They dedicate money to staff for workshops, conferences, and classes toward advanced degrees. For managers who have completed a degree in parks and recreation, this is just the first step in the learning process. Good managers will develop their intellectual abilities throughout their careers.

## Outcomes-Based Management

Many of the management and leadership theories that have been discussed thus far were developed in the commercial sector and most likely with big businesses. However, **outcomes-based management** has strong roots in the nonprofit and public sectors. It is particularly strong in parks and recreation.

The purpose of outcomes-based management is to uncover what programs and services actually mean to users. It moves away from counting the number of people served, the number of programs offered, or the number of units sold to identifying how people benefit from the programs. The United Way has been a front-runner in developing outcomes-based management. Their model (figure 1.7) has four elements: inputs, activities, outputs, and outcomes (United Way of America 1996).

Inputs are the resources dedicated to the program such as staff, money, volunteers, and facilities. Activities are the result of the inputs, and in recreation they include programs or products. Outputs are the volume of activities. In this field, we have a tendency to count the number of programs offered per season, the number

**outcomes-based management**—A management philosophy in which the agency carefully plans and sets priorities with the purpose of realizing quality results rather than quantified results.

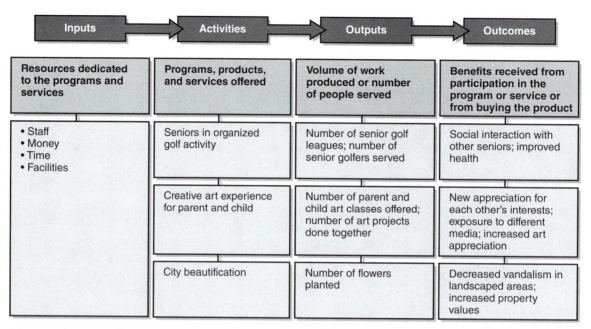

| Inputs | Activities | Outputs | Outcomes |
|---|---|---|---|
| **Resources dedicated to the programs and services** | **Programs, products, and services offered** | **Volume of work produced or number of people served** | **Benefits received from participation in the program or service or from buying the product** |
| • Staff<br>• Money<br>• Time<br>• Facilities | Seniors in organized golf activity | Number of senior golf leagues; number of senior golfers served | Social interaction with other seniors; improved health |
| | Creative art experience for parent and child | Number of parent and child art classes offered; number of art projects done together | New appreciation for each other's interests; exposure to different media; increased art appreciation |
| | City beautification | Number of flowers planted | Decreased vandalism in landscaped areas; increased property values |

**Figure 1.7** Performance outcome model.

Adapted from: Measuring Program Outcomes: A Practical Approach (1996). Used by permission, United Way of America.

of memberships sold, or the number of people in the facility each hour. Up to this point, the model looks like systems theory. However, outcomes-based management goes one step further by adding the outcomes variable. Outcomes are the benefits people receive from participation in the program or purchasing the product. Outcomes can be "related to behavior, skills, knowledge, attitudes, values, condition, or other attributes" (United Way of America 1996, 2).

In the early 1990s, the National Recreation and Park Association (NRPA) and the Canadian Parks and Recreation Association (CPRA) developed benefits programs to help agencies better position themselves so that the community can see what they get from programs rather than just the program itself. These benefits are actually outcomes. Many of the benefits efforts were marketing driven. They then moved to being management driven with the introduction of benefits-based management, which gave the field a clearer understanding of the management process and resulting outcomes.

Outcomes/benefits-based management has been used in parks and recreation agencies such as the U.S. Forest Service (Lee and Driver 1992), countless cities, counties, and park districts across the United States, and the U.S. Bureau of Land Management (BLM) (Bureau of Land Management n.d.).

Understanding the concept of benefits and outcomes seems logical, but what does it have to do with management? Outcomes can serve several management functions. First, they make agencies accountable for resources. Resource usage should tie directly to the outcomes received. A program that demands a large proportion of staff time should prove to be worth that expenditure in terms of what people get from the program. Second, outcomes demonstrate how organizations make a difference in the community by promoting the value of programs and services. This leads to increased public support, which is needed for such things as funding and capital projects. Third, having a clear understanding of outcomes often leads to more focused and productive staff (United Way of America 1996). Finally, outcomes drive program decisions, such as when an organization expands programs that are delivering the outcomes it has deemed important according to its values, vision, mission, and goals.

## Strategic Management and Leadership

**Strategic management** and leadership are based on the concept of strategic planning. Strategic planning guides the staff of an organization in envisioning its future and then developing an outline of what they need to do in order to become that organization over a certain time frame (e.g., five years). Strategic planning requires agencies to follow several steps, including the following. (These steps are further explained in chapter 6.)

1. Develop and clarify values, vision, mission, goals, and objectives.
2. Complete a performance analysis to determine what the organization does right.
3. Complete a SWOT (strengths, weaknesses, opportunities, threats) analysis.
4. Identify strategic issues and strategies.
5. Approve and implement the plan.
6. Monitor, review, and update the plan.

> **strategic management—** A management philosophy that assumes planning improves performance by setting strategies that the staff tries to achieve to strengthen the overall organization.

The main premise of strategic management and leadership is that planning improves performance. It shows the organization what its strengths are and matches those strengths with customer needs. The developed strategies help the organization get stronger and better able to compete in the market, and they ensure that all staff members are headed in the same direction.

Strategic management and leadership have been embraced by managers. Many park and recreation agencies are committed to regularly creating strategic plans, and a number of educational sessions on strategic planning are offered each year at professional conferences. Twenty years ago, agencies created strategic plans because they were good public relations tools or they were needed to apply for grants. However, these plans were rarely implemented. Today, strategic plans are highly valued and seen as a must in the field. It is not unusual for agencies to refer to their strategic plan as a scorecard where they track what strategies and actions have been implemented and make decisions based on the plan. Managers plan, organize, and direct employees to make decisions and achieve goals and objectives set by the strategic plan. Leaders use their interpersonal influence over their staff to achieve the same organizational goals, objectives, and strategies.

## Competency-Based Management

**Competency-based management** requires that the agency implement strategies to improve the competencies of its staff at all levels—from the board of directors to entry-level employees. This means that the agency provides resources to develop its staff and ensure that competencies are the cornerstone to human resources management, organizational goals and objectives, strategic planning, succession planning, and more.

> **competency-based management—** Implementation of management practices and strategies to improve skills, knowledge, and abilities through such tools as competency-based job descriptions, hiring practices, and training.

Competency-based management has several key elements:

- *Competency-based job description.* A detailed job description for each position within the agency, listing the job demands and the competencies needed for the position. It should be reviewed and updated regularly to reflect the job.

- *Competency-based hiring.* Competency-based hiring practices so the people hired can meet the job demands. Applicants should be screened based on the competencies outlined in the job description, and interview questions should directly relate to demonstrating these competencies.

- *Assessment of competency gaps.* Employee assessment to determine competency gaps—the gap between the current skill level of the employee and where he or she needs to be. Part of this assessment is to create individual development plans for career advancement.

- *Systematic training plan.* Development of a systematic training plan designed to direct resources to close competency gaps.

- *Skills and strategy alignment.* Development of a strategic plan for the agency and aligning competencies and job demands to help the agency achieve its goals and objectives.

- *Succession plan.* Development of a succession plan at all levels of the organization. This includes such things as assessing the "bench strength" at each level to determine what positions have talented staff in the pipeline for the position if needed. The bench strength assessment also shows where staff weaknesses exist. The succession plan builds skills in employees for the present and the future.

## Competency Use for Managers

Competency-based organizations determine the skills, knowledge, characteristics, and abilities needed for different jobs and then use them to increase efficiency and effectiveness.

There are four main uses of competencies in organizations (Hurd 2005):

1. Competencies establish training and development benchmarks. Employees can use competencies to measure their own skills and address any deficiencies through training and development. Students can also measure their current skills and get experience during their internships that will build competencies, better preparing them for an entry-level position upon graduation.

2. Competencies establish hiring criteria. Although job descriptions are required for all jobs, they are usually broad. Competencies can be added to job descriptions to make them more specific. These competencies ensure that new employees fully understand what is required of them. In addition, they ensure that the hiring committee is looking for the same competencies from each candidate by guiding interview questions. Competency-driven interview questions are more specific than broad questions about education and general experience (see table 1.4).

3. Competencies are used for evaluation. Developing competencies and using them for evaluation purposes is at the core of human resources management (Oss 2004). Competencies set performance standards and expectations for employees that should be measured during performance appraisals.

4. Competencies form the basis of career advancement. Most professionals will want to move beyond being frontline managers to being middle- or top-level managers, and competencies can help direct this process. An entry-level professional is most likely to rely on the agency or a mentor to help with career development, whereas a more experienced professional will move toward

**Table 1.4** Competency-Based Interview Questions

| Broad Interview Questions | Competency-Driven Interview Questions |
|---|---|
| What experiences have you had in dealing with angry customers? | Give us an example of an issue brought to you by a disappointed customer. What was the issue and how did you solve it? |
| Describe your ability to work in a team. | Describe a project where you were required to work in a team. What did you bring to the team? What could you have done to be a better team member? |
| Evaluate your ability to deal with conflict. | Give an example of when you had to deal with conflict in a work environment. How did you handle it? What would you do differently the next time? |

self-directed career development. Career development happens through training and setting career goals. Competencies can be used to set career goals by detailing what experiences are needed.

Although the uses of competencies discussed here focus on entry-level positions, competencies exist for CEOs, middle managers, and board members of leisure services organizations. As careers change and progress, so do the competencies needed to succeed.

Competency-based management can be seen in many parks and recreation agencies. For example, the Woodlands Community Association in Texas uses competencies as part of their internship program by outlining what interns will learn and experience during their 12- to 16-week endeavor.

# OUR COMPETENCY-BASED APPROACH

Although there are any number of ways we could organize this text, we chose to follow a competency-based approach. Each chapter in this book is designed to help an entry-level professional build skills and gain an understanding of what it will be like to be a manager in this profession. The competencies required for a successful leisure services manager are broad, as can be seen from the diversity of topics covered in this text. By no means are entry-level employees expected to be experts in all areas, but new managers must be proficient enough to make good decisions and be willing to ask the right questions of people who are experts in various areas.

## Entry-Level Management Competencies

Academic preparation to become a leisure services professional develops a knowledge base leading to a set of skills that can be used in an entry-level position. The ultimate goal of a degree program is to get a job, but many students question whether they are skilled in the right areas to be competitive in the job market. We propose that there is a competency set that students should strive to attain in order to reach the goal of being hired in an entry-level position upon graduation. Each chapter focuses on different parts of this competency framework.

Developing competencies for a broad profession such as parks and recreation is a difficult task. As you will see throughout this book, the different sectors have special challenges in terms of management, particularly structure and funding. However, research on competencies in the public sector (Hurd 2005), recreational sport (Beggs et al. 2018), commercial recreation (Hammersley and Tynon 1998), park and recreation professional certification specifications, and the nonprofit sector has been used to create a competency model to guide the development of qualifications for entry-level positions in the park and recreation field. The topics discussed in this text will help build these competencies and the competency portion of the model of effectiveness.

The competencies for entry-level park and recreation professionals can be categorized into six general categories: business acumen, communications, community relations, interpersonal skills, management techniques, and planning and evaluation (table 1.5). Not every entry-level position in the field will require all of these competencies, but they are an excellent starting point for future professionals to gauge their strengths and weaknesses. Similar to a strategic plan for an organization, these competencies can serve as a scorecard for developing the skills to be a better manager and increasing your chances of being hired. Each chapter provides a snapshot of the competencies that can be met by acquiring the knowledge from that chapter.

## Competency Scorecard

Throughout the text, references are made to the competency scorecard. This scorecard includes the competencies needed for entry-level professionals, as outlined in table 1.5. Content is directed at enhancing knowledge in many of these areas. Remember that competencies are skills, knowledge, abilities, and characteristics that entry-level professionals need to be successful, and a single course in management cannot totally prepare students for their first job. If that were the case, you would not need the other courses required in the major! Furthermore, some of these competencies are **characteristics** and will come with experience. For example, the interpersonal skills of the competency framework include aspects that will either develop over time or are part of someone's personality; it is difficult to teach patience, enthusiasm, and initiative in the classroom.

**characteristics**—
Distinguishing qualities, attitudes, personality factors, or mental traits needed to perform a job.

Before beginning the journey through this textbook, let's develop a picture of where you are in terms of your own competence to become a manager in an entry-level position. Table 1.6 is a rating sheet listing all of the entry-level competencies. Rate yourself in terms of your skill, knowledge, ability, characteristics, and experience. You may feel you have knowledge in an area but have not had an opportunity to put it to work yet. In this case, you may rate yourself lower on experience than on competence. Rating all the competencies in this fashion can determine how current skills compare to those needed in entry-level positions. Many of you will not have any experience in most of these areas, which is understandable because you are still students. Do not forget that not all learning comes from the classroom. While you are building these competency areas in class, complement that learning through experiences in the field, such as working in an afterschool program, volunteering at special events, or shadowing a manager in a resort. Once you complete this management course and have read the text, rate yourself again to see how you have improved, and do it a third time once you complete your final field experience. You will see how far you have come and how prepared you are to become a manager in this dynamic field.

Notice how the competencies in table 1.6 are numbered. These competencies are listed for each chapter using the same numbering. Thus, when you reach a specific chapter, you can see the competencies that will be covered and refer back to your own ratings to see what you need to learn in a specific area. This allows you to track your progress through your management course.

**Table 1.5** Entry-Level Competencies

| General Competency Categories | Specific Competencies |
|---|---|
| Business acumen | Understand financial processes (i.e., purchasing, budget). <br> Develop, monitor, and stay within a budget. <br> Possess knowledge of management principles. <br> Demonstrate basic knowledge of laws and legal matters affecting the field. <br> Understand technology and how to use it. |
| Communications | Clearly communicate with staff, customers, and the public. <br> Possess effective written and oral communication skills. <br> Listen to staff and customers. <br> Implement marketing techniques. <br> Communicate the organization's values, vision, and mission. |
| Community relations | Know the community and its needs. <br> Understand customer service practices. <br> Have the ability to deal with the public. <br> Develop partnerships with other organizations. <br> Work with boards and elected officials. |
| Interpersonal skills | Be creative and innovative. <br> Be flexible. <br> Have patience. <br> Be enthusiastic and have a positive attitude. <br> Be open-minded. <br> Deal with personality conflicts. <br> Understand the concept of criticism and accept constructive criticism. <br> Take initiative. |
| Management techniques | Use effective problem-solving and conflict-resolution skills. <br> Make ethical decisions. <br> Understand the hiring process. <br> Supervise, discipline, and evaluate a diverse staff. <br> Motivate employees. <br> Have leadership skills and abilities. <br> Be able to work in a team. <br> Use effective organizational skills. <br> Prioritize and manage multiple tasks. <br> Demonstrate effective time-management skills. <br> Conduct program evaluations. <br> Schedule programs, leagues, and staff. <br> Network within and outside the profession. <br> Participate in policy formation, evaluation, and revision. |
| Planning and evaluation | Provide input on strategic, master, recreation, marketing, and technology plans. <br> Conduct research and evaluation. <br> Conduct needs assessments. |

## Table 1.6  Sample Competency Assessment

| Competencies | SKILL, KNOWLEDGE, ABILITIES | | | | EXPERIENCE | | |
|---|---|---|---|---|---|---|---|
| | Excellent | Good | Fair | Poor | A lot | Some | None |
| **1.** Understand financial processes (i.e., purchasing, budget). | 4 | 3 | 2 | 1 | 3 | 2 | 1 |
| **2.** Develop, monitor, and stay within a budget. | 4 | 3 | 2 | 1 | 3 | 2 | 1 |
| **3.** Possess knowledge of management principles. | 4 | 3 | 2 | 1 | 3 | 2 | 1 |
| **4.** Demonstrate basic knowledge of laws and legal matters affecting the field. | 4 | 3 | 2 | 1 | 3 | 2 | 1 |
| **5.** Understand technology and how to use it. | 4 | 3 | 2 | 1 | 3 | 2 | 1 |
| **6.** Clearly communicate with staff, customers, and the public. | 4 | 3 | 2 | 1 | 3 | 2 | 1 |
| **7.** Possess effective written and oral communication skills. | 4 | 3 | 2 | 1 | 3 | 2 | 1 |
| **8.** Listen to staff and customers. | 4 | 3 | 2 | 1 | 3 | 2 | 1 |
| **9.** Implement marketing techniques. | 4 | 3 | 2 | 1 | 3 | 2 | 1 |
| **10.** Communicate the organization's values, vision, and mission. | 4 | 3 | 2 | 1 | 3 | 2 | 1 |
| **11.** Know the community and its needs. | 4 | 3 | 2 | 1 | 3 | 2 | 1 |
| **12.** Understand customer service practices. | 4 | 3 | 2 | 1 | 3 | 2 | 1 |
| **13.** Have the ability to deal with the public. | 4 | 3 | 2 | 1 | 3 | 2 | 1 |
| **14.** Develop partnerships with other organizations. | 4 | 3 | 2 | 1 | 3 | 2 | 1 |
| **15.** Work with boards and elected officials. | 4 | 3 | 2 | 1 | 3 | 2 | 1 |
| **16.** Be creative and innovative. | 4 | 3 | 2 | 1 | 3 | 2 | 1 |
| **17.** Be flexible. | 4 | 3 | 2 | 1 | 3 | 2 | 1 |
| **18.** Have patience. | 4 | 3 | 2 | 1 | 3 | 2 | 1 |
| **19.** Be enthusiastic and have a positive attitude. | 4 | 3 | 2 | 1 | 3 | 2 | 1 |
| **20.** Be open-minded. | 4 | 3 | 2 | 1 | 3 | 2 | 1 |
| **21.** Deal with personality conflicts. | 4 | 3 | 2 | 1 | 3 | 2 | 1 |
| **22.** Understand the concept of criticism and accept constructive criticism. | 4 | 3 | 2 | 1 | 3 | 2 | 1 |
| **23.** Take initiative. | 4 | 3 | 2 | 1 | 3 | 2 | 1 |
| **24.** Use effective problem-solving and conflict-resolution skills. | 4 | 3 | 2 | 1 | 3 | 2 | 1 |
| **25.** Make ethical decisions. | 4 | 3 | 2 | 1 | 3 | 2 | 1 |
| **26.** Understand the hiring process. | 4 | 3 | 2 | 1 | 3 | 2 | 1 |
| **27.** Supervise, discipline, and evaluate a diverse staff. | 4 | 3 | 2 | 1 | 3 | 2 | 1 |
| **28.** Motivate employees. | 4 | 3 | 2 | 1 | 3 | 2 | 1 |
| **29.** Have leadership skills and abilities. | 4 | 3 | 2 | 1 | 3 | 2 | 1 |
| **30.** Be able to work in a team. | 4 | 3 | 2 | 1 | 3 | 2 | 1 |
| **31.** Use effective organizational skills. | 4 | 3 | 2 | 1 | 3 | 2 | 1 |
| **32.** Prioritize and manage multiple tasks. | 4 | 3 | 2 | 1 | 3 | 2 | 1 |
| **33.** Demonstrate effective time-management skills. | 4 | 3 | 2 | 1 | 3 | 2 | 1 |
| **34.** Conduct program evaluations. | 4 | 3 | 2 | 1 | 3 | 2 | 1 |

**Table 1.6** *(continued)*

| Competencies | SKILL, KNOWLEDGE, ABILITIES | | | | EXPERIENCE | | |
|---|---|---|---|---|---|---|---|
| | Excellent | Good | Fair | Poor | A lot | Some | None |
| **35.** Schedule programs, leagues, and staff. | 4 | 3 | 2 | 1 | 3 | 2 | 1 |
| **36.** Network within and outside the profession. | 4 | 3 | 2 | 1 | 3 | 2 | 1 |
| **37.** Participate in policy formation, evaluation, and revision. | 4 | 3 | 2 | 1 | 3 | 2 | 1 |
| **38.** Provide input on strategic, master, recreation, marketing, and technology plans. | 4 | 3 | 2 | 1 | 3 | 2 | 1 |
| **39.** Conduct research and evaluation. | 4 | 3 | 2 | 1 | 3 | 2 | 1 |
| **40.** Conduct needs assessments. | 4 | 3 | 2 | 1 | 3 | 2 | 1 |

From A. Hurd, R. Barcelona, J. Zimmermann, and J. Ready, *Leisure Services Management*, 2nd ed. (Champaign, IL: Human Kinetics, 2020).

 Check out the web study guide for additional material, including learning activities, sample documents, interactive case studies, web links, CPRP exam connections, and more.

# Conclusion

Management is the process of coordinating and integrating resources in order to achieve organizational goals. Many different elements are required for the manager to be successful, and a driving force behind these elements is competencies. It is hoped that by the time you reach the end of this text, you will have stepped into the shoes of the manager to build an understanding of what a manager does and all the aspects that go into being effective and efficient.

# Review Questions

1. Define *management*.
2. Describe how competencies can be used in a competency-driven agency.
3. Give examples of competencies needed by entry-level professionals.
4. Describe the model of effectiveness for managers.
5. Compare and contrast leadership and management.
6. Describe the four eras of leadership theory and how they are used today.
7. Describe the four categories of management theory. Which theories are still in use today?
8. Which management theories sound the most similar to leadership?
9. Which leadership theories sound the most similar to management?
10. Can an organization be both a learning organization and implement strategic management? Why or why not?
11. Select two management trends and discuss their importance to the field.

# 2

# Leisure Services Managers

## Learning Outcomes

- Understand the interrelationship between the levels and functions of managers.
- Demonstrate knowledge of the four main resources within an organization.
- Describe how managers experience career progression.
- Compare and contrast values, vision, and mission statements.
- Formulate goals and objectives.
- Differentiate between efficiency and effectiveness.

responsibility, authority, resources, mentorship, management drivers, values, shared values, vision, mission, goals, objectives, efficiency, effectiveness, cultural competency, sustainability

## Competency Check

Refer to table 1.6 to see how you assessed this related competency.

10. Communicate the organization's values, vision, and mission.

## A Day in the Life

A typical day for me starts at home, checking my messages to ensure there are no staff who can't attend work that day. If needed, I'll arrange casuals (an Australian term for part-time employees without guaranteed hours) or shuffle staff members, even allocate management staff, to work in the program. If the Cottage rings me because a driver is away and no volunteer drivers are available, then I need to arrange another staff to shuffle roles or drive for the morning, as getting the clients to the Cottage is priority. Now I get time to check my calendar and organize my day. There are set days for regular tasks like undertaking the payroll procedure and local networking meetings. Then there is the prioritizing of tasks on my work plan, which includes any projects, allocating students for placements, preparing reports for the board meeting, organizing regular and skill development training for staff, conducting staff mentoring or appraisals as well as attending my own appraisal. I have learned along the way that a manager needs to be flexible to support staff, volunteers, and the clients of the service. They need to be resourceful—not necessarily have the answer, but know where to get the answer—keep up to date, and be able to promote the organization at conferences and other guest speaking opportunities.

Margaret Donnelly
Assistant Manager
Myrtle Cottage Group Inc.
Ingleburn, Sydney, Australia

Chapter 1 outlined a foundation and historical perspective of management, allowing you to see where management and leadership started and where they are today. Now that we've established the big picture of management, it is time to look at the details, the nuts and bolts of daily management activity. Discussion in this chapter focuses on what a manager does, different levels of management within an organization, management resources, what drives management, and organizational efficiency and effectiveness. Together these things represent the total manager and give a picture of what to expect as a manager.

# LEVELS AND FUNCTIONS OF MANAGERS

A soon-to-be graduate probably wants to know what managers do and where they are in the organization. Regardless of whether the manager works in a resort, a city park and recreation agency, or a nonprofit organization, the functions and levels of management are similar. The two are tightly connected, with the level of management dictating many functions.

## Levels of Management

Managers are found throughout an organization with varying levels of responsibility and authority. A discussion of what managers do cannot happen without understanding what these two terms mean. **Responsibility** refers to the aspects of the organization that the manager is in charge of, such as arts, sales, sport, or the Midwest region. **Authority**, on the other hand, is the power that comes with the position a manager occupies in the organizational chart (Hersey, Blanchard, and Johnson 2012). Authority is given to managers who oversee employees or certain areas of the organization. Both responsibility and authority change as managers change levels in the organization.

**responsibility**—Designated area of the organization that an employee is in charge of.

**authority**—The right to exercise influence, give directives, or make certain decisions within a designated area of an organization.

Managers can be classified into three levels (figure 2.1). The base of any organization is its frontline managers or direct service providers. Managers at this level are responsible for dealing with day-to-day production and service issues related to such things as teaching aerobics or dance classes, preparing ball diamonds for play, or leading activities at a resort. Frontline managers generally work directly with nonmanagement staff, which can require them to supervise other full- or part-time employees. These jobs are usually considered entry-level positions and are the most plentiful in an organization.

The next level in the organization consists of middle managers, who supervise the frontline managers. Middle managers are often considered department heads, such as director of sales, cultural arts manager, or coordinator of interpretive programs. They have responsibility and authority over a particular area in the organization and are often required to develop tactics, policies, and short-term plans to help guide the employees they supervise.

At the top of the organization are the upper level or senior managers—the chief executive officers (CEOs), presidents, and vice presidents. They make up a small group of senior executives responsible for managing the entire organization. They supervise the middle managers and have ultimate responsibility for all aspects of the organization from finance and facilities to planning and marketing. They should be the ones who develop long-term plans for the organization to thrive and produce value for stakeholders.

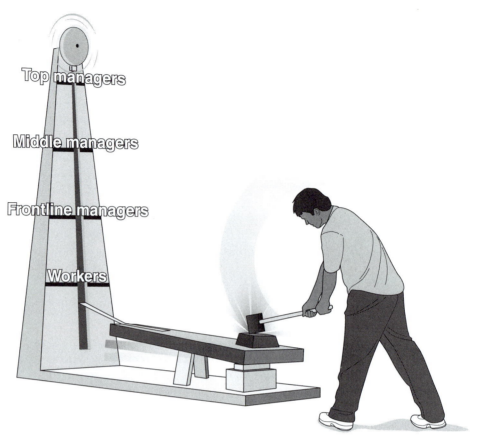

**Figure 2.1** Levels of management.

As a manager moves up the levels of management, the number of positions decreases; there are only one or two people within an organization at the top level of management. Also, as a manager moves up through the three levels, responsibility and authority will increase, with the top-level manager having the most responsibility and authority.

## Functions of Management

At each level in the organization the manager has specific functions and, similar to varying responsibilities, these functions change as the manager moves up in the organization. There are two approaches for discussing the functions of a manager. The first focuses on the conceptual, human relations, and technical functions of managers. The second looks at the specific functions of planning, organizing, leading, and controlling (introduced in chapter 1).

### Conceptual, Human Relations, and Technical Approach

The conceptual, human relations, and technical functions of managers are most often examined in connection with the three levels of the organization. Technical functions are job-specific knowledge and techniques that enable employees to do their jobs effectively and things done by the manager in order to accomplish tasks and complete procedures. Technical skills are predominantly a function of frontline managers. Going back to the competencies discussed in chapter 1, technical functions require competencies such as conducting program evaluations, developing budgets, and implementing marketing techniques. When comparing the levels of management and their functions, the frontline managers are the most likely to use technical skills, followed by middle managers and then top managers. Thus, technical skills are stressed during undergraduate and graduate education to prepare future managers for entry-level positions.

Human relations functions deal with internal customers (i.e., employees) and external customers (i.e., participants and visitors) and include the ability to work with, lead, and understand other people, including both individuals and groups. Human relations competencies include the ability to deal with the public, to work in a team, and to deal with personality conflicts. Human relations functions are used extensively by all levels of management, with no one level performing this function more than others. However, the ways in which these functions manifest themselves at each level may be quite different. For example, a CEO may use human relations skills to work with potential donors, the board, or CEOs of other organizations, whereas the frontline manager is most likely to use human relations skills with participants by leading activities, teaching fitness classes, or registering participants.

The last function of management is the conceptual function. This is the big-picture function where managers view the organization as a whole and make decisions based on how they will affect everyone in the organization. Conceptual skills allow a manager to analyze situations from multiple perspectives, determine cause and effect, and come up with solutions to challenges. The top-level manager has a much larger conceptual function than the middle or frontline manager. As far as entry-level competencies go, conceptual skills are limited, other than problem-solving skills. However, several CEO competencies demonstrate conceptual functions, including the ability to create a vision or direction for the agency and to make effective long-range plans (Hurd and McLean 2004).

Table 2.1 depicts a sample of competencies needed at the three organizational levels, categorized by function. It is clear that competencies change as the level of the manager changes within each function. Although these functions are universal to management in all fields, seeing them in the context of parks and recreation can aid in understanding what a manager actually does in this setting.

## Planning, Organizing, Leading, and Controlling Approach

The planning, organizing, leading, and controlling approach was first introduced by Henri Fayol, the same person who introduced the 14 principles of management discussed in chapter 1. Despite the development of management theory, this concept has remained a prominent school of thought regarding what a manager does.

The planning function involves establishing goals and objectives, as well as strategies for achieving them (Dumler and Skinner 2005). The planning function sets a course of action for the organization through short-term and long-term goals. Short-term goals should be accomplished within a year, whereas long-term goals are designed to be achieved within 5 to 7 years (goals and objectives are discussed later in this chapter). The planning function of management can take on many forms, including planning staff goals and objectives, long-range strategic planning that drives agency operations over a longer time frame, marketing planning, and master planning for land and facility acquisition and development. Planning is more fully addressed in chapter 6.

The organizing function results from the planning function. It takes the plans and assigns them to the proper staff to carry out. In other words, organizing is the

**Table 2.1**  Function and Competency Comparison

| Function | Frontline Managers | Middle Managers | Top Managers |
|---|---|---|---|
| Conceptual | — | — | Understand organizational dynamics |
| | — | — | Possess knowledge of business and administrative principles |
| | — | Possess knowledge of organizational goals | Set goals and objectives |
| | Know the mission of the agency | Possess working knowledge of agency mission | Operate according to agency mission |
| | Possess basic planning skills | Have the ability to plan | Make effective long-range plans |
| | Possess general knowledge of the park and recreation profession | Possess knowledge of all jobs within their area of responsibility | Possess comprehensive knowledge of the park and recreation profession |
| Human resources | — | — | Work effectively with a board or elected officials |
| | — | — | Establish positive public relations |
| | Lead staff | Develop staff | Develop staff |
| | — | Understand personality styles | — |
| | — | Be a good mediator or negotiator | Be an effective facilitator |
| | — | Build partnerships and collaborations within the community | Build partnerships and collaborations within the community |
| | Possess effective written and oral communication skills | Possess effective written and oral communication skills | Possess effective written and oral communication skills |
| | Possess good listening skills | Possess good listening skills | Possess good listening skills |
| Technical | Develop and stay within a budget | Possess budgeting and financial management skills | Possess sound overall financial management skills |
| | Understand the hiring process | Possess knowledge of effective and legal hiring practices | Understand personnel law |
| | Program activities and events | Possess knowledge of programming skills | — |
| | Conduct program evaluations | Conduct program evaluations | — |
| | — | Manage contracts | Manage contracts and projects |
| | — | Solicit donations and raise funds | Raise funds |
| | Schedule programs, leagues, and staff | — | — |

---

### Something to Think About

- Plan—"If you fail to plan, you plan to fail"
- Organize—if you can't organize yourself, you have little chance of organizing others
- Control or monitor—answers the question "How are we doing?"
- Lead—Support, guide, influence and inspire

---

mechanism that puts plans into action (Certo 2003). This includes setting up an appropriate structure of employees within the organization, as well as hiring and training staff so they can do the necessary tasks to accomplish goals and objectives. The organizing function of a manager in parks and recreation is quite prominent. Programs, events, as well as staff and volunteers must all be organized. A major portion of a manager's job in this profession is planning and organizing.

The leading function involves influencing staff to carry out the assigned tasks. This function is obviously staff focused because of the need to respect staff, to motivate staff to achieve established goals, to be honest and ethical with staff, and to be an overall good leader.

The controlling function is the evaluation part of management where performance is measured. Managers establish performance standards and use these standards as benchmarks for achievement. The manager's role with this function is to address how employees can improve as well as how the organization as a whole can improve. The controlling function includes program evaluations, employee evaluations, monthly sales reports, event and program implementation results, and so on.

### Summary of Functions of Management

Two approaches for discussing the functions of management have been presented. Technical skills are present within all four functions (i.e., planning budgets, hiring staff), the human relations functions are closely aligned with the leading function, and conceptual skills are most prevalent within planning and controlling. The two approaches to functions of management share many similarities; the major difference lies not in what the manager does but in how it is labeled.

## RESOURCES TO MANAGE

There has been much discussion on the history, competencies, levels, and functions of managers, but nothing has outlined what resources managers actually manage. Resources can come in many different forms. For our purposes, **resources** are the financial, physical, technological, and human assets that organizations need for the production of goods or services.

Financial resources (discussed in detail in chapters 11 and 12) drive many of the decisions managers make. Budget restrictions, available capital, and monthly sales numbers affect what things managers do and how they do them. For example, managers are responsible for determining how money will be spent throughout the year, what programs or events can be planned, and what equipment can be purchased. Financial management may also mean deciding where to cut a budget, how

**resources—**
Financial, physical, technological, and human assets that organizations need for the production of goods or services.

to deal with unanticipated decreases in revenue throughout the year, or simply how to allocate resources. Few agencies have unlimited financial resources, so taking care of them is a large part of management. The higher the level of the manager in the organization, the more responsibility the manager will have for financial resources.

Physical resources are those things that people can see and associate with the agency. They may include a high-end resort, a roller coaster at an amusement park, an ice rink, or a store. In addition to large facilities and amenities such as these, physical resources also include equipment, such as mowers, water fountains, treadmills, and banquet tables.

Technological resources aid in the creation of products or the provision of services. Technology is changing so rapidly that it is difficult to keep up with. For many agencies this is often due to the limitations of financial resources. Larger agencies may have a staff member or department dedicated to technology, whether it is a registration system, computer-aided design (CAD) used for parks and facilities, or web-based evaluation systems. Years ago, managers spent little time on this resource, but today's managers need to manage technological resources—and rely heavily on technology to do so.

The last, and arguably most important, resource is people. Chapter 1 discussed in detail how employees are used in organizations. They are the impetus behind production, and they require a great deal of time from managers. Employees need to be trained, motivated, and evaluated. They also need to be allowed to take risks and be innovative. It is people who are the focus of almost all park and recreation agencies.

Managers have a lot on their plates. They have to manage people, finances, physical resources, and technology. They have different responsibilities and parameters of authority. They serve a variety of functions from technical to conceptual, and they are responsible for planning, organizing, leading, and controlling various parts of the organization.

## CAREER PROGRESSION OF MANAGERS

People who are new to the field and equipped with a degree in parks and recreation will most likely find themselves in a frontline management position. However, many frontline managers aspire to middle management and possibly top management. This career progression starts by gaining experience in the field and building competencies needed for the next level. Functions change from level to level, but it is necessary to gain an understanding of how competencies change as well so that managers can put their career progression into perspective. Table 2.1 demonstrates competencies of frontline, middle, and top managers grouped by function.

Several competencies will be important throughout a manager's career regardless of level, such as public speaking and written and oral communication skills. However, there are far more differences than similarities in the competencies needed by managers at different levels. These differences are not drastic; they are subtle increases in the skills, knowledge, and abilities required for increased responsibility and authority. When considering career progression, look at the conceptual competencies of knowledge of the profession (table 2.1). Competence moves from a general knowledge of the field for frontline or entry-level employees, to knowledge of a specific area such as sport for middle managers, to comprehensive knowledge of the profession for top managers. Within the technical functions, a steady progression of all three levels can be seen in hiring competencies. For example, a manager moves from understanding the process to knowledge of effective and legal hiring practices to understanding personnel law.

Although a manager's job and competency requirements change, this does not mean the knowledge and skills learned as a frontline manager can be forgotten. It is more accurate to assume that some of the competencies are not used as much but still serve as foundational knowledge needed for supervising other staff. Take programming, for example. Both frontline and middle managers have programming skills listed as a competency, but the top-level manager does not. This is because both frontline and middle managers are responsible for planning programs. Furthermore, middle-level managers are most likely supervising people who are running the programs. Although top-level managers are probably not programming at all, they supervise people who program or oversee programmers. The CEO, however, makes decisions every day that require program knowledge, such as how much space is needed for youth and adult soccer fields and what sorts of programs could operate on each field size. This example illustrates the relationship between levels and technical, human relations, and conceptual skills.

Career progression is an ongoing concern for managers. Everyone will approach it differently, but there are several common practices. First, learn to manage yourself and your responsibilities. If you can't do that, you have no hope of moving up in an organization.

Second, professionals should gain experience in different areas of the organization. They might begin as a student through internships and summer jobs. Positioning oneself for career progression means gaining as much experience as possible. Once in the field, experience is gained through daily tasks and taking on added responsibilities. This will help improve skills in both communication and technical competencies.

Third, **mentorship** has helped many managers move up within the profession. Learning from others is a good way to learn the behind-the-scenes information. Mentors guide their mentees in making good career choices, advising them on what additional responsibilities to take on and how to network with others in the profession. Mentors can be within the same agency or in a different one.

**mentorship**— Professional relationship established between a more experienced employee (mentor) and a less experienced employee (mentee) designed to guide career development.

Finally, career progression happens with education. Just because the degree is in hand does not mean that education stops. Many middle- and top-management positions require master's degrees and several years of experience. In addition, education is not just gained through universities. It is also obtained through state and national conferences, workshops, and professional development seminars. The park and recreation profession has a number of professional certifications that require more education and are highly respected in the hiring process (table 2.2).

Although career progression may seem like a simple concept, it takes a lot of planning to achieve the desired goals and level in the profession.

## MANAGEMENT DRIVERS

Thus far this chapter has focused on what managers do and what functions they play in the organization. Several underlying premises require further discussion. Roles and functions define what a manager does, but the organization's values, vision, mission, goals, and objectives drive the roles and functions of the manager. These **management drivers**, as we will call them, guide how managers make decisions, solve problems, allocate resources, and train staff. They also help people become more efficient and effective managers and improve the overall organization.

**management drivers**—Elements that influence how managers make decisions, solve problems, use resources, and function within an organization.

**Table 2.2** Select Certification Opportunities in the Field

| Certification | Website |
| --- | --- |
| Aquatics Facility Operator (AFO) | https://www.nrpa.org/certification/AFO/ |
| Certified Heritage Interpreter | www.interpnet.com |
| Certified Interpretive Manager | www.interpnet.com |
| Certified Interpretive Planner | www.interpnet.com |
| Certified Meeting Professional (CMP) | https://www.mpiweb.org/education/certified-meeting-professional |
| Certified Park and Recreation Professional (CPRP) | https://www.nrpa.org/certification/CPRP/ |
| Certified Playground Safety Inspector (CPSI) | https://www.nrpa.org/certification/CPSI/ |
| Certified Special Events Professional (CSEP) | http://www.ileahub.com/CSEP |
| Certified Therapeutic Recreation Specialist | www.nctrc.org |
| Leave No Trace Master Educator | https://lnt.org/learn/master-educator |

# Values

**values**—Beliefs held by an organization.

**shared values**—Values that are accepted and embraced by the entire staff of an organization.

**Values** underline the agency's reason for existing. They are the principles, qualities, and beliefs regarding the organization. Values have the greatest influence in an organization when they are shared by the staff. These **shared values** are embraced by all staff from the top managers to those on the front line. Organizational values are the underlying principles that drive decision making, corporate culture, and priorities. They are formed by merging three value systems—member values, leader values, and societal values (McLean, Bannon, and Gray 1999).

Member values come from the staff. Many people are drawn to companies because their own values match those of the company. Research has shown that when employee and company values match, employee loyalty, creativity, quality and accuracy of communication, and integrity of decision making increase (Kouzes and Posner 2017). For example, take Patagonia, a company that manufactures clothing and accessories for outdoor recreation adventures from surfing to alpine climbing to fly fishing. The company demonstrates its commitment to the environment by reducing pollution during manufacturing, contributing a percentage of sales to grassroots environmental groups, and using organic materials when possible. Because of these values, Patagonia is looking for staff with similar values. Patagonia's job announcements state, "We're especially interested in people who share our love of the outdoors, our passion for quality and our desire to make a difference" (Patagonia 2017a).

Leader values come from top managers. Leaders have their own values that guide organizational values. The impact of leader values within an organization will change with each company. Some will subtly influence organizational values whereas others will be a driving force, as is the case with Ben and Jerry's ice cream. Ben Cohen and Jerry Greenfield started their ice cream shop in 1978 in Burlington, Vermont. Their personal values are the impetus behind the company values, which include peace, environmentalism, and social responsibility (Ben & Jerry's Homemade Ice Cream 2007).

Societal values come from the community, customer, and society in general. They influence agencies, especially public agencies that have a responsibility to their community. This is not to say that pockets of vocal constituents with particular values could influence the value system of an entire organization, however. Societal values are adopted based on the good of the entire community, not just a select few. For example, societal values have changed the way food is prepared in New York City. As of July 2008, all restaurants must eliminate trans fat from their food (Jones and Hellmich 2006). This change resulted from the national obesity epidemic and concern over growing rates of heart disease. Changes in how people value health will affect organizational policy, decisions, and operations for years to come.

With values coming from three perspectives, an organization must bring all of these perspectives together to form shared values. Shared values drive the entire organization and are supported by the staff, owners, and customers, not just upper management. Shared values make sure everyone in the organization is operating from the same perspective regarding customer service, working relationships with peers, and the reasons the organization is in business. Furthermore, shared values result in more ethical behavior among employees, reduced stress and tension on the job, increased pride in the company, and increased understanding of job expectations (Kouzes and Posner 2017). Having shared values thus results in a more successful organization.

Here are a few examples of values statements.

## PARK DISTRICT OF OAK PARK, OAK PARK, ILLINOIS

### Our Values

Partnerships: We will work collaboratively with others in our community.

Responsible Leadership: We will create a high performing, engaged, and accountable organization.

Integrity: In all that we do, we will adhere to moral, honest, and ethical principles and work toward accessibility and inclusion.

Innovation: We will continuously try new methods and ideas, adapt services according to trends, and continuously improve processes in order to exceed the needs of our customers.

Sustainability: The District will endure through renewal, maintenance, stewardship, and stability in all aspects of operation.

Reprinted by permission from Park District of Oak Park, Illinois. Available: www.pdop.org/about/mission-vision-values/.

## MYRTLE COTTAGE GROUP INC., INGLEBURN, NEW SOUTH WALES, AUSTRALIA

Myrtle Cottage Group Inc. (Sydney, Australia) endeavors to operate in a professional and caring manner that promotes:

- Respect, dignity, and informed choice for clients, volunteers, and staff
- Integrity, honesty, and transparency in business conduct
- Diversity and inclusion

From Myrtle Cottage Group Inc. Ingleburn, NSW Australia. Available: http://myrtlecottage.org.au/about/.

## Vision

In a study involving more than 75,000 managers on six continents, it was determined that honesty is the most important characteristic workers want in their leaders. The second most important characteristic is forward thinking—having a vision (Kouzes and Posner 2017). Kouzes and Posner defined **vision** as an ideal and unique image of the future for the common good. Similar to values, a vision must be shared among the workers in an organization. This shared vision is derived from the organizational values and depicts what the company will look like in 5 to 20 years. Having a shared vision requires the entire staff to work together to see what the company can be. Good vision statements should be realistic and achievable, as well as optimistic and ambitious. To get a better idea of what vision statements are, here are two examples.

**vision**—Realistic and desirable view of where an organization will be in the future.

### BRENHAM PARKS AND RECREATION, BRENHAM, TEXAS

The vision for the future of Brenham Parks and Recreation is to provide families and visitors a safe, accessible, and high quality park system that provides diverse recreation opportunities.

From Parks & Recreation, The city of Brenham, Texas. Available: http://cityofbrenham.org/parks /documents/rec-masterplan-2015.pdf.

### BOYS & GIRLS CLUBS OF AMERICA

Vision: Provide a world-class Club Experience that assures success is within reach of every young person who enters our doors, with all members on track to graduate from high school with a plan for the future, demonstrating good character and citizenship, and living a healthy lifestyle.

From Boys & Girls Clubs of America. Available: https://www.bgca.org/about-us/our-mission-story.

Managers play a major role in the development and achievement of the vision. They should not create the vision on their own; instead, they work with staff to look at the history of the organization, assess where it is today, and create a vision for where it will be in the future. Although the manager facilitates creation of the vision, the staff has a major role in its creation. This involvement reinforces staff commitment to achieving what they create, making this a shared vision. A shared vision results in significantly higher job satisfaction for workers, who are more motivated, committed to the organization, and productive (Kouzes and Posner 2017). In an attempt to make management drivers more relatable for both staff members and the community, many organizations are developing unique ways to illustrate their values, vision, mission, and goals.

**mission**—Statement of purpose for an organization that describes who the customers are, what services are provided, and how the services are delivered.

## Mission

A **mission** is a more detailed extension of the values and vision of an organization. Specifically, a mission statement addresses who the customers are, what services the organization provides, and how services are provided (McLean, Bannon, and Gray 1999). Mission statements are much more readily publicized than values and vision statements even though they are no more important to the organization than

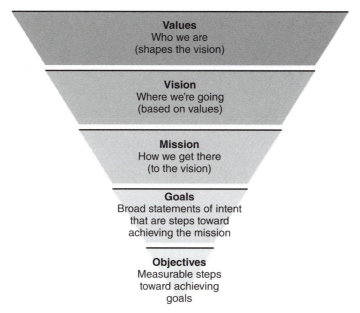

**Figure 2.2** Values, vision, mission, goals, and objectives.

the other two. Overall, a mission statement is a concise purpose statement reflecting what the company does. Here are a couple of examples.

## SCHLITTERBAHN WATERPARKS

Schlitterbahn Waterparks exist to provide wholesome family fun at the hottest, coolest places in Texas and Kansas. A less visible part of our mission is to make tomorrow a little brighter for as many children as possible.

From Schlitterbahn Waterparks. Available: http://www.schlitterbahn.com/community/mission.

## TEXAS PARKS AND WILDLIFE DEPARTMENT

Mission: To manage and conserve the natural and cultural resources of Texas and to provide hunting, fishing, and outdoor recreation opportunities for the use and enjoyment of present and future generations.

From Texas Parks & Wildlife Department. Available: https://tpwd.texas.gov/about/mission-philosophy.

Values, vision, and mission function together and are tightly entwined. Think of them as an inverted pyramid (figure 2.2) to see how they work together to drive the day-to-day operations of managers. The values are the overarching premise of the organization and are general guiding principles resulting in a more specific vision, leading to the most specific of the three, the mission. Even more specific than these three are the goals and objectives, which together form stepping stones to achieving the mission and thus the vision, while keeping in mind the values upon which the organization is founded.

## Goals

Sometimes the terms *goals* and *objectives* are used interchangeably when in fact they are distinct. **Goals** are broad statements of intended actions. They outline what an agency wishes to accomplish, which helps move the organization in the desired

**goals**—Broad statements of intent set by organizations to guide actions.

direction to fulfill its mission and achieve its vision. Here are some examples of goals.

## SPORT AND RECREATION VICTORIA, AUSTRALIA, HAS THE FOLLOWING FOUR GOALS.

1. Improve the health and well-being of Victorians
2. Build stronger and more connected communities
3. Deliver economic growth and jobs
4. Enhance livability

From Sport & Recreation Victoria, Australia. Available: http://sport.vic.gov.au/about-us/what-we-do.

## THE USDA FOREST SERVICE LISTS THE FOLLOWING GOALS IN THEIR STRATEGIC PLAN:

Sustain our nation's forests and grasslands

Deliver benefits to the public

Apply knowledge globally

Excel as a high-performing agency

From US Forest Services. Available: https://www.fs.fed.us/sites/default/files/strategic-plan%5B2%5D-6_17_15_revised.pdf.

Goals can be short term, achievable in a year or less; intermediate term, achievable in one to five years; or long term, achievable in five to seven years. Agencies set short-, intermediate-, and long-term goals to drive decision making and carry out planning functions. They set goals for marketing, productivity, and the use of financial resources.

Although the focus thus far has been organizational goals, goals are infused throughout the organization, right down to individual employees. Each department within an organization may have its own goals. In that instance, it is important that the department goals link back to the vision, mission, and goals of the organization. Furthermore, employees may have annual, semiannual, or biannual goals for themselves. Often these goals are used as performance measures during employee evaluations and should also relate to what the department and/or organization is striving to achieve.

Participation in organizational goal setting is a must. The people responsible for achieving the goals know the ins and outs of the area better than upper management would. Also, staff members need to feel they have a role in determining the direction of the organization. This increases their commitment to achieving the goals. Research has indicated that when people set goals, they outperform those who do not set goals (Locke 1968). When difficult goals are set and accepted, a higher level of performance results.

## Objectives

**objectives**—Direct statements that serve as steps to achieving goals.

In order to achieve goals, it is necessary to establish objectives. **Objectives** are measurable steps to achieving goals. In essence, goals are what an agency wants to accomplish, and objectives are how the staff is going to accomplish them.

## SMART Objectives

Few organizations develop well-written objectives. A well-written objective should be SMART—specific, measurable, achievable, realistic, and time-related (Drucker 1954). Objectives are far more difficult to write than goals because of the need to make them SMART. Let's use the following objective for a convention and visitors' bureau to demonstrate the SMART acronym.

Objective: The sales and marketing staff is responsible for bringing three new conferences to the Binghamton Convention Center by the end of 2019.

### Specific

Objectives should clearly state what is to be accomplished. They should be detailed, focused, and concrete as to what is to be achieved. For the sample objective, there is no doubt what is to be achieved. The sales staff knows they need to find three new clients and get their conferences scheduled at the convention center.

### Measurable

Objectives should be written so that they can be assessed as to whether or not they are achieved. The specification of three conferences makes this objective measurable. A manager should be able to answer yes or no as to whether or not three conferences were booked and thus the objective was achieved.

### Achievable

If objectives are not achievable in the near future, staff will not stay motivated to complete them. For example, if the convention center did not have space for three more conferences until 2021, this objective would not be achievable. Or if the date to fulfill this objective is set four years into the future, it is too far away to keep staff committed to it, again making it unachievable. Objectives are regularly reviewed either semiannually or annually to update progress, add new objectives, and change objectives that are not achievable.

### Realistic

A good objective must be realistically attainable; the organization needs to have the appropriate resources such as staff and budget. Assume the sales and marketing department consists of two people who have a lot of responsibility and who are short-staffed. A few more conferences might be realistic, but if the objective was changed to 20 new conferences, two people realistically could not accomplish it. Although this example is exaggerated to illustrate a point, it shows why staff at all levels should be involved in setting goals and objectives—they have intimate knowledge of what objectives are realistic.

### Time-Related

In order to know if the agency is on target to achieve the goals, the objectives must be time-related, meaning there is an established time frame or deadline, such as a year, a month, a specific date, or a season, that indicates when the objective will be achieved. This is where many objectives fall short. The objectives may follow SMART in everything but the component that makes the objective time-related—the deadline. This is not to say that the deadline cannot be changed. It is not always possible to predict when an objective can be achieved. For example, assume an agency evaluates its employees based on employee- and manager-determined objectives each year. During the employee evaluation meeting, progress on objectives is discussed. If an objective was scheduled to be completed by the evaluation meeting and it was not, the objective can be carried over to the next evaluation with a new deadline (if feasible) and a discussion can be held to ascertain why the objective was not met.

### Three Types of Management Objectives

Following the SMART method of writing objectives will provide a solid framework of work to be accomplished over a certain length of time. However, managers should not only be concerned with how objectives are written, they should be concerned with the type of objectives they are writing as well. There are three types of management objectives: process, impact, and outcome objectives (March of Dimes 2007).

*Process objectives* hold agencies accountable for whether and how they accomplish things. These objectives could pertain to staff or customers. For example, a process objective could be the following:

By December 2019, the customer service staff will explore the use of new technology that could be used to communicate with and engage customers.

This objective is designed to examine the current process and to make suggestions for improving it.

*Impact objectives* focus on changes in attitudes, knowledge, perceptions, and other behaviors, such as the following objective for the Park District of Oak Park (Illinois):

Fitness staff will create a community-wide wellness campaign, possibly exploring partnerships with local partners and/or other national campaigns such as the Surgeon General's walking campaign, by the end of 2020.

*Outcome objectives* focus on the end result of an action. As mentioned in the discussion of outcomes-based management in chapter 1, outcomes can be skill, knowledge, attitude, value, and condition oriented (United Way of America 1996). To help clarify the distinction between impact and outcome objectives, consider the following outcome objective. Now that the staff has started their community-wide wellness campaign, as outlined in the impact objective, the next objective is outcome based:

The Park District of Oak Park will strive to earn a Community Impact Award from the Illinois Park and Recreation Association based on its programs and reputation as contributing to the health and wellness of its citizens.

Goals and objectives have been a common topic of study in beginning leadership and programming courses as well as in more advanced evaluation and management courses. The need to work with goals and objectives will also be a mainstay throughout a manager's career.

## EFFICIENCY AND EFFECTIVENESS

New organizations open every day, from restaurants to fitness centers to outdoor recreation equipment stores. Some close within a few months whereas others thrive for years. What makes organizations successful? There are many answers to this question, but one key is whether an organization is efficient and effective. The most important goal of this book is to teach you to be an efficient and effective manager, which will lead to an organization that has a much better chance of succeeding. Since these two terms will be used throughout the book, it is important to understand what they mean.

**Efficiency** is concerned with minimizing the amount of resources that an organization wastes. An efficient organization does not waste resources such as money, people, or technology. All of these resources cost money, and quality organizations do not waste resources. Examples of wasted resources include keeping lifeguards on the clock and paying them to do nothing when the pool is closed due to inclement weather or buying 20 more staff uniforms than are actually needed.

**Effectiveness** refers to how capable an organization is of achieving its goals and objectives. An agency might strive to increase membership by 20 percent, to sell 20 percent more units each quarter, or to operate at 85 percent of room capacity each month. The degree to which the organization meets these goals and objectives is a measure of its effectiveness.

Efficiency and effectiveness are measured in numerous ways and from many perspectives. Customers measure them through participation in programs, facility use, and product purchases. The community as a whole can evaluate efficiency and effectiveness by passing referenda and valuing the quality of life that results from agency products and services. Internally, organizations can measure efficiency and effectiveness by looking at how monetary and human resources are used in relation to quality of products and services or how well the organization is meeting the needs of the community.

Do not assume that all organizations that have been in business for years are both efficient and effective. Efficiency and effectiveness can be measured on a continuum from efficient to inefficient and effective to ineffective (figure 2.3).

**efficiency**—
Minimizing the waste of human, financial, technological, and physical resources.

**effectiveness**—
Capability of an organization to achieve its goals and objectives.

**Figure 2.3** Efficiency versus effectiveness.

Organizations can have varying levels of each, and these levels can change over time. So, how can organizations remain both efficient and effective? That question will be answered throughout this book by providing insight into how to be a better manager. For example, managers must be efficient and effective employees themselves. Most park and recreation agencies have limited resources, and employees are expected to be as efficient as possible while still providing quality services. Managers are also responsible for measuring the efficiency and effectiveness of employees through employee evaluation and continual feedback on performance (chapter 9), having sound financial management processes (chapters 11 and 12), and evaluating the effectiveness of programs and services (chapter 13). All of these and more contribute to the efficiency and effectiveness of organizations.

# CRITICAL MANAGEMENT ISSUES

Managers face many challenges in their day-to-day tasks. While there are many issues that could be classified as critical, it is important to mention two that have grown in importance over the last decade: managing a diverse workforce and sustainable business practices.

## Managing a Diverse Workforce

**cultural competency**—Ability to learn and build understanding between people of varying cultures; being respectful, enriched by, and celebrating of differences within and between groups of people.

Perhaps one of the most challenging aspects of managing people is the diversity found in today's workforce. Thirty-five percent of the workforce is nonwhite, and that figure continues to grow each year. Managing a diverse workforce involves respect, acceptance, and acknowledgement that individuals are different from each other (Lumadi 2008). Diversity is a complex issue and can be related to a variety of factors, including age, culture, education, employee status, family status, gender, national origin, physical appearance, race, regional origin, religion, sexual orientation, and thinking style. Developing **cultural competency** will greatly assist managers working with both a diverse workforce and a diverse community. According to Alpert (2015, 1) "culture refers to the values, norms, and traditions that affect the way a member of a group typically perceives, thinks, interacts, behaves, and makes judgments. It even affects perceptions of time, which can impact day-to-day scheduling and deadlines."

There are many challenges to managing a diverse workforce.

- Full cultural integration can be inhibited by prejudice, stereotyping, and discrimination.
- Colleagues from some cultures may be reluctant to speak up and let their opinions be heard.
- Communication styles and language can be misinterpreted.
- Understanding visa status and employment laws can be difficult and expensive.
- Proper etiquette can vary by culture (Hult International Business School 2017).

The benefits of a diverse workforce outweigh these challenges. They include such things as:

- Increased productivity, creativity, and business image
- Infusion of varying viewpoints, perspectives, and experiences
- Opportunity to interact with people who do not think like you
- Ability to draw from a diverse talent pool, which allows organizations to hire high-quality employees
- Allows for a broader cross section of programs and services
- Provides greater opportunity for personal and professional growth

If managers are to be culturally competent, they must be able to interact effectively with people from different cultures. In order to be successful, managers must first have an awareness of their own cultural worldview. It is then necessary to learn about other cultural practices and worldviews, develop tolerant attitudes toward cultural differences, and practice cross-cultural skills at every opportunity. Shaban (2016) details seven specific steps managers can take to improve their ability to manage a diverse group of employees:

- There must be a commitment by top management to diversity.
- Increase diversity awareness within the organization by allowing "differences to be celebrated instead of being tolerated" (79).
- Increase diversity skills in communication; recognize that both verbal and nonverbal communication may mean different things to different people.
- Encourage flexibility in approaches to completion of tasks as well as scheduling.
- Establish clear and objective performance standards.
- Empower employees to "challenge discriminatory behaviors, actions, and remarks" (80).
- Reward employees for effective diversity management.

Managing a diverse workforce will require the manager to continually grow and develop as a person and a professional. Our world is changing so fast that good managers cannot rely on the workforce looking like it always has and being able to treat everyone the same. They will have to broaden their perspectives and best utilize the talent within their department. Even if the agency itself has limited diversity among the staff, park and recreation professionals will face changing demographics within the community. They will need the expertise and staff to meet the needs of that diverse community.

## Sustainable Business Practices

Further complicating the job of a manager is the need for implementing sustainable business practices. Many agencies and organizations are now concerned with more than just the financial bottom line. They are placing an emphasis on what is referred to as a triple bottom line: people, planet, and profit (figure 2.4) (University of North Florida 2017). The triple bottom line goal is to create strategies that preserve the long-term viability of people (social responsibility in and toward community and beyond), planet (stewardship of the environment), and profit (economic value to stakeholders).

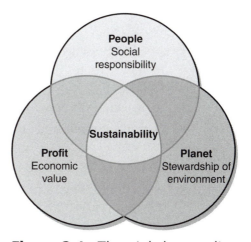

**Figure 2.4**   The triple bottom line.
University of Northern Florida.

**Sustainability** requires that we see the world as an integrated system that connects businesses to society and the environment through both space and time. Pollution in one part of the world affects others thousands of miles away.

The people component of the triple bottom line includes both social and corporate responsibility strategies. Social and corporate responsibility not only affect communities today but also leave lasting impressions for generations to come. Sustainable business practices consider resource scarcity and how we use limited

**sustainability**— Responsible use of resources so as not to deplete or permanently damage them for future generations.

resources. One of the leaders in social and corporate sustainability is Patagonia. They diligently abide by international labor and human rights standards by protecting migrant workers, and assist supply chain partners in meeting human rights standards, particularly in the areas of human trafficking and child labor. They carry fair trade certified products where a portion of the sales go back to the workers to use for projects such as a day care center within the plant (Patagonia 2017b).

Sustainability for the planet is a vast undertaking. It can include such things as efforts to reduce a company's environmental footprint, reduce waste, or enhance environmental stewardship. One example of this is the LEED (Leadership in Energy and Environmental Design) building rating system. LEED is an independent verification of a building's or neighborhood's green features, including the design, construction, operations, and maintenance of resource-efficient, high-performing, healthy, cost-effective buildings (LEED 2017). Another example is ecotourism, which strives to support conservation of natural areas, minimize pollution, respect cultural traditions, plan activities to avoid physical or environmental degradation, and efficiently use limited and nonrenewable resources (Greenloons 2017).

For many agencies and companies, profit can be a driving force in making sustainability decisions. Some sustainability initiatives can be quite expensive in terms of both financial and human resources. However, some efforts over the long term can save the company money and build the bottom line. For example, a LEED gold-certified building can save utility costs, decrease maintenance expenditures, and reduce waste sent to landfills. The challenge for managers is determining what level of sustainability the agency should achieve. Parks and recreation by its very nature is often seen as a profession that should be wedded to sustainable practices. Here are a few things managers can do to enhance sustainable business practices:

- Top executives need to instill the awareness that sustainability is both serious and a priority for the agency.
- Start small and build. For example, go paperless, install energy efficient lighting, use environmentally safe cleaning products.
- Set goals, targets, and priorities on what to accomplish and when to accomplish it.
- Involve employees in creating initiatives.
- Learn from other similar agencies. Find out what works for them and what does not. Learn from their mistakes.

Both of these critical management issues can essentially be tied to the culture of the organization. Managers will have to lay the groundwork, demonstrate the importance of diversity and sustainability, and work with staff to implement education programs and processes to support the efforts aimed at achieving goals. Through strong management practices, agencies can create a diverse workforce and implement sustainable business practices.

 Check out the web study guide for additional material, including learning activities, sample documents, interactive case studies, web links, CPRP exam connections, and more.

## Conclusion

Regardless of what level manager you are and what agency you work for, several things will hold true. First, efficiency and effectiveness will always be a vital part of success in an agency. Second, managers will be driven by values, vision, and mission statements so they know where the company is headed and how they are going to get there. Finally, a manager can always count on having goals and objectives that guide the agency, the department, and the individual employee. All of these things working together form what managers do, why they do it, and how they get it done.

## Review Questions

1. Discuss the three levels of management and give an example of each.
2. How do the three levels of management relate to the technical, human relations, and conceptual functions of managers?
3. Differentiate among the planning, organizing, leading, and controlling functions of management.
4. Define *responsibility* and *authority*. How do they change as a person moves up the three levels of management?
5. Give examples of the four types of resources a manager must deal with in the workplace.
6. How do competencies change in terms of career progression and the functions of management?
7. Define *values*, *vision*, and *mission*. How do they each drive management?
8. Differentiate between goals and objectives, and then write an objective that follows the SMART acronym.
9. Discuss efficiency and effectiveness. Give examples from your own experience of good and poor efficiency and effectiveness.
10. Describe how managers experience career progression in terms of competencies needed from entry-level through top-level managers.
11. Define diversity.
12. Give an example of sustainable business practices.

# 3

# Legal Foundations for Managers

## Learning Outcomes

- Identify legal issues in recreation management.
- Distinguish between the three types of torts.
- Describe important considerations in contracts.
- Describe the risk management process.
- Compare the employment laws of the United States, the United Kingdom, Canada, and Australia.

## Key Terms

civil law, criminal law, torts, negligence, assumption of risk, intentional torts, battery, assault, defamation, false imprisonment, strict liability, contract, legislation, gross negligence, Good Samaritan statutes, risk management, employment laws

## Competency Check

Take another look at table 1.6 to see how you assessed this related competency.

4. Demonstrate basic knowledge of laws and legal matters affecting the field.

## A Day in the Life

Legal and risk management concerns are a big part of my job. I review contracts and pass them on to our insurance company for approval of coverage for programs and events. When volunteers rent vehicles to transport athletes to various competitions, it is important to ensure that there is an automobile insurance policy in place. I also make sure that every athlete has a medical release form and that each volunteer completes a background check and an online protective behavior course before working with our athletes. Once volunteers are cleared to work with our athletes, I provide incident report forms so that records of incidents can be captured should an incident happen at a program site. In addition to contract review, insurance concerns, and risk management procedures, my organization recently discussed the Fair Labor Standards Act and whether wage employees are being paid in accordance with statutory law. Knowledge of law and risk management concepts is a critical part of my job and key to ensuring our organization can continue to provide services to athletes in our community.

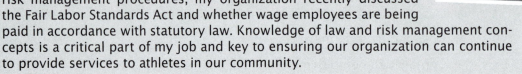

Alyssa Truesdale
James River Region Director
Special Olympics Virginia
Richmond, Virginia

The authors thank contributors Angela Hayslett and Katharine Nohr for writing this chapter.

A basic understanding of legal concerns is crucial for students who will soon be working in the leisure services industry. Whole courses are devoted to legal concerns and risk management. Even some of the subtopics of this chapter, such as negligence and contract law, are given semester-long coverage in law schools, business schools, and other curricula. Therefore it is not the purpose of this chapter to provide a complete understanding of legal concerns or to provide legal advice. The intent of this chapter is to introduce legal concepts and applications to prepare you for further study or on-the-job learning.

It would be rare indeed if you did not encounter a situation in your career or personal life that required your involvement in litigation to some extent. You might merely work for an agency or business that is involved in a lawsuit, or you might be a direct part of a lawsuit in your capacity as an employee or manager. If this happens, an understanding of legal implications may empower you to better handle the legal process and the subsequent decisions that you will make with the aid of your attorney.

This chapter addresses major legal topics in the context of specializations within the field of leisure services. The chapter first introduces current trends, then provides an overview of relevant legal terms and concepts, and finally provides an overview of legal issues and risk management principles with unique applications for managers.

The U.S., Australian, and Canadian legal systems were influenced by the British legal system. Understand that there are many similarities and differences between these legal systems, but this chapter focuses more on the U.S. system. However, U.S., U.K., Australian, and Canadian terminology are very similar.

# CURRENT LEGAL ISSUES AND TRENDS

The importance of understanding legal issues and risk management in leisure services management is unique to each student. A few students may wish to pursue future legal studies by choosing law as a profession. For this group, understanding legal issues is the first small step in a long journey of learning about legal issues and risk management. Some students may become risk managers for their organization, with the specific job of managing risk, improving safety, and limiting the liability of the organization. Others will be involved in risk management and reducing the risk of liability through their roles as managers and leaders in various organizations. And for those who become personally involved in a lawsuit, a basic understanding of legal issues might bring empowerment to better handle the litigation process.

Regardless of your specialization in the field, the possibility of a lawsuit is ever present. You can likely imagine the many situations in leisure services where injury and subsequent lawsuits can occur. For example, in natural resources management, lawsuits have resulted from the following categories of potential harm:

- Water features such as fast-moving rivers and streams, lakes, and ocean currents
- Encounters between humans and carnivorous animals such as bears, cougars, and alligators
- Scenic overlooks and high cliffs
- Search-and-rescue operations

In the area of hospitality and tourism, litigation has arisen from the following categories of events:

- The serving of alcohol
- Swimming and diving in hotel pools
- Hotel security
- Cruise ships and ports of call
- Travel and tour planning

In the area of recreational sport, the following categories encompass litigated areas:

- Facilities such as basketball courts and fitness centers
- Supervision of sport activities
- Equipment

In municipal recreation, areas of concern for litigation include the following:

- Youth supervision
- Lightning preparedness
- Facilities and equipment
- Playground safety

In the nonprofit sector, litigated areas include the following:

- Protection of lakes and streams
- Protection of endangered species

In recreation therapy, important legal issues include the following:

- Employment of people with disabilities
- Inclusion and safety in sport
- Communication regarding participant disabilities

**civil law**—Laws that regulate the private rights of people and provide legal remedies regarding disputes between individuals on matters like torts and contracts.

Even with the most strict safety standards, their diligent execution and care, injuries will occur and lawsuits will arise. For all students, a basic understanding of key legal concepts is important for the leisure services manager. Knowledge of the basics is the first step toward becoming empowered and understanding the rationale behind preventive risk management and safety measures.

## CIVIL AND CRIMINAL LAW

**criminal law**—Laws that define crimes and conduct that threatens public safety and welfare and warrants punishment by the government

Leisure service managers will most often be concerned with **civil law**, applicable when one person or company files a lawsuit against another. The party filing the lawsuit alleges that the other party, the defendant, breached a contract or a duty owed and caused damages or injury. In civil cases, the plaintiff seeks an award of monetary damages to be paid by the person at fault.

**Criminal laws** protect people from harm caused by others and result in prosecution by a state or federal government entity. If a person is convicted of a criminal offense, the punishment will most likely be imposition of a fine or prison sentence.

# Torts

A **tort** is an important concept in civil law, referring to a wrongful act or omission. If a wrongdoer or tortfeasor is found liable for a tort, an award of monetary damages will be made requiring the tortfeasor to pay the injured person. If more than one person commits a tort, they are joint tortfeasors. There are three types of torts:

1. Negligence torts
2. Intentional torts
3. Strict liability torts

**torts**—A wrongful act or omission in civil law that may result in negligence, intentional torts, or strict liability.

## Negligence

**Negligence** represents the most likely type of lawsuit a leisure services manager might face when someone is injured on the property of the organization. Negligent conduct occurs when a defendant fails to meet the standard of care for the protection of others and as a result someone or someone's property is harmed.

**negligence**—Conduct that fails to meet the standard of care for the protection of others and as a result someone or their property is harmed.

**Four Elements of Negligence** In order to pursue a negligence cause of action, one must prove the existence of four elements (figure 3.1). These elements are duty, breach of duty, causation, and damages.

The first element, duty, is a special relationship established inherently, voluntarily, or statutorily between a service provider and participant. Managers of leisure services typically owe a duty to provide a reasonably safe environment and keep participants from an unreasonable risk of harm. Establishing the standard of care (the duty or responsibility of the plaintiff) is critical to whether a case is won or lost. Following is a list of factors that a court might consider when determining whether the standard of care was met. Often, a combination of factors determines whether the standard of care was met.

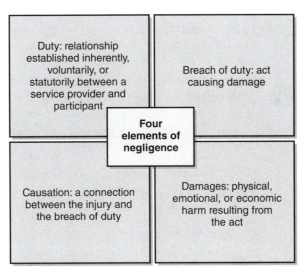

**Figure 3.1** Elements of negligence.

- *Case precedent.* Courts will look to the outcomes of previous cases to determine the standard of care.

- *Rules and regulations.* The standard of care might be written in a rule put forth by a regulatory agency (e.g., pool safety standards regarding the proper number of lifeguards for a pool of a given size).

- *State and federal laws.* Legislation may mandate a certain act. For example, in some states, fitness centers, high schools, and park and recreation agencies are required to have automated external defibrillators (AEDs) on the premises.

- *Community practice or industry standard.* The standard of care might be influenced by what others in the industry or community are doing. For example, do other playgrounds in the city or state adhere to certain guidelines?

- *Federal regulatory agencies.* The Consumer Product Safety Commission (CPSC) has guidelines for playground safety that are often used by courts in determining whether the standard of care was met for playgrounds.

- *Professional associations.* Position statements are often published by organizations such as the National Collegiate Athletic Association (NCAA), the American College of Sports Medicine (ACSM), the National Recreation and Park Association (NRPA), and the National Athletic Trainers' Association (NATA) that provide guidelines on subjects as diverse as lightning safety and equipment safety. These guidelines might be used by the courts in determining the standard of care.

- *Agency manuals.* The policy and procedure manuals of organizations might be used in determining whether they met their own standards.

- *Expert opinion.* The opinions of experts from various fields might be used to help a court determine the standard of care.

The second element, the breach of duty, or the act causing damage, may be either a commission (something you did) or an omission (something you did not do but should have). Failure to properly supervise young children at soccer practice is an example of omission, whereas removing warning signs from a lakefront swimming area is an example of commission.

The third element to be proved is that there is a connection between the injury and the breach of duty. Causation is the crucial link between the act and the damages.

Finally, damages are simply the injury received. In order to pursue a negligence claim, the plaintiff must show that some physical, emotional, or economic harm resulted from the act.

**assumption of risk**—An effort to shift the responsibility for the injury back to the plaintiff.

Defenses to negligence claims emanate from three sources of law: common law, contract law, and statutory law. **Assumption of risk** is a legal theory that falls under the common-law category. Under this theory, plaintiffs may not recover for damages if they were injured as a result of a risk inherent to the activity and they voluntarily exposed themselves to a danger that was known and understood. Some courts recognize that three elements must exist for an assumption of risk defense to shield the defendant from liability:

1. The risk must be inherent to the activity.
2. The plaintiff must voluntarily consent to participate in the activity.
3. The plaintiff must have knowledge, understanding, or appreciation of the risks involved in the activity.

Note that the interpretation of this doctrine varies from state to state, and some states no longer recognize it. The interpretation in this section is but one example.

Providers of leisure services must ensure that patrons know of the risks inherent in an activity. They can tell patrons about the risks either verbally, such as in a short presentation before a rafting trip, for example, or in written form, such as on a warning sign or in a document that lists the risks. Often a waiver will contain language that warns of the risks in an activity. When risks are told or written, the assumption of risk that might protect the service provider is termed *express assumption of risk*.

Another way that participants might be held to have knowledge of risk is through their background, experience, or common knowledge. A skilled climber, for example, might be held to assume the risks in climbing, just as an experienced athlete might be held to assume the risks inherent to a particular sport. When knowledge of the risk comes from a person's background, experience, or common knowledge, the assumption of risk that might be raised as a defense is termed *implied assumption of risk*.

Finally, certain risks that are deemed to be inherent to certain activities are written in state laws. For example, in some states, a collision with a tree would be a risk assumed by a snow skier. It would not be feasible to remove all trees bordering a ski slope. Trees are part of the experience and an inherent risk in skiing.

Another method by which defendants might seek to protect themselves by shifting responsibility is the comparative negligence defense. With this defense, a plaintiff might be entitled to only that part of the final judgment for damages for which the court determines the defendant to be responsible. For example, where a defendant is found 60 percent responsible, the plaintiff is found 40 percent responsible, and the total verdict is for $100,000, the plaintiff would only recover $60,000, the proportional amount by which the defendant was found responsible. This type of defense is called *pure comparative negligence*. Other forms of comparative negligence might proportion damages only if the plaintiff is less than 50 percent at fault.

In addition to these defenses, there is a maximum amount of time that a plaintiff can wait before bringing a lawsuit. This is called the statute of limitations. As an example, if the plaintiff brings a lawsuit after three years and the statute of limitations is two years, the defendant may be able to successfully dismiss the lawsuit.

Release or waiver is another defense used in negligence cases. A waiver signed by an activity participant will have exculpatory language protecting the service provider from ordinary negligence. A well-written waiver releasing a leisure services provider from liability for ordinary negligence while participating in an activity can be enough to protect an organization from liability for a negligence claim. Some jurisdictions have determined that such documents are against public policy, and even if they are signed, the participant can recover against the negligent organization. Other states allow releases and waivers as long as they are signed and understood by the participant.

Governmental immunity, known as sovereign immunity, is a defense that may be available to local, state, or federal governmental entities that might be immune from lawsuits unless they prove their consent. In 1946, the U.S. Congress passed the Federal Tort Claims Act, which replaced governmental immunity and allowed the government to be held liable for certain negligent acts. State legislatures also enacted their own tort claim acts to enable people to file negligence claims against public entities at the state level.

Because of this movement to abrogate governmental immunity, there has been an increase in the number of statutory defenses to negligence for public, private, and nonprofit entities. These include tort immunity statutes, such as recreational user statutes and sport safety statutes that require a higher level of negligence for liability to be found, and caps on damages for negligence claims.

Recreational user statutes are legislative acts established in all states for the purpose of protecting landowners from liability if they permit the public to use their property at no cost for recreational activities. Since the inception of recreational user statutes in the mid-1960s, the statutes have been interpreted in a variety of ways at the state level and have evolved to protect both private and public landowners.

Sport safety statutes exist in most states to limit the liability of certain commercial leisure enterprises. The theme of these laws is to shift responsibility to participants for risks that they voluntarily assume. The most common types of sport safety statutes provide legislative protection for snow skiing, roller skating, and equestrian activities. In addition, the list of protected activities has expanded to include limitations on liability for activities as diverse as hang gliding, snowmobiling, and white-water boating. Additionally, some states have enacted statutory provisions that provide blanket protection to all sport and recreational activities.

**Alternative Ways to Prove Negligence**   Plaintiffs may use the following theories in an effort to prove negligence against one or more defendants in a lawsuit:

- Negligent entrustment
- Vicarious liability
- Joint and several liability
- Negligence per se
- *Res ipsa loquitur*

Negligent entrustment arises when a person or organization entrusts a person to use their motor vehicle or dangerous object and an accident occurs, causing injury. The plaintiff claims that the person or entity was negligent for allowing an incompetent or unfit person to use a dangerous object, such as a car. The plaintiff will attempt to prove that the defendant knew that the driver had a bad driving record, used drugs or alcohol, was not licensed, or there were other facts to establish the driver incompetent or unfit.

Vicarious liability occurs when the actions of an organization's agents, employees, volunteers, or others acting on their behalf cause injury or damages for which the organization may be at fault. The organization is deemed to be legally responsible for those persons acting on its behalf. If an employee is acting within the scope of his employment when committing a tort, an employer might be held liable under the master–servant rule, also known as the *respondeat superior* doctrine. Under this doctrine, a lawsuit might be filed against the employee, alleging negligence, and against the employer, alleging vicarious liability.

Joint and several liability might come into play if your organization is one of multiple defendants in a lawsuit. The defendant is responsible for paying the entire judgment if it is even 1 percent responsible if another defendant cannot pay its portion of the judgment.

Negligence per se is when an act is inherently negligent because of a statute or an ordinance that prohibits such act. If there is a violation, the plaintiff will not have to prove there was a breach of a duty of care.

*Res ipsa loquitur* is a legal doctrine applicable when negligence is inferred simply by the accident occurring when the cause of the accident is in the exclusive control of the defendant. This might occur where there is a machine, such as an elevator, that caused the accident. The plaintiff would only have to prove that the machine was in the exclusive control of the owner of the facility, that the accident would not have happened in the ordinary course of events, and that he or she did not contribute to the cause of the accident.

**intentional torts**—A purposeful action conducted by a person who intends to harm another person or knows with substantial certainty that his or her conduct will harm another person.

## Intentional Torts

As mentioned previously, the most common type of lawsuit in recreational settings is negligence, since most managers and staff do not intend to act in such a way that will bring harm to others. In some cases, however, intentional acts are committed that result in harm to participants. The following are **intentional torts** that might be alleged (see also figure 3.2).

**Battery and Assault**   The law often makes a technical distinction between assault and battery that differs from common perceptions of the two. The distinction is that battery involves the touching of another whereas assault involves the threat of that touching. **Battery** is generally defined as the touching of another that is intentional, harmful or offensive, unprivileged, and unpermitted. The intentional aspect refers to the intent to make contact with another, either directly or indirectly (e.g., throwing a baseball at someone). The touch can be either harmful, meaning that the victim does have

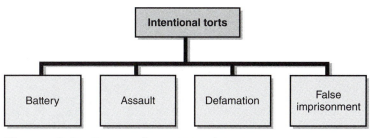

**Figure 3.2** Types of intentional torts.

to be bruised or physically hurt, or it can be offensive, such as an inappropriate touch associated with sexual harassment. Harmful touching is common in sport but often there is no liability because it is permitted (or consented to) as part of the game. Examples of situations where battery might come up include referees getting into fights with college intramural players or a counselor touching a camper inappropriately. Rules regarding appropriate touching, methods of discipline, and referees not taking matters into their own hands are put in place to avoid situations that might lead to battery and subsequent lawsuits against the organization.

**battery**—Touching of another that is intentional, harmful or offensive, unprivileged, and unpermitted.

Assault is closely associated with battery but differs in that assault is the threat of battery. An organization might be held liable for the acts of an employee who threatens to touch someone in a harmful or offensive way. Again, it is important to instruct staff on not taking matters into their own hands by threatening another person. Waiting for the proper authority to handle a heated situation is often the best measure to take.

**assault**—The threat of battery.

**Defamation**   Most people have heard about the intentional tort of **defamation** (figure 3.3). Gossip in the workplace; media outlets that write harmful, untrue things about certain people to increase sales; untrue negative remarks that are made without knowing that they were overheard; and negative untrue evaluations of work performance can all lead to defamation under the right circumstances. *Defamation* is an umbrella term for two specific types of defamation: libel and slander. Slander represents the verbal form of defamation, and libel represents the written form. In defamation lawsuits, plaintiffs have been injured as a result of something written or spoken about them that was untrue, harmful, and made public.

**defamation**—Causing harm to another person's reputation by making a false statement.

The law uses certain terms to describe that which is harmful and made public. The term used for harm is *defamatory*. Therefore, one element of defamation is making a statement that is defamatory. The term used to describe a statement that is made public is *published to a third party*. This means that a third person, someone other than the person making the statement and the person affected by the statement, has heard what was said.

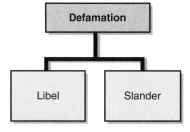

**Figure 3.3** Types of defamation.

The rules for defamation differ for public figures and ordinary citizens. Public figures generally have less protection against statements about them that are untrue and negative. Also, certain categories of defamatory statements are potentially more libelous, including statements about someone's moral character (e.g., falsely calling someone a child molester), a person's chastity (e.g., sexual promiscuity), and specific diseases, as well as statements that affect a person's occupation and profession.

To avoid defamation, managers must discourage gossip in the workplace, back up performance evaluations with objective factual information, and not say anything if they are unsure of the truth in a given situation.

**false imprisonment**—The intentional and unlawful detention of another person.

**False Imprisonment**  Another intentional tort that leisure services providers should be aware of is the tort of **false imprisonment.** The word *imprisonment* brings to mind prison bars or being locked in a room. However, confinement does not necessarily have to occur. Depending on the court and jurisdiction, people may be imprisoned merely if they believe that they cannot leave a certain location (e.g., a child is told by an adult to stay in one place for an unreasonable amount of time or a person cannot leave an area without fear of being harmed). False imprisonment may arise from seemingly innocent situations. Children might be held against their will as punishment without the supervisor realizing the error in keeping them from leaving a certain area for an unreasonable amount of time, or an innocent person might be held because a manager believed that the person had stolen an item from the organization.

Because of the potential for false imprisonment claims, the leisure services manager should be extremely careful in making decisions that could result in people being held against their will. Managers of commercial establishments must consider the reasonableness of their actions. For example, did the manager have reasonable suspicion to detain the person, was the person detained for a reasonable amount of time, and was the use and amount of force reasonable? If theft is at issue, was the person brought back into the place of business after they left (in order to determine intent to steal merchandise, one must wait until the person leaves the store to show that it was actually stolen)? These are all concerns that the leisure services professional should consider and discuss with legal counsel before acting.

Other intentional torts that will not be described in detail here are false arrest, invasion of privacy, malicious abuse of process, intentional infliction of emotional distress, and intentional torts involving property.

## Strict Liability

**strict liability**— A legal doctrine that makes a person liable for his or her actions regardless of whether the person was at fault.

The third type of tort is strict liability. The legal doctrine of strict liability means that a person is liable for his or her actions regardless of whether the person was at fault. This occurs in situations with inherently dangerous activities; an example is the use of elephants in a circus. Product liability claims are based on strict liability rather than negligence. Under a theory of strict liability, the manufacturer of a football helmet can be held liable even if it did not act negligently.

# Contracts

**contract**— An agreement between people that is enforceable by law.

A **contract** is an agreement between people that is enforceable by law if certain conditions are met. Contracts are usually agreements of exchange for tangible items such as money for food or beverages. However, the leisure services industry often has intangible forms of exchange such as an agreement where participants pay money (a tangible item) for an experience such as white-water rafting (an intangible item). The field may also have agreements (contracts) where neither item is tangible. For example, participants may sign a waiver (a contract) where they give up the right to prevail in a lawsuit if they are injured in exchange for the right to participate in the activity.

Contracts are common in the leisure services profession. In hospitality, the hotel or resort might have contracts with food and beverage providers, linen services, and security companies, as well as employment contracts with hotel and resort employees. With guests, the hotel might have contracts related to lodging, food and beverage, and the provision of hotel services. In tourism, contracts exist for travel package agreements, agreements with cruise lines, and air and ground transportation. Parks and public lands contract with concessionaires who run hotels or restaurants on public land. Public and private recreation providers often require waivers from participants. In sport, players and coaches' contracts are common agreements. You can probably think of many more examples.

To have a valid and enforceable contract that will bind the parties to an agreement, you must have a valid offer and acceptance. As such, a contract is an exchange. It is an agreement to offer a product, service, or experience that requires acceptance of the terms of that offer. Two important concepts form the basis for an enforceable contract: fairness and the ability of the person or organization to understand the terms of the contract. Factors that influence the ability to understand the language of a contract come from several sources, including the characteristics of the person agreeing to the terms of the contract and the way the contract is written.

What factors might make it difficult for someone to understand the terms of a contract? One that probably comes first to mind is the age of the person. Contracts signed by a minor (a person under the age of either 18 or 21, depending on the state) are unenforceable. The law uses the term *capacity* to describe the ability to understand. A person under the state-mandated legal age of majority does not have the capacity to enter into a contract. Another issue related to capacity is the mental status of the person agreeing to the terms of a contract. Mental status can be influenced by health status, disability, alcohol, or drugs. Therefore, when contracting for products or using waivers, it is important for managers to understand the mental state and age of the person signing the contract.

A second issue that relates to the ability to understand a contract is how the contract is written. For example, a contract written in confusing language with a lot of legalese may be difficult for the average person to understand. A waiver is an example of a contract where the language is crucial. For instance, another term for waiver is *exculpatory agreement*. It would be better to use the word *waiver* than the term *exculpatory agreement* since many would not understand the meaning of the latter term. Additionally, the size and type of font should be easy to read and understand.

The fairness of the contract is another overriding principle that governs the enforceability of contracts. The term *equal bargaining power* is often used in determining whether a contract was fair. This term means that one party should not be overwhelmed or unduly intimidated by the status and power of the other party. For example, governments and some large organizations have far superior bargaining power. Situations might arise where one party has no choice but to accept the terms of a contract given the power of the other party. In these cases, unequal bargaining power might be brought up as an argument for voiding a contract.

It is often said that a waiver is not worth the paper it is written on; however, this blanket pronouncement is false. As with any contract, a waiver may be binding (valid) if it meets the necessary contractual requirements. Courts will uphold waivers and make them binding on both parties if the requisite contractual elements are met.

Another issue of fairness involves whether a party has voluntarily entered into a contract. Contracts may be deemed unenforceable if one side is forced or tricked into signing. Managers should be aware of situations where people may feel they have lost their choice in entering a contract. An example might be where people participating in a dangerous outdoor climbing experience are given the waiver halfway through the activity. There would be no choice except to sign the waiver and continue under the guidance of experienced climbers or else try to make it back to safety on their own.

When dealing with contracts, managers should be aware of the bargaining power of both parties, the characteristics of the person signing the contract, and the language of the contract. All of these considerations should be taken into account and discussed with a competent attorney when contracts are drafted and administered.

# LEGISLATION

**legislation**—Federal and state laws enacted by the legislature.

**gross negligence**—Higher level of negligence (subjectively determined) where a defendant has demonstrated a high degree of carelessness.

**Good Samaritan statutes**—Laws that limit liability for laypersons who provide assistance (often medical) to someone in need.

**Legislation**, or federal and state laws enacted by the legislature, greatly influences leisure services management. In some cases, immunity, or protection from liability, is provided by state and federal laws. As mentioned previously, recreational user statutes protect both public lands and private landowners who lease their property for recreational pursuits. This protection is provided by an increase in the standard by which these entities are judged in negligence suits. The standard rises from ordinary negligence to a higher level often termed *willful and wanton behavior*, or **gross negligence**. The interpretation of these terms is subjective and depends on the circumstances of individual cases.

Another type of law provides some protection for commercial recreation. For example, some sport organizations (e.g., skiing operations, skating rinks, equestrian activity providers) are protected from liability when someone is injured due to an inherent risk in participation. Examples of injuries from inherent risks protected by statute include when someone hits a tree on a ski slope or when a horse is spooked and the rider is injured. The reasoning behind these laws is to protect an industry that provides economic support for the affected region.

Other types of legislation include liability protection for organizations that have AEDs, commonly used in such recreational places as fitness centers, golf courses, and stadiums. In addition, legislation provides protection for those who come to the aid of someone in need (e.g., a hotel guest providing cardiopulmonary resuscitation [CPR] to a stranger on the property) and do not owe some preexisting duty (e.g., a swimmer doesn't owe the same duty that the lifeguard owes to pool patrons). These laws are commonly known as **Good Samaritan statutes**.

In addition to providing protection from liability, some laws mandate certain actions by leisure services providers. For example, certain states have enacted legislation that mandates the placement of AEDs and their use by trained responders in fitness centers. Others have mandated AEDs in city parks, and still others require that high school athletic departments have AEDs.

Other types of legislation that are designed to protect include dram shop laws, which were created to protect people who suffer as a result of the illegal sale of alcohol. These laws should be known and understood by managers, particularly those in the restaurant and hotel industry. Dram shop laws impose liability on those who sell alcohol to a minor or to someone who is visibly intoxicated and then injures another person, usually by way of an automobile accident.

Another form of legislation relevant to leisure services is enabling legislation. Enabling legislation is either state or federal law that gives certain officials the authority to enforce the law. Enabling legislation is often connected to the creation of parks and public lands. Federal land such as a national park, for example, will have enabling legislation. This legislation is an act of the U.S. Congress that creates the park and authorizes actions to set the park up. Examples of federal enabling legislation include the following:

- The Wilderness Act of 1964 mandates that federal land management agencies identify public lands suitable for wilderness designation and provide guidelines for their classification and management.

- The National Park Service Organic Act of 1916 established the national park system on the principle of conservation.

- The National Environmental Policy Act (NEPA) of 1969 requires environmental impact statements for significant changes contemplated by the National Park Service (NPS) in the management of its lands.

Another important type of legislation involves volunteer immunity. Volunteers for government and nonprofit entities are often protected from liability through state legislation and federal law. It is important for managers to know whether their state has a volunteer immunity law and, if so, what that law covers. Protection might not be available under certain conditions. For example, volunteers might not be protected from liability if, in the act giving rise to the lawsuit, they committed a criminal act, a sexual act, or an act of discrimination, or if they were under the influence of alcohol or a drug. Another common exception to the protections afforded by legislation is where the volunteer committed an act that rose above ordinary negligence to one categorized at a higher level, such as recklessness, gross negligence, or willful and wanton misconduct. Further, for the protections to apply, the volunteer must have been acting within the scope of employment when the incident occurred.

In addition to state laws, the leisure services manager should understand, with the advice and assistance of competent legal counsel, the Volunteer Protection Act of 1997. This federal law offers additional provisions that might influence the liability protections afforded to volunteers. Volunteers are often vital to the functioning of a leisure services organization; therefore, knowing the laws that offer protection for them is an important management function.

# RISK MANAGEMENT

**Risk management** is the process of decision making and implementation so as to minimize injuries or loss to an organization, facility, or event. Risk managers are often hired or appointed to oversee an organization's risk management program, and committees may be appointed to address risk management issues and tasks. Risk management programs involve risk assessment, risk control, and risk financing (figure 3.4).

**risk management**— Process of decision making and implementation so as to minimize injuries or loss to an organization, facility, or event.

## Risk Assessment

Risk assessment means identifying and analyzing the risks or loss exposures of a particular activity, event, or organization. Loss exposures can be placed in four categories: property, liability, personnel, and net income.

Property loss exposures arise out of the possibility of damage, destruction, or disappearance of property resulting from a peril or cause of loss. Such losses could be to buildings, personal property, or land. For example, a hurricane could damage a gym, which could

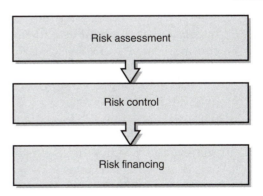

**Figure 3.4** Elements of risk management programs.

include not only the facility but also the office with its files and computer equipment.

Liability loss exposures arise from an organization having a legal responsibility to pay a claim for bodily injury or property damage sustained by another party. Such loss exposures arise out of torts (negligence, intentional torts, and strict liability torts as described previously), contracts, and by statutes (e.g., workers' compensation).

Personnel loss exposure occurs when an employee, manager, or owner with special skills or knowledge resigns, retires, or dies.

Net income loss exposure occurs when circumstances affecting the organization reduce net income. Examples are economic downturn or the impact of a lawsuit.

There are many loss exposures to assess, and every organization will have different loss exposures to consider. The following list includes some of the loss exposures to consider: premises liability (safety from slip-and-falls and accidents on the premises); automobile liability; watercraft liability; workers' compensation (work-related injuries and diseases); intellectual property (copyrights, trademarks, and patents); criminal loss (burglary, robbery, shoplifting, fraud, embezzlement, counterfeiting, forgery, terrorism, arson, vandalism, computer crime, etc.); and disaster loss (fire, explosion, flood, windstorm, hurricane, tornado, snowstorm, earthquake, lightning, avalanche, etc.).

When assessing potential risk, all aspects of a property should be considered. For example, a risk assessment of a sport stadium would include evaluation of the parking lot, traffic, environmental elements, locker rooms, public restrooms, stands and viewing areas, entryways and exits, concession areas, ticket booths, press box, field of play, protective gear and equipment, as well as many other potential loss exposures. Other aspects of a risk assessment on such a facility and events held in the facility would include violence and unruly behavior of athletes and spectators, supervision of minors if applicable, air space (drone use), and first aid for players and spectators.

## Risk Control

Once an organization has completed a thorough risk assessment, the risk control phase should begin. This involves taking conscious action and planning to control risks, rather than be subjected to sudden, unplanned events that can be catastrophic to the organization. An example of planning for a foreseeable event is to install AED machines in strategic locations so that a heart attack victim's life might be saved.

Risk control means developing comprehensive safety plans, safety rules, and emergency procedures in every aspect of the organization. Such plans must be communicated to personnel and volunteers and practiced. Safety rules should be communicated and consistently enforced. Crowd management, provision of security, and planning for possible terrorism are all aspects of risk control.

Risk control also encompasses facility and equipment inspection, cleaning, maintenance, and repair. Preparing the field of play or the place where an activity will take place so that all visible hazards are removed or warned against is another way to control risks. Risk control also means use of safety gear, such as helmets, mouth guards, and padding. It also means protecting spectators from harm by installing nets or warning of danger.

Any organization can control risks of slip-and-fall hazards with planned and regular inspections, mop and cleaning schedules, and provision of warning cones that can be quickly placed when a slip hazard is noticed. Risk of lightning and other weather hazards can be controlled in leisure environments by checking weather forecasts. Activities may need to be delayed or cancelled in order to control the risks of harm to participants.

## Risk Financing

An important means of planning for risks is the risk financing phase. Risk financing requires consciously deciding whether or not to generate funds to pay for potential losses, by means of transfer and retention.

Risk transfer means purchasing insurance or using noninsurance techniques to pay for losses. When transferring possible financial consequences to an insurance company, your organization will pay premiums. In return for the premium, the insurance carrier will pay those losses that are covered by the insurance contract as well as provide claims-handling services and hire an attorney to defend the organization in the event of a lawsuit. A noninsurance risk transfer means using another method to transfer all or a portion of the financial consequences of a loss to another party. This can be done contractually in a hold harmless agreement.

Risk retention can be used by an organization if it prefers not to transfer the risk. Planned risk retention means that the organization deliberately assumes the loss. They can fund the risk with their own funds or borrow money to pay the loss. If the risk retention is unplanned, the organization has not taken any steps to plan for funding in advance. An example of this occurs when a hurricane destroys property and there is no insurance coverage or funds allocated to pay for the damage. Risk financing can include a combination of risk transfer and risk retention.

# LEGAL ISSUES IN EMPLOYMENT

It is important for leisure services managers to understand legal concerns associated with employment. The remainder of this chapter addresses a number of issues relevant to employment. It would be wise to supplement your knowledge of employment law with a thorough reading of the literature on this topic. Table 3.1 provides a comparison of the protected classes in the countries discussed in this section.

## United States Employment Laws

U.S. federal **employment laws** extend protection to potential employees as well as current and former employees. Federal employment laws, though, do not extend protection to all employees of all employers. Ultimately, a qualifying employer is prohibited from discrimination, harassment, or retaliation against a person who belongs to a protected class. Employers may have a responsibility to protect its employees from discrimination or harassment from management, other employees, and even customers. Discrimination is treating someone differently on the basis of his or her belonging to a federally protected class. Even a seemingly neutral policy or practice that has the result of discrimination toward a protected class can be in violation of a federal employment law. Harassment is unwelcome conduct based on a protected class and the conduct is conditioned upon employment or severe or pervasive enough to create a hostile work environment. Retaliation is treating a person differently because of a claim of a violation of a federal employment law. Federal employment laws often make allowances or exceptions for when it is appropriate to treat one employee differently from another. In the United States, the Equal Employment

**employment laws**—Extend protection to certain groups of potential, current, and former employees from discrimination, harassment, or retaliation.

**Table 3.1** Comparisons of Protected Classes

| Protected Class | United States | United Kingdom | Australia | Canada (Ontario Province) |
|---|---|---|---|---|
| Race | X | X | X | X |
| National, ethnic social origin, ancestry | X | X | X | X |
| Color | X | X | X | X |
| Age | X | X | X | X |
| Religion (creed) | X | X | X | X |
| Sex | X | X | X | X |
| Sexual orientation | X | X | X | X |
| Gender identity, transgender status, gender expression | X | X | X | X |
| Disability | X | X | X | X |
| Marital status and civil partnership | X | X | X | X |
| Pregnancy | X | X | X | X |
| Family or caregiver's responsibilities | | | X | |
| Family status | | | | x |
| Record of offenses | | | | X |
| Political opinion | | | X | |

Opportunity Commission (EEOC) enforces federal employment laws where an employee has faced discrimination, harassment, or retaliation in employment.

## Race, Color, Religion, National Origin, or Sex

Title VII of the Civil Rights Act of 1964 prohibits discrimination, harassment or retaliation in the workplace for those who belong to protected classes.

- *Protected class(es).* Race, color, religion, national origin, or sex (expanded to include pregnancy, sexual orientation, transgender status, or gender identity)
- *Qualifying employer.* An employer with 15 or more employees working for 20 or more weeks in a year
- *Prohibition.* Discrimination, harassment, or retaliation
- *Miscellaneous.* Additionally, employers must provide a reasonable accommodation for an employee's religious observance, practice, and belief unless it creates an undue hardship on the employer.
- *Exceptions.* Employers may treat an employee differently if it is on the basis of an employee's seniority or merit, or for a bona fide occupational qualification (reasonably necessary to the business).

Hiring decisions must be made with respect to Title VII. As such, you should also know about the Equal Employment Opportunity Commission (EEOC), the governmental agency that monitors compliance with Title VII and other federal employment law statutes. If qualified applicants feel they have been discriminated against, they can file a charge with the EEOC. The EEOC then decides whether to investigate the charge and take action. If they decide not to take action, the applicant may bring a lawsuit directly against the manager and the organization.

Discrimination charges can be brought on the basis of either intentional or unintentional acts of the employer. Decisions about hiring, promotion, and retention must be based solely on job-related qualifications and cannot reflect discriminatory practices. This is the basic requirement of Title VII.

If employees or prospective employees feel that they are being unintentionally discriminated against, their claim would rest on disparate impact discrimination. This might happen where an organization hired a disproportionate number of people from the same class. A potential defense to this claim would be the business necessity defense. This defense arises where an organization requires as a condition of employment that applicants be able to meet certain criteria essential to the job that have an unintentional discriminatory effect on a certain protected class.

If applicants feel that they have been intentionally discriminated against, they have to prove three things: that they are a member of the protected class (e.g., by race, color, or national origin), that they are qualified for the job, and that the job remained open or was offered to someone not in the protected class. This type of intentional discrimination is termed *disparate treatment discrimination*. If a case for disparate treatment discrimination can be shown, the organization has the burden of proof in defending its actions. One type of defense is the bona fide occupational qualification (BFOQ) defense. This defense arises when a particular trait is necessary for a particular job.

## Sexual Harassment

Sexual harassment is an employment issue that is critical from both an ethical and legal standpoint. Guidance on sexual harassment comes primarily from the EEOC and the Supreme Court. Additionally, many organizations and municipalities have attorneys on staff who communicate to management the important points regarding sexual harassment. Leisure services managers should educate themselves about sexual harassment from a valid and reliable source as a first order of business.

Sexual harassment can include unwelcome sexual advances, requests for sexual favors, or even offensive comments about a person's sex that create a hostile work environment. Sexual harassment therefore is conduct that is sexual in nature and can occur between any combination of genders. It is also conduct that is not consensual between both parties, meaning that one party does not want or agree to the sexual conduct. Physical conduct may first come to mind, but verbal conduct can amount to sexual harassment under certain conditions as well. The determination of a hostile and abusive work environment is the central issue in many sexual harassment claims. In general, it means that someone finds the sexual conduct so offensive or intimidating that it negatively affects job performance.

Leisure services managers should have policies and procedures to manage sexual harassment claims and to promote a work environment where all employees are treated with dignity and respect and where everyone knows that sexual harassment will not be tolerated. Managers should also take every sexual harassment claim seriously and initiate the proper agency protocol for handling the situation, such as notifying the proper people in the chain of command and following the proper procedures for interviewing both the victim and the accused. If your organization does not provide guidance on sexual harassment, a competent outside source should be consulted. The proper handling of sexual harassment claims is not only the right thing to do, it is also important for protecting both the manager and the organization from liability.

## Affirmative Action and Equal Employment Opportunity

Affirmative action is a proactive process whereby employers take specific hiring and promotion actions to seek out, hire, and promote qualified individuals in protected classes. It is designed to reduce or eliminate discriminatory practices in hiring, promotion, and retention of employees by providing increased employment opportunities to people in protected classes and ensuring equal opportunity in employment. Although not a requirement under Title VII, it helps to understand and be aware of affirmative action requirements when advertising and writing descriptions and applications for job positions. Managers should seek guidance on affirmative action statements regarding women, minorities, and other protected groups, as well as the provision of advertisements in publications, online sources, and venues specific to protected groups.

### Equal Pay

Equal Pay Act of 1963 (EPA) requires equal pay for employees.

- *Protected class.* Persons of the opposite sex are required to be paid the same for substantially equal work in the same workplace.
- *Qualifying employer.* All employers
- *Prohibition.* Discrimination or retaliation
- *Exceptions.* Seniority, merit, quantity or quality of production, or other nondiscriminatory factor

The Equal Pay Act of 1963 predates Title VII, but it is still relevant. Equal pay not only applies to salary but to benefits offered to employees. An employer is not permitted to reduce compensation for the person of the opposite sex in order to resolve an inequity in compensation. Under the EPA, a person has up to two years to file a lawsuit and can go directly to court or to the EEOC. The statute applies to virtually all employers. In contrast, with a Title VII claim, a person only has 180 days to file, the charge with the EEOC, and the statute does not apply to all employers. All leisure services managers should evaluate whether employees are being equally compensated for performing substantially equal work in the same workplace.

### Disabilities

Title I of the Americans with Disabilities Act of 1990 (ADA) governs persons with disabilities in the workplace.

- *Protected class.* Person with a qualifying disability or person regarded as having a qualifying disability
- *Qualifying employer.* An employer with 15 or more employees working for 20 or more weeks in a year
- *Prohibition.* Discrimination or retaliation
- *Miscellaneous.* Employers must provide a reasonable accommodation for an employee that would enable the employee to perform the essential functions of a job.

- *Exceptions.* An accommodation that creates an undue hardship on the employer; job-related and necessary selection criteria that cannot be met with a reasonable accommodation

The passage of the Americans with Disabilities Act (ADA) of 1990 greatly affected the leisure services industry. The intent of the ADA was to make places of public accommodation accessible to people with disabilities (e.g., providing full and equal access). However, part of the ADA requires that employers make a reasonable effort to accommodate the workplace needs of an employee with disabilities. The legal term *reasonable accommodation* applies to situations where an employer finds work responsibilities and environments that place employees with disabilities in a position to be successful in performing their job functions. However, not every employee will be suited for all positions, and sometimes providing an accommodation may cause an undue hardship on the employer. Even with a reasonable accommodation, an employee will still need to perform the essential functions of an employment position. An employer is not required to provide any and all accommodations, only those that are reasonable and do not cause the employer an undue burden. Ultimately, if an employee is not able to perform the essential functions of a job, even with accommodation from an employer, then the employee is not qualified for the job.

## Age Discrimination

Age Discrimination in Employment Act of 1967 (ADEA) protects persons 40 years of age and older in the workplace.

- *Protected class.* Person 40 years of age or older
- *Qualifying employer.* An employer with 20 or more employees in a business that affects commerce
- *Prohibition.* Discrimination, harassment, or retaliation
- *Exceptions.* Seniority or bona fide occupational qualification (reasonably necessary to the business)

Leisure services managers need to be aware of the Age Discrimination in Employment Act (ADEA). This federal law prohibits employment discrimination on the basis of age for people at least 40 years old. It applies to businesses that have 20 or more employees and whose activities affect commerce. If a qualified applicant is 40 years of age or older, you must ensure that there is no implication of discrimination in the hiring process, as well as in promotion and termination.

## Employee Health

Managers owe a duty to their employees to provide a reasonably safe work environment. Aside from this legal duty, there is also an ethical duty to protect those under their care. The U.S. government has taken this a step further by passing legislation that provides for the safety of employees. The most common and arguably most important law providing for the safety of employees is the Occupational Health and Safety Act. This federal law, enacted in 1970, established the Occupational Safety and Health Administration (OSHA), a federal regulatory agency with oversight responsibilities for safety and health in the work environment. There are many health hazards that employees might face in the work environment, including exposure to dangerous chemicals, airborne hazards, and dangerous equipment or facilities.

Leisure services managers should have a good understanding of OSHA regulations and their implications. This information can be obtained from various sources and should be implemented in consultation with qualified legal professionals.

## United Kingdom Employment Laws

The United Kingdom has similar laws regulating employers and protecting employees from discrimination in the workplace. The Equality Act 2010 replaces prior employment law discrimination legislation and protects employees from discrimination, harassment, or victimization (retaliation) based on any of the following protected characteristics (The National Archives, n.d.):

- Age
- Disability
- Gender reassignment
- Marriage and civil partnership
- Pregnancy and maternity
- Race, ethnic or national origins, nationality, or color
- Religion or belief
- Sex
- Sexual orientation

The Equality Act 2010 also requires employers to make reasonable adjustments for persons with a disability.

## Australia Employment Laws

Australian federal law has similar protections to U.S. law against discrimination and harassment for employees.

- Age Discrimination Act 2004
- Australian Human Rights Commission Act 1986
- Disability Discrimination Act 1992
- Racial Discrimination Act 1975
- Sex Discrimination Act 1984
- Fair Work Act 2009

Essentially, Australian legislation prohibits all employers from discriminating against a potential or current employee on the basis of any of the following attributes (Fair Work Ombudsman, n.d.):

- Race
- Color
- Sex
- Sexual preference
- Age
- Physical or mental disability
- Marital status

- Family or caregiver's responsibilities
- Pregnancy
- Religion
- Political opinion
- National extraction or social origin

Any adverse action taken against an employee can be considered discrimination.

## Canada Employment Laws

Canada operates differently than the United States in that employment laws, particularly laws about discrimination, largely are enacted by each province and not by the federal government. Thus, employment law in Canada may vary by locality. For instance, in Ontario, the following statutes apply to employment law (Queens Printer for Ontario, 2018):

- Pay Equity Act (PEA) (equal pay for jobs of equal value)
- Employment Standards Act, 2000 (similar to U.S.'s Equal Pay Act)
- Ontario Human Rights Code

The Occupational Health and Safety Act (OHSA) requires employers to protect employees from workplace violence and to create a workplace harassment policy and program that is conveyed to employees. Workplace harassment includes sexual harassment on the "basis of sex, sexual orientation, gender identity or gender expression . . . or an unwelcome sexual solicitation or advance" by a person in a position of power (Queens Printer for Ontario, 2018).

The Ontario Human Rights Code prohibits discrimination and harassment in employment on the basis of any of the following:

- Race
- Ancestry
- Place of origin
- Color
- Ethnic origin
- Citizenship
- Creed (religion)
- Sex (including pregnancy)
- Sexual orientation
- Gender identity
- Gender expression
- Age (18 and over)
- Marital status (including same-sex partners)
- Family status
- Disability (including actual or perceived, past or present)
- Record of offences

Additionally, the Ontario Human Rights Code makes it illegal for a person in a position of power to convey an unwelcome sexual solicitation.

Check out the web study guide for additional material, including learning activities, sample documents, interactive case studies, web links, CPRP exam connections, and more.

## Conclusion

As you can see from this chapter, a large part of management in the leisure services industry involves legal issues and a closely related concept, the management of risk. Often the steps needed to prevent or greatly reduce the chance of lawsuits are simple. Understanding key legal and safety concerns is a great place to start. Further coursework and on-the-job training likely lie ahead for you. Hopefully this chapter has sparked your interest in increasing your knowledge of legal issues, with the ultimate goal of managing risk in order to provide a safe, enjoyable, and tolerant environment for both employees and patrons. Keep in mind that there are many resources available to help with legal issues. In addition to those already listed in this chapter, both the NRPA Law Review column in *Parks and Recreation* magazine and the *Journal of Physical Education, Recreation and Dance* law articles are good sources of legal and risk management information for practitioners.

# Review Questions

1. Describe at least one legal issue or trend in leisure services management.

2. Explain why an understanding of legal issues is important to leisure services professionals.

3. Describe the concept of negligence and its relevance to leisure services management.

4. Describe how and why intentional torts might occur when managing leisure programs and services.

5. Describe a potential issue in regard to contracts that may be used in leisure services management.

6. Apply the risk management process to a hypothetical situation in your area of specialization.

7. Choose at least one statutory law and describe its relevance to leisure services management.

8. Describe the key federal employment laws discussed in this chapter and their relevance to leisure services managers.

# 4

# Organizational Structure

## Learning Outcomes

- Compare and contrast the public, nonprofit, and commercial sectors.
- Identify different types of organizations within each sector.
- Evaluate the interrelationship between organizational structure and design.
- Gain an understanding of the three types of boards and their roles and responsibilities.

## Key Terms

public sector, municipal organizations, nonprofit sector, voluntary sector, nongovernmental organizations, commercial sector, unlimited liability, limited liability, C corporation, shareholders, organizational structure, organizational design, simple structure, unity of command principle, organizational culture, boards, self-perpetuating board, quorum, closed sessions

## Competency Check

Refer to table 1.6 to see how you assess this related competency.

15. Work with boards and elected officials.

## A Day in the Life

My first full-time job just happened to be my dream job. Starting as an intern, I was hired after only one and a half months, and I immediately fell in love with my career path. A typical day for me is anything but normal. Working for an NGB (national governing body), my typical day can range anywhere from answering phone calls and emails to helping both organize and work National Championship events. Working in the membership department, I get to interact with both domestic and international players, coaches, and administrators. Whether it is processing international tours, issuing certificates of insurance, or creating new clubs in our database, there is always something to do. I have met the USA National team, played touch rugby with both All-American staff and world renowned referees, spoken with Olympians, and interacted with rugby clubs on all levels. The best part of my job is being able to see the game grow and knowing that every day I am helping make a difference, no matter how small, in someone's life.

Jessica Dombrowski
Membership Services Coordinator
USA Rugby
Lafayette, Colorado

The organizational structure is how interrelated components of an agency are constructed in order for it to function. It is first influenced by whether the agency is in the public, nonprofit, or commercial sector and then by what type of agency it is within that sector, such as a federal agency, voluntary organization, or S corporation. These structural elements also drive the configuration of the board, whether it is an independent, semi-independent, or advisory board.

All of these complex factors form the skeleton of the organization, which greatly influences how managers communicate, how efficient and effective they are, and how they make decisions. Many aspects of organizational structure are well established and ingrained in day-to-day operations. Managers need a thorough understanding of these aspects because they can be changed to improve the organization. This chapter presents the three sectors that park and recreation managers may work in (public, nonprofit, and commercial), as well as organizational topics such as the organization of jobs, work environments, governing boards, and organizational culture.

# THREE SECTORS

Park and recreation agencies can be found in the public sector, the nonprofit sector, and the commercial sector. The nonprofit sector is also known as not-for-profit, the voluntary sector, or nongovernmental organizations (NGOs). Each sector has unique characteristics in terms of governance, financial resources, and organization.

## Public Sector

Recreation agencies in the **public sector** are formed through legislation at the local, state or provincial, and federal levels. Recreation and park-oriented programs, services, and facilities are run by governmental agencies for citizens of the community, state or province, or country. These agencies receive operating money from taxes, such as property and sales taxes, which is one of the unique features of the public sector. A closer look at the three levels of public recreation is needed to get a better understanding of how these organizations are formed and managed.

### Local Park and Recreation Agencies

Local park and recreation agencies, also called **municipal organizations**, can be found in cities, townships, counties, and boroughs. They are operated through municipal government, county government, and special districts. In Canada, municipalities offer recreation, parks, sport, and culture through commissions, boards, and civic departments. Both the United States and Canada have local recreation agencies that are funded largely through property taxes. Some of these agencies have special laws that regulate how they are established and special structural concerns that are an important part of management. There are several laws in the United States that affect the formation of local park and recreation agencies, including special recreation and park laws, special district laws, enabling laws, home rule legislation, and manager–council and mayor–council structures.

**Special Recreation and Park Laws**  Special recreation and park laws were enacted to empower cities and towns to establish park and recreation agencies. The laws gave these agencies authority to tax, float bonds, and administer themselves. Under these laws, county and municipal agencies provide services for their designated

**public sector—** Organizations formed through legislation at the local, state or provincial, or federal levels dedicated to providing services to citizens at these levels.

**municipal organizations—** Administrative entities at the local level, such as a city, county, or town governed by a mayor, city manager, or council.

areas. Not all counties have a county department; instead, they rely on the city park and recreation agency to provide services. When a county has both a separate county and city park and recreation department, differences between the two emerge. County agencies usually provide services for a more rural area, whereas city agencies predominantly provide services within the city limits. In addition, county agencies may oversee regional parks and facilities, special facilities, and programs that are more conducive to rural areas, such as outdoor recreation.

**Special District Laws**  The United States has special districts that are independent governing bodies with a clearly defined geographic area, their own taxing authority, and their own administration and power. The number and types of special districts vary by state. Nine states have more than 1,000 special districts, including Illinois (3,227), California (2,861), Texas (2,600), and Pennsylvania (1,756). Almost 20 percent of the 37,203 special districts in the United States perform functions related to natural resources, including soil and water conservation and flood control (U.S. Bureau of the Census 2013). In Canada and Australia, the park district system does not exist, and parks and recreation are only administered within the municipality.

Special districts differ from city-operated parks and recreation departments in that they are stand-alone agencies located within the city but are not part of city government. Districts receive funds directly from taxpayers rather than through the city council as a department does, where they would be seeking the same funds as police, fire, and other city services. Since districts are not part of the city, they cannot rely on city units for services such as police or fleet (cars, dump trucks, bucket trucks, etc.) without paying for these services. In addition, districts have their own independent board rather than a city council (discussed later in the chapter).

**Enabling Laws**  Enabling laws are enacted by the state or province to enable local governments to acquire, develop, and maintain recreation areas, including parks, programs, and facilities. These laws set parameters for the types of governments that may operate park and recreation agencies, fiscal practices, types of governing boards, and operational authority. Enabling laws are permissive rather than mandatory since the local government is not required to establish a recreation agency. For example, the Golden Gate National Recreation Area was established by enabling legislation on October 27, 1972, through Public Law 92-589. This law mandates that the secretary of the Interior shall preserve the recreation area, as far as possible, in

## Special District Provides Recreation for People with Disabilities

An example of a special district is the Western DuPage Special Recreation Association (WDSRA), which provides recreation opportunities for people with disabilities. It is a cooperative entity among nine park districts in the western suburbs of Chicago, and the board of directors consists of a staff person from each park district. The WDSRA provides programs at member districts' facilities, and it also provides assistance to each district when people with disabilities want to participate in programs through their home district rather than the WDSRA.

its natural setting and protect it from development and uses which would destroy the scenic beauty and natural character of the area (National Park Service 1972).

**Home Rule Legislation**   Home rule legislation allows local governments to control issues at the local level without the interference of state government, and it shifts decision making from the state to local level. Home rule municipalities have greater control over zoning regulations, greater flexibility in using new funding sources, and reduced regulation from state mandates.

**Strong Mayor–Council or City Manager–Council**   Local legislation establishes the structure for municipal parks and recreation. Municipalities that are not considered special districts typically have one of two types of structures, either a strong mayor–council or a city manager–council. With a strong mayor–council form of government, the elected mayor has administrative control over the municipality. In many respects, mayors operate as CEO of the city. They have the power to hire and fire department heads, make decisions, and prepare and present budgets. The council acts as the legislative body for the city and works with the mayor. Strong mayor–council forms of government mean that the mayor is elected and can make political appointments and remove staff from positions upon election. Strong mayor–councils can be found in such cities as New York City, Los Angeles, and Chicago, but the strong mayor–council is not found in Canada or Australia.

The city manager–council form of government, on the other hand, hires a professional city manager to serve as the CEO of the city. In Canada, the municipalities call this person the chief administrative officer (CAO). This person works with the council and has the authority and responsibilities of the mayor in the strong mayor–council form of government. The city manager–council form often also has an elected mayor, who presides over the council meetings, serves as a spokesperson for the community, and assists the council in decision making and policy setting. The mayor does not have as much authority for overall operation of the city as in the strong mayor–council structure; instead, this role is left to the city manager. City manager–council forms of government can be found in counties and cities

## Canada's National Recreation Statement of 1987

Canada's National Recreation Statement of 1987 outlined the roles and responsibilities of federal, provincial, and municipal governments in Canada.

*Municipal parks and recreation.* Suppliers of services because they are closest to the people; as a result, sport, recreation, and health are of particular importance.

*Provincial and territorial governments.* Responsible for coordinating programs and providing information and financial resources for service delivery; rarely a direct service provider.

*Federal government.* Focus is on recreation on a national scope and under the jurisdiction of federal government.

(Stanton, Markham-Starr, and Hodgkinson 2013)

including Charlotte, North Carolina; Clark County (Las Vegas), Nevada; and Winnipeg, Manitoba.

## State or Provincial Park and Recreation Agencies

The next level of public agencies is state or provincial parks and recreation. Most state park and recreation agencies in the United States focus on outdoor recreation, resource management, arts, and tourism. All 50 states have state park systems with varying park lands and acreage. Legal authority for the development of state park and recreation areas comes from the Tenth Amendment of the U.S. Constitution. This amendment gives states all the powers that the Constitution does not give to the federal government or take away from the states. The amendment is also referred to as the *states rights amendment*. State legislation has established such departments as fish and wildlife, state forests, tourism bureaus, and arts commissions.

### Sample Statistical Report of State Park Operations: FY 2016

In the United States, state parks account for:

- 8,495 state park areas comprising 18,597,527 acres
- 9,067 trails over 38,200 miles total length
- 241,255 campsites with 61.4 million campers
- 9,457 cabins and cottages with 4.7 million cabin guests
- 161 lodges in 39 states with 7,420 rooms serving 1.6 million lodge guests
- 142 golf courses, 146 ski slopes, and 320 marinas
- 791,510,058 annual visitors; 373 million visitors to fee areas
- 19,296 full-time state park personnel and 26,855 total personnel (including part-time and seasonal)

(National Association of State Park Directors 2017)

In Canada, the provinces have ministries or departments that oversee recreation. At this level, the ministries serve more as coordinators of programs and providers of information and financial resources than direct service providers (Stanton, Markham-Starr, and Hodgkinson 2013). For example, the Ministry of Tourism, Culture and Sport was established to provide tourism and recreation experiences for travelers to Ontario. The ministry contributes to planning and education, and it gives financial assistance to agencies that make tourism services available (www.ontario.ca/page/ministry-tourism-culture-and-sport). In Saskatchewan, the Ministry of Parks, Culture and Sport focuses on the cultural, artistic, recreational, and social life of people in Saskatchewan through partnerships and legislative initiatives (www.pcs.gov.sk.ca/Recreation). The government of South Australia has an Office for Recreation and Sport, which distributes resources and advice to industry partners, collaborators, and communities so they are able to provide recreation and sport to the people of South Australia (www.ors.sa.gov.au).

## Federal Park and Recreation Agencies

The highest level of public park and recreation agencies is the federal level. The primary functions of federal park and recreation agencies entail management of outdoor resources, conservation, preservation, open-space development, resource reclamation, advisory and financial assistance, and research and technical assistance (McLean, Hurd, and Anderson 2019). Authority for the two types of agencies—

natural resources management and welfare of people—is not specifically outlined in the U.S. Constitution. However, it is provided under "broad authority of the general welfare (Art. I, sec. 8, cl. 1), commerce (Art. IV), and property (Art I, sec. 8, cl. 13) clauses" (Moiseichik and Bodey 2005, 31). This legislation has granted the establishment of such federal agencies as the National Park Service (NPS), U.S. Forest Service, Bureau of Land Management, and Tennessee Valley Authority, just to name a few.

The federal government in Canada has responsibility over various arts, culture, sport, and fitness programs. Although parks and recreation is not specifically outlined in the constitution of Canada, the constitution has a section giving the government the power to act on behalf of the citizens, and it is felt that recreation is in the best interest of Canadians. Parks Canada, the equivalent of the National Park Service in the United States, oversees four areas: national parks and reserves, national historic parks and sites, national canals, and national marine conservation areas. In addition to Parks Canada, the Canadian Wildlife Service is responsible for national wildlife areas and migratory bird sanctuaries (Eagles and Hallo 2016).

Australia has a unique approach to national parks. Four percent of Australia's land is designated and protected as national park lands. Rather than the federal government managing these lands, they are mostly managed by the states and territories. The federal government oversees only fifteen parks and reserves (http://www.australiannationalparks.com/).

## Nonprofit Sector

The **nonprofit sector**, called the **voluntary sector** in Canada and **nongovernmental organizations** in Australia, is extensive both in the number of agencies in existence and the scope of services they provide. Nonprofit organizations provide services that meet a need in the community, including public services; thus, they are also called *quasi-public* and *semipublic*. The Canadian voluntary sector is so called because of its heavy reliance on volunteers and Canada's strong commitment as a nation to volunteerism. About 50 percent of Canadians volunteer annually (Vézina and Crompton 2012) and give an average of 168 hours per year, compared to 25 percent of the population in the United States, who average 52 hours per year (U.S. Bureau of Labor Statistics 2016) and the 36.2 percent of the population of Australia, who average 56 hours per year of volunteer work. Interestingly, 37 percent of all volunteers in Australia focus on sport and recreation (Volunteering Australia 2015). Examples of nonprofit organizations include the Boys & Girls Clubs, New York City Marathon, Special Olympics, International Sport Alliance, and Metropolitan Museum of Art. Nonprofit agencies rely on fund-raising, grants, and program fees for sustenance. They do not typically receive funds from taxes or city government.

The nonprofit sector is far more broad than many people realize. In the United States, there are more than 20 types of nonprofit organizations under the Internal Revenue Code. The most common are 501(c)(3) organizations that are religious, charitable, or educational and exist for the public benefit. These organizations are exempt from paying taxes, can apply for government and foundation grants, and can receive tax-deductible donations.

In addition to 501(c)(3) organizations, nonprofits can organize under the following, among others:

- 501(c)(4): Civic leagues, social welfare organizations, and local associations of employees

**nonprofit sector**—The U.S. term for a sector with nongovernmental and noncommercial organizations that are formally constituted for the public benefit.

**voluntary sector**—The Canadian term for a sector with nongovernmental and noncommercial organizations that are formally constituted for the public benefit.

**nongovernmental organizations**—Another term for nonprofit organizations that is used extensively in Australia and on a more limited basis in the United States and Canada.

- 501(c)(6): Business leagues, chambers of commerce, real estate boards, and boards of trade
- 501(c)(7): Social clubs organized for recreation and other purposes for the benefit of their members

There are several differences among these types of nonprofit organizations. For example, 501(c)(3) organizations are prohibited from any political activity whereas the other three can participate in political activity but are taxed on it (Internal Revenue Service 2016).

Because the 501(c)(3) is by far the most common recreation-related nonprofit organization, it is the focus of this section. Nonprofit organizations can organize as a coalition, an unincorporated trust, or a corporation. The nonprofit corporation is most common because it protects board members from personal liability based on the actions of the agency.

Establishing a nonprofit organization is a relatively straightforward process, yet it takes a considerable amount of time to complete the overwhelming amount of paperwork. To become a nonprofit organization, articles of incorporation must be developed, much like a business would file to incorporate itself. The articles of incorporation outline such things as the name and purpose of the organization, duration of its planned existence, office location, people and board members involved, regulatory authorities to be followed (i.e., state and federal), how to change the articles of incorporation, and how to dissolve the organization.

In addition to the articles of incorporation, bylaws must be written. Bylaws describe how the organization will be administered and operated; the authority, decision-making power, and responsibility of the board and staff; and the creation of the board, election of members, and procedures that will be followed.

The last major step in forming a nonprofit organization is to apply for tax-exempt status. The tax-exempt status for a 501(c)(3) means the organization is exempt from federal tax, sales tax, and real property tax, and donations made to the organization are tax deductible. Furthermore, a large majority of government and foundation grants are only given to 501(c)(3) organizations, so this status is vital to many organizations.

Nonprofit organizations, while incorporated, do not have owners like businesses do, but they do often have members. Nonprofits can operate in any number of ways. They can have a board of directors who govern the organization through their own volunteer efforts or they can hire a chief executive officer (CEO) to manage the organization. This CEO is then an employee of the board of directors and can be fired by the board.

Although the name might suggest otherwise, nonprofit organizations can make a profit. If a profit is made, it is reinvested in the organization rather than distributed to staff or board members. A portion of the organization may make a profit on products or services that are not substantially related to the mission outlined in the articles of incorporation. If this happens, the organization must pay what is called *unrelated business income taxes*.

Recreation-related nonprofit organizations include Scouts Canada, Girl Guides, the YMCA and YWCA, and 4-H. Many public park and recreation agencies are also starting their own nonprofit organizations for fund-raising purposes in the form of friends groups, trusts, and foundations. For public agencies, establishing a nonprofit agency allows donations to be tax deductible. It also allows the public agency to apply for grants that are only available to 501(c)(3) organizations. Examples of public agencies with nonprofit organizations include the San Francisco Parks Alliance, which raises money and partners with the San Francisco Recreation and Park

Department (San Francisco Parks Alliance 2017), and the Montgomery County Friends of Recreation, which seeks funding from the commercial sector for the Montgomery County Department of Recreation in Maryland (Montgomery County Friends of Recreation 2017).

# Commercial Sector

The **commercial sector** consists of profit-motivated businesses, and the drive to make a profit sets it apart from the public and nonprofit sectors. These businesses can be categorized into three types—sole proprietorships, partnerships, and corporations. Each has its advantages and disadvantages.

**commercial sector**—Sector with legally recognized businesses established for the purpose of generating a profit.

## Sole Proprietorships

Sole proprietorships are unincorporated businesses that have only one owner. This owner is totally responsible for the business without reliance on partners or shareholders. The business and the owner are not separate in terms of financial responsibility, liability, and closure of the business upon death of the owner. Because of this lack of separation, if a business fails financially, then the personal assets of the owner can be taken to pay debts. Sole proprietorships are simple to start and dissolve and do not require extensive paperwork. However, there are state and local regulations such as zoning ordinances, licenses, and building codes to consider. Sole proprietorships are also exempt from corporate taxes since the owner includes the profits from the business on personal income taxes. An example of a sole proprietorship is Capt. Brian Caudill Inshore Fishing Charters, in Clearwater, Florida. Captain Caudill owns and operates the business, which will dissolve when he stops running trips, passes away, or sells the business.

**Advantages:**

- Total control over decision making
- Revenues taxed only once
- Great flexibility
- Easy to form
- All profits retained by owner
- Less concern about confidentiality
- Easy to sell
- Fewer government restrictions

**Disadvantages:**

- Limited managerial experience
- Unlimited personal liability
- Lasts only as long as the owner lives
- Limited access to capital funds

Reprinted by permission from G. Fried, S. Shapiro, and M. Mondello, *Sport Finance*, 3rd ed. (Champaign, IL: Human Kinetics, 2013), 91.

## Partnerships

When two or more entities form a business, it is called a *partnership.* Partnerships can be either general or limited. Both types of partnerships are relatively simple to form and have state and local regulations similar to those for sole proprietorships.

**unlimited liability**—When business owners are personally responsible for any debt or legal problems within the business and may lose an unlimited amount of money.

**limited liability**—A form of business in which business owners are only responsible for debts up to the amount of their investment.

If the partners share equally in the profits, liability, and management of the business, it is considered a general partnership. There is **unlimited liability** in this business structure as well, meaning that the owners are personally held liable for any debt or legal problems with the business, and they can lose an unlimited amount of money.

In limited partnerships, one or more of the partners is limited in that the partner did not invest as much capital in the business, does not have as much responsibility, or does not share equally in the profits. Limited partners have **limited liability** in that they are only responsible up to the amount of their investment. Limited partners also are not actively involved in the management of the business. If they do assume a management role, the individual must become a general partner and assume unlimited liability.

Partnerships are limited in their ability to raise capital compared to a corporation, which can sell shares to raise capital. For a partnership, the capital comes from the owners themselves. Furthermore, a partnership legally ends when a partner dies, goes bankrupt, or engages in illegal activity. An example of a partnership is Dvorak Expeditions in Nathrop, Colorado, a rafting and fishing company owned by Bill and Jaci Dvorak. This partnership assigns unlimited liability to both parties.

**Advantages:**

- Some control over decision making
- Revenues taxed only once
- Great flexibility
- Easy to form
- All profits retained by owners
- Easy to sell
- Fewer government restrictions

**Disadvantages:**

- Limited managerial experience
- Joint personal liability
- Limited access to capital funds
- Lasts only as long as the partnership survives

Reprinted by permission from G. Fried, S. Shapiro, and M. Mondello, *Sport Finance*, 3rd ed. (Champaign, IL: Human Kinetics, 2013), 91.

**C corporation**—For-profit business that has been established as a separate legal and taxed entity from its owners (shareholders).

**shareholders**—Individuals or companies who own shares in a company and are considered an owner of that company.

## Corporations

When a business is formed as a corporation, also called a **C corporation**, it is seen as a fictional, legal person. This means the corporation has many of the same rights and responsibilities as a person does, such as the right to own, manage, and sell property; to sign binding contracts; to sue and be sued; and to pay taxes. Owners of corporations are called **shareholders** and have limited liability for debts and obligations up to the amount of their investment. Corporations are formed by special charter of the state, province, or federal government and exist after the death of an owner. Like a nonprofit organization, C corporations must have bylaws and articles of incorporation upon formation.

An advantage of a corporation is the ability to raise capital by selling stock or borrowing money using company assets as collateral. In addition, ownership transfer is easy; it simply involves buying and selling stock. Disadvantages of corporations are that they have a complex formation process, they face extensive government regulations, and they are double taxed in that the corporation itself is taxed as well as the shareholders who make a profit on the stock. Furthermore, the process and expense of forming a C corporation can be extensive. The paperwork associated with it is voluminous as are state and federal filing fees, legal representation, and accounting costs.

**Advantages:**

- Unlimited life of the corporation
- Liability limited to the extent of corporate assets
- Creditors not permitted to come after individual investors for payment beyond their equity investment
- Ownership interest easily transferable in the form of shares
- Ability to hire a broad base of talented managers
- Tax benefit: dividends paid to corporation are 70 percent tax free
- Greater bargaining position with vendors who are more willing to provide credit to a corporation versus a single owner
- Ability to issue publicly traded debt and equity

**Disadvantages:**

- Complex formation process
- Need to answer to shareholders who might have ulterior motives
- Sometimes onerous government regulations
- Double taxation

Reprinted by permission from G. Fried, S. Shapiro, and M. Mondello, *Sport Finance,* 3rd ed. (Champaign, IL: Human Kinetics, 2013), 91.

**S Corporations**   The formation of S corporations (also called Subchapter S corporations) is similar to that of C corporations. However, S corporations can avoid double taxation because the "income flows through the corporation to the shareholders, who pay taxes as personal income" (Fried, DeSchriver, and Mondello 2013, 93). Although S corporations are taxed as a sole proprietorship or partnership, they are also responsible for certain taxes on capital gains and some other income.

It may seem that the S corporation is more beneficial, but a C corporation would not want to seek S corporation status if it is not going to distribute all profits to the shareholders. Regardless of whether shareholders receive the income, they are taxed on it. For example, if an S corporation makes $2 million in profit in a given year and decides to give $1 million to the shareholders and reinvest the other $1 million in the company, the shareholders are still taxed on all $2 million of the profit rather than the $1 million they actually received. S Corporations have fallen out of favor over the last several years as limited liability companies became more popular. They are easier to form and manage than S corporations. However, some still exist in sport and recreation (Fried, DeSchriver, and Mondello 2013).

**Limited Liability Companies and Limited Liability Partnerships**   Limited liability companies (LLCs) and limited liability partnerships (LLPs) are a mix of partnerships and corporations, and owners are called *members* rather than *partners* or *shareholders.* The primary benefit of the LLC or LLP is that it is taxed as a partnership

**Table 4.1** Funding and Formation of Business Structures

| Sector | Type | Funding Sources | Formation |
|---|---|---|---|
| Public | Local | Taxes (often predominantly property taxes), fees, and charges | Enabling laws |
| | State | Taxes (often predominantly sales taxes), fees, and charges | Enabling laws |
| | Federal | Taxes (often predominantly income taxes), fees, and charges | Enabling laws |
| Nonprofit | 501(c)(3) | Fund-raising, fees, and charges | Articles of incorporation and bylaws |
| Commercial | Sole proprietorship | Owner resources, income from services or products | Obtain a local license |
| | Partnership | Owner resources, income from services or products | Obtain a local license |
| | C and S corporations | Shareholders, income from services or products | Extensive filing of forms, articles of incorporation, and bylaws |
| | Limited liability companies and limited liability partnerships | Owner resources, income from services or products | File application with the state |

but has the limited liability of a corporation. In addition, it is easier to form an LLC or LLP than a C or S corporation. A disadvantage of the LLC or LLP is that it dissolves when a member dies, goes bankrupt, or wants out of the business. LLCs and LLPs are still relatively new, so there are limited standards and regulations in place for these businesses. An example of an LLC Is Vision Sports, LLC, which represents sport broadcasting talent such as Stephen Bardo, Doris Burke, and Kenny Smith.

Recreation and sport agencies and businesses span all three sectors and all types of business structures. The main differences in all of these are funding sources and the formation process (see table 4.1).

# ORGANIZATIONAL STRUCTURE, DESIGN, AND CULTURE

Once an organization is established as public, nonprofit, or commercial, attention turns to how the organization is structured internally in order to deliver the services outlined in its mission statement. Organizations are made of people and groups who are goal directed. In other words, the organization exists for a purpose, and the roles and responsibilities are assigned to each employee to deliberately achieve organizational goals. Organizational structure, design, and culture work together to define the grouping of jobs, division of responsibilities, levels of authority within the organization, and formal reporting procedures.

**organizational structure**—Process by which managers arrange and coordinate positions within an agency.

Organizations have both formal and informal structures. Informal structures, or organizational culture, are the ways that people interact, communicate, and behave and are discussed in detail later in the chapter. Formal structures, on the other hand, are the controlled and well-defined part of management. Formal organizations are controlled by policies, procedures, and organizational charts. A major element of formal organizations is **organizational structure** and organizational design.

# Organizational Structure

Organizational structure is a means to define how job tasks are organized, divided, and grouped so the organization can operate efficiently and effectively. This allows workers to understand their roles and positions within the organization. The organizational structure is best depicted using an organizational chart, a schematic drawing showing jobs, reporting lines, and departments. The organizational chart allows managers to better understand the six elements of organizational structure: work specialization, departmentalization, chain of command, span of control, centralization, and formalization.

## Work Specialization

Work specialization describes how narrow the focus of a job is. A highly specialized job requires a small variety of tasks or functions. An assembly line in a boat factory is a prime example of a highly specialized job; a person has one task to do in building the boat. People become quite skilled at their one task, but boredom and absenteeism are prevalent in jobs that are highly specialized.

In the park and recreation profession, managers take a broader approach to work specialization by hiring people with expertise in certain areas such as media relations, fund-raising, and sales. These people are considered specialists rather than generalists, although the work is not so specialized as to be monotonous.

## Departmentalization

Once work specialization is determined, jobs must be departmentalized, or grouped according to function, product, geography, or customer. Departmentalization according to function groups similar jobs together. A resort may choose to have a landscape and maintenance division where groundskeepers and horticulturists are in the landscaping department and pool maintenance and carpenters are in the maintenance department. Departments may include arts, events, sports, sales, catering, membership, facilities, and so on.

Jobs also can be departmentalized based on products or services. For example, Walt Disney Company has departments for different functions such as Walt Disney International, parks and resorts, ESPN and media networks, and consumer products and media. Geography is another common departmentalization method. Jobs are grouped based on where customers are or geographic regions. The National Park Service uses this method and has staff based in the various parks across the United States rather than only in Washington, D.C. The Minneapolis Park and Recreation Board uses a combination of organization by services. They have three main service divisions—environmental stewardship, planning services, and recreation services. Within recreation services, the community centers are divided based on four geographic regions.

Finally, jobs can be departmentalized by customer. Customers may be departmentalized by need, as corporate or individual customers, or as retailers, wholesalers, or government clients. For example, the National Recreation and Park Association has member networks for those interested in such things as aquatics, armed forces recreation, and parks and conservation, among others.

## Chain of Command

Chain of command has had a presence in organizational structures since the Industrial Revolution. It describes the line of authority, or who answers to whom in the organization. The organizational structure determines the direct supervisors of

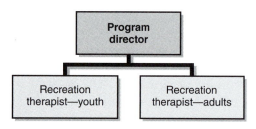

**Figure 4.1** Chain of command.

specific areas. In figure 4.1, the two recreation therapists are supervised by the program director. This is a direct chain of command.

## Span of Control

Span of control is the number of people a manager can supervise effectively. With a small span of control, a small number of employees report to a manager, whereas a large number of people report to a manager with a large span of control. Typically there is a smaller span of control at the top of the organization, with two to four people reporting directly to the CEO. The span of control increases further down the chart, and research on span of control indicates that five to seven is the optimum number a manager should supervise (Chamberlain and Wheeler 2016). However, this number may vary depending on the type of work being done and the skill of the supervisor and employees. For example, when the work tasks are very similar among employees, a manager is able to supervise more people than when the jobs are more diverse with different tasks. Also, if the staff are highly skilled, a manager can more easily supervise them than staff members who are less highly skilled. Highly skilled staff need less direct supervision by the manager.

## Centralization

Organizational decision making is a key structural concern. Organizations can have varying degrees of centralization, which is the extent to which decision making is concentrated at one or a few points in the organization. In a centralized organization, top managers make all of the decisions. Although this brings consistency to decision making, it makes for a slow process because issues must move up through the chain of command. A completely centralized structure is most useful in a small company such as a sole proprietorship or partnership where the layers of management are limited.

With a decentralized organization, decision making occurs further down in the organization by managers who are closest to the situation, and more than one person in the organization can make decisions. This form of organizational structure leads to faster decision making and allows for more input from employees. A large organization is more likely to function efficiently and effectively with a decentralized structure. In a decentralized organization, managers delegate authority to the staff. This allows staff to carry out their responsibilities and make decisions within the scope of their job. Managers must trust staff to do the job, as delegation can increase morale and self-esteem, build staff skills, create a team approach to the work, improve efficiency, and increase staff creativity and innovation (Chamberlain and Wheeler 2016).

## Formalization

The last element of organizational structure to consider is formalization. Formalization is the level of standardization in a job. In a highly standardized job, an employee has little control over how, what, and when things need to get done. Little decision making is involved because policies and procedures are detailed. A less formalized structure gives employees freedom and allows for creativity, decision making, and control over work. In parks and recreation, an agency is most likely to be less formalized, with employees having structured jobs but the ability to make decisions about how to do those jobs. Keep in mind there is a difference between formalization and work specialization; work specialization focuses on how many different tasks a person performs, whereas formalization focuses on the freedom of how, when, and where tasks are done.

## Summary of Organizational Structure

Organizational structures vary from agency to agency regardless of the sector. Managers will need to consider how different structures influence the efficiency and effectiveness of production and program delivery. Look at the differences in how organizational structure can affect two managers.

- Manager 1: The organization is departmentalized geographically and has a wide span of control (eight people), decentralized decision making, and lower levels of formalization.
- Manager 2: The organization is departmentalized by formalized functions and has a small span of control (three people) and centralized decision making.

Manager 1 supervises many employees. These employees have significant control over how they do their jobs and decision making because the manager has many staff to work with directly. Manager 2 only has a few employees to supervise and thus may spend more time interacting with them and discussing potential decisions. Jobs are highly formalized without much freedom for how to do them, and the employees are in specialized areas such as arts or fitness. All decisions must go to the top of the organization. Manager 1 would most likely be present in a large organization whereas manager 2 is better suited for a smaller one.

# Organizational Design

Once structure has been established, **organizational design** is considered. The design is shown in an organizational chart that illustrates how the different elements of the organizational structure are arranged and incorporated. Designs change fairly regularly as jobs are changed or combined, new products and services are developed, or changes in management are needed to make the organization more efficient and effective.

There are four types of designs: simple designs, bureaucracies, team-based designs, and matrix designs.

**organizational design**—The means of arranging and incorporating organizational structure, which is typically depicted in the form of an organizational chart.

## Simple Designs

A **simple structure**, also called *entrepreneurial startup*, is considered a flat organization (figure 4.2). Simple structures are characterized by a wide span of control, low degree of departmentalization, little formalization, and centralized decision making. These structures operate best in small agencies where the CEO has the decision-making power yet the employees have some freedom in how they get things done (Robbins and Coulter 2016). Although there is little formalization, tasks get done effectively because of centralized decision making. Many sole proprietorships and partnerships begin as simple structures and morph into other structures and designs as they grow.

**simple structure**—Organizational design that is flat, or has few levels of authority. In simple structures, most people answer to the same supervisor.

**Figure 4.2**  Simple structure.

## Bureaucracies

Bureaucracies were first introduced by Max Weber (see chapter 1). They consist of highly formalized jobs that are guided by rules, regulations, and policies. This strong adherence to policies guides decision making and keeps decision making centralized. Most bureaucracies have a narrow span of control with jobs grouped by function. Because they are somewhat resistant to change, bureaucracies work best in stable environments that can be standardized. Bureaucracies often have a negative stigma, but they do have some positive aspects. Their strengths lie in the ability to perform standardized tasks efficiently and to function well with less talented employees due to the high level of standardization.

Bureaucracies still exist extensively in the park and recreation profession. Agencies make the bureaucracy work by reducing the level of specialization and decentralizing decision making to lower levels in the organization. These agencies are still guided by rules, regulations, and policies and have a functional division of labor, but they are not so structured as to make the organization rigid and unresponsive to change (figure 4.3).

## Team-Based Designs

The term *team* is often misused in the workplace. It has become a popular management approach that many agencies adopt, yet they are merely renaming work groups without actually instituting teams. A work group is a collection of people

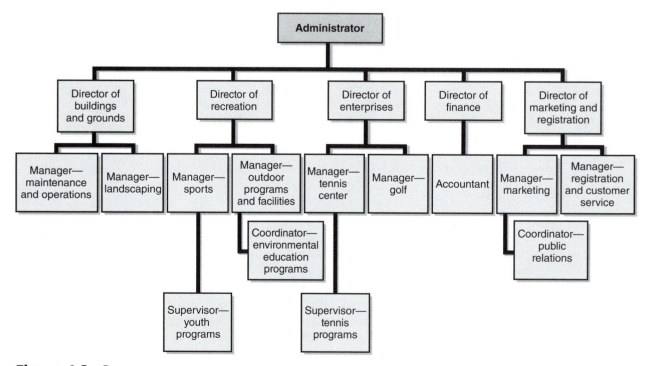

**Figure 4.3**  Bureaucracy.

## Reading Organizational Charts

Organizational charts show the relationship of positions within the organization. Lines connect positions to show levels of authority. In figure 4.3, for example, the direct line between the director of recreation and the manager of sports shows that the director of recreation supervises the manager of sports, who supervises the supervisor of youth programs. Organizational charts also demonstrate different levels in the organization by title and by placement on the chart. Job titles should be consistent across levels, showing that the jobs at a particular level are relatively equal within the organization. For example, if an organization had four job classifications—director, manager, coordinator, and supervisor—there would be four horizontal levels on the chart. In figure 4.3 you can see that the directors are on the same level, followed by managers, then coordinators, and then supervisors. If an area does not have a coordinator position, as is the case with tennis, then the supervisor's position is dropped lower on the chart to be in line with other supervisors rather than directly under the manager at the coordinator level.

In addition to demonstrating different levels in the organization, the organizational chart demonstrates pay levels. Most organizations have set pay for each level on the chart. These levels are ranges where employees usually start when assuming a particular position.

working on a project who have their own responsibilities, complete them individually, and come back to the group to share information on their progress. The group most likely has a designated leader who facilitates meetings and oversees project progress.

A team, on the other hand, has more interaction and interdependence. The team creates a synergy where the whole is greater than the sum of the individual parts. Work teams break down traditional barriers and department structures in the organization and move decision making to the team level. The team is given a project and members bring their individual skills together in such a way that innovation, creativity, and high performance result. Teams do not simply report what they have accomplished in meetings but use knowledge of each other to complete projects through discussion and active problem solving (figure 4.4).

The two most common types of teams are self-managed and problem-solving teams. Self-managed teams work together to perform a function or produce a product or service. The team has control over how tasks get done and are fully responsible for the quality and efficiency of the output. For example, an organization may have a marketing team that includes people in the areas of sponsorships, market research, media relations, public relations, and advertising. This self-managed team works together to market products and services for the agency.

Problem-solving teams, or task forces, come together with the purpose of solving a problem. Once this goal is achieved, they disband. An example of a problem-solving team is a team assigned the task of determining whether an indoor golf driving range is financially feasible for an organization.

Chamberlain and Wheeler (2016, 85) suggest that for teams to be successful they need people with

- a clear understanding of the outcome and goals,
- technical expertise to carry out the assigned task,
- problem-solving and decision-making skills to identify issues, generate alternatives, evaluate those alternatives, and make competent decisions,
- good interpersonal skills such as listening, feedback, and conflict resolution,
- accountability for their individual contribution to the project, and
- commitment to complete the project.

Teams can be challenging to work in but can produce excellent results if managed well.

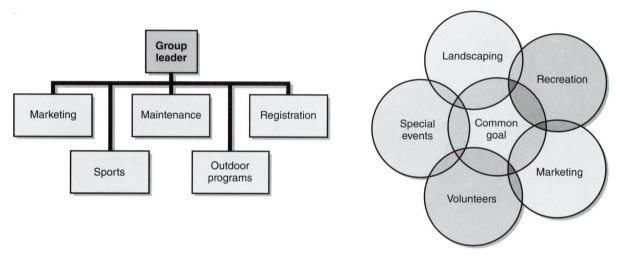

**Figure 4.4**   Group structure (left) versus team structure (right).

## Matrix Designs

The matrix structure brings together the concepts of teams and bureaucracies. It is a combination of both function and departmentalism where teams are created by bringing together select people from different departments for a specific function or problem. These are also called *cross-functional teams*. For example, the agency depicted in figure 4.3 is planning a triathlon for an anticipated 1,000 participants. The director of recreation decides to create a project team for this event with staff from different departments who have the needed areas of expertise. Figure 4.5 demonstrates the nine people who will be working on the triathlon, including three people from sports, two from outdoor programs and facilities (because the lake will be used for swimming), two from maintenance (because of the course setup), and one each from marketing and registration. For this event, the project team members will answer to the director of recreation as well as to their original supervisor.

The matrix structure brings together expertise from different areas and can be highly efficient and effective; however, its weakness is that it breaks the **unity of command principle**, which asserts that each employee should have only one identifiable supervisor. Employees in a matrix structure have two supervisors during the project. Once the project is complete, the group disbands and unity of command is reestablished.

**unity of command principle**—When employees have only one identifiable supervisor.

Matrix structures are used extensively in parks and recreation due to the nature of the business. Our products and services require knowledge of several areas that one person rarely possesses. Assembling people who have various knowledge areas for a project is an effective means of accomplishing a goal.

## Organizational Culture

As previously mentioned, organizations have formal and informal elements. The formal aspects are structure and design, and the informal structure is the **organizational culture**—shared norms, values, beliefs, and expectations that bind employees together and distinguish the agency from others. In essence, organizational culture is the personality of the organization.

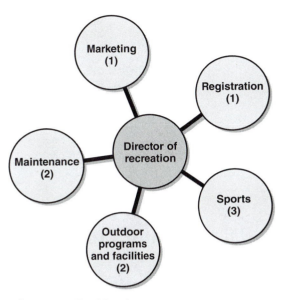

**Figure 4.5** Matrix structure.

Schein and Schein (2017) describe three levels of organizational culture from very tangible to almost subconscious: (1) artifacts, (2) espoused beliefs, and (3) underlying assumptions. Artifacts, the most tangible level, are things that can be seen and touched, as well as less tangible things such as the climate of the organization. Artifacts may include the look of the facilities and furnishings, the way the staff dresses, how the staff interacts with each other and the public, the language used, or how people address each other. A new manager coming into an organization can immediately get a feeling about the organization by observing these cultural indicators.

A new manager may also observe the next level of organizational culture, espoused beliefs. Espoused beliefs are those things that the staff have developed to show the outside world who the organization is, including slogans, credos, and values, vision, and mission statements. For example, Patagonia, a company that makes clothing and accessories for outdoor recreation, is known for its environmentally conscious behavior. A statement on their website demonstrates their professed culture:

> *For us at Patagonia, a love of wild and beautiful places demands participation in the fight to save them, and to help reverse the steep decline in the overall environmental health of our planet. We donate our time, services and at least 1 percent of our sales to hundreds of grassroots environmental groups all over the world who work to help reverse the tide. We know that our business activity—from lighting stores to dyeing shirts—creates pollution as a by-product. So we work steadily to reduce those harms. We use recycled polyester in many of our clothes and only organic, rather than pesticide-intensive, cotton. Staying true to our core values during thirty-plus years in business has helped us create a company we're proud to run and work for. And our focus on making the best products possible has brought us success in the marketplace (Patagonia 2017a).*

The third and most deeply ingrained level of organizational culture is underlying assumptions, which are the unwritten rules that guide behaviors. As new staff members come into the organization, they are socialized into the culture. Assumptions may include such things as expectations of team performance, risk

**organizational culture**—Shared norms, values, and expectations that bind employees together and distinguish an agency from others.

taking, creativity, or competitiveness. New managers will often find it difficult to quickly gauge this level of organizational culture, but it will become more visible over time. It is very important for new managers to learn the culture. Even a highly skilled manager may not succeed if they do not understand this aspect of the job.

It is difficult to change organizational culture because it is so deeply ingrained in employees. Although the formal structure of an organization can readily change on paper, certain elements of the informal culture will need special attention and time in order to change. Many staff see their culture as "this is who we are" and strongly identify with that image. This makes a change in organizational culture even more difficult.

## Summary of Organizational Structure, Design, and Culture

As you can see, organizations have extensive organizational structures, designs, and cultures, as well as formal and informal structures and expectations. These factors work together to make the organization what it is and how it operates.

Bringing together structure, design, and culture takes a great deal of time and consideration. The melding of these three aspects forms the roots of the organization. They dictate responsibility, the chain of command, the span of control, how specialized and formalized each job is, how jobs are grouped, and expected behavior. All which drive efficiency and effectiveness within an organization and require continual attention and monitoring so that improvements can be made.

# WORKING WITH BOARDS

**boards**—Governing bodies within organizations that can have authority ranging from setting policies to advising management.

Once the organizational structure and design are determined, the manager may have another major organizational factor to consider: boards. **Boards** are governing bodies within agencies. Many park and recreation agencies work with some form of board, and there are roughly 3.5 million boards in the United States (Pointer and Orlikoff 2002), though not all are in park and recreation agencies. Public and nonprofit agencies will most likely have a board, as will major corporations. In general, the only agencies not governed by boards are sole proprietorships, partnerships, and LLCs.

There are three types of boards—independent, semi-independent, and advisory—and they have several titles, such as trustees, commissions, councils, and directors. Each type of board has different powers, responsibilities, and authorities. Table 4.2 gives an overview of these differences and similarities.

## Independent Boards

Independent boards can be found in all three sectors. These boards have the most responsibility and authority of the three types. In the public sector, recreation agencies that are independent taxing bodies, such as special districts, have independent boards. These boards, such as the Foothills Park and Recreation District board of directors in Colorado, have the authority to assess taxes, purchase land, hire and fire the CEO, and set policy. Independent board members are most often elected by the general public.

In the nonprofit sector, boards such as the YMCA of Metropolitan Minneapolis are composed of members, whereas a board in the commercial sector, such as the

**Table 4.2** Summary of Board Responsibilities and Authority

| | Independent Board | Semi-independent Board | Advisory Board |
|---|---|---|---|
| **SECTOR** | | | |
| Commercial | ✓ | — | ✓ |
| Public | ✓ | ✓ | ✓ |
| Nonprofit | ✓ | — | ✓ |
| **POSITION ATTAINMENT** | | | |
| Elected members | ✓ | — | ✓ |
| Appointed members | — | ✓ | ✓ |
| **AUTHORITY** | | | |
| Set policy | ✓ | Limited | — |
| Ultimate financial responsibility | ✓ | — | — |
| Assess taxes | Some may (e.g., park district) | — | — |
| Hold property title | ✓ | — | — |
| Power | Full power | Dependent on independent board | Power limited to advise |

Disney Corporation board of directors, is made up of shareholders who are elected by other shareholders. Because they are not public agencies, these boards do not have the ability to levy taxes.

An independent board has three core functions: policy formation, decision making, and oversight (Pointer and Orlikoff 2002). All board responsibilities fall within one of these core areas. Responsibilities include:

- Determining the values, vision, mission, goals, and objectives of the organization
- Selecting, evaluating, and replacing the CEO
- Providing advice to top management
- Approving and monitoring programs, services, and corporate actions
- Providing sound financial management
- Formulating and approving policies that guide the agency
- Ensuring the organization complies with laws and regulations

Independent board members also have fiduciary duties. Fiduciary duties require that board members do what is best for the organization, showing impartiality by acting in good faith, and treating all stakeholders, members, and user groups equally and fairly. Fiduciary duties outline the obligations of board members to avoid conflicts of interest. For example, a conflict of interest would occur if a landscaping company owned by a board member was contracted to mow parks and install flower beds. Board members are required to act in the best interest of the agency and put their personal well-being aside.

## Board Member Competencies

Not only do managers need to be skilled at their jobs, board members do too. Agencies under a board's jurisdiction cannot thrive unless the board is competent, active, and working in the best interest of the agency and not as individual board members. As discussed in chapter 1, competencies are the knowledge, skills, and abilities needed to be successful in a job. Research on public park and recreation boards has identified several competencies that board members need in order to be effective (Hurd 2004). Table 4.3 shows a selected listing of these competencies.

**Table 4.3** Board Member Competencies

| Public Sector | Nonprofit Sector |
| --- | --- |
| Be willing to study issues before making decisions. | Have long-range and short-range planning skills. |
| Be willing to participate in committee and board meetings. | Have fiscal management skills. |
| Have the ability to make decisions. | Determine the mission, vision, goals, and objectives of the organization. |
| Be objective and fair. | Ensure efficient operation of the board. |
| Read and understand supplied information before board meetings. | Select the CEO. |
| Be prepared to give time to the board and agency. | Raise money. |
| Understand the role of the executive relative to the board. | Gain constituent support. |
| Be accountable to the public. | Select and orient new board members. |
| Understand the budgeting process. | Understand board functions. |
| Be supportive of staff. | Be able to problem solve. |

In addition to these responsibilities, it is often expected that nonprofit board members will help raise funds for the organization. This is not the case with corporations and is only occasionally expected with boards in the public sector.

## Semi-independent Boards

Semi-independent boards exist in the public sector only. These boards are most often found within city government where a city council has the ultimate authority over the park and recreation department but appoints a board to work directly with the department. For example, the city council in Bloomington, Indiana, has appointed a board of park commissioners to serve as the governing board. This board has many of the same powers and fiduciary duties as an independent board, but it relies on an independent board (the city council) for the ultimate authority. A semi-independent board has the authority to direct policy formation, decision making, and oversight, yet budget approval and major policies often require the approval of the independent board. Although this type of board has a great deal of control over an agency, it also has limitations, such as fiscal control lying with a higher board.

## Advisory Boards

Of the three types of boards, the advisory board has the least amount of authority and responsibility. All three sectors have advisory boards; however, corporate entities use them a bit differently than public and nonprofit organizations do. Nonprofit and public agency advisory boards are established as links between the agency and the community or members. They have advisory responsibility and do not take on any policy or oversight duties. Members are a sounding board for problems and ideas, and the board serves as a means of citizen involvement. Advisory boards can be created to advise an entire agency, such as the Wake Forest, North Carolina, Recreation Advisory Board and the Parks and Recreation Advisory Board in Bellingham, Washington. They can also advise particular areas, such as the Teen Advisory Board for the Speed Art Museum in Louisville, Kentucky, or the Park Advisory Board for the Gulf Islands National Park Reserve in Canada.

Corporate organizations, on the other hand, have experts on their advisory boards rather than people who represent the general population. These experts are usually from other corporations, have specific areas of expertise, and receive a modest retainer fee for serving on the board. The advisory board commitment is short (one to two years), and the board meets two to four times a year. The corporate advisory board reviews business plans, strategic plans, and special concerns and gives feedback to the company. As with public and nonprofit advisory boards, the corporate advisory board has limited legal responsibility for the organization. The corporate world uses these boards more as consulting firms than advisory boards.

## Board Structure

As with any organization, boards require structure. Board structure comes in the form of board qualifications and elections, board size, terms and term limits, board governance, and board meetings.

### Qualifications and Elections

Strong boards in the nonprofit and commercial sectors seek members with diverse expertise, demographics that reflect the constituents, and knowledge of and connections to the community. Expertise areas include marketing, finance, volunteer management, fund-raising, business planning, and so on. In the commercial and nonprofit sectors, the current board or a nominating subcommittee nominates potential candidates. Members or shareholders then vote on the slate of candidates to elect the members. Some organizations have a **self-perpetuating board** in which board members themselves vote for new members to the board.

**self-perpetuating board**—System where current board members elect new board members.

Boards in the public sector have slightly different ways of obtaining new members. The two predominant means of becoming a board member in a public agency are election and appointment. Park and recreation independent board members are elected by the community. For example, Illinois park districts are considered special districts. Rather than the board nominating potential members for the community to vote on, people choose to run, get signatures on a petition, and are then placed on the ballot to be voted on during a general election within the community.

In this situation it is virtually impossible to control for expertise, demographic diversity, or community knowledge.

If boards in the public sector are appointed, usually by the city council, they may be political appointments that are made because of the connection between the new board member and the members of the city council. Appointments also may be made when the council interviews those who apply for the position and then chooses the candidate who best fits the board and the philosophy of the council.

## Board Size

Board size will vary from board to board and by sector. Public boards tend to consist of 5 to 15 people, with 7 to 9 being standard (Moiseichik 2016). Corporate boards average 9 people (Kirdahy 2007) and nonprofit boards average 16 people (Dambach, Davis, and Gales 2009). Nonprofit organizations tend to have larger boards for fund-raising purposes—there is often an underlying expectation that members will donate money themselves or work to raise funds.

Small boards are advantageous in that they allow for more participation from board members. However, all of the work must be shared by the select few. Large boards, on the other hand, can share the responsibilities, but their numbers can inhibit participation and slow progress.

## Terms and Term Limits

A term is the length of time that the board member serves without being reelected or reappointed. Rarely does a board member join a board for only a one-year term; two- to four-year terms are more common. A short time on the board does not give members time to make a meaningful contribution because they are still learning about the organization, and longer terms prohibit new people and their ideas from influencing the board. Although there is much variance in term lengths among the three sectors, 64 percent of all boards in the Nonprofit Governance Index Report have three-year terms (BoardSource 2012).

With term lengths come term limits. Term limits are the number of consecutive terms a person can serve on a board. Many organizations institute term limits so that one person does not get on the board for perpetuity and the board does not stay the same over a number of years. Term limits also allow new people to be involved. Two-term limits are standard, along with the ability to be off the board a year before coming back on. The board members should have a staggered rotation system where part of the board rotates off each year rather than having an entirely new board in a given year (table 4.4). A good rule of thumb is to never have more than one-third of the board rotate off each year.

## Board Governance

Boards operate according to their bylaws and their policies and procedures manual. Bylaws are the formal rules governing the internal operations of the organization. They establish the size of the board, terms, term limits, board member rotation, officers, meeting procedures, quorum, proxies, board vacancies, dissolution of the agency, and so on (figure 4.6).

Just as the staff has policies, procedures, and operating manuals, so does the board. This manual is given to board members at the start of their term so they understand how the board operates and what its roles and responsibilities are. A board manual will contain some of the following items:

- *Legal documents.* Bylaws, articles of incorporation, 501(c)(3) papers
- *Organizational information.* Agency history; values, vision, and mission statements; goals and objectives; strategic plan; staff and board organizational charts; staff policies; program descriptions
- *Board operations.* Ethics statement, conflict of interest statement, board attendance and expectations for committee participation, board member job descriptions, board evaluation procedures, professional development expectations, standing committees
- *Meeting procedures.* Board meeting information packets, agendas, minutes
- *Financial information.* Policies, procedures, budget and financial reports and statements, previous and current budget

An important piece of information that must be included in the policies and procedures manual is the board's role in day-to-day operation of the organization. All too often boards overstep their jurisdiction and attempt to control more of the agency than they should. The role of a board is to advise management, not to run the agency. The only person who answers to the board of directors is the CEO. The remaining staff members either directly or indirectly report to the CEO. A well-designed policy manual can help alleviate some of these problems.

Both the bylaws and the operations manual can serve as an orientation for board members. All new board members should follow a structured orientation process and be assigned a current board member as a mentor. This will enable the new board member to become an active and contributing member more quickly. In addition to helping new board members, the bylaws and operations manual will guide the board in adhering to its roles and responsibilities, thus strengthening both the board and the agency.

## Board Meetings

Board meetings are most likely to happen biweekly, monthly, or quarterly. They usually follow a standardized procedure that includes board packets, meeting announcements, agendas, and parliamentary procedure.

**Board Packets**   Most agencies send board members packets with detailed information before meetings. Such packets should be received a minimum of one week

**Table 4.4**  Sample Board Rotation System

|  | Year on the Board | Year off the Board |
|---|---|---|
| Board member 1 | January 1, 2020 | December 31, 2022 |
| Board member 2 | January 1, 2020 | December 31, 2022 |
| Board member 3 | January 1, 2021 | December 31, 2023 |
| Board member 4 | January 1, 2021 | December 31, 2023 |
| Board member 5 | January 1, 2022 | December 31, 2024 |
| Board member 6 | January 1, 2022 | December 31, 2024 |

This six-member board has three-year terms and a rotation system where two people leave and two new people join the board each year. Assume there are four board members continuing from 2019 with two new members coming on the board in 2020.

---

## Article II—Board of Directors

### Section 1

Board size and composition: The board shall be composed of nine members. There must be six members who represent each district in the region. The remaining three board members are considered at-large members and may come from any of the six districts, with no more than two people from any one district.

### Section 2

The board of directors will meet quarterly at an agreed-upon time and place.

### Section 3

Board elections: Board members will be elected annually by the members of the organization through an electronic ballot.

### Section 4

Terms: All board members shall serve three-year terms but are eligible for reelection one time so as not to serve any more than two consecutive terms. Once the two consecutive terms are served, the member must remain off the board for one year before being reelected to the board. Board members will serve staggered terms so that three people rotate off the board each year.

---

**Figure 4.6** Sample section of bylaws.

before the meeting. The packet includes minutes from previous meetings and any committee meetings that have occurred between board meetings, financial statements for review, study materials for issues to be discussed, and so on. Board members are expected to thoroughly review these materials so they are prepared to discuss the issues at hand and make sound decisions at the board meeting.

**Meeting Announcements**  Meeting announcements should be made to the community, members, and shareholders in advance. This is particularly important for public agencies in the United States because they are legally required to do so based on the Open Meetings Act. Although the details of the act vary from state to state, the act generally states that public agencies must notify the public that a meeting is to be held and that the public is invited to attend. A meeting is defined as a gathering of a **quorum** of board members who gather to discuss business pertaining to the agency. The size of the quorum is often 50 percent of the board members plus one, but it does not have to be; it can be a smaller or larger number of board members based on the state's law. The Open Meetings Act does not mean that all aspects of agency business are open to the public. State laws dictate which items are to be discussed in **closed sessions**. For example, personnel concerns such as the annual performance evaluation of the CEO are discussed in closed sessions to protect the rights of employees.

**Agendas and Parliamentary Procedure**  The meeting agenda is the roadmap that guides the business of the meeting. The agenda will often follow *Robert's Rules of Order*, also called *parliamentary procedure*. These rules delineate how meetings are

**quorum**—Minimum number of board members needed to conduct official board business.

**closed sessions**— Board meetings that are not open for the public to attend. Closed sessions are held for such things as personnel concerns, litigation, or collective bargaining.

started and ended and how votes are presented to the group, discussed, amended, and voted upon. A typical agenda looks something like this:

1. Call to order
2. Roll call of members present
3. Reading and approval of minutes
4. Officers' reports
5. Committee reports
6. Old business
7. New business
8. Announcements
9. Adjournment

**Meeting Minutes**   The board secretary or other designated officer is responsible for the minutes of the meeting. The minutes detail the date, time, and place of the meeting. They also include members present and absent, a summary of the discussion and deliberation, and any votes that were taken. The minutes serve as a record of the meetings and are usually saved for the life of the organization. For public agencies, the Open Meetings Act requires minutes to be taken and made available to the public within a specified amount of time. Some organizations will record the meeting and have verbatim minutes and others will have abbreviated, but thorough minutes.

## Summary of Board Structure

Board structure is just as complicated as agency structure. It requires time and attention in order for the board to function well. Boards have a tremendous amount of influence on organizations, especially independent and semi-independent boards that influence policy and financial decisions. A well-structured board that is able to conduct productive meetings is a true asset to an organization. It is in the best interest of managers to develop a positive working relationship with board members so that the staff and board are working together toward common goals rather than as two separate entities dividing the agency.

# FORM OF GOVERNMENT AND ORGANIZATIONAL STRUCTURE AND DESIGN

Many aspects of an organization drive its structure, including the sector in which the agency exists, organizational culture, type of board, and strengths and weaknesses of staff. For example, a public agency that was established as a special district has an independent board. This gives the organization more freedom to adopt the structure that best fits its need. On the other hand, a public agency with a semi-independent board within a city system may have to follow a pre-established organizational structure that has set job titles such as coordinator, supervisor, or manager. These titles will most likely have comparable pay grades across the city. Furthermore, when developing its structure, the organization must consider the city council or a semi-independent board that answers to the city council.

A commercial agency will rely on advice from shareholders who examine the strengths and weaknesses of staff to determine organizational structure. The same can be said for nonprofit organizations, which also have an independent board that may or may not have valuable input on how jobs are structured and designed.

Finally, culture plays an important role in structuring an organization. Underlying assumptions and espoused beliefs and actions can drive an organization. Even when staff members say they want a change in the structure, it is often difficult to deviate from the norm because the people making the changes are the ones who have internalized the values, beliefs, and assumptions that have driven the organization for years.

 Check out the web study guide for additional material, including learning activities, sample documents, interactive case studies, web links, CPRP exam connections, and more.

## Conclusion

Given the sector, structure, design, and board concerns presented, it is easy to see that organizations are quite complex. The organizational structure and design can change as the agency's goals, objectives, and needs change. Since change is inevitable in any agency, managers need a solid understanding of structure, design, and board responsibilities. In addition, state and federal legislation dictates such things as funding, profit distribution, and board meetings. A lack of knowledge in these areas can have a negative impact on the efficiency and effectiveness of the entire organization.

# Review Questions

1. Differentiate between strong mayor–council and city manager–council forms of municipal governments.
2. Differentiate between a district and a department.
3. Outline how a manager might start a nonprofit organization.
4. Compare and contrast partnerships, sole proprietorships, and corporations.
5. Explain how organizational structure and design interrelate.
6. Describe organizational culture and its tangible and intangible elements.
7. What are the three types of boards, and how do they differ?
8. What items are contained in board bylaws?
9. What items are contained in board operating manuals?
10. What is the Open Meeting Act?

# 5

# Coordination of Resources, Programs, and Services

## Learning Outcomes

- Understand the connection between various management functions (planning, organizing, leading, and controlling) and the coordination of agency resources, programs, and services.

- Define the functions used for intra-agency coordination, including vertical and lateral coordination.

- Provide examples of planning and control systems used to coordinate and control agency work processes, including performance control and action planning.

- Define management roles for leisure services provision in the three sectors (public, nonprofit, commercial) and identify the opportunities for coordination both among and within sectors.

- Identify the methods for coordinating interorganizational efforts, including both inter- and intrasector partnership strategies.

## Key Terms

functional resources, organizational resources, structural differentiation, structural integration, suboptimization, vertical coordination, human capital, policies, policy making, procedures, rules, standard operating procedures, standards, accountability, action planning, performance control, management by objectives (MBO), horizontal coordination, teams, task forces, synergy, intersectoral partnership, partnership, collaboration, alliance, administrative consolidation, joint programming (joint facility use), networks, partnership integration, joint venture, merger

## Competency Check

Refer to table 1.6 to see how you assessed these related competencies.

14. Develop partnerships with other organizations.
37. Participate in policy formation, evaluation, and revision.

## A Day in the Life

I am the executive director of a university-affiliated nonprofit organization that specializes in community-based recreational therapy and adaptive sports. In my world, I have three primary areas of concern: the internal climate of the organization, including celebrations, stressors, challenges, and successes, to keep the team operating at its full potential; fund development to keep the organization replete with the resources necessary to run efficiently and effectively; and program development that advances the profession and keeps our organization on the leading edge.

Each day I arrive early to catch staff on their way out to programs to wish them well, then I triage the priorities for the day. On any given day I will deal with one or more of these areas through meetings, email, or written proposals and reports. I work in teams and on my own based on the project. There is always much to be done.

Jill Gravink
Executive Director
Northeast Passage Adaptive Sports
Durham, New Hampshire

The four major functions of management are planning, organizing, leading, and controlling. Together they provide the foundation for another important aspect of management—coordination. Coordination ability is one of the core competencies of organizations, and the capacity of an organization to coordinate **functional resources** (human assets) and **organizational resources** (physical, financial, and technological) has been linked to overall effectiveness and to competitive advantage (Jones 2012). All four functions of management contribute to coordination ability. Successful coordination includes planning (setting goals), organizing (identifying and coordinating resources to achieve goals), leading (encouraging personnel to contribute to organizational success), and controlling (evaluating goals and developing processes to improve organizational performance).

To a large extent, coordination is a component of organizational structure (see chapter 4) and requires successful communication (see chapter 8). As organizations grow in size and scope, they become more complex. Complex organizations have higher degrees of **structural differentiation**—there are many people and units fulfilling diverse and varied organizational roles. The challenge for managers is to find an efficient and effective method for organizing and allocating work. This is accomplished primarily through organizational design (chapter 4). However, allocating work is just one piece of the puzzle; once it is allocated, it must be coordinated. Without coordination, an organization runs the risk of being disorganized, competing against itself, duplicating efforts, and squandering scarce resources. This chapter focuses on the process of coordination both from an intraorganizational and interorganizational perspective. Specifically, it examines methods for achieving organizational integration, as well as methods and best practices for coordinating interorganization collaborative efforts.

**functional resources**—Personnel skills and knowledge.

**organizational resources**—Financial, physical, technological, and human assets that organizations need for the production of goods or services.

**structural differentiation**—Structural condition in complex organizations where many people and units must fulfill diverse roles.

## INTERNAL ORGANIZATIONAL COORDINATION

The process of coordinating organizational tasks, roles, functions, and units so that they work together effectively is called **structural integration**. Creating a structure that clearly defines work roles is a necessary component of organizational design. However, structural differentiation alone cannot address coordination and control. Coordination is necessary when the tasks of organizational units are highly interdependent. Specifically, coordination helps to

**structural integration**—Coordinating organizational tasks, roles, functions, and units so that they work together effectively.

- achieve consistency for both staff and customers,
- ensure fairness and equity, and
- avoid duplication of efforts or unnecessary internal competition.

Consider the university campus recreation organization depicted in figure 5.1. The organization consists of six different functional units: sport clubs, instructional classes and programs, facilities, intramural sports, fitness and wellness, and outdoor adventures.

Each unit is responsible for a unique aspect of campus recreation programming, yet many of the units are functionally interdependent. For example, the intramural sport and sport club units rely on available and adequately prepared facilities to ensure that programs run effectively. Similarly, policy must be coordinated among units to ensure consistency. Suppose that access to the recreation center requires a valid student or member identification card. Eligibility for participation in an intramural basketball game would need to be limited to students or campus recreation members to ensure that participants would be able to access the facility.

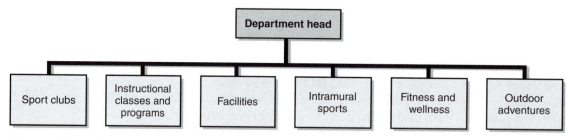

**Figure 5.1** University recreation organization.

Other policy areas such as program pricing and risk management require a coordinated effort to achieve consistency and fairness. For example, it might be unfair for intramural sport programs, which are typically male dominated, to be free of charge whereas group fitness classes, which tend to attract female participants, are offered for a fee. Finally, it is important that units do not compete against each other for participants and resources or unnecessarily duplicate efforts. If a department goal is to provide alternative late-night programming to discourage students from drinking or engaging in other risky behavior, it would not be wise to offer several competing late-night programs at the same times and on the same nights, especially if those programs attempt to attract the same participants.

Although certain courses of action might benefit a particular unit—such as allowing nonmembers to participate in intramural sport contests or charging fees for a kickboxing class—they might have a negative impact on the overall organizational effort. If the actions of individual units work against the mission of the organization, then inconsistency, inequity, and inefficiency are likely to occur. Ultimately, effective coordination helps to curtail this process of **suboptimization**, or emphasizing unit goals rather than the larger goals of the organization (Bolman and Deal 2013). The central challenge for managers is to balance differentiation and integration so that both simple and complex organizations have the necessary systems to ensure effective coordination. Both too much and too little coordination lead to organizational inefficiency. For example, too much coordination wastes time and resources, and too little coordination leads to the problems discussed previously.

The structures that organizations use to coordinate internal efforts comprise two major areas: vertical coordination and horizontal coordination. Both vertical and horizontal coordination place high premiums on effective communication down, up, and across the organizational chart (see chapter 8).

**suboptimization—** Emphasis on achieving unit goals rather than focusing on the larger goals of an organization.

## Vertical Coordination

**vertical coordination—** Formal systems of control typified by hierarchies and authority; policies, rules, and standards; and accountability systems.

**Vertical coordination** involves formal systems of control and is typified by use of the following:

- Organizational hierarchies and authority
- Policies, procedures, rules, and standards
- Accountability systems

### Organizational Hierarchies and Authority

One of the principal methods for coordination and achieving integration involves structures of authority. Authority refers to power that is achieved through the position that a particular leader occupies in the organizational chart (Hersey,

Blanchard, and Johnson 2012). Coordination can be achieved by instituting a clear hierarchy of authority that leaves little room for unit or individual decision making that might work against overall organizational goals. In such organizations, leadership has the authority to act by making rules, allocating resources, controlling access to information, rewarding individual and team performance, and meting out punishment and discipline (George and Jones 2011).

One strength of hierarchical, authority-based organizations is their ability to achieve organizational integration. Recent management and organizational theory has raised the question as to whether such authority-based systems achieve integration at the expense of employees and whether **human capital**—the wealth of knowledge, skills, and abilities that individual employees possess—is wasted. Although authority might be granted by position, leadership is typically earned. In other words, employees matter. An organization might be able to achieve integration and coordination through draconian methods of command and control yet ultimately waste the potential that exists in individual employees.

At the same time, horizontally coordinated organizations, which are discussed later in the chapter, struggle with organizational integration and suboptimization, and therein lies a classic paradox. John Gardner, in his classic book *On Leadership*, asks the question this way: "Should there be a high degree of structure . . . a clear hierarchy of authority with emphasis on detailed assignments and task specifications? Or should the relationship be more informal, less structured, with leaders making the goals clear and then letting [employees] help determine the way of proceeding?" (Gardner 1993, 25).

A case study examining this paradox of coordination and control in the airline industry suggests that the answer might be a little bit of both (Gittell 2000). By reorganizing management operations and strengthening the role of supervisors, Southwest Airlines was able to increase organizational coordination without sacrificing employee empowerment. Increasing the number of supervisors and decreasing management spans of control—the number of employees that each supervisor was responsible for—led to greater coordination among frontline employees. In the process, Southwest Airlines committed to ensuring that the relationship between supervisor and employee was a cooperative one. Supervisors were present to ensure that goals and standards were upheld (i.e., on-time flight departures) by facilitating organizational learning among frontline staff. This was accomplished through troubleshooting problems and determining solutions in the context of Southwest's overall goals, such as what could be done better to ensure on-time flight departures. In this context, increased authority led to greater coordination and integration by providing frontline staff with the tools, resources, and support necessary to accomplish tasks.

**human capital**—The knowledge, skills, and abilities possessed by individual employees.

## Policies, Procedures, Rules, and Standards

Policies, procedures, rules, and standards limit discretion and guide organizational practice (Bolman and Deal 2013). One method for limiting discretion and standardizing processes is to establish a clear set of guidelines that steer behavior. This is important because organizational situations often require a uniform and predictable response. It would be unfair to a customer, for example, if the same situation were handled differently depending on who happened to be managing the situation on any given day. For example, suppose a local sports club has a policy that limits participation in a soccer program to children over the age of six. Parents who register their children in such a program would expect to be treated in the same manner, regardless of who was taking registrations. It would be unfair if one parent was allowed to register a child who was soon to be six years old, but another parent in a similar situation was denied the same opportunity.

Similarly, it may be unfair for employees in the same organization to be treated differently based on who their direct supervisor happens to be. For example, suppose a large outdoor outfitter company has a corporate policy that encourages employees to take a set number of days off with pay to engage in outdoor recreation activities to promote knowledge of the equipment they are selling to customers. An employee in one unit who makes a request to take time off under this policy should be treated the same way as another employee in another unit in the same organization. In this case, coordination across units is important to achieve fairness and equity.

Policies, procedures, rules, and standards are all mechanisms that organizations use to coordinate the actions of employees and units. **Policies** are broad statements that provide direction for an organization and flow from its goals and objectives. In the previous examples, the organizations set policies to ensure predictability and to limit discretion in terms of how various cases are handled. Ideally, policy in both cases was set in accordance with the values, vision, mission, goals, and objectives of the organizations.

Policies can be both informal and formal. Informal policies are not put in a policy manual and given to staff as a directive but result from the day-to-day activities of the organization itself. Informal policies are derived from organizational culture where norms and customs emerge and guide behavior. An informal policy may be that all staff members work the major special events that the agency holds. This is more of an expectation than a directive and thus is considered an informal policy.

Formal policies are more structured and closely followed. They are written in a policy manual, approved by a governing board, and implemented as guidelines for behavior. Formal policies direct organizations in how to accomplish things such as hiring and accounting procedures. Policies can be established to prohibit behaviors as well. They may prohibit people under the age of 18 from renting boats or other equipment at a resort, or they may prohibit groups renting rooms at a hotel from using their own caterers for food and beverages. Finally, policies can regulate behaviors of staff and customers, such as employee or customer dress codes or standards. Policies that are implemented must be fair and equitable. In Canada, the government of British Columbia recently moved to ban policies requiring female employees to wear high heels on the grounds that such policies were discriminatory and unsafe (BBC News 2017).

**Policy making** is the process of establishing policies and involves a number of people, including staff, the public, and the board. Policy making starts by identifying the need for policies. This identification may come from the strategic plan or from customer actions that require an organization to deal with a certain issue. Once the problem areas are identified, information is gathered. This information may include policies from other agencies; local, state, and federal laws that could affect the policy; and input from the community. Regardless of sector, the public can also be involved in the policy-making process. It probably is not feasible to involve the public in formulating smaller policies, but major changes in policies require input from constituents. This input gives the agency a different perspective, resulting in better policy making.

Once the issues are defined and information gathered, a policy is drafted, often by a small group of staff members. The policy draft is then discussed among the staff and the public if warranted. Changes are made after the staff and public

**policies**—Broad statements that flow from goals and objectives and provide direction.

**policy making**—Establishing policies by identifying critical issues and gathering information.

review the policy, and this step is repeated as necessary until a final draft of the policy is developed. Then it goes to a policy-making board such as the board of directors or city council. Once approved, the policy is implemented and reviewed for effectiveness. Figure 5.2 shows the process for policy making from start to finish.

**Procedures** are specific actions or steps that help carry out policy. Let's consider the sport club's eligibility policy for the youth soccer program discussed previously. Assume the policy states that the program is available for children who are six years old on the first day that the program begins. How do employees who are staffing the registration process determine a child's date of birth? Absent a procedure that details how the policy is to be carried out, this can be open to interpretation. One staff member might take a parent's word for the birth date, whereas another might request some form of official identification, such as a birth certificate. A procedure that specifically states the action to be taken in order to carry out the policy (i.e., verification of age by birth certificate or government-issued identification card) would be necessary in order to coordinate the actions of staff and to ensure consistency and fairness.

**Rules** are developed to govern behavior. Whereas policies and procedures guide behavior, rules focus on governance and, in some cases, they spell out consequences. Rules generally flow from policies and procedures. For example, in the case of the sport club's youth soccer program, there is a specific eligibility policy that lists the age that a child must be to participate. Staff members must ask parents to produce an official identification document (birth certificate or government-issued identification) to verify a child's eligibility to register for the program. A program rule might state that failure to produce such a document would prevent the child from participating. In this case, the consequences are clear: no proof of identification, no participation. The more clarity and less ambiguity there is, the easier it is to coordinate actions among staff members and participants.

In more complex processes where specific actions are necessary, standard operating procedures may be used. **Standard operating procedures (SOPs)** are clear action guidelines that may not deviate. For example, in the case of an injury in an athletic contest, on-site staff must follow a specific set of guidelines and standard operating procedures to protect the safety of the participant and to minimize risk to the athletic organization. Provo, Utah's parks and recreation department has a clear set of standard operating procedures (SOPs) for the management of the Provo Shooting Sports Park. The SOP document includes the history, purpose, and mission of the Shooting Sports Park, a safety plan and range rules, and range operations (Provo Shooting Sports Park Standard Operating Procedures 2015). In this case, a clear set of policies, procedures, and rules must be in place because of the need for risk management and to provide for a safe environment for shooting sports.

Finally, **standards** are measures that help gauge quality and determine when a particular organizational goal has been accomplished (Bolman and Deal 2013;

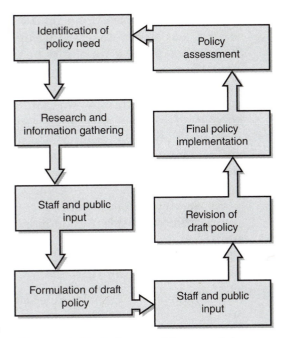

**Figure 5.2**  Policy making model.

**procedures**—Specific action steps that help carry out policy.

**rules**—Statements that govern behavior, flow from policies and procedures, and spell out consequences.

**standard operating procedures**—Guidelines for performing an action that are absolute and cannot be deviated from.

**standards**—Measures that help gauge quality and determine when a particular goal has been met.

Hersey, Blanchard, and Johnson 2012). Standards are useful for ensuring that both services and staff are measuring up to the quality expected by the organization. Standards minimize variability because they clearly state the minimum requirements for performance. Programs, facilities, and staff can also be measured against a desired standard. One of the challenges in managing leisure services is their variable nature. It is difficult to standardize a leisure experience because many variables are outside the influence of management.

Consider snow skiing as an example. Each ski experience is likely to be somewhat different based on variables such as weather, crowd density, and snow conditions. However, service encounters between resort staff and customers, especially in positions with a lot of customer contact, can be standardized to minimize variability in customer service. Likewise, management can create standards for facility safety and cleanliness that clearly communicate expectations and coordinate maintenance efforts.

## Accountability Systems

Famed management scholar Peter Drucker once stated, "What the business enterprise needs is a principle of management that will give full scope to individual strength and responsibility, and at the same time give common direction of vision and effort, establish team work, and harmonize the goals of the individual with the commonweal" (2001, 125). Drucker was talking about a system of accountability for both individual objectives and larger organizational goals.

**accountability**—The responsibility of organizations or individuals for their actions and to justify their decisions to stakeholders.

There is no shortage of definitions for accountability. It has become a buzzword that defines management practice in all three institutional sectors (public, nonprofit, commercial). Definitions of **accountability** are varied, yet almost all refer to the responsibility of organizations or people for their actions, particularly the responsibility to explain or justify their decisions to stakeholders. Leisure services organizations have multiple stakeholders, including taxpayers (in the public sector), direct users, suppliers, and boards, among others. Leisure services managers are also accountable at multiple levels. They are accountable for their own performance, the performance of their unit, and their contribution to the overall goals of the organization.

Most accountability systems start with a set of goals that are clearly articulated and can be easily measured. The organization sets goals and objectives through the strategic planning process. Organizational goals and objectives are worked into unit, program, and performance goals and objectives for managers and employees.

### Action Planning and Performance Control

Mintzberg (1979) specifies two types of planning and control systems: action planning and performance control.

**action planning**— The specific processes that are undertaken to achieve organizational objectives that are not easily measured.

**Action planning** involves the specific processes that are undertaken to achieve an objective that is not easily measured. For example, a municipal park and recreation department that is primarily taxpayer funded is accountable for the money that it spends on recreation supplies, equipment, and other expenditures. To cut down on overspending and waste (the objective, or outcome), a department might specify a process for bidding purchase requests (chapter 12) to three or more private vendors if the purchase is more than $500. The department would then compare the bids and contract with the lowest bidder for the purchase. As part of the action plan, the department specifies exactly how the bid process should be managed. In this way, the department is accountable to its taxpayers by spending money wisely, and it also promotes a level playing field for the business community by avoiding cronyism and other types of exclusivity in contracting. The key to action planning is specifying the objective and clearly articulating the steps for achieving the objective. This system tends to be most effective when the ultimate outcome is not easily measured (eliminating wasteful spending) but can be justified through specific staff or management activities (Bolman and Deal 2013).

**Performance control** is less prescribed and tends to be used when objectives are easily measured, when there are multiple methods of achieving objectives, or when the methods taken to achieve objectives are best left to the individual employee or unit. For example, a local middle school might have an objective to increase participation in an after-school program by 10 percent over the course of the next academic year. How the leaders of the after-school program achieve the outcome is up to them. The ultimate outcome is easily measured and can be used to assess the performance of the program staff at the end of the academic year. The staff members are accountable for their performance in achieving the participation targets outlined beforehand. Performance control works best when the ultimate objective is easily measured, such as an increase in participation.

Both action planning and performance control are intimately connected to the overall planning process. Strategic planning helps an organization to articulate its values, vision, mission, goals, and objectives and to outline key organizational priorities (see chapter 6). Action planning and performance control help to enact the planning process by specifying the processes and outcomes necessary for employees to achieve the goals and objectives of the organization. They fulfill a necessary coordinating function by standardizing processes and outcomes, building accountability for performance, and limiting employee discretion in important areas.

**Management by Objectives**    Management by objectives (MBO) is an accountability mechanism that was popularized by Peter Drucker. It is a performance control system where managers and supervisors jointly set objectives and evaluate results (George and Jones 2002). In Drucker's classic work *The Practice of Management*, he asserts that the busy work lives of managers help them fall into an activity trap where they focus so much on their daily activities that they forget the bigger picture (Drucker 1954). MBO keeps managers focused on their responsibilities to the objectives of their unit and the larger organization. A key aspect of MBO is that the manager's objectives should reflect the larger objectives of the organization. MBO also emphasizes participatory decision making; both managers and supervisors have input in determining and evaluating performance objectives. MBO is typically implemented at the management level, but its principles might be used at other levels of the organization as well.

For MBO to be successful, objectives must be clear, specific, and measurable. Drucker suggests that managers and their supervisors should write SMART objectives (see chapter 2 for more details):

- Specific
- Measurable
- Achievable
- Relevant
- Time-related

MBO entails a considerable amount of trust between supervisors and managers. Without trust and good communication, managers may try to set objectives that are too easy to achieve, or managers may be vague or unrealistic in their expectations. Finally, organizations and managers must have a clear idea of their objectives in

**performance control**—The methods that are used to achieve organizational objectives that are easily measured.

**management by objectives (MBO)**—Performance control system where managers and supervisors jointly set objectives and evaluate results.

order to implement such a system. That said, MBO can be another tool for coordinating individual efforts and building accountability to organizational goals.

# Horizontal Coordination

**horizontal coordination**—
Integrating the efforts of units or positions across the organizational chart.

**Horizontal coordination** focuses on lateral techniques for integrating the efforts of units or positions across the organizational chart. Horizontal coordination generally uses the following techniques:

- Meetings and direct contact
- Teams and task forces
- Integrated roles or coordinated units
- Electronic networks

## Meetings and Direct Contact

One method for coordinating the efforts of people or units involves direct contact. In most organizations, this takes the form of regularly scheduled meetings that are used to review goals, discuss progress, assign responsibilities, and address concerns relevant to the group. Regular meetings serve an important integrating function. There may be few opportunities for organizational members to actually meet face to face, especially in highly specialized work environments. In some cases, relatively autonomous units may actually begin to work toward their own goals and purposes because they have little understanding of the roles played by other units. Organizational meetings can be motivating and can help remind people and units of their connection to larger organizational goals. They can help employees get to know the job roles of other people and units in the organization. Regular direct contact between people in different units can facilitate interaction among staff and managers, and it can help develop personal relationships that will facilitate cooperation on difficult goals.

Meetings have a potential downside as well, however. Too many meetings can waste time and organizational resources; time spent in meetings means less time spent taking care of organization or customer concerns. Managers should constantly review their need for meetings, taking into account both the value and cost of such encounters. Hartman (2014) suggests the following seven steps for running effective meetings:

1. Make your objectives clear.
2. Invite only those who really need to be there.
3. Create an agenda, send it in advance, and stick to it.
4. Establish ground rules to avoid monopolization of the conversation.
5. Start on time, end on time.
6. Ban technology.
7. Follow up with highlights, task assignments, and deadlines.

Meetings require the right balance of coordination—too many meetings, and time and resources are wasted; too few meetings, and staff can get off track. Often, the default coordinating tool for managers is a meeting. However, there may be more effective ways to achieve organizational integration, depending on the goals of coordination. Managers should continually review the need for and frequency of meetings. Technology has helped reduce the need for face-to-face meetings. Web conferencing tools such as Zoom, Adobe Connect, and GoToMeeting provide flexible alternatives to getting people in the same room at the same time. File and folder sharing tools such as Dropbox allow collaborators to review shared documents. Collaborative editing tools such as Google Docs or other wiki platforms provide opportunities for people to edit the same document at the same time from different locations.

Using meetings as a horizontal coordination tool often works best in smaller, less complex organizations. Large organizations with complex operations spread over large geographic areas may be less conducive to face-to-face meetings because of the coordination challenges involved in getting people to attend the meeting in the first place. When used effectively (sparingly and purposefully), however, meetings are a key component for organizational integration.

## Teams and Task Forces

Recall that in chapter 4, teams were introduced as a strategy for organizational design. Both teams and task forces are formal work groups put together by the organization in order to meet organizational goals. Teams and task forces differ in their permanence. **Teams** consist of a group of organizational members who work together to accomplish common organizational goals. **Task forces**, also called problem-solving teams, are assembled for the purpose of accomplishing a specific organizational goal. After the goal is accomplished, the task force is usually disbanded, although longer-term goals or organizational problems may be addressed through standing committees or task groups (George and Jones 2012).

Both teams and task forces aid in horizontal coordination when they comprise members from different functional specializations, departments, or divisions. For example, a team or a task force set up by a city park and recreation department to manage a large community festival might consist of members representing the programming, facilities, marketing, customer relations, risk management, and human resources units within the department. On a larger scale, the city itself might set up a team or task force with members of city departments, including parks and recreation, police, emergency medical service, legal counsel, community schools, buildings and grounds, housing, and transportation. Increased coordination and integration occur by including team members from different functional units.

Teams and task forces are highly goal oriented—they exist to achieve specific ends. They require a large degree of commitment and interaction among group members. Teams or task forces are usually created for the following purposes:

- To coordinate work processes across various functions (management teams)
- To study an overarching organizational concern and recommend action (task forces or problem-solving teams)
- To produce a specific product that requires input from a variety of organizational functions (work teams)
- To examine and refine organizational policies or address organizational problems (quality circles)

The coordination and control challenges that teams and task forces are designed to alleviate may also negatively affect team functioning. Some challenges to team performance include the following.

**Lack of Leadership** The lack of strong leadership is one of the many challenges to team performance and can be the cause of many of the other challenges listed

**teams**—Groups of organizational members who work together to accomplish common goals.

**task forces**—Organizational members who come together for the purpose of accomplishing a specific organizational goal and normally disband after the goal has been achieved.

below. In some cases, teams may be assembled without an officially designated leader—there is no one person who articulates the team's vision, sets the agenda, guides the work process, or holds team members accountable for performance. This challenge might be resolved merely by designating a team leader. However, if the leader does not have official authority to engage in the functions of leadership, or if the person does not have the respect of the other team members, team performance is bound to fail.

**Lack of Shared Values among Team Members**   Teams are often based on the desired qualities and competencies of people from various units within the organization. Because of this, team members may not share the same values or have a unified sense of purpose. High-performing teams have a strong shared vision and purpose.

**Lack of Resources and Commitment to the Team's Purpose**   Organizations must commit to the goals and work processes of teams and task forces. Much like larger organizational units, teams and task forces must have resources in order to effectively meet their goals. Resources could include office space, administrative assistance, financial support, workload allocation for team tasks, or some combination of these. For teams to effectively solve problems, provide solutions, and achieve their goals, they must have the commitment of the organization.

**Lack of Accountability for Team Members' Performance**   One of the reasons teams fail is a lack of accountability. Most people have had the experience of working with team members who did not pull their weight. This often results in a lack of trust in individual members, and if the problem is widespread, it can severely affect team morale and undermine the team's ability to function properly. When individual team members do not make meaningful contributions to the team's work, their capacity and talents are wasted, ultimately diminishing the team's effectiveness. Effective teams have built-in accountability mechanisms for individual and group performance. Organizations should include team or task-force duties in the performance appraisal process, and they should consider the feedback of team leaders and members. Team or task-force leaders can be evaluated on their ability to meet the team's charges.

Ultimately, organizations need to devote resources to team and task-force duties; that is, teamwork should not be seen as simply one more thing to do. It should have meaning for both the employee and the organization, and it should be job enhancing rather than just job enlarging. Team tasks and duties should be incorporated into the overall scope of an employee's job responsibilities.

**synergy**—Situation where the whole is greater than the sum of the individual parts.

**Lack of Synergy**   Synergy refers to the idea that the talents and capacities of individuals are maximized when working with others—that production outcomes are maximized through shared effort rather than working alone. Sometimes organizational cultures favor individual effort. From a management perspective, it may be easier to evaluate an employee's effectiveness, and from an individual perspective, an employee need not worry about coordinating efforts with others. Although structuring work for individuals may have some advantages, it can also lead to wasted energy, duplicated efforts, and, ultimately, inefficiency. In addition, individual talents are often amplified when working with others. Effective teams coordinate efforts, but they also draw on the unique capabilities of members to achieve group goals, motivate other team members, and help develop individual talents.

A useful model for team development is Tuckman's (1965) concept of forming, norming, storming, and performing. According to this theory, team building happens in stages over time. Team members need to get to know one another, build relationships, get into disagreements, and learn to work through their disagreements before they can expect to be productive. Tuckman's theory has been applied in a variety of fields, including recreation (Jordan 2007).

**Lack of Group Cohesiveness**   In order to achieve synergy, teams need to function as cohesive units. This can be difficult to achieve, especially when teams are made up of members from different organizational divisions. Sometimes teams can provide forums for turf fighting or other kinds of disagreements, and conflict among team members may undermine group efforts. Teams often react to conflict by attempting to keep disagreement to a minimum or trying to arrive at compromises that ultimately do not resolve problems.

Surprisingly, though, conflict does not necessarily undermine productivity or team cohesiveness. Conflict among members can be good for organizational effectiveness, up to a point. Acknowledging conflict can facilitate team and organizational learning, redirect organizational efforts, and lead to shared understanding (Jones 2012). Of course, team leaders need to be able to effectively manage group conflict before it begins to undermine team goals or render the team completely ineffective. This can be accomplished by discussing team goals and working toward shared understanding from the beginning, as well as depersonalizing discussions so that they focus on team goals rather than on individual ones.

## Coordination of Units

One answer to some of the challenges that face formal work groups is the creation of coordinating units or the designation of specific people with integrating roles. These organizational members or units are designed to help other organizational members with the integration effort. For example, consider the case of a large, complex campus recreation organization. The organization sponsors 34 sport clubs and provides intramural sports, open recreation, special events, outdoor recreation, sport instruction, inclusive recreation, and fitness opportunities.

Recreational sport opportunities take place at more than 20 different facilities on campus. In many cases, these facilities are shared by multiple sports and across multiple programs (e.g., intercollegiate, intramural or club, open recreation). In order to coordinate the facility needs of the various sport and program areas, a coordinating unit was set up to manage facility scheduling and access. Before each semester, meetings are held with representatives of various program areas to discuss facility and other space needs. A facilitator is present to manage the process and work out conflicts. During the course of the semester, the facility coordinating unit handles additional requests, troubleshoots problems, and works with the diverse program areas to ensure that facility needs are being met.

In this way, individual program areas are able to express their facility needs while the entire process is integrated by a centralized coordinating unit. Needless to say, given the diverse programming areas and needs, the facility management process could easily devolve into intergroup fighting over specific needs and priorities. Using a coordinating unit to help bridge the gap between diverse program areas, handle the details of facility scheduling, and take facility management out of the hands of individual programs has helped to alleviate conflict and develop a coherent approach to a complex process. Using a coordinating unit or designating a person to serve in an integrating role works when the process is relatively complex, such as the example described here. Simple group tasks probably do not require such an involved step.

### Electronic Networks

Many of the horizontal coordinating roles that are described here can be easily retooled for use with virtual or electronic networking. Consider the facility management example in the previous section. The large recreational sport department combined the use of a work team (facility management working group) with a coordinating role (facility management unit) and used face-to-face meetings to achieve integration of a complex system. It is possible to replace both the work team and the regular meetings with an internal electronic network that guides the facility management process.

For example, representatives of various sport programs (e.g., athletic teams, intramural sport, sport clubs, informal sport) might have access to a dynamic online scheduling system. All potential users of the network are able to log in and view available athletic facilities. Clicking on available days and times triggers a pop-up window calling for additional information. Filling out the requested fields and hitting Send places the request in a queue and allows the facility manager to review the request, follow up with the person making the request, and check to see if the request is allowed based on preset criteria. Electronic networks can be used for other types of scheduling, purchasing requests, inventory control, group communication, or product development as well. This kind of network can also be used in a vertically coordinated organization; however, the ideal organization is both vertically and horizontally coordinated, using a balance of these strategies. There are many proprietary software systems that can accomplish these tasks. Some systems are run through downloaded software, and others are web- and cloud-based. Examples include RecTrac, EZFacility, ACTIVE Network, and eTrak, among others.

## EXTERNAL ORGANIZATIONAL COORDINATION

Leisure services organizations, and municipal park and recreation agencies in particular, have a long tradition of engaging in partnerships with other entities to deliver recreation programs and services. Municipal recreation departments and schools in many communities throughout the United States and Canada, for instance, have historically been linked through shared programs, staff, and facilities. Following World War II, public investment in municipal parks and recreation precipitated a shift away from the joint provision of recreation services and led to the proliferation of stand-alone park and recreation departments responsible for the direct delivery of community recreation (Crompton 1999). Publicly funded park and recreation facilities, programs, and services arose to meet the demands of a growing population.

However, a climate of dissatisfaction with government spending and tax increases since the 1970s has put pressure on municipal recreation departments to do more with less and to find ways to meet the demands of the community without adding to the already overburdened public funding base. One result of this shift has been a return to the collaboration networks of the past and the potential of partnerships for increasing leisure options. Other types of organizations engage in collaborative efforts to provide recreation and leisure services in addition to public parks and recreation departments. These types of partnerships are described below.

### Intersectoral Partnership

Leisure services delivery in communities involves a complex system of service providers in three primary institutional sectors—public, nonprofit, and commercial (see chapter 4 for more on these three sectors). Municipal park and recreation agencies, YMCAs, voluntary youth sport organizations, state or provincial park systems, commercial sport and fitness businesses, nonprofit/voluntary youth organizations, and community schools are all examples of leisure services providers. Meeting the leisure and recreation needs of a community is not the sole responsibility of any one organization. Rather, a multitude of direct and indirect service providers form an interdependent web of leisure services in communities. In many cases, organizations from all three sectors coordinate their efforts and engage in partnerships to help facilitate leisure services delivery. The term **intersectoral partnership** refers to partnerships that occur among organizations in different institutional sectors.

Although there are considerable differences in the service mandates, organizational philosophies, and funding mechanisms for each sector, there are many examples of collaboration and cooperation between sectors to enhance recreation services. Even well-funded organizations find that they need to work with other providers to better meet the needs of their constituents. Suppose a municipal park and recreation department has primary responsibility for sport and athletics facilities throughout the city. They operate indoor and outdoor swimming pools, several outdoor multisport complexes, baseball and softball fields, a skate park, an ice arena, and an indoor gymnasium. They also offer a variety of in-house youth sport programs, such as a league basketball program for middle and high school students.

Provision of youth sport programs, however, is not the sole responsibility of the municipal recreation department. A number of parent-led, voluntary sport organizations also provide youth sport opportunities in baseball, softball, cheerleading, soccer, football, lacrosse, and ice hockey. These voluntary sport organizations work with the recreation department to secure facility space, partner with the local business community for funding support, and affiliate with national organizations (such as Little League Baseball) for competitive structure, insurance, and standardized rule sets.

What seems at first to be a fairly simple service is actually a complex set of relationships that needs to be managed. It would be nearly impossible for any one organization to provide such services in isolation. Given the interdependence that exists in the delivery system, some form of partnership must exist in order to effectively and efficiently manage the process. The term **partnership** describes the voluntary sharing of resources between two or more parties to achieve mutual goals (Mowen et al. 2009). Partnerships can be classified by both the levels and areas of integration between organizations (Kohm, La Piana, and Gowdy 2000). The partnership matrix in figure 5.3 depicts the range of partnership classifications.

## Collaborations

**Collaboration** anchors the left side of the partnership matrix. It is the process of two or more stakeholders working together to solve a set of problems that neither can solve alone (Crompton 1999). In the context of the partnership matrix, collaborations leave high levels of autonomy to each partner organization. Although the organizations work together to achieve mutual goals, authority and decision making are left to the individual organizations. Collaborations tend to lack permanent structures. This does not suggest that collaborations are informal structures—they can be highly formalized—but each organization retains the right to act on its own behalf.

In the previous municipal park and recreation example, collaboration takes place among the various members of the local recreation delivery system. Each organization

**intersectoral partnership**— Partnership among organizations in different institutional sectors.

**partnership**— Relationships between two or more parties for the purposes of addressing a common challenge.

**collaboration**—Two or more stakeholders working together to solve problems that neither can do alone.

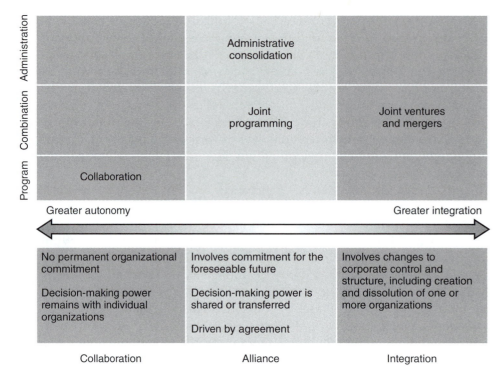

**Figure 5.3** Partnership matrix.

Adapted with permission from La Piana Associates, Inc.

**alliance**—Strong partnership effort categorized by high levels of commitment between organizations and some sharing of authority and decision making.

**administrative consolidation**—Alliance where organizations agree to share, exchange, or contract administrative functions to increase efficiency.

**joint programming (joint facility use)**—Alliance that focuses on the combined management efforts (shared programming or facility use) of organizational partners to further the mission of the alliance.

**networks**—Organizations that are connected through formal or informal channels or are linked through mutual webs of connections.

works together to achieve its own individual goals and retains ultimate decision-making authority. For example, the park and recreation department may decide to limit the number of voluntary sport organizations it works with, or a sport organization may choose to change affiliations with its national governing body.

## Alliances

An **alliance** is a stronger partnership effort and is categorized by higher levels of commitment and some sharing of authority and decision making. Whereas collaborations may be driven by formal agreements, alliances are defined by such agreements. Alliances may include **administrative consolidation**, where organizations agree to share, exchange, or contract administrative functions to increase efficiency (Kohm et al. 2000). An example might be to share fund-raising efforts between organizational members or to pool purchasing decisions in order to receive bulk discounts. Alliances may also include joint programming and facility use. **Joint programming** and **joint facility use** focus on the combined management efforts of organizational partners to further the mission of the alliance. An example of joint programming might be an after-school program run by a community youth development alliance, where administrative, fiscal, personnel, and facility resources are pooled to facilitate program design and delivery.

Alliances are often formed by organizations that are already collaborating through formal or informal channels or are linked through mutual webs of connections. These **networks** of organizations can often be the seeds of alliance formation in the future. An example of this type of coordinated effort is the formation of the Dover Kids Cabinet, a grassroots alliance of youth development organizations in the Dover, New Hampshire, community.

## Dover Kids Cabinet: An Alliance for Youth

The Dover Kids Cabinet was formed in response to cuts in funding to the Dover Middle School Leaders' Project, an after-school program that served more than 200 children per year. In response to these changing conditions, Leaders' Project staff and friends identified other youth development organizations and support organizations and called a meeting to discuss the implications of losing the program. The network members represented at the meeting—including the park and recreation department, community schools, the local teen center, the police department, the YMCA, the public housing authority, university faculty, parent volunteers, and stakeholders from the business community—decided to form an alliance to influence youth development programming in the area. The Dover Kids Cabinet is an alliance of organizations representing all three institutional sectors (public, nonprofit, and commercial) and the voluntary, frontline, local, state, regional, and national levels.

The Dover Kids Cabinet identified five primary goals for the alliance:

- To coordinate community resources and agency activities to improve health, education, and recreational opportunities for children, youth, and adolescents in the Dover community
- To promote collaboration between youth-supporting programs and agencies in the Dover community
- To facilitate the participation of community members in a positive agenda for the development of children, youth, and adolescents in the Dover community
- To provide leadership and advocacy for comprehensive and efficient services for children, youth, and adolescents in the Dover community
- To provide leadership on issues involving sustainability for programs serving children, youth, and adolescents in the Dover community

Almost all of the benefits of partnerships noted in this chapter are represented in the goals of this alliance, including collaboration, coordination to avoid duplication, community building, shared resources and expertise, and creation of a synergistic relationship among network members.

## Partnership Integration

**Partnership integration** is the strongest level of partnership and is typified by a structural change in one or more partners to create an entirely new organization (Kohm et al. 2000). Integration includes both joint ventures and organizational mergers. A **joint venture** is a shared project between two or more organizational partners that results in a new corporate entity represented by each partner organization. In this arrangement, partners typically share governance of the new corporate entity. An example is the Central-Clemson Recreation Center, a joint venture between the Town of Central and the City of Clemson, South Carolina. The Central-Clemson

**partnership integration**—The strongest level of partnership, typified by a change in organizational structure in one or more partners to create an entirely new organizational entity.

**joint venture**—Shared project between two or more organizational partners that results in a new corporate entity represented by each partner organization.

Recreation Center is a full-service recreation and fitness center offering basketball and volleyball courts, group fitness classes, two swimming pools, and a variety of youth and adult sports opportunities (Central-Clemson Recreation Center 2018).

**merger**—Strong partnership that occurs when one or more organizational partners dissolve themselves into an existing partner, resulting in a new organization.

A **merger** refers to the dissolution of one or more organizational partners. Mergers can either result in

- the incorporation of all or part of one or more organizations into another organization, or
- a new organization that includes some or all aspects of the old organizations.

A defining characteristic of mergers is that one or more of the original partners gives up autonomy and decision-making authority to the new organizational entity. Mergers may be the result of a desire to increase efficiency, better manage scarce fiscal resources, or improve the coordination of related management efforts. An example of a merger between recreation organizations is Recreation Nova Scotia, which resulted from the merger of three organizations: the Recreation Association of Nova Scotia, the Recreation Council on Disability in Nova Scotia, and Volunteer Nova Scotia. The new organization advocates for access to quality recreation services on behalf of all Nova Scotians (Recreation Nova Scotia 2018).

## Partnership as Exchange

Typically, partnership efforts are best viewed as exchange relationships—they must provide benefits to all parties in order to flourish. Partnerships are advantageous when organizations receive benefits that they might not otherwise receive and when individual players would not be able to function as effectively or efficiently (or in some cases, at all) if the partnership did not exist. This is an important consideration in managing partnerships because it forces managers to think in terms of what they can offer to the partnership as well as thinking about what they may gain. When partnerships are one-way efforts, they tend to break down.

Consider cases where organizations must engage in some level of partnership as a precondition for existence. For example, organizations that do not have access to their own facilities to run programs, such as the Boston Ski and Sports Club (BSSC), must seek out partners to provide facility access. The partnership arrangement benefits the BSSC—joint facility-use agreements allow their programs to happen—and the host organization receives a facility rental fee that provides an additional revenue source. In some cases, this type of arrangement allows a host organization, such as a large municipal park and recreation department, to outsource the day-to-day operations of a specific program (in this case, adult sport and recreation) to an outside group while still providing some level of service to the existing customer base. This type of arrangement represents a classic win-win scenario that typifies partnerships as exchange relationships. Organizations in both the commercial sector and the public sector benefit from the arrangement.

## Benefits of Partnerships

The list of benefits from partnerships goes beyond resource acquisition. Partnerships have been justified by their ability to yield a number of organizational benefits, including the following (Andereck 1997; Bruton et al. 2011; Mowen et al. 2009):

- Gaining access to new resources (facilities, staff, equipment, financial capital)
- Creating synergy between partnering organizations where joint efforts produce more than what either partner could produce alone

- Avoiding duplication of services and unnecessary competition for scarce resources
- Enhancing efficiency by creating a more flexible organizational structure
- Better meeting the needs of customers by being able to offer a wider range of services
- Enhancing expertise in specialized areas
- Building and developing community
- Enhancing organizational prestige

Several of these benefits speak to the importance of coordination as a key component in the formation and functioning of partnership efforts. For example, public and nonprofit or voluntary organizations may find it advantageous to coordinate efforts so they are not unnecessarily duplicating services, competing for scarce resources, or unintentionally creating gaps in service provision for underserved groups. Organizations may also find it necessary to coordinate their efforts to maximize talents and capitalize on the strengths of other organizational partners (through pooling or sharing physical, financial, technological, or human resources). Coordinating efforts may also allow smaller organizations to achieve more power for influencing the causes they care about.

## Making Partnerships Work

For collaborative relationships to succeed, network partners need to benefit individually and collectively from the arrangement. These relationships often fail because the partners do not feel they have benefited from their involvement. Collaborative relationships also tend to break down—or fail to get off the ground—because they do not respond favorably to what Ferguson and Dickens (1999, 44) refer to as the four trust questions:

1. What are the motives of current or potential allies?
2. Are they competent? Can they do the job, or are they at least willing to learn?
3. Will they be dependable in fulfilling their responsibilities?
4. Will they be collegial? Can partners get along?

According to the authors, these four trusts—motive, competence, dependability, and collegiality—are the foundation for partnerships. Unless these basic questions are answered in the affirmative, most will fail.

Bocarro and Barcelona (2003) provide six suggestions for encouraging effective partnership formation:

- Encourage different types of partnerships. Not all partnerships are built around resource acquisition. Indeed, many partnerships are focused on other goals, including coordinating shared efforts, sharing resources and expertise, leveraging power in numbers, and creating synergistic relationships among network partners.
- Ask "What can I offer?" as well as "What can I gain?" Partnerships need to be viewed as mutually beneficial relationships. Thinking of partnerships as a meaningful exchange with both parties giving and receiving helps to frame the relationship.
- Clearly articulate the needs, roles, and responsibilities of each partner. Who is responsible for what? What talents, skills, and responsibilities does each partner

bring to the group? What are the unique needs of partners that need to be accommodated? Considering these questions up front can help prevent trust breakdowns later on.

- Make partnerships more formal. Formalized, written agreements that detail the responsibilities of all partners can help coordinate a diverse group of network members. Many of the coordination strategies discussed earlier in the chapter can help formalize the relationship, including designating group goals and holding regular meetings. Partnership agreements should attempt to address at least some of the following areas: the purpose of the partnership, partner roles and responsibilities, governance and the decision-making process, the communication process, deliverables (products of the partnership), time lines, resource transfers, and evaluation of the partnership results. It is always advisable for managers to consult with legal counsel when entering into formal, written agreements.

- Engage in power-with rather than power-over relationships. In partnerships, power issues will arise. Partnerships will have little chance to get off the ground if partners engage in power struggles and feelings of superiority.

- Create an organizational commitment to partnering. It is often easy to work in isolation; however, collaborating with other organizations can result in more effective and efficient provision of services. Managers should recognize the value of partnerships and devote organizational resources to developing these types of relationships.

 Check out the web study guide for additional material, including learning activities, sample documents, interactive case studies, web links, CPRP exam connections, and more.

## Conclusion

The ability to coordinate organizational resources is one of the core competencies of leisure services managers. Coordination includes all four functions of management—planning, organizing, leading, and controlling. Balancing coordinating mechanisms is an important consideration for managers. Vertical coordination focuses on formal systems of control, whereas horizontal coordination focuses on lateral techniques that integrate the efforts of units or positions across the organizational chart.

Partnerships can also coordinate the efforts of organizations operating in interdependent systems. Leisure services in a community are typically delivered through public, nonprofit, and commercial providers. Although these providers are distinct entities, sometimes organizations must collaborate to provide services to their clientele. Intersectoral collaboration can maximize resources, create synergy among network partners, avoid duplication of services and unnecessary competition, enhance efficiency, consolidate power, and strengthen community. Organizations engage in partnerships because there are mutual benefits to such relationships. Partnerships are built on trust and depend on the motives, competence, dependability, and collegiality of network partners.

# Review Questions

1. What is the difference between structural differentiation and integration?

2. What is suboptimization? How can effective coordination be used to limit this organizational challenge?

3. What tools and techniques can managers use to enact both vertical and horizontal coordination?

4. Define and differentiate the concepts of policies, procedures, rules, and standards.

5. What is accountability? How can action planning, performance control, and management by objectives (MBO) be used to increase accountability?

6. What is the difference between a team and a task force? What are their general purposes?

7. What are the main coordination and control challenges that face teams and task forces? What can managers do to avoid these challenges?

8. Provide an example of an intersectoral partnership in leisure services. Is this partnership a collaboration, alliance, integration, joint venture, or merger? Why?

9. What are the main benefits of partnerships?

10. How can managers maximize partnership effectiveness?

# 6

# Planning and Decision Making

## Learning Outcomes

- Compare and contrast the six plans most used in the recreation profession.

- Describe the decision-making process.

- Differentiate between programmed and nonprogrammed decisions.

- Explain the four approaches to ethical decision making.

## Key Terms

strategic planning, performance analysis, SWOT analysis, focus group, master planning, business plan, revenue facilities, decision making, problem solving, programmed decisions

## Competency Check

Refer to table 1.6 to see how you assessed these related competencies.

24. Use effective problem-solving and conflict-resolution skills.

25. Make ethical decisions.

38. Provide input on strategic, master, recreation, marketing, and technology plans.

## A Day in the Life

Many might say that there is nothing typical about a day in the life of a parks and recreation director—and that may be true. However, there are certain hallmarks of this industry that I can count on occurring on a daily basis. These are engagement, progress, and laughter. There is rarely a day that we don't engage with a resident or visitor. Whether we are leading a stakeholder input meeting for the development of a new park or recreation center, attending a city council meeting, taking a call from a concerned citizen about a situation on a bike trail, or simply having a conversation with a participant as they walk into a program, our entire team is engaging in meaningful conversation with the community. This constant engagement helps us be responsive to their needs and gain the support we need to make progress to achieve our vision. Regardless of the magnitude of progress, it occurs as a result of collaboration between our team and countless park fans who choose to dedicate their time, treasure, and/or talents to the cause. Together we build amazing communities. Though achieving amazing things is always hard work, this is parks and recreation—if we are not having fun along the way, we are doing it wrong. It is rare that I walk through our offices and there is not someone smiling or laughing. The commitment that parks and recreation professionals show to their teammates and for meeting their goals has always been inspiring to me. On those rare occasions when the process itself might challenge the constant joy, I can always step into a recreation center or by the playground and instantly be reminded of why we walk in the door each day.

Stacie Anaya
Director
Lewisville Parks and Recreation
Lewisville, Texas

This chapter presents two tightly linked management practices that serve as a foundation for management and the operation of an organization. In management, planning is the process of creating a direction for one or more parts of the organization. Planning guides decision making—when decisions need to be made, managers will look to their plans to ascertain what can be done to solve the problem that best meets the goals, objectives, and future direction of the agency. This chapter goes through the process of planning and decision making, including ethical decision making.

# PLANNING

Planning serves several purposes in addition to guiding decision making. First, agencies make plans to achieve their vision. The vision statement is a declaration of where the organization wants to be in 5 to 10 years, and planning outlines the necessary steps to reach this vision. Chapter 2 discussed the role and importance of having a vision, and planning is the path to accomplishing this vision.

Agencies also plan in order to enhance efficiency and effectiveness. As discussed throughout this book, efficiency and effectiveness involve using resources to minimize waste and reach goals and objectives. Neither would be consistently possible without a plan outlining both resource use and the goals and objectives to be accomplished over a certain time frame.

In addition, planning helps agencies deal with change. Change is inevitable and often difficult. When establishing a vision for an organization, change is always at the forefront. Planning helps the organization and the people within it to change. It can be a step-by-step process to deal with something such as a major change in technology, or it can serve as a guide for more complex issues such as shifting population demographics in a community.

Planning also helps agencies to be proactive. Solid organizations are proactive rather than reactive. Good managers envision trends in the field and develop a plan to meet these trends. Being proactive means solving problems before they occur, and planning helps managers anticipate community needs, changes, and desires. Reacting to a situation instead of being proactive places undue stress on both financial and human resources.

For example, for the past 10 years, a school district has leased an unused elementary school to the local park and recreation department for use as a community center. The school district has given notice that due to projected population increases, the district is being proactive and terminating the lease to the facility in three years. In this situation, a plan is necessary to determine where all the recreation programs will go, how the building will be converted back to a school, and whether the park and recreation department should look for a different facility to lease or build a new one. This is a situation where good planning can help ease the stress of decision making and allow the agency to be proactive rather than reactive.

There are a number of plans that are useful in the park and recreation profession, including master plans, recreation program plans, marketing plans, and capital development plans, just to name a few. Regardless of the type of plan, the main purpose is to have a written document of what the organization wants to achieve in the future. Some agencies are equipped with the staff expertise to develop their own plans, and others hire a consulting firm to facilitate the planning process. It is impossible to thoroughly cover all of the plans that may be used by an organization. In this chapter we'll look at six types: strategic, master, business, marketing, program, and technology plans. Strategic plans and master plans are more comprehensive and might involve consultants. The other four are less comprehensive and are more likely to be created by staff.

# Strategic Plan

Probably the most widely used type of plan in parks and recreation, **strategic planning** involves envisioning a future state of the organization and designing strategies and tactics to reach that vision. Strategic planning relies on managers' conceptual skills to see the big picture of the organization. The term *strategy* is used because this type of plan is a purposeful process to make the organization better.

Strategic plans cover anywhere from three to five years and establish guidelines on what organizations need to do, why they need to do it, and how they will get it done. These plans are not designed to make decisions for the organization but are used as reference points to guide decision making. Strategic planning guides decision making by establishing priorities for the organization. This is a difficult process, but it assists the organization in determining what is most important, what goals should be accomplished, and how to manage resources in doing so.

Although strategic planning could be done by the staff within an organization, it is probably best to hire a consultant to facilitate the process. This is not to say that the consultant will develop a plan and tell the organization what it needs to accomplish; rather, the consultant will facilitate the planning process with the staff. Consultants see the organization from an unbiased perspective, which is difficult, if not impossible, for staff. Furthermore, consultants who do this type of work are trained facilitators and can move a group through the process more efficiently and effectively than a manager within the organization can.

Although the consultant is facilitating the strategic planning, staff at all levels of the organization must be involved. This increases the amount of information available for making decisions, and it increases buy-in from the very staff members who will be responsible for implementing the plan. In addition to staff, stakeholders should help formulate the plan. Stakeholders are those people who have a vested interest in or impact on the organization, including stockholders, users, neighbors, or volunteers.

Several models can be used in the strategic planning process. Regardless of the model, McLean, Bannon, and Gray (1999) argue that a strategic plan should answer three questions.

1. *Are we doing the right things?* Managers must examine what services or products are currently offered, what the quality of those services and products is, and whether enough products and services are being produced.

2. *Are we doing things right?* This question analyzes delivery systems, efficiency, and effectiveness. The planning process explores how programs are delivered, where they are delivered, what goals are being met, and how resources are being used.

3. *What should we do next?* The final question is a direct result of the other two and focuses on the outcomes (discussed in chapter 2) the organization is seeking. This is the vision piece of the plan and includes an outline of strategies to reach the vision.

Figure 6.1 shows a basic six-step strategic planning model, while figure 6.2 shows how Fairfax, Virginia, chose to illustrate the planning process for their staff and community.

## Step 1: Develop and Clarify the Values, Vision, and Mission

Previous discussion on values, vision, and mission outlined the interconnectedness of these three concepts and how each one drives the next. The premise of strategic planning is to show organizations how they can achieve the vision set out by the staff. Without this step, the plan will have no direction and will not be grounded in a solid philosophical foundation. This step prepares an agency to answer the first question, "Are we doing the right things?" which is addressed in the next step.

## Step 2: Complete a Performance Analysis

During a **performance analysis**, an organization studies its core competencies. Much has already been said about competencies in relation to individual employees, but an organization itself has core competencies

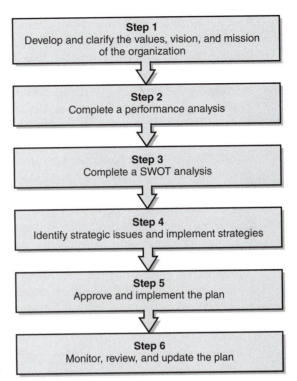

**Figure 6.1** Strategic planning model.

**performance analysis**—Examining core competencies to determine strengths and weaknesses of an organization.

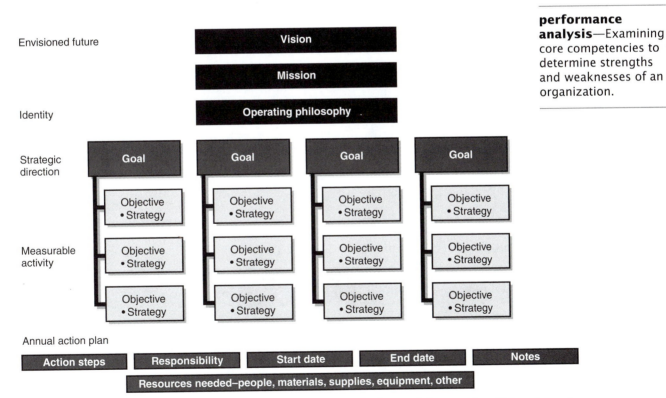

**Figure 6.2** Strategic planning process used by the Parks and Recreation Department in Fairfax, Virginia.

Reprinted by permission from city of Fairfax, VA.

too. Organizational core competencies are "capabilities held by people within a firm that, when applied to create products and services, make a critical contribution to corporate competitiveness" (Edgar and Lockwood 2011, 61).

In addition to examining core competencies, the performance analysis step addresses the question "Are we doing the right things?" The actions of the organization need to match the values, vision, and mission statement. If they do not, then the strategies developed in a later step should address the inconsistencies. Each area of the organization will go through its programs, products, and services to ascertain whether it should continue what it is doing. Divisions may find they are providing services that they should not be based on their mission or they do not have the core competencies to be offering such services. In essence, this step in the planning process looks at whether the agency should be in the business of providing certain products or services. For example, the mission of Toronto Parks, Forestry, and Recreation is as follows:

> *The Parks, Forestry and Recreation Division ensures that people in the diverse communities of Toronto have full and equitable access to high-caliber, locally responsive recreational programs, efficiently operated facilities, and safe, clean and beautiful parks, open spaces, ravines and forests (Toronto Parks, Forestry, and Recreation 2018).*

Given this mission, the agency can complete a performance analysis of the programs currently offered or desired, such as the analysis depicted in table 6.1.

## Step 3: Complete a SWOT Analysis

**SWOT analysis**—A planning tool that identifies the strengths, weaknesses, opportunities, and threats of an organization.

A **SWOT analysis** of strengths, weaknesses, opportunities, and threats (SWOT) is the next step in the strategic planning process. This is where the agency begins to answer the second question, "Are we doing things right?" Strengths and weaknesses are considered to be internal to the organization, whereas opportunities and threats are external to the organization. The strengths and weaknesses of the organization may include

- its products and services,
- connection to vision and mission,
- unique resources, including advantages over other agencies,

## Table 6.1 Sample Performance Analysis

Does This Program, Product, or Service Support the Values, Vision, and Mission of the Organization?

| | Definitely Supports | Moderately Supports/ Not Sure | Does Not Support |
|---|---|---|---|
| Miniature golf course | | | ✓ |
| Zoo | ✓ | | |
| Youth-at-risk programs | | ✓ | |
| Youth scholarship program | ✓ | | |
| Programs specifically for people with disabilities | | ✓ | |
| Open space | ✓ | | |

- the organization, training, and education of the staff,
- management of the organization, including training and education, number of managers, and abilities,
- budget and financial resources,
- information and communication, including reports, records, marketing, and access to information, and
- customers, especially meeting their needs and having customer knowledge (Gray and McEvoy 2005; Jordan 2016).

All of these strengths and weaknesses focus on the organization and its operations, which is why they are considered internal operations. Table 6.2 is a sample SWOT analysis. The agency lists elements of operations and rates the elements as strengths or weaknesses.

Opportunities and threats are external factors that have an impact on the agency (table 6.3). This sort of analysis would focus on

- demographics of customers and the community,
- community assets,
- economic trends and factors that could affect the organization,
- demand trends such as an increase or decrease in demands for products,

## Table 6.2 Sample Strengths and Weaknesses Analysis

| | Major Strength | Minor Strength | Neutral | Minor Weakness | Major Weakness |
|---|---|---|---|---|---|
| **MARKETING** | | | | | |
| **1.** Company image | | | | | |
| **2.** Product demand | | | | | |
| **3.** Media relations | | | | | |
| **4.** Public relations | | | | | |
| **BUDGET AND FINANCE** | | | | | |
| **5.** Cash flow | | | | | |
| **6.** Accounting procedures | | | | | |
| **7.** Investment policies | | | | | |
| **SERVICES** | | | | | |
| **8.** Facilities | | | | | |
| **9.** Variety of services | | | | | |
| **10.** Reputation of services | | | | | |
| **MANAGEMENT** | | | | | |
| **11.** Trained and knowledgeable staff | | | | | |
| **12.** Trained and knowledgeable managers | | | | | |
| **13.** Visionary staff | | | | | |

**Table 6.3** Sample Opportunities and Threats Analysis

| | Impact Level | | |
|---|---|---|---|
| | High | Medium | Low |
| **1.** Increase in baby boomers | | | |
| **2.** National obesity rate | | | |
| **3.** Economic decline | | | |
| **4.** Ability to grow | | | |
| **5.** Aging population | | | |
| **6.** Increased competition from nonprofit agencies | | | |
| **7.** Funding received from federal government | | | |
| **8.** Changing family structure | | | |
| **9.** Risk management and increased lawsuits | | | |

- prospective growth or enhancement of technology,
- government and public policy trends such as limitations on taxing authority or child care regulations, and
- societal and macroenvironmental trends such as ethical and legal concerns, population growth, and the obesity epidemic (Gray and McEvoy 2005; Jordan 2016).

Opportunities and threats in particular could be identified by external stakeholders such as user groups or volunteers because they may be more open-minded and less ingrained in the organization itself. It is not unusual—and most often beneficial—to include the public in the planning process. They may serve on planning subcommittees or as participants in a **focus group** or community meeting.

**focus group**—
Means of gathering information from a group of participants where semistructured questions are asked and responses from the group are received.

## Step 4: Identify Strategic Issues and Implement Strategies

Thus far in the strategic planning process, the agency has gathered information from managers and stakeholders, solidified a vision for the future, and analyzed the current state of the organization and its environment. Now they can begin to answer the third question, "What do we do next?" Using this information as a foundation, the organization identifies strategic issues and then creates strategies to address the issues. Strategic issues are the guiding forces behind the strategic plan. They are the overarching step to achieving the vision, which is the purpose of the strategic plan. The issues and strategies are the major outputs of the entire plan. Here is an example to get a better understanding of this step.

*St. Paul Parks and Recreation Department updated their strategic plan, which was originally completed and implemented in 2002. The plan, which is updated annually, identifies the issues and strategies according to year they will be completed, with the current plan spanning from 2016 to 2020.*

www.stpaul.gov/depts/parks/administration/comp-plan.html (St. Paul, MN Parks and Recreation, 2016)

## Strategic Issue #1

Promote Active Lifestyles.

Strategy (2 of 19):

Implement construction or renovation of deteriorated outdoor court areas through the Citywide Outdoor Court Restoration Program based on asset management system priorities.

Responsibility: operations manager, asset management team, design manager, design staff

Budget impact: $251,000 CIB

Strategy (3 of 19): Complete annual audit of 16 children's play areas and make necessary updates to CIB play area rankings.

Responsibility: operations manager, support maintenance supervisor, recreation maintenance supervisor

Budget impact: staff time

## Strategic Issue #2

Create Vibrant Places.

Strategy (3 of 58):

Complete annual review of Como Park Zoo and Conservatory education animal protocols and update.

Responsibility: zoo curator, zoo staff, operations manager, education staff

Budget impact: staff time

Strategy (6 of 58):

Implement the Great River Passage Master Plan. Seek private foundation grant funding to match the City's portion for the new GRP Division. Prioritize projects and programs for implementation. Manage the ongoing community alignment around communication, advocacy, and fundraising.

Responsibility: director, design manager, design staff, special services manager, city lobbyist

Budget impact: unknown

Notice that the strategies in the example also outline who is responsible for implementing them and how they will affect the budget. These things help make the strategy actionable. Remember when the functions of a manager were discussed in chapter 2? The responsibility and budget elements in the example are the organizing part of those functions that result from the overall planning.

## Step 5: Approve and Implement the Plan

Once the strategic issues and strategies are identified, the plan is ready for approval and implementation. Depending on the type and structure of the agency, various approval processes must be followed. The plan may need the approval of the board of directors, the advisory council, or top management. This approval process should not be lengthy since the approving body and staff should be involved in the development of the plan from the beginning.

Implementing the plan means integrating each strategy into the daily responsibilities of the appropriate staff. A well-written plan that includes the responsibilities and dates for accomplishing each action makes implementation easier than if these things were left up to the staff to determine after the plan was approved. The strategic plan of the St. Paul Parks and Recreation Department will be easy to implement because the responsible entities know what and when they should accomplish each strategy.

Countless agencies have ended their strategic planning efforts right before implementation. They spent hundreds of hours formulating the plan just to let it sit on the shelf to gather dust. Some agencies do this because they lack support for the plan from staff. Others only complete strategic plans so they can be eligible for grants and awards or as a public relations tool so that the community thinks they are attempting to be better. When a strategic plan is created but not implemented, a great deal of money and other resources are wasted. If the plan is done well, it can improve the overall efficiency and effectiveness of the organization. One way to improve the chances of staff staying engaged is to create a visual that makes it easy to see the main elements on which you want people to focus. See appendix B for an example of an image created by the Parks and Recreation Department in Fairfax, Virginia.

### Step 6: Monitor, Review, and Update the Plan

The final step in the strategic planning process occurs once the plan has been implemented. The plan should be continually monitored to ensure that the responsible staff members are following through on the strategies and that the strategies are achievable. This monitoring can be done as an entire agency, by a department, or at the individual level. The main goal of monitoring the plan is to determine what outcomes have occurred as a result of accomplishing the strategies.

The plan should be reviewed and updated annually. Even with all of the foundational information used to formulate strategies, a strategic plan can require changes. The annual review of the plan should highlight accomplishments. Many agencies use their plan as a report card they can present to their customers. It gives them an opportunity to celebrate accomplishments and brag a little about what they were able to achieve over a certain amount of time.

During this review process, major changes in the agency may require modification of the plan. In a sense, a mini-SWOT analysis is done to determine any major shifts to address in the plan. For example, a major change that had a large impact occurred within the City of Las Vegas Department of Leisure Services. It was determined that parks would be better housed in the Department of Public Works, and less than a year later they were moved to a newly created department—Field Operations—which included fleet services, building maintenance, park maintenance, and streets. Losing a major part of an agency or department such as this requires a change in the strategic plan.

Lastly, the annual review serves as a launching point for the strategies to be accomplished during the next year. This monitoring and review step is an ongoing process and must be done in order to carry out the strategic plan and reach the ultimate goal of achieving the vision set by the organization.

**master planning—**
Planning for land, facilities, and natural resources.

## Master Plan

The terms *strategic planning, comprehensive planning,* and **master planning** are often used interchangeably. The differences among them vary with the agency, geographic location, and setting (Wolter 1999). According to Sawyer, Hypes, and Gimbert (2013, 4), "master planning is a process structured to promote cost-effective development decisions that best serve the goals and objectives of the organization." For our purposes, the master plan covers land, facilities, and natural resources, whereas the strategic plan focuses on the entire organization. Master planning includes such factors as how land will be used; what facilities will be purchased, built, or renovated; what park land will be purchased; and preservation and conservation initiatives.

Master plans generally cover a period of up to 10 years and are completed for several reasons. First, master planning is a means of getting public input on facilities and parks. As is the case in strategic planning, involving the public is beneficial. Public input gives a different perspective and provides valuable insight into the process.

Second, master plans are created so that agencies can apply for grants. For example, the Land and Water Conservation Fund (LWCF) provides matching grants for states to acquire and develop outdoor recreation sites and facilities. These funds are usually distributed to departments of natural resources and local park and recreation departments. In order for states to be eligible, they must have a statewide comprehensive outdoor recreation plan (SCORP), and the applying agencies must have a master plan for the proposed site of development. In addition, the project must fit with the SCORP.

Master planning is also done to establish a capital improvement plan over an extended length of time. A master plan will show major projects to be completed as well as land acquisition, facility construction, and large-scale maintenance. This planning purpose is vital to developing annual budgets and establishing priorities for capital development.

Finally, master plans are developed to protect historical, ecological, and environmental areas. Natural resources are shrinking because of urban sprawl, overuse, and exploitation. Master plans outline how to protect these resources.

The master planning process is quite similar to strategic planning. The Complete Communities Toolbox created by the Institute for Public Administration (IPA) at the University of Delaware outlines a four-step parks and recreation master planning process that centers around the engagement of stakeholders (see figure 6.3). The four steps are as follows:

1. *Review existing conditions.* This step requires the agency to research existing conditions and trends, conduct site inventories, review permitted land uses, conduct an inventory and analysis of current parks facilities and recreation programs, map data, and address accessibility.

2. *Analyze needs and preferences.* This step reviews previous plans and studies, assesses community needs, and conducts a needs analysis, including a preliminary level of service assessment of facilities.

3. *Develop a prioritized action plan.* This step requires the agency to describe

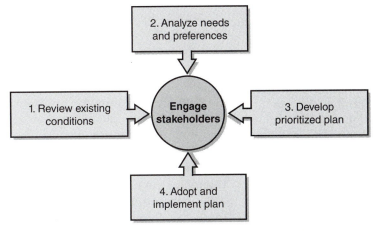

**Figure 6.3** Four-step process for parks and recreation master planning.

Scott, Marcia. (2014). *Steps to complete a parks and recreation master plan.* Delaware Complete Communities Planning Toolbox. Institute for Public Administration, University of Delaware. www.completecommunitiesde.org/planning /healthy-and-livable/steps-parks-rec-master-plan/.

and rank-order priorities related to new or upgrades to existing facilities, recreation programs, and management operations.

4. *Adopt and implement the plan.* This final step formalizes the plan so that it can serve as a decision-making tool for local government officials to provide a high level of parks and recreation services. Information in the plan should inform the operating budget as well as help identify capital projects for the identified timeline.

While the four steps provided by the University of Delaware are good, the list is really incomplete without considering how the agency will monitor and evaluate how the implementation process is going. This is a vital step to include in any planning process.

After reading about both strategic planning and master planning, it may seem as though there is considerable overlap between the two processes. This is true—they follow the same steps. In addition, the master plan may be a part of the strategic planning process or vice versa. Together the plans give an organization a more comprehensive look at what it must do to reach its vision.

As with a strategic plan, a master plan can be done by the staff without the aid of a consultant. However, a more detailed plan requires the hiring of an outside group to facilitate the process. Consultants can quickly become expensive, but a well-developed plan is worth the expenditure. Due to the nature of these two plans, they will most likely require different planning consultants. Master planning requires consultants with specific expertise such as architecture, landscape design, engineering, and accessibility knowledge.

## Business Plan

**business plan—**
Document detailing how a business venture will be operated, what will make it successful, and what short- and long-term finances are needed.

A **business plan** details how a business venture will operate. Business plans are created for two reasons. First, the business plan serves as a blueprint for success because the plan requires managers to look at all aspects of the business and think about how the organization will operate. Second, a business plan is needed if loans or investors are being sought. The plan will give the details needed to make financing decisions. Although this type of plan is for commercial businesses, this does not mean that nonprofit and public agencies do not have business plans. Agencies in each sector may have entrepreneurial elements, such as **revenue facilities**, that operate as businesses.

**revenue facilities—**
Facilities that are expected to make a profit and are not supported by taxes or other means.

A quick Web search will overwhelm you with the hundreds of companies that help develop business plans for a fee and commercial software products that walk you through the process. There are also various formats for business plans. In this section, we will use the format developed by SCORE as an example. SCORE is a nonprofit organization partnered with the U.S. Small Business Administration that provides free advice to people interested in starting a new business. They have helped start such businesses as Imagine Escape Games, Gator Bait Adventure Tours, Pilates on the Bay, and Phamily Fun & Fitness (SCORE 2017a). They have more than 320 offices throughout the United States and provide how-to advice, business templates, and even mentoring for new entrepreneurs. Canada's version of SCORE exists as a provincial agency in British Columbia. Small Business BC helped establish such businesses as Western Martial Arts Assembly and Men In Kilts (Small Business BC 2017). A standard SCORE business plan contains the following sections (SCORE 2017b).

- *Executive summary.* The executive summary summarizes everything contained within the plan. It is a stand-alone document that may be the only section read by a decision maker. Executive summaries are found in many types of plans and reports, not just business plans.

- *General company description.* The description details what the business will be, including the mission statement, goals, objectives, philosophy, description of the industry, company core competencies, and ownership (e.g., sole proprietorship, partnership).

- *Products and services.* This includes a detailed description of products and services, factors that give the organization a competitive advantage, and pricing details.

- *Marketing plan.* A marketing plan outlines market research on the products and business, economics of the industry, features and benefits of the product, who the customers are, who the competition is, marketing strategy, distribution, and sales projections. Marketing plans are discussed in more detail in the next section.

- *Operational plan.* This section of the plan describes how and where the business will function. It includes product development, inventory control, production techniques and costs, accounting systems and policies, type of location (such as storefront, Internet, or mail order), and so on.

- *Management and organization.* This portion of the plan outlines the personnel and their structure, any contractual personnel, and the board if applicable.

- *Startup expenses and capitalization.* This section details the expenses involved in opening for business and how much capital will be needed.

- *Financial plan.* The financial plan is completed with a 12-month profit and loss projection, cash-flow projection, a projected balance sheet, break-even calculation, and use of capital.

- *Appendixes.* Don't slow your readers down by cluttering your business plan with supporting documents, such as contracts or licenses. Instead, put these documents in the appendixes, and refer to them in the body of the plan so readers can find them if needed. These documents might include:

  - Agreements (leases, contracts, purchase orders, letters of intent, etc.)
  - Intellectual property (trademarks, licenses, patents, etc.)
  - Résumés of owners and key employees
  - Advertising and marketing materials
  - Public relations and publicity
  - Blueprints and plans
  - List of equipment
  - Market research studies
  - List of assets that can be used as collateral

A business plan is an extensive undertaking but one that will increase the chance of success for an organization.

## Marketing Plan

In this chapter, we focus on the planning aspects of marketing; for more on the importance and details of marketing, see chapter 7. Marketing plans are common in the public, nonprofit, and market sectors. Similar to the other plans discussed, marketing plans can be created by staff or by a hired consultant. Marketing plans can range from two to five years, with most covering just a couple of years at a time. They have several sections, some of which are the same as other planning documents discussed.

- *Executive summary.* This is the same as described for the business plan; it summarizes the entire plan.
- *Situational analysis.* This includes the values, vision, and mission of the organization; history of the organization; a SWOT analysis; and a product analysis.
- *Customer analysis.* This includes demographics, psychographics, segmentation strategies, and the target market.
- *Marketing issues and strategies.* This includes short- and long-term marketing goals and strategies to address them.
- *Implementation and control.* This includes the action plan for who will do what and when it will be accomplished. It also details the budget required to complete the strategies and the evaluation procedures for the plan.

Here is an example of marketing strategies from the Newfoundland and Labrador Tourism Marketing Division Marketing Plan titled "Uncommon Potential—A Vision for Newfoundland and Labrador Tourism." In the plan they list seven strategic directions; one of them is listed below:

## Goal 1.1

Continue the alignment of tourism board partners and tourism industry stakeholders to strengthen communications and engagement.

### Actions

1. Reap the benefit of the defined roles and responsibilities of Tourism Board partners and industry stakeholders ensuring continued alignment of strategies for industry development.
2. Embrace best practices for governance and industry leadership for continued alignment of key tourism industry partners, not-for-profits and organizations to support Vision 2020.
3. Develop two-way communications and engagement processes with tourism stakeholders to regularly discuss Vision priorities and expectations.
4. Continue to release Vision 2020 Milestone Evaluations as a tool to measure progress towards Vision goals and to ensure partner accountability.

(Newfoundland and Labrador Canada, Department of Tourism, Culture, Industry and Innovation, Tourism Division, 2016)

# Recreation Program Plan

A recreation program plan follows the same format as the others but with an emphasis on recreation programs and services. Rather than reiterate the planning process, the more unique features of program plans will be explored.

A recreation program plan uses public input to a greater extent than the other planning processes. Needs assessments are done via a number of methods, including community surveys, focus groups, web surveys, public meetings, and surveys of nonusers. Advisory boards (see chapter 4) also play a key role in giving community feedback.

In addition to public input, a recreation plan inventories and analyzes what other recreation providers offer the community in order to minimize duplication of services. This means looking at agencies from all three sectors to determine what they do and how well they do it. Duplicating services that others offer may not be an efficient use of resources, particularly for agencies with limited funds. This part of the recreation plan helps make those decisions.

Finally, a recreation program plan includes a service segmentation analysis, which requires the agency to look at its programs from four perspectives (DiGrino and Whitmore 2005).

1. Programs should be categorized according to their target market. For example, they can be categorized as preschool programs, teen programs, and programs for people with disabilities, among others.

2. Programs can be divided according to type, including arts, sports, outdoor recreation, and aquatics.

3. Programs can be categorized by the facility in which they are held, such as at an ice rink, community center, or resort.

4. Programs can be classified by the geographic region in which they are held.

Categorizing programs in so many ways reveals weaknesses in service offerings. For example, when categorizing the programs in each of the ways suggested, it may be easier to see that arts programs are missing for teens in the northwest section of the city.

A recreation plan allows an organization to examine its services from a multitude of perspectives, analyze what the community needs, and plan recreation services accordingly. This plan may be part of the overall strategic plan and is also likely to interface well with a master plan in terms of what programs and services can be offered in facilities and parks.

## Technology Planning

Technology planning is not much different from other organizational planning efforts. Similar to other plans, the technology plan should be a component of the overall strategic plan and work with the larger strategic initiatives and goals of the organization. Successful technology plans demonstrate how an investment in technology contributes to the mission of the organization. For example, a municipal park and recreation department might have a mission to increase the health and well-being of the community by encouraging active participation in community resources. A plan that specifies how technology might be used to achieve that mission—making more information available through the Internet, perhaps, or reducing participation barriers by streamlining activity registration using online applications—is more effective than simply stating that the organization needs to buy more computers. Ultimately, technology planning maps the path between where an organization is currently and where it wants to be in the future.

Technology should not be seen as an end in itself. It must provide technological solutions that enhance organizational effectiveness; otherwise, investments in technology may be unnecessary and a waste of scarce resources. Just because a tool exists does not mean that it has to be used or that it is the most effective tool for the job. Like any tool, the solution that is chosen will be based on a variety of factors, including availability of the resource, time, budget, competence of the user, and so on. By linking the technology plan with the strategic plan, technology becomes a tool for achieving the mission of the organization.

Technology planning helps provide the technical direction of the strategic plan (Farris 2005). The strategic planning process is typically conducted every five years or so, but the technology plan should be revisited more frequently to keep up with the rapid pace of technological change. Consider Moore's Law, which suggests that computing power is essentially doubled for half the cost every 18 months (Drucker 2001).

Technology planning involves the following steps:

1. Assembling a planning team
2. Examining the vision, mission, goals, and objectives of the organization
3. Assessing current technology infrastructure
4. Identifying new technology solutions that work to achieve organizational goals
5. Developing implementation strategies, time lines, and costs
6. Understanding and involving end users
7. Assessing effectiveness
8. Making adjustments by repeating the process

Each step of the process is described in the following sections.

## Assembling a Planning Team

As in any planning process, involving key stakeholders is critical for receiving input, understanding needs, assessing alternatives, and creating buy-in. The leader of the technology planning team should be familiar with a broad range of technological applications. This person may be the chief information officer (CIO), director of computing technology, managing systems administrator, or other staff member with leadership, planning skills, and technological competence. In some cases, it may be advantageous to work with an outside consultant who specializes in technology planning and solutions. This option may be cost intensive; however, if the organization is committed to technology planning and considers the expense to be a necessary component of strategic planning, the organization may benefit from fresh ideas and outside-the-box thinking. Either way, it is important that technology planning be conducted at the organizational level and include representatives from all relevant units in order to achieve a system that is integrated and creates the kind of boundaryless structures that encourage innovation.

## Examining the Vision, Mission, Goals, and Objectives

As stated previously, technology planning should be seen as an extension of the strategic planning process. It needs to be connected to the overall mission, goals, and objectives of the organization. Clearly articulating the goals of an organization and how technology might be employed to achieve them is at the forefront of technology planning.

## Assessing Current Technology Infrastructure

Technology planning should take stock of existing technological infrastructure, including digital hardware, software, and networks. Hardware consists of the physical components of computers and other digital or electronic systems. Historically, computer hardware included the monitor, keyboard, and central processing unit (CPU). However, as technology continues to evolve, agencies are also likely to have laptops, all-in-one desktops and even hand-held devices that are used in the field. Hardware can also include peripheral machinery such as printers, faxes, modems, docking stations, and the concept can be extended to an array of computing, communications, and multimedia devices. Software consists of the programs that allow these devices to function. Computing software may include operating systems as well as specific technological functions such as word processing, spreadsheets, databases, website development, presentations, and multimedia applications.

The ability to develop networks connecting customers, organizations, and employees is a powerful tool, and the wider the network, the more powerful the tool (Lovelock 2001). Organizations should examine their access to and use of the Internet, extranet, and intranet. The Internet is publicly accessible by everyone who can log on to a computer. Open-access websites that provide information can be viewed anywhere there is a computer with Internet access. A German citizen who is planning to take a trip to Canada can access the National Parks of Canada website from Berlin and find public information related to Glacier National Park, for example.

Extranets have more restrictive access. Organizations define the boundary of the network and provide access to specific users through secured portals. For example, a sport organization may make general information publicly accessible through its Internet site but make specific information available only to season-ticket holders or club sponsors through a password-protected security system. Intranets are the most restrictive and are generally only accessible by employees or members of the organization. System administrators provide network security to prevent access from unauthorized parties. Intranets may link or network different employees or units within an organization and can greatly enhance communication and the exchange of information.

## Identifying New Technology Solutions

In examining the strategic plan of the organization, the technology planning team should devise technological solutions that help advance the organization's goals and objectives. These solutions may include using current technology resources more effectively, integrating existing systems, or adopting brand-new technological applications. Regardless of the proposed strategy, the planning team must demonstrate how the technological solution can help bridge the gap between where the organization is currently and where it wants to be.

For example, the three-year information technology (IT) plan for the city of Palo Alto, California, identified four strategic goals: (1) deploy digital city capabilities, (2) implement IT governance, (3) standardize and enhance service delivery, and (4) upgrade technology infrastructure and formalize information security. With this plan, IT expected to lower costs, increase quality and efficiency, and provide opportunities for greater innovation (City of Palo Alto 2013).

## Developing Implementation Strategies, Time Lines, and Costs

Technology solutions need implementation strategies. As a rule, complex solutions requiring major additions to the existing technology infrastructure or changes in organizational systems need to be phased in over time. Managers should expect some resistance to changes in technology and systems, and a realistic time frame should be allowed for wholesale buy-in of new technology solutions. Managers must also consider the costs involved in implementing new technology. They extend beyond just the cost of the technology and include staff (or customer) training and the potential for lost productivity while personnel get up to speed on new systems. The following steps represent a plan for implementing new technology within an organization.

1. Develop a time line and budget for implementation of new technology.
2. Develop an information campaign for staff and customers.
3. Train a few personnel or customers on the new technology as a test run.
4. Install new technology systems.
5. Test new systems solutions in mock or artificial environments.
6. Evaluate performance, obtain feedback from stakeholders, and make adjustments where appropriate.
7. Pilot test new systems in a limited manner.
8. Evaluate performance, obtain feedback from stakeholders, and make adjustments where appropriate.
9. Train all staff and customers on the new technology.
10. Implement the new system.

### Understanding and Involving End Users

Technology planning should develop strategies with the end user in mind. Each step of the process should involve users such as employees or customers to ensure a successful transition to new technological systems. Personnel and key customers should be included in the process of designing strategies or systems, provided with training on new systems, and asked to provide input for the purposes of evaluation and as a precursor to future change. By including staff and customers in the planning process, resistance to change can be reduced.

It is also important to consider the current capacity of people to use new technologies. Staff and customers will undoubtedly need information, orientation, or training on the use of new systems. Access is another factor to consider. For example, if an organization is planning to go paperless by moving program registration, facility reservation requests, and payment for services online, then it is imperative that potential users be able to access those systems. Internet use continues to grow, and in the United States at least, it is almost a universally accessed technology. The U.S. Census Bureau reported that 89.2 percent of American households have at least one computer in the home, and 91 percent of those households have Internet access (U.S. Census Bureau 2016). Moving to an Internet-based registration and payment system may be a good idea for a variety of reasons; however, the organization must create an implementation plan for ensuring that all customers can access and use the new system. For example, in trying to bridge the digital divide, a public park and recreation organization might provide digital kiosks in convenient locations throughout a municipality, allowing constituents without Internet access to register for programs, reserve facilities, and make payments.

### Assessing Effectiveness, Making Adjustments, and Repeating the Process

Technology planning is a process. As with any plan, organizations should continually evaluate, revisit, and adjust their strategies and solutions. Obtaining feedback from key users is a valuable method for evaluating the effectiveness of technology strategies. A system for data collection and ongoing assessment of organizational systems and technology use can help drive future planning efforts.

## Summary of Plans

The plans discussed in this chapter are used in all sectors of the leisure services profession. Different agencies may have different plans depending on their needs. An agency might also have one comprehensive plan that encompasses a strategic plan, a master plan for facilities, a recreation program plan, a marketing plan, and a technology plan.

# PROBLEM SOLVING AND DECISION MAKING

The ability to solve problems and make decisions is a highly rated competency for both entry-level and top managers (Hurd 2005). Furthermore, decision making falls within the planning aspect of the managerial functions.

The terms *problem solving* and *decision making* are often used interchangeably due to their close relationship. **Decision making** is choosing between two or more alternatives, whereas **problem solving** is determining solutions to correct the discrepancy between a desired state and current reality (Dumler and Skinner 2005). When problems arise that need to be solved, a decision must be made on how to solve the problem. However, not all decision making deals with problems. We make hundreds of decisions every day without even thinking about them—we choose what clothes to wear, what route to take to work, what to have for dinner, and so on.

Decisions fall on a continuum from programmed to nonprogrammed (Certo 2003). **Programmed decisions** are the routine decisions managers make. These decisions may be policy or planning driven, so the manager already knows what to do. Programmed decisions are usually less time consuming and difficult to make than nonprogrammed decisions. For example, a programmed decision may be whether to close a pool and spa in an electrical storm or whether to cancel a class based on low enrollment.

Nonprogrammed decisions are more challenging because they are often new or unique. Problems usually require nonprogrammed decisions. These situations take more thought and time to look at every angle of the situation in order to make the decision and solve the problem. Nonprogrammed decisions could include how to define *family* for membership purposes or how to deal with an undesirable group that requests the use of a park for a controversial rally.

Making decisions requires a process. Although programmed decisions will be made without consciously thinking about these steps, nonprogrammed decisions require careful consideration and follow six steps (figure 6.4).

## Step 1: Identify and Define the Problem

Identifying and defining a problem is not as easy as it may appear. Sometimes when managers look at problems, what they are really seeing are symptoms of a larger problem. This requires that the manager look deeply into the situation. To identify the real problem, managers must see what barriers are standing in the way of achieving goals and get multiple viewpoints of the situation (Arnold, Heyne, and Busser 2005). Multiple viewpoints provide a different perspective from what the lone manager sees. These multiple viewpoints can come from fellow managers or from people external to the agency. Someone without any history of the situation

**decision making**—Choosing from two or more alternatives through a process of analyzing the situation, evaluating options, and selecting a course of action.

**problem solving**—Creating solutions to correct the discrepancy between a desired state and current reality.

**programmed decisions**—Routine decisions that managers face on a daily basis.

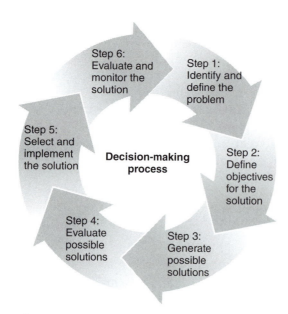

**Figure 6.4** Decision-making process.

may shed new light on the root of the problem rather than the symptoms.

To illustrate the decision-making model, assume you are a manager in the Jefferson Parks and Recreation Department. You are faced with the question of whether or not to ban sledding in parks. The major concerns are liability and damage caused to the golf course.

## Step 2: Define Objectives for the Solution

The next step is to determine the objectives of the solution, or what the end result should achieve. In determining the objectives, it is important to consider everyone involved with the problem. More people may be affected than those within the agency; there are also customers, community members, shareholders, and other stakeholders to consider. Their reaction to the solution may require consideration. For our sledding problem, here are a few examples of objectives:

- Protect the golf course from turf damage.
- Provide safe activities for city residents.
- Provide a variety of free indoor and outdoor winter activities for city residents.

Each objective is specific enough to guide you through the next step of generating possible solutions.

## Step 3: Generate Possible Solutions

Few problems have only one solution, so looking for multiple solutions is advised. Inexperienced managers may be too timid to generate creative solutions for fear of rejection. However, creative problem solving makes you a better manager. We have all heard the phrase "think outside the box." This is especially true when generating possible solutions for a problem.

Sometimes the generation of solutions is inhibited for various reasons. Ideas may be stymied because of emotional attachments to programs, products, or places. For example, a popular preschool arts program instructor was fired for insubordination, not following through on responsibilities, and not staying within the program budget over several years. This instructor was so popular that upon her firing, past program participants spoke out expressing their disbelief. They caused quite a media stir and much headache for the agency. The solution to this problem is inherently connected to emotional ties from the community. When generating solutions, the agency needs to consider such emotional ties but should not be held hostage by them.

Solution generation can also be inhibited by change. People have varying degrees of success when dealing with change. Walk into any agency as a new manager and listen to people describe processes in the organization. Undoubtedly, the phrase "we've always done it that way" will emerge. When ways of doing things become ingrained in the culture of the organization, they are sometimes difficult to change. A radical solution to a problem may be a great idea, but if it is not the typical response, it may cause some resistance. However, this is not an excuse to avoid generating good ideas. Change is the only constant within an organization!

Here are some possible solutions to the sledding problem:

- Ban sledding at the golf course and allow it at other parks.
- Post signs at dangerous sledding spots to warn of dangers and take extra precautions to protect sledders, such as fencing in areas where sleds go off course.
- Hire a supervisor at the golf course to monitor for safety and damage.
- Stop sledding at all parks and golf courses.

## Step 4: Evaluate Possible Solutions

All solutions need to be screened based on the objectives for the solution. This step allows managers to compare the solutions, adapt them if needed, and even combine possible solutions. Once a change is made to a solution, it needs to be evaluated just as the original solutions were. In this step, all solutions should have a devil's advocate to think of the alternatives, the what-ifs of a solution. Table 6.4 shows one example of how to evaluate the solutions to the sledding problem.

## Step 5: Select and Implement the Solution

After evaluating possible solutions, one is chosen and implemented. Each solution will have some level of risk. Selecting a solution means determining which one will be the most beneficial and least detrimental to achieving the goals, objectives, mission, and strategic plan of the organization. After much thought and discussion with staff, board, and community, sledding is banned from the golf course and extra safety precautions and signage are installed at other parks.

**Table 6.4** Evaluation of Solutions

| Solution | Pros (+) | Cons (−) |
|---|---|---|
| Ban sledding at the golf course and allow it at other parks. | Stops damage to the golf course. Keeps sledding as a free winter activity. | Damage occurs in other parks. Liability is still an issue. |
| Post signs at dangerous sledding spots to warn of dangers and take extra precautions to protect sledders, such as fencing in areas where sleds go off course. | Keeps sledding as a free winter activity. Somewhat protects the agency in case of lawsuits | Makes people aware of the dangers. Does not necessarily prevent injuries and accidents |
| Hire a supervisor at the golf course to monitor for safety and damage. | Reduces injuries. Reduces damage if sledding is stopped in time. | Does not eliminate injuries and accidents. Adds the expense of a supervisor. May need to charge to sled, thus eliminating a free winter activity. |
| Stop sledding at all parks and golf courses. | Stops turf damage at the golf course and parks. Eliminates a liability issue. | Eliminates a free winter activity. Major elimination for a minor and controllable problem. |

## Step 6: Evaluate and Monitor the Solution

Decision making does not end with the implementation of the solution. Managers learn a lot from evaluating and monitoring their decisions. Once the solution is implemented, managers should measure whether the desired effect has occurred. Evaluating and monitoring means examining the consequences of the decision, measuring the outcomes, and determining if it was the right decision. If it was not the right decision, then the process begins again.

As for our sledders, after the first winter the agency evaluated the new policy and how it met the needs of the community. The solution seemed to work. However, if it had not, the agency could go back and look at other solutions to the problem.

Even following this decision-making process does not automatically result in the right decision every time. Decision making is not foolproof because there are so many uncontrollable and sometimes unforeseeable aspects to various situations. Using the sledding example, a number of variables could have come into play to affect the quality of the decision. It could have been a snowy winter, and the number of sledders was well beyond projections and the turf suffered; it could have been a mild winter with little snow, yet many sledders used the park anyway and destroyed the turf; or unforeseen risk areas in the park might have resulted in a higher number of injuries than in the past. As managers gain experience, they become better at identifying problems, defining objectives, developing creative solutions, predicting consequences, and choosing the right solutions. This takes experience, and it takes making both good and bad decisions.

# ETHICAL DECISION MAKING

The decision-making process covers all decisions regarding everything from human resources to participants. It is impossible to discuss decision making without discussing the ethical implications of decisions. Ethics are principles of behavior encompassing goodness, fairness, and doing what is right. Ethical decision making takes into account the results of a decision and how it affects others.

Rather than reinventing the decision-making process, it is only necessary to consider the ethical implications. To do this, the manager assesses the situation to see if there are legal, personal, or social issues that could cause conflict. For example, it is unethical for a supervisor to ask a staff member to do personal errands or jobs for the supervisor. A supervisor asking a landscape specialist to plant a flower bed at the supervisor's house while being paid by the agency is considered unethical.

When an issue is defined as ethical, extra care must be taken during the decision-making process. When generating possible solutions (step 3) for an ethical decision, the solutions can be categorized in several ways. Let's use the following scenario to look at the various ethical decision-making approaches. The local YMCA has a competitive soccer program for young people. This program has a widespread reputation for being one of the best for player development. Many players in the league went on to earn college scholarships and even play professional soccer. The teams are ranked in terms of talent. A local businessperson is upset to hear that his son made the second team and not the first, which has the top players and gets the most exposure to large universities. This person offers the YMCA $25,000 to make much-needed renovations to the soccer fields. The only thing the agency needs to do is move his son to the first team.

The first approach to ethical decision making is the utilitarian approach, where the decision results in the greatest good for the greatest number. It can be viewed as the decision that does the least amount of harm. With this approach, the manager would place the son on the top team. It is only adding one more person, and the young man has talent since he was originally placed on the second team. The most good will come to future players because they will have state-of-the-art facilities on which to play.

A moral approach to ethical decision making requires the manager to do what is right regardless of the consequences. If using a moral approach, the manager would not move the player to the top team or accept the donation, because the young man did not earn the spot on the first team and the money was not given in good faith.

A universalist approach requires the manager to look at the situation and how it affects everyone else. In this case, the manager must assess how everyone else would feel if they knew how the new soccer fields were funded and that the player was moved up to the first team. This requires thinking like those who are affected to determine whether they would rather have new fields or give the space on the first team to a more talented player.

Finally, a cost–benefit analysis requires the manager to examine the costs and benefits of the decision. The manager would need to look at the cost (beyond just dollars and cents) of this move to the reputation of the program and how the ability to buy a child's way into a program goes against all that the organization stands for in its mission. The benefits of accepting the money include the ability to put other resources originally earmarked for field renovations into other aspects of the program and the ability to draw state and national tournaments on much-improved fields (Poznak Law Firm, Ltd. 2007).

Ethical decision making requires an extra step to identify the issue as ethical. An "ethical yardstick" can be used to see if ethics are involved (Elliot and Mink 1995). Ask yourself the following questions:

- Do your chosen courses of action seem logical and reasonable?
- If everyone followed this course of action, would the results be beneficial for all?
- What effect will this plan of action have on others? On you?
- When you look back on what you've done, what will you think of yourself?
- How would the person you admire the most handle the problem?
- What difference would it make if everyone knew about your decision? (Chances are that decisions one makes hoping no one will find out are not ethical.)

Once you have determined if ethics are involved, you need to determine which of the ethical approaches discussed earlier is the most appropriate given the situation. All other aspects of ethical decision making follow the presented process and should result in a decision meeting the needs of the organization. That doesn't mean the decision will be easy to make. Making ethical decisions requires a manager to develop three very important competencies: the competence to recognize ethical situations and think through alternate solutions; the self-confidence to seek out different points of view, and decide what is right for that time and place; and finally, the tough-mindedness to emerge with a solution when there are no set solutions (Elliot and Mink 1995).

Check out the web study guide for additional material, including learning activities, sample documents, interactive case studies, web links, CPRP exam connections, and more.

## Conclusion

This chapter focused on two concepts that are strongly interrelated. First, planning was introduced as a guide to reach the vision an agency sets for itself. Planning goals, objectives, strategic issues, and strategies help an agency prioritize what it should do, why it should do these things, and how they should be done. Second, decision making and problem solving are affected by planning and policies. Although planning does not determine decisions, managers refer to plans when evaluating the solutions to problems.

Planning and decision-making skills are interwoven with many aspects of being a manager, from setting goals and objectives to creating budgets. Neither will be instantaneous skills for new managers; they will build over time and with experience. They require the involvement of others both inside and outside the organization to be effective.

# Review Questions

1. Compare and contrast strategic planning, master planning, and recreation program planning.
2. Explain the four approaches to ethical decision making.
3. Explain a SWOT analysis and give an example of each element.
4. Why should organizations plan?
5. Discuss the role of public input in planning and policy making.
6. Explain programmed and nonprogrammed decisions and give an example of each.
7. Discuss the decision-making process.

# Marketing and Public Relations

## Learning Outcomes

- Explain marketing and its importance in leisure services.
- Differentiate between market segmentation and target marketing.
- Examine the marketing mix and describe how to incorporate it into leisure services organizations.
- Understand the use of social media in leisure services.

## Key Terms

marketing, market segmentation, target marketing, mass marketing, market, demographics, psychographics, marketing mix, product life cycle, direct distribution, indirect distribution, intensity of distribution, promotion, promotions mix, advertising, sales promotions and incentives, personal selling, public relations, media relations

## Competency Check

Refer to table 1.6 to see how you assessed this related competency.

    9. Implement marketing techniques.

## A Day in the Life

My day-to-day job pulls me in all different directions from interacting and communicating with the public to working on various publications. Doing public relations for a village is very different than if I was just focused on a park district, as I am supporting all the various departments within the village, which includes the Parks, Recreation and Facilities Department. Overall, my key job responsibilities include website design, social media, designing flyers, creating advertisements, designing newsletters and other mailer publications, visual media, photography, community outreach, writing press releases, and interacting with the media.

With the constant growth of technology and social media, I rely heavily on these various platforms to communicate to the public. On a daily basis, I update the village website, social media, and electronic marquees with relevant and up-to-date information. The recreation division, special events committees, and all of the various departments within the Village of Glendale Heights rely on the public relations division to let the residents and public know what is happening in their community. The job responsibilities are endless as new challenges arise every day. However, just like with any position, staying positive and taking on these responsibilities has helped me grow into a career that I truly love and appreciate!

David Genty
Public Affairs Coordinator
Village of Glendale Heights
Glendale Heights, Illinois

The authors thank Haley Palmer for her contribution to this chapter.

For many years, marketing was not a part of the park and recreation profession in the public and nonprofit sectors. Agencies hired people to plan and implement programs but no one to tell the public about them. Marketing was left to the programmer and may have consisted of developing a flyer, distributing a brochure, or sending out a news release.

Until the last two decades or so, few park and recreation curricula required students to take a marketing course. However, this has changed, as has the concept of marketing. Marketing in leisure services has moved beyond flyers and brochures to integration of the marketing mix, marketing plans, target marketing, and market research.

Marketing can take on many faces within an organization. Some agencies have employees whose only job is to market products and services. Other agencies have an employee who is responsible for some marketing but also has other responsibilities, and then there are agencies where staff members do their own marketing. Marketing is an innovative area, and rarely can an agency attract too many people to use its programs and services. Thus, it is important to know the fundamentals of marketing in order to increase use of programs and services to the desired level.

For those who have the luxury of a marketing department to carry out marketing functions, it is still necessary to understand marketing basics. This knowledge allows for a team approach to marketing with input from the manager as well as the marketing staff. The manager has much more intimate knowledge of the product, service, or program than the marketing staff does, and vice versa in terms of marketing. If the two sides can come together and speak a common language through an understanding of marketing, the organization will be able to better utilize resources and capitalize on marketing efforts than if the manager does not understand marketing beyond a flyer and news release. This chapter outlines the foundations of marketing and introduces concepts needed in order to market programs and services effectively.

## DEFINITION AND HISTORY OF MARKETING

**Marketing** can be defined as the purposeful planning and execution of the pricing, place, and promotion of ideas, goods, and services (the product) to create an exchange of time or resources that results in the satisfaction of individual needs and organizational objectives (figure 7.1).

Marketing has not always been defined and executed in this fashion. Marketing history can be divided into four eras (O'Sullivan 1991): the production era, the sales era, the marketing era, and the service marketing era (figure 7.2).

**marketing—**
Purposeful planning and execution of the pricing, place, and promotion of ideas, goods, and services to create an exchange of time or resources that results in the satisfaction of individual needs and organizational objectives.

### Production Era

The Industrial Revolution changed how people worked and spent their money. More and more people worked in factories and were able to mass-produce products for consumers. In this era, businesses focused on what they did best and produced those products while trying to reduce costs. People were able to buy many things for the first time, and demand often exceeded supply. There was little regard for what customers wanted, and goods were the focus rather than services. Manufacturers

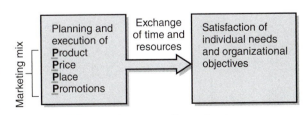

**Figure 7.1** Definition of marketing.

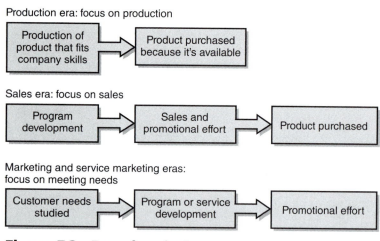

**Figure 7.2** Eras of marketing.

Adapted from D.R. Howard and J.L. Crompton, 1980, *Financing, Managing, and Marketing Recreation and Park Resources* (Dubuque, IA: Wm. C. Brown Publishers), 307, by permission of The McGraw-Hill Companies.

simply had to put the product on the market and people bought it.

## Sales Era

Beginning in the 1930s during the Great Depression, supply exceeded demand for most products. Companies were still producing the products they wanted based on their own strengths. Sales techniques were used to stimulate demand and align customer wants with production capabilities. During this era, sales and marketing became synonymous. Also during this time, a lot of advertising was done by people who had virtually no control over the product. This approach is still seen today in many leisure services agencies where the responsibility of the marketing staff is to sell programs to users without having any input on the programs.

## Marketing Era

This era, which began in the early 1980s, derived from increased competition and saw organizations becoming more responsive to the needs of consumers. Marketing staff studied consumer needs and then developed products to meet those needs. Marketing thus became an integrated function of product development because it was customer driven rather than product driven. It was also during this era that park and recreation agencies saw the value in marketing and started marketing their programs.

## Service Marketing Era

The service marketing era is similar to the marketing era, except it has increased the focus on marketing services and ideas in addition to products. This era started in the early 1990s and continues today. It remains customer focused, and the value of services as a product is strongly emphasized.

## Summary of Eras

The leisure services profession has moved through all four eras of marketing. The commercial sector was ahead of the public and nonprofit sectors in doing so, but the latter two sectors are quickly catching up and valuing the benefits of marketing as much as the commercial sector does. This is especially true now that the marketing of services has become a focus.

# MARKET SEGMENTATION AND TARGET MARKETING

Because not everyone has the same wants and needs, watches the same television programs, or uses the same products and services, market segmentation and target

## Shifts in Demographics in the United States and Canada

The demographic profile of the United States is rapidly changing. Minority groups are growing so quickly that there is no majority race in California, Hawaii, New Mexico, the District of Columbia and Texas (U.S. Census Bureau 2012). The same is true in Canada, where 19 percent of the population is a visible minority. (A visible minority is a person who is non-Caucasian in race or nonwhite in color.) In Toronto, one of the world's most diverse cities, 47 percent of the population identified as a visible minority (De Souza 2013).

Given this growth in minority populations, it is easy to see that targeting minority markets is a necessity. Not only is there a desire to meet the needs of these markets, but there is a wealth of buying power as well. Buying power is the total post-tax personal income that is available to spend on goods and services, also called *discretionary income*. For example, buying power for Hispanics has reached $1.3 trillion, followed by African Americans ($1.1 trillion) and Asians ($770 billion) (University of Georgia 2013). Clearly, minority groups have a large amount of disposable income to spend on leisure services, which makes targeting minority markets a necessity.

marketing are needed. **Market segmentation** is the process of dividing a heterogeneous market into smaller homogenous subgroups that are similar in terms of wants, needs, demographic profiles, and how they respond to the marketing mix (Mullin, Hardy, and Sutton 2014). **Target marketing** selects one or more market segments on which to focus the marketing mix.

Before target marketing is possible, the market must first be segmented. A market is all the actual or potential buyers of a product. Market segmentation allows an agency to look at its different markets, their individual needs, and the products that meet those needs rather than taking a mass-marketing approach. Mass marketing assumes that all people want the same things, and one product is expected to appeal to all people. **Mass marketing**, or undifferentiated marketing, is defined as a marketing strategy that ignores market segments and tries to reach as many people as possible.

## Selecting a Segmentation Strategy

When determining whether to segment a **market**, it is important to establish if the market is identifiable, accessible, and responsive. In a market segment that is identifiable, the people within the segment can be distinguished from the general population, which will reveal the size of the market, its purchasing power, and its sustainability. For example, let's say the local senior center offers a trip to New York City that includes airfare, a hotel room for five nights, tickets to two Broadway shows, and all meals at a cost of $4,500 per person. In a mass-marketing approach, the organization would direct promotions for this trip to the entire community of 250,000 people rather than focusing on likely buyers. Market segmentation would allow the agency to identify market segments in the community based on such characteristics as income, age, education, and travel interests—all identifiable characteristics.

**market segmentation**—Process of dividing a heterogeneous market into smaller homogenous subgroups who are similar in terms of wants, needs, demographic profiles, and how they respond to the marketing mix.

**target marketing**—Selecting one or more market segments and focusing the market mix on this segment.

**mass marketing**—A marketing strategy that ignores market segments and tries to reach as many people as possible.

**market**—All the actual or potential buyers of a product.

The market should not be so small as to be a poor use of resources but not so large as to resemble a mass market. In this trip example, certain income levels will be more prone to respond to this trip than others. A middle or upper income segment is more likely to respond than a lower income due to the cost of the trip alone.

A viable market segment should also be accessible. The people within the segment must be able to be reached and served by distribution and promotion of the product. For example, isolated seniors may prove to be a difficult group to access regardless of the value of offering this trip to them.

Lastly, market segments should also be responsive to the marketing mix. There are two aspects of responsiveness: the ability of the program to meet the needs of the segment and the responsiveness of the segment to the marketing initiatives. Our sample trip will only be effective if this is an activity people actually want and we align marketing efforts that reach them.

## Bases of Segmentation

Bases of segmentation are ways in which a mass market can be segmented into smaller, more homogenous groups. Although this can be done in a number of ways, typically leisure services use four different bases: demographics, geography, psychographics, and behavioral characteristics.

**demographics—**
Population characteristics used to gather data on groups of people (e.g., sex, age, race).

The most common method to segment a market is **demographics** and includes income, age, gender, race and ethnicity, sexual orientation, education, and family life cycle (how people progress through various stages of life; see table 7.1). Many leisure services providers use demographics to segment their market. For example, the Carmel Clay Parks and Recreation Department in Indiana divides programs into parent–child, preschool, youth, and adult programs, among others. Demographics data are available through most cities, libraries, and the census bureaus.

Demographics can be quite powerful in identifying markets in sport and leisure services. For example, the National Golf Foundation knows that their largest group of beginning golfers is 18 to 39 years of age, which accounts for more than half of all beginners. This information helps golf courses focus efforts on new golfers in that age range more than younger or older age groups. (Stachura 2015).

A second segmentation base is geography. This variable considers such factors as geoclusters (how closely people live to each other) and proximity. Geoclusters assume that people living close together, as in neighborhoods or zip codes, share many of the same characteristics. It is possible to develop a market segment based on a neighborhood and determine a demographic profile of this geocluster to learn even more about it.

Similar to geoclusters, proximity identifies how close people are to the service. There is a strong relationship between proximity to a service and use of that service. A person who lives five minutes from a beach is much more likely to use the beach than someone living an hour away. Because of proximity concerns, the YMCA of Greater Des Moines has seven branches located throughout the city. Members can use any branch, but most will use the one closest to where they live or work.

**psychographics—**
Values, attitudes, beliefs, personality, motivation, and lifestyle variables that define a person.

**Psychographics** include personality, motivation, and lifestyle or social class variables. Psychographic data can be difficult to gather, yet they can be beneficial if used in conjunction with demographic data. Lifestyle variables are of particular interest to park and recreation professionals. These variables are a combination of activities such as vacations, hobbies, and entertainment; interests such as family, community, and work; and opinions such as politics, social issues, and culture. For example, the Ventana Big Sur resort and spa in Big Sur, California, provides an elegant resort

**Table 7.1** Sample Demographic and Geographic Segmentation Variables for Consumer Markets in the United States

| Variable | Typical Breakdown |
| --- | --- |
| **GEOGRAPHIC** | |
| Region | Pacific, Mountain, West North Central, South Central, East North Central, South Atlantic, Middle Atlantic, New England |
| City or metro size | Under 5,000; 5,000–20,000; 20,000–50,000; 50,000–100,000; 100,000–250,000; 250,000–500,000; 500,000–1,000,000; 1,000,000–4,000,000; 4,000,000 and over |
| Density | Urban, suburban, rural |
| **DEMOGRAPHIC** | |
| Age | Under 6; 6–11; 12–19; 20–34; 35–49; 50–64; 65+ |
| Family size | 1–2; 3–4; 5+ |
| Family life cycle | Young and single; young, married, no children; young, married, youngest child under 6; young, married, youngest child 6 or over; older married, with children; older married, no children under 18; older single; other |
| Income | Under $10,000; $10,000–$15,000; $15,000–$20,000; $20,000–$30,000; $30,000–$50,000; $50,000–$100,000; $100,000+ |
| Occupation | Professional and technical; managers, officials, and proprietors; clerical, sales; craftspeople, foremen; operatives; farmers; retired; students; stay-at-home wives or husbands; unemployed |
| Education | Grade school or less; some high school; high school graduate; some college; college graduate; postgraduate work; postgraduate degree |
| Race | African American; American Indian; Asian; Caucasian; Hispanic; other |
| Nationality | American; British; French Canadian; German; Italian; Japanese; Australian; Latino |
| Social class | Lower lower; upper lower; working class; middle class; upper middle; lower upper; upper upper |

## Grassroots Marketing

Knowing a lot about a specific population in a community allows for grassroots marketing—where marketing professionals focus on making marketing efforts personally relevant to consumers. For example, when Nike was a much smaller company, they focused on grassroots efforts by sponsoring local events and teams, providing equipment to local schools, and conducting clinics in neighborhoods. They wanted to build their business via individual communities (Kotler and Keller 2016). Grassroots efforts can be particularly successful for local park and recreation agencies and small businesses.

experience that caters to a high-end lifestyle, including formal dining with caviar, oysters on the half shell, and foie gras as appetizers; rooms starting at $700 per night; and a spa featuring massages, body treatments, and Reiki therapy (Ventana Big Sur 2018). This type of vacation destination would appeal to a specific lifestyle and market segment. Ventana Big Sur understands the need to expand their market and has done so by introducing glamping in the redwood forest to appeal to upscale outdoors enthusiasts. Glamping (glamour camping) at Ventana Big Sur includes a safari-style canvas tent on a platform, a king-sized bed, daily housekeeping service, a bath house with teak-enclosed showers, ingredients for s'mores and other provisions, and hot water bottles to warm up the bed sheets before retiring. Businesses such as Ventana Big Sur greatly benefit from psychographic data.

The last base of segmentation is behavioral characteristics. A market segmented according to behavioral characteristics considers how much and how often consumers purchase a product, their skill level related to the product, product benefits, and their product loyalty.

In response to the different segments of buyers and how often they purchase, the WNBA's Indiana Fever understands the value of behavioral segmentation by offering different ticketing options for different levels of users. The options include a season ticket (18 games), a fan's choice pack (5 games), 2-for-1 Wednesdays, and single-game tickets (Indiana Fever 2017). These options are offered in response to attendance behaviors of several segments.

In addition, skill level plays a significant role in targeting people for certain activities based on their experience. For example, Clear Creek Rafting Company in Idaho Springs, Colorado, offers trips for a variety of abilities, including beginner trips, intermediate trips, advanced trips, evening trips, and multiday trips (Clear Creek Rafting Company 2017). Each user level has different trip expectations and different desires for increased challenges. To a business such as Clear Creek Rafting Company, demographics, geography, and psychographics may give good insight into the market segment, but behavioral characteristics should be a primary base used in combination with the others.

Benefits-based behavioral characteristics segmentation separates homogenous groups based on what they want to gain from the product. For example, Dagger Kayaks offers a fit guide that asks potential buyers what benefits are important to them and then finds the kayak that is the best choice based on those benefits, such as a touring kayak that is durable, affordable, and stable with a lot of storage (Dagger Kayaks 2017). The company has a full line of kayaks and targets benefits rather than demographics, psychographics, or other segmenting methods.

Finally, loyalty status is a means of behavioral market segmentation, and Kotler and Keller (2016, 282) suggest there are four consumer groups based on brand loyalty:

- Hard core loyals, who buy only one brand at a time
- Split loyals, who are loyal to two or three brands
- Shifting loyals, who shift loyalty from one brand to another
- Switchers, who show no loyalty to a particular brand

Marketing efforts for each of these groups will differ. For example, with those who have no brand loyalty, efforts should be made to understand why they shift or switch brands, and then address those reasons in marketing efforts. Keep in mind that brand loyalty may not only be a result of a quality product; it may simply be a habit. Other causes of brand loyalty include indifference to other brands out there, low price, high switching cost, or the unavailability of other brands (Kotler and Keller 2016).

# Selecting a Target Market

Once a market has been segmented into different groups, target markets must be selected. Determining which segments to target will depend on several factors, including resources available and likelihood of the segment to respond to marketing efforts. However, there are three basic strategies to selecting a target market: undifferentiated, differentiated, and concentrated strategies (figure 7.3). An undifferentiated approach ignores the different market segments and focuses on all of them as one large market. This approach assumes the mass-marketing mentality that everyone will be reached by one marketing approach. Of the three sectors, the public sector is most likely to use this method because market research skills, time, and money limit a better segmentation strategy.

Differentiated market segmentation recognizes that market segments require different marketing strategies. A number of segments are identified, and specific marketing plans are developed for each segment. Agencies such as the YMCA may take a differentiated marketing segmentation approach, especially if they offer programs and services for a variety of age groups and income levels. All sectors are prone to this approach.

The commercial and nonprofit sectors are more likely to use a concentrated target marketing strategy than the public sector. This selection approach identifies a clearly defined target market and focuses its resources and marketing efforts on that particular market. Ventana Big Sur, for example, knows that its target market is educated, high-income, middle-aged to older adults who value prestige, relaxation, and escape. This is the market they will target, and though others are always welcome to come to the resort, they are not the focus of marketing efforts.

Many leisure services agencies show their marketing weaknesses by disregarding market segmentation and target marketing. Managers are expected to use limited resources as best as possible, and any manager attempting to mass-market a product is wasting resources. People are different and want different things. By clustering people into groups and then focusing on those segments that would best be served by the product, the manager is making wise use of time, money, and effort. Furthermore, with target marketing there is a far better return on the marketing investment if the manager understands who the prime candidates are for the marketing exchange.

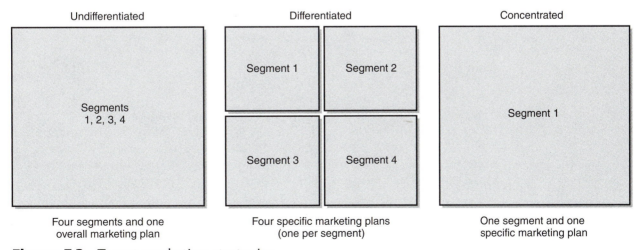

**Figure 7.3** Target marketing strategies.

# MARKETING MIX

**marketing mix**—Integration of product, place (or distribution), pricing, and promotion.

Once a target market is selected, the **marketing mix** for that market must be outlined. The marketing mix encompasses the four Ps: product, place, pricing, and promotion. It is the careful and purposeful combination of these elements that makes marketing effective. Although many people view marketing as simply advertising, several additional aspects are required in order for it to work. A logical starting point is the product.

## Product

A product is anything offered to a market with the intent of satisfying wants or needs. This means that a product can be a tangible good or a service. Many products in the recreation profession are services, such as programs, events, and other experiences, but goods also exist in such things as sports equipment, all-terrain vehicles, and art supplies. Product-related issues to consider include goods versus services, the product life cycle, and product extension strategies.

Products have many layers to them. They can be thought of as a bundle of benefits directed at satisfying needs. This is considered your core product. Beyond the core benefits of many products is the augmented product—the parts of the product that go beyond expectations, such as an on-site massage therapist at a fitness facility, turn-down service at a hotel, or free tune-ups for the life of a bicycle. For recreation and sport there are many aspects of the product that can positively or negatively affect the core product, including such things as star players or coaches, the fans or spectators, equipment, facilities, music, or food. For example, imagine a major music festival with poor or too few restroom facilities, a weak sound system, and limited food options. Many visitors would be leery of returning to this sort of event in the future simply because of the augmented product.

---

### Market Position and Branding

Throughout the discussion on the marketing mix, two key concepts will repeatedly emerge: market position and branding. Market position is how the community perceives the agency and its services. Agencies strive to position themselves positively as well as position themselves uniquely from the competition. Agencies with unique products, high-quality services, excellent staff, or a quality storefront location are often positioned better in the eye of the consumer.

Branding is the process an agency uses to create an image of that agency in the minds of the consumer. They will use such things as the agency name, logo, colors, or product image (Mulvaney and Hurd 2017). Good branding ensures that when a community member sees the logo, they know what the agency is. Think about the Nike swoosh. There is no need to label the logo with the company name because of the outstanding branding that Nike has done.

## Goods versus Services

When looking at goods versus services, there are four main differences: intangibility, inseparability, heterogeneity, and perishability.

Services are considered intangible whereas goods are considered tangible. Tangible goods can be sensed through touch, such as a bicycle, a football, or hiking boots. On the other hand, services are considered intangible. The consumer experiences a service, such as a swim lesson, but the service itself cannot necessarily be physically touched.

Second, services and products differ based on the inseparability of services and their creators or producers. Services must be consumed at the place they originate, and they must be used at the time they are produced. Using the swim lesson example, the lesson must be used when the instructor creates it at the pool. Consumers cannot take this service home and use it when they want, unlike a product such as a bicycle that can be ridden at any time the buyer chooses.

Third, there is more heterogeneity, or inconsistency, in services than in goods. For example, let's say you have decided to purchase a Specialized Sirrus Comp road bicycle. There are four bicycles on the floor, each in a different color. Because the products are homogenous, there is no reason to ride a bicycle in each color to determine which one feels best. The bikes are standardized, and production and assembly are rigidly controlled and inspected before distribution. Conversely, most services do not have the luxury of these control factors, making them more heterogeneous. The swim lesson will change based on the preparation, mood, or experience of the instructor, the aesthetics or location of the facility, and even the weather. Since people cannot be totally standardized, services will always have some variability.

Finally, services differ from goods in terms of perishability. Services are highly perishable because they cannot be inventoried or stored. The unsold bicycles remain available for consumer purchase long after their production, whereas a swim lesson held on Tuesday for an hour is gone once the lesson time passes. Furthermore, bicycle manufacturers can mass-produce their bicycles in advance for the summer season. Swim lessons cannot be mass-produced in the winter, stored, and then used in the summer.

The recreation profession deals with both goods and services, whether it is selling outdoor adventure equipment or running the Thunderbird Lodge in Manitoba. Because of this, *goods* and *services* will be used interchangeably throughout this chapter.

## Life Cycle

From the time a product is first offered until its discontinuation, it goes through a **product life cycle**. As it passes through each of the five phases—introduction, growth, maturation, saturation, and decline (figure 7.4)—the marketing strategy is adjusted to respond to customer behaviors. Inexperienced managers might focus solely on advertising a product, but there are several strategies that can be used to extend the life cycle of the product. In order to make these adjustments, an understanding of what happens in the life cycle is needed.

**product life cycle**— Phases that products go through from inception to death, including introduction, growth, maturation, saturation, and decline.

**Introduction**  During the introduction phase, the product is first released to the market. Typically there are only a small number of participants and little profitability. Marketing efforts are employed to expose people to the product and convince them to try it. This is done through heavy promotions, such as two-for-one deals, buy one

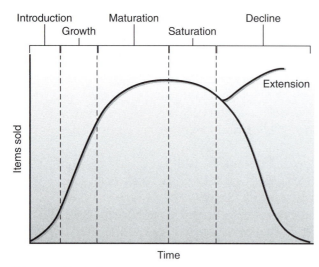

**Figure 7.4** Product life cycle.

get one free, a month's free membership, or Sunday nights free with a Friday and Saturday stay.

**Growth** The product begins to experience a rapid growth in the number of participants as the early consumers continue participating and new consumers emerge. During this phase of the life cycle, there is a heavy reliance on word of mouth and various promotional efforts to lengthen the growth phase as long as possible. In the growth stage of the life cycle there is also opportunity to improve the core and augmented product quality and features, enter new market segments, or lower prices to reach the next level of price-sensitive consumers.

**Maturation** Growth slows in this phase as the product has gained acceptance by potential buyers. It is at this point profits will stabilize or slightly decline due to increased competition (Kotler and Keller 2016). Products often stay in the maturation stage longer than any of the others, sometimes for several years. Most marketing efforts are directed at mature programs because they are solid programs that are still seeing growing numbers. At this stage, different markets can be explored or program modifications made (Rossman and Schlatter 2015). As a result, advertising campaigns are changed to accommodate these changes or to simply attract more people.

**Saturation** At the saturation stage, sales level off and the number of consumers peaks. Those who are loyal to the product keep purchasing at a steady rate; this is called *brand loyalty*. Any people who drop out are replaced by new purchasers, thus keeping steady numbers of consumers. Promotional efforts may change to attract new users and maintain loyalty.

**Decline** When there is a steady decrease in consumers, the product has moved into the decline phase. During this phase, decisions about what to do with the program need to be made. Program options include petrification, death, and extension. If petrification is chosen, the program is left as is and will phase itself out until there are no more consumers. The program can also experience a death in that it is simply stopped. The most elaborate response to the decline phase is to use extension strategies that manipulate the product or the target market (figure 7.5): market penetration, market development, product development, product replacement, and diversification (Howard and Crompton 1980).

● *Market penetration.* When an existing product that has been targeted to a specific market slides into the decline phase, market penetration can be used to extend the life of the product. Market penetration leaves the existing product as is and goes deeper into the existing target market. This may mean adjusting the marketing strategies to attract competitors' consumers or using heavy promotion to convince nonusers within the target market to become consumers. For example, the Greater River Area Family YMCA in Chillicothe, Missouri, offers an aquatics fitness program called Rusty Hinges that targets seniors who need a low-impact aerobic workout.

With market penetration, increased promotional efforts are used to target people in this market who have the intention to participate but have not yet done so.

● *Market development.* Market development looks for a new market segment for the existing product. Using the Rusty Hinges example, if attendance began to drop, the YMCA could target a younger population with physical disabilities who would benefit from the program.

● *Product development and product replacement.* Both product development and replacement are extension strategies for a new product and an existing market. With product development, the old program is replaced by an entirely new program, whereas with replacement, the old program is replaced by an improved version of the same program. Using the Rusty Hinges example, a product development strategy would replace Rusty Hinges with another program aimed at the same target market, whereas a replacement strategy would make improvements to Rusty Hinges and reintroduce the improved version to the same target market.

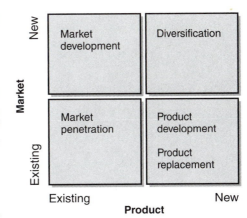

**Figure 7.5** Product extension strategies.

Adapted from D.R. Howard and J.L. Crompton, 1980, *Financing, Managing, and Marketing Recreation and Park Resources* (Dubuque, IA: Wm. C. Brown Publishers), 397, by permission of The McGraw-Hill Companies.

● *Diversification.* Diversification, the last extension strategy, begins the product life cycle over again since it introduces a new product to a new market segment. For example, the Rusty Hinges program would no longer be offered and its time slot and pool space would be used for a different program targeted toward a different segment, such as young people. With diversification the decision is made to move in an entirely different direction.

# Place

The second *P* in the marketing mix is place. Sometimes referred to as distribution, place is how organizations get the product to the consumer. Place may include parks, recreation centers, golf courses, resorts, stores, and so on.

It is not by chance that a business finds itself in a certain section of the community or that certain programs are only offered in select recreation centers. In-depth research is carried out on distribution channels and intensity, community composition, location accessibility, and atmosphere (figure 7.6).

## Distribution Channels and Intensity

Since parks and recreation is a diverse profession and encompasses the public, nonprofit, and commercial sectors, distribution channels vary widely. However, distribution channels are either direct or indirect. In **direct distribution**, a product goes directly from the producer to the consumer, whereas an **indirect distribution**

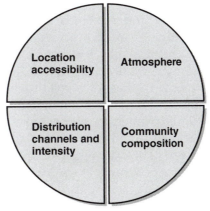

**Figure 7.6** Elements of place.

**direct distribution—** Sending products straight from the producer to the consumer.

**indirect distribution—**The means by which a product reaches the consumer; there is an intermediary entity between the producer and the consumer.

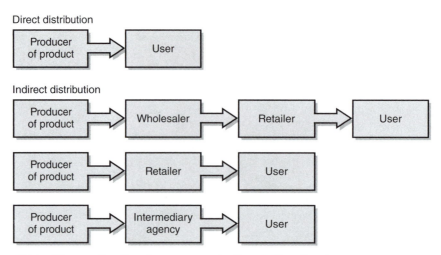

**Figure 7.7** Direct distribution versus indirect distribution.

channel has a facilitating agent between the producer and the consumer. All those involved in the distribution of products are considered channel members. The public and nonprofit sectors usually have fewer channel members and a more direct distribution route. For example, the Bloomington Parks and Recreation Department in Indiana runs a premier farmers' market on Saturday mornings. They deliver the farmers' market directly to area residents without involving any other channel members—they plan and implement the program for the community without going through any other leisure services providers or distributors (figure 7.7).

Commercial recreation agencies such as a resort will also often use a direct channel of distribution for many services, such as room nights or meeting and convention services. However, the commercial sector in particular may also use an indirect channel of distribution. This means of distribution involves wholesalers and retailers. The wholesaler serves as a broker who works for the producer to get products to retailers. For example, a sporting goods store will work with a wholesaler of Under Armour products to get the goods in the store in order to sell them to the customer. Since the products come from a wholesaler rather than directly from Under Armour, the distribution method is indirect.

Another example of indirect channels of distribution in the commercial sector occurs within resorts. Many resorts do not provide their own recreation programs and services but hire companies to do this for them. For example, the American Hospitality Academy hires recreation workers who are assigned to various resorts where they plan and implement activities and events (American Hospitality Academy 2017).

Although an indirect channel of distribution is widely used in the commercial sector, the public and nonprofit sectors use this distribution method as well. For example, Portland Parks and Recreation in Oregon offers adult basketball leagues. Because the agency owns limited gym space, the leagues use local elementary and middle school gymnasiums. In another example, the Champaign County YMCA in Illinois wanted to offer swim lessons for people with disabilities in order to meet the needs of an underserved market segment. Since the YMCA did not have staff expertise in this area, they contracted with Champaign-Urbana Special Recreation to offer programs at the YMCA. These are both examples of public and nonprofit agencies using an indirect channel of distribution as well as collaborative efforts.

In addition to the channels of distribution, there is intensity to consider within the marketing mix (figure 7.8). **Intensity of distribution** is the "relative availability

**intensity of distribution**—Number of events, programs, services, and facilities available in a community.

of a service to the consumer" (Crompton and Lamb 1986, 193). Given the nature of the recreation profession, intensity is a factor regarding both facilities and services. Facility intensity is concerned with such things as the number and location of golf courses, pools, resort rooms, and bike trails. Also of interest for many agencies is the location of facilities. Many large communities, for example, are cognizant of the need to have recreation centers in different neighborhoods, including low-income neighborhoods. Service distribution has many of the same concerns regarding the number and variety of programs offered in each location.

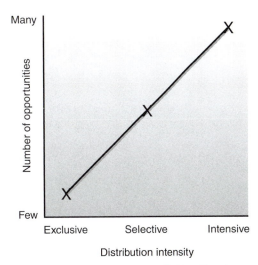

**Figure 7.8**  Intensity of distribution.

Not all service providers in the recreation profession have the same intensity of distribution. Three levels of distribution intensity are used in the leisure profession—intensive, selective, and exclusive (McCarville 2002). *Intensive distribution* "creates maximum numbers of opportunities to enjoy a program" (182). Parks and playgrounds are prime examples of intensive distribution because many communities strive to provide both within a short distance of all residents in a community. For example, Dallas Park and Recreation in Texas has 382 parks, 4,658 acres of water, and 145 miles of trails (Dallas Park and Recreation 2017).

At the other end of the spectrum is exclusive distribution, where facilities or programs are limited to a select few. An elite golf league, an ice rink, and an urban whitewater rafting facility are examples of exclusive distribution. In Dallas, the park and recreation department operates the city's only arboretum and botanical gardens.

In the middle of these two intensity levels is selective distribution. Selective distribution assumes that a program can be held at a few locations or a few sessions of a program are offered throughout the year at one or more facilities. For example, the Wisconsin Department of Natural Resources has 53 state parks distributed within its borders. Although there is not a state park in every city, there are quite a few within 45 to 60 minutes of residents (figure 7.8).

## Community Composition

Understanding the composition of the community is an important element that cannot be emphasized enough. Most communities have several neighborhoods, each with its own characteristics, people, and work and leisure activity. What goes on in a neighborhood and what is located there will have a tremendous impact on whether it is a good distribution channel. Gaining a clear picture of community composition includes breaking down the city by neighborhood and investigating

- what businesses are in the community,
- the nature of the businesses (i.e., industrial, technological, or large versus small businesses),
- overall education of the community and potential workers for the business,
- cost of living,
- economic viability and a plan to either maintain or grow economically, and
- direct and indirect competition in the area for the proposed business.

---

## Equitable Distribution of Resources

Equity of programs is a major issue in public recreation and refers to how programs, services, facilities, and other resources are distributed throughout the community. Three models of equity are used to distribute these resources (McCarville 2002).

- The compensatory model provides resources based on who needs them the most. For example, an agency may determine that more free youth programs are needed in a low-income segment of the community.

- The equal opportunity model dictates that resources are distributed equally to all residents. This would mean that neighborhood parks are distributed within a certain distance of every home in the community so everyone has access close to home.

- The market equity model provides services for those who are willing and able to pay for them. This means of distribution is most often used by the commercial sector, but it is also seen in the public and nonprofit sectors for such things as fitness memberships or aquatics facilities.

---

All of these factors set the stage for whether the proposed business will succeed or fail. For instance, a nonprofit organization whose mission is to provide services for teens from low-income, single-parent families would not choose a highly industrialized neighborhood with many high-tech businesses where the few households that are in the area belong to young, single professionals. The organization would miss its target market segment simply by choosing the wrong location. However, this same location may be well suited for a hotel that caters to business travelers.

## Location Accessibility

Location decisions for service distribution may mean finding a facility to buy and renovate, finding land on which to build a new facility, or choosing which of the current facilities to offer programs through. Regardless of the situation, several things need to be considered when addressing the accessibility of current and future locations.

Transportation is the main factor concerning location accessibility. It includes bus systems, train systems, airports, interstates, ease of traffic flow, and availability of parking. Even with the best marketing efforts, if people cannot easily get to a location, the product is bound to fail. The adage "build it and they will come" is risky at best and probably not the most sound means of addressing location.

Even within the same industry, different transportation concerns affect where a business is located. For example, Motel 6 builds properties near major highways because its customers are most likely to be driving, whereas Sheraton Hotel knows that a large portion of its guests are businesspeople, thus driving the decision to locate hotels in business districts and near airports.

Transportation barriers that hurt businesses can be physical, such as mountains, unbridged rivers, or freeways without access ramps, or they can be social, such as congested traffic, unsafe neighborhoods, or industrial areas. Agencies use several tactics to overcome these barriers. For instance, Disneyland sits directly off the Santa Ana Freeway, which allows easy access. Imagine if Disneyland were located at the end of a two-lane road! In another example, the Chicago Cubs' Wrigley Field is located on the north side of the city and has no parking deck or designated lots. The Cubs organization uses free remote parking at lots away from Wrigley Field and runs shuttles, but fans are strongly encouraged to use public transportation such as buses, trains, and shuttles from the suburbs. Although locals are used to the parking situation, it can be difficult for people from out of town.

Another important accessibility consideration is drawing radius. Drawing radius is the time and distance a person is willing to go to reach the facility. The type of facility will dictate the amount of time people are willing to spend. For example, people are willing to travel about an hour to a professional sports arena or field. That distance increases as the frequency of events decreases. Based on this idea, a season ticket holder is willing to travel farther to attend an NFL game than a season ticket holder for MLB would travel. Drawing radius is also affected by such things as emotional commitment to the players (e.g., a child playing in Little League), perception of the quality of the game, or star players playing (Mullin, Hardy, and Sutton 2014).

## Atmosphere

The last element of place involves the facility itself. The atmosphere, or the appearance of the facility and its neighborhood, can attract or eliminate potential customers. Our perception of a business is derived through the senses. Colors, brightness, smells, noise level, and shape are a few ways we use our senses to develop perceptions. A low-lit, quiet, elegant restaurant and a multicolored, bright, noisy bar are different experiences and create different expectations. Las Vegas uses light, sound, and pedestrian pathways in a very effective way that makes the Las Vegas Strip unique.

Using these sensory elements together can create the desired image of a facility. For example, the Champaign Park District in Illinois renovated a historic post office in the downtown area. The purpose of the Springer Cultural Center was twofold: To provide a place for art programs to reach a specific target market and to offer a variety of general preschool and youth programs. These two program types were sometimes in conflict in terms of image. To remedy this problem, the top floor of the building was set aside for art programs and was decorated formally with off-white walls, cool colors (i.e., blues and grays) on the floors and furniture, dark wood trim and flooring, and professional artwork on the walls. This floor was fairly quiet even with a large number of people in the building. The bottom floor became the youth floor and was painted with primary colors. It had tile floors for easy cleanup and smelled of tempera paint, clay, and many other things associated with high-energy children's programs. This noisy, fun floor was quite a contrast to the one above it simply because of its atmosphere. The atmosphere of each floor created the image desired by the park district.

# Pricing

The third *P*, pricing, is the total value assigned to a product and is a major factor in purchasing decisions. It is the only element of the marketing mix that brings in revenue, yet it is the least understood aspect of the mix. When thinking about price, most of us only think about the dollar amounts, or monetary costs of the price. Pricing is far more complex than simply assigning a dollar amount to a product or service. In addition to monetary price, recreation products have opportunity, effort, and psychological costs that make up the total value of products and influence the marketing mix (Brayley and McLean 2008).

Monetary costs are the typical costs associated with a product. Let's use an Indianapolis Colts football game as an example. The direct monetary costs for attending the game include the game ticket, parking fees, a Colts sweatshirt to show fan loyalty, and visits to the concession stand. There are also indirect costs such as gas to get to the game and a babysitter for the children at home. All of these things require an exchange of actual money. Furthermore, opportunity costs also exist. In other words, what is the fan giving up in order to attend the game? For students, it may mean time studying or working on a project or time away from family. For parents, it may mean missing their child's soccer game.

Effort is also a cost to consider, including physical energy expended, logistics of participation, and commitment. Effort costs for Colts games may be high if the game is sold out and tickets are difficult to get, if personal schedules need to be arranged, or if it is hard to find someone to attend the game with. In terms of effort costs and commitment, attending a game requires a large time and resource commitment. If the Colts fan is a season-ticket holder, considerable time and money are given to the team in comparison to attending just one game.

The last aspect of cost is psychological. Psychological aspects can be both positive and negative and may include how much fun the game will be, uncertainty of whether the Colts will win or lose, and embarrassment if they lose by a wide margin. For a volleyball league or fitness program, another psychological cost may be that the person experiences low self-esteem or feels they lack the skill needed to participate in activities such as these.

These four cost elements make pricing quite complex. Remember that the definition of marketing is creating an exchange to satisfy wants and needs. Before Colts fans will commit to buying the ticket and going to the game, they need to think about whether the game experience will outweigh all of the costs. That is where marketing comes in. Effective marketing helps a potential customer see the value of the product, eases participation through such things as distribution, and communicates how the product meets the needs of the consumer, thus helping the consumer decide to make the purchase. Knowing the costs associated with a product and realizing how few of them are strictly money driven aids in understanding how instrumental pricing is to the marketing mix. Other aspects of pricing include the psychology of pricing and changing prices.

**Psychology of Pricing** Psychological aspects of pricing move beyond the economics of setting a price and cost recovery; they appeal to emotions more than logic. The psychology of pricing focuses on how people respond to set prices, and is key to understanding where to set prices. In chapter 11, you will learn how to set prices from a loss, breakeven, and profit perspective. The psychological aspect moves beyond this to consider where products are priced so that people are more likely to buy them. One of the most important aspects of the psychology of pricing is the reference price—the price the consumer thinks that something should be. There is a range within the reference price that people find acceptable. If the price of a service is within that range (or even increased within that range), the individual is willing to make the purchase. If the price falls below the reference price, people will perceive the item to be inexpensive. If it falls too far below the reference price, there is risk that the item is seen as being cheap or of poor quality. Items priced above the acceptance zone can cause consumers to refuse to make the purchase. Consumers are more sensitive to prices above the acceptance zone than they are below it. There are several things that can expand the acceptance zone for products and services. For example, the acceptance zone is increased for higher priced items more than for lower priced ones; the more discretionary income a person has, the more they expand the acceptance zone; and those loyal to a program, facility, or instructor better accept price increases (Crompton 2015).

Dr. John Crompton (2015, 2016) is considered to be a leading expert on pricing within leisure services management. His research offers practitioners helpful ideas about establishing prices. Here are a few examples:

- *Price–quality relationship.* Consumers establish a price–quality relationship where they perceive price as equal to value. In other words, a more expensive service may appear to be better. For example, in searching for a hotel room in San Francisco, a $50 room and a $250 room are found to be available. Right away, most travelers would doubt the quality of a $50 room in a major city, and they would assume that the $250 room offers many amenities.

- *Odd number pricing.* Products ending in the digit nine are seen as being less expensive than those ending in a five or zero. A product priced at $19.99 is perceived as more attractive than if it were priced at the rounded-up $20. Even though the price difference is minute, people perceive it as a greater difference than it actually is. This is why stores rarely price products at even dollar amounts; they price just below the rounded-up price. This slightly lower price results in increased revenue because of the odd/even pricing phenomenon.

- *Bundling services.* Consider bundling services and presenting packages to consumers. For example, if you are planning a trip designated for adults, having an all-inclusive package and a flat price is more palatable than establishing a price for transportation and hotel and then additional add-ons for food and activities.

- *Electronic payments.* Set up options to pay with a credit card, monthly bank draft, or other electronic means. These methods of payments cause less angst for people than parting with actual cash. They are more willing to purchase if they do not have the actual cash outlay.

- *Annual fee options.* Annual fees for services such as after-school care or a health club can be placed on payment plans, such as one payment per year, two payments per year, quarterly, or monthly. Those paying monthly have a tendency to use the service more than those selecting other payment options because they see their monthly investment more frequently and want the benefits of it.

- *Ticket booklets.* If people buy season tickets and receive each individual ticket in a booklet or bundle, they are more likely to attend more events than if they are given one pass or ticket to use at all events.

- *Enterprise fund effect.* The enterprise fund effect suggests that people are more supportive of price increases if they see the increased revenue being used toward the service they are paying for. For example, if a round of golf is increased from $30 to $40, people are more accepting of the $10 price increase if they see that it is being used to improve the quality of the greens. These are seen as direct benefits to the user.

- *Positive price differentials.* Frame price differentials positively rather than negatively when listing different fees. For example, rather than pricing 18 holes of golf as $50 for residents and $75 for nonresidents, say that 18 holes cost $75 and residents receive a $25 discount.

- *Promotional pricing.* Use promotional pricing carefully so as not to reestablish an individual reference price to the discounted rate. Discounts should be short, temporary, and infrequent so that the price stays in short-term memory and does not become the new reference price.

The sport industry has been quite cutting edge in studying price, especially in terms of tickets. A couple of examples of pricing strategies in sport include:

- *Dynamic pricing.* A relatively new pricing strategy in sport, dynamic pricing dictates the ticket prices will change on a daily or hourly basis. If a team is hot, then ticket prices will go up to capitalize on the demand. Of course, dynamic pricing can backfire if a team is not doing well, and demand drops significantly. This means that ticket prices must decrease to a point below what a ticket would be set at in the beginning of the season.

- *Premium pricing.* Consider premium pricing for products or events that will sell out quickly. Price key games higher, such as MLB opening day or Cubs versus Cardinals rivalry games. This also works in the arts. For example, Broadway can increase ticket prices for a new show with a big name such as Bette Midler, and then drop the price once a lesser-known actor takes on the lead role (Mullin, Hardy, and Sutton 2014).

**Changing Prices**  Rarely will a price remain the same throughout the entire life cycle of a product. Adjustments will be made, most likely to increase the price. Keep in mind that the reference price is the cornerstone of price changes. Increasing prices is a difficult decision to make. It is tricky to know if the increased revenue will offset the customers lost due to price increases. However, careful marketing can reduce the number of lost customers and enable people to more easily adjust their acceptance zone. Crompton (2015, 2016) suggests a few ways to make price increases more acceptable to leisure services consumers:

- *Benefits approach.* Explain the details and benefits of the program and the reasons for the change. Let's say the after-school program at the city park and recreation department decides to raise its price from $60 per month to $80 per month. In order to help parents understand the price increase, the program supervisor can show that the new price is $2 per program hour, with which children get quality staff trained in recreation leadership, a daily snack, a monthly field trip, and daily education and recreation activities. Without the price increase, the snack, field trip, and two leaders would be eliminated from the program.

- *Program comparisons.* A different approach with the same program is to compare the after-school program with others like it. For example, the park and recreation department can compare its after-school program to those offered at the YMCA and the private sport complex in town. This comparison should highlight the advantages of the after-school program of the park and recreation department.

- *Discounts vs. lower fees.* Many public and nonprofit leisure services agencies have a tendency to keep prices low so that low-income customers can afford services. Rather than keeping prices low for a group of people, set prices where they need to be and offer discounts to those who need the financial assistance.

- *Price and image congruency.* Set prices so that they are consistent with other services within the organization. For example, an $8 piece of cheesecake at McDonald's would probably not see many purchases, but the same piece of cheesecake at a high-end restaurant at the same price would be quite acceptable. McDonald's is known for its low-cost meals, and an $8 item is inconsistent with the rest of its menu options.

• *Reduce services.* When it is difficult to change a price, agencies may reduce the services provided or quantity of the product to reduce costs. This was first labeled as "candy bar pricing" (Blinder et al. 1998) where candy bar companies wanted to keep the same price, so they reduced the size of the bar but continued to use the same sized package to make consumers think they were getting the same thing they always had.

Given the different aspects of actual costs, psychology of pricing, and price change strategies, it is easy to see why pricing is so complex and a major factor in marketing. It is never easy to align all of these factors and set a price that entices consumption of a product. However, when pricing is used in conjunction with the other parts of the marketing mix, the chance of successfully marketing a product increases.

# Promotion

The last piece of the marketing mix is promotion. Although many people equate marketing and promotions, this assessment is inaccurate. **Promotion** communicates the value of the product—it is the mouthpiece of the program, so to speak.

With parks and recreation in particular, many products are actually services. As discussed, a major difference between the two is tangibility. When a tangible product is promoted, the product can be displayed in advertisements. However, a service does not have that luxury. Instead, a benefits approach is taken to make a service seem more tangible. A benefit is anything of value to a consumer, so rather than promoting a service as just a service, it should be promoted as a bundle of benefits that a consumer will receive from the service.

The NRPA and the Canadian Parks and Recreation Association (CPRA) have been at the forefront in helping leisure services professionals understand that their true product is not a swim lesson or an aerobics class but rather a bundle of attributes, characteristics, and outcomes that people get from these programs. These benefits can be likened to the outcomes component in outcomes-based management (chapter 1).

The NRPA and CPRA outline four categories of benefits—individual/personal benefits, economic benefits, social benefits, and environmental benefits (figure 7.9).

Not every program has all four types of benefits, but many have several. For example, a midnight basketball league for teens has several individual and social benefits, including increased self-esteem for players, lower vandalism rates in the city, increased skill and fitness levels for players, and an opportunity for players to interact with each other in a positive environment. A new park built within a city has a number of benefits as well, particularly economic and environmental benefits. The new park increases the property values of neighboring houses, the mature trees provide shade and reduce power bills, green space is preserved in a rapidly expanding city, and environmentally conscious products and equipment were used to build the park.

When it is time to promote an event, facility, or program, a promotions mix is used. The **promotions mix** is the means by which the organization communicates the benefits of its products. This is done through advertising, sales promotions and incentives, personal selling, and public relations. To be successful, the promotions mix should follow the AIDA approach (Mullin, Hardy, and Sutton 2014):

• Increase awareness (A)

• Attract interest (I)

• Arouse desire (D)

• Initiate action (A)

**promotion**—Communication designed to facilitate an exchange between potential consumers and an organization.

**promotions mix**—Use of advertising, sales promotions and incentives, personal selling, and publicity to communicate an exchange between potential consumers and an organization.

## Benefits Categories and Examples

**Personal and Individual Benefits**
- Fitness and wellness
- Relaxation and stress relief
- Skill building

**Social Benefits**
- Reduced loneliness
- Strong families
- New friends

**Economic Benefits**
- Preventative health
- Reduced costs of vandalism
- Increased sales revenue into a community

**Environmental Benefits**
- Conservation
- Environmental rehabilitation
- Lower energy costs

**Figure 7.9** Benefits categories and examples.

This acronym is a sequential process where the manager strives to increase awareness of products. Exchange of resources cannot happen if people do not know about the product. Once awareness exists, promotion is designed to attract interest. This phase of promotion requires more in-depth information about the product in order to develop promotions that will arouse the desire to purchase or participate. This phase will most likely focus on conveying the benefits of participation. It is hoped that people will begin to move from intent to participate to action where the actual exchange of resources takes place.

This approach leads a potential consumer from learning about a product to consumption. Different elements of the promotions mix help marketers achieve different aspects of AIDA.

### Advertising

**advertising**—Paid communication through a media outlet where the sponsor of the message is identified.

**Advertising** is any form of communication through the media that is paid for and controlled by the sponsoring agency. This means that an organization buys ad space and has control over what goes into that ad. There are many options for buying media, including television, radio, newspaper, magazines, display boards, Internet advertising, social media, and logo placement opportunities such as dasher boards on ice rinks.

Choosing which media to buy is a difficult task at best. First, consider the preferences of the target market. Find out what media they watch, read, or listen to as a group. Media preferences differ significantly by market segments. For instance, consider the differences between students and professors. Compared with professors, students are more likely to read the university paper than the local paper. Professors are more likely to watch the evening news than students, and students are more likely to pay attention to chalked sidewalks and flyers hanging around campus or the latest social media trend.

Second, the type of product dictates what type of media to buy. Some products are better suited for certain types of media. For a new luxury resort, a luxury travel magazine might be a good option if the advertisements are targeted to the right groups. A local bar advertising a band playing on a Friday night would choose media that best reflect the activity, such as flyers on campus, radio ads, or social media.

Cost is also a media determinant and the one that may be the most influential for park and recreation agencies. Television ads can be expensive, whereas radio and newspaper ads may be more affordable. This is not to say that television would be prohibitive for public and nonprofit agencies; there are deals and less expensive ads that may be perfect for a certain target market. However, the price of some media and the return on that investment may be prohibitive. For example, Troy Parks and Recreation in Michigan offers Anyone Can Paint, a class for 10 adults at a cost of $24 per person. Given the product, the registration fee, and the low maximum number of participants, running advertisements on television would not be the best use of money. Instead, Troy Parks and Recreation may promote their class by creating an event on social media, allowing members of the community to share the event. This type of social media promotion is focused on consumer-to-consumer advertising, significantly reducing the cost for the agency.

The last media buying consideration is the message. If the message to be communicated is simple, then newspapers and billboards may be good options because of the limited space available and the short amount of time people can look at a billboard while driving. If the message is more complex, then radio or television might be a better option.

Let's say there is a major special event coming up. This event has been going on for years and is well known throughout the area. It would require a simple message letting people know the date and time of the event and maybe an activity or two that will be going on during the event. This simple message opens a lot of opportunities for advertising. A billboard on a major thoroughfare, posters placed around town, and carefully placed ads in the newspaper may be all that is needed to advertise the event.

However, the first year this event was held would have required far more complex advertising since it was in the introductory stages of its life cycle. Advertisements had to be more complex since more information was needed about the new event. This detailed information would not be effective on a billboard where the information people can absorb while driving by is limited. This event may have required larger, more detailed newspaper ads, as well as ads on television and radio.

## Sales Promotions and Incentives

**Sales promotions and incentives** have a financial value to the consumer and are used in the short term to stimulate awareness or lead people to participation. This type of promotion can be categorized as promotional pricing, free offers, prizes, and celebrities.

**sales promotions and incentives**— Promotion of a program or service that has a financial value to the consumer.

- *Promotional pricing.* Buy two get one free, half-off admission, family discount night, discounted entrance fees with a soda can

- *Free offers.* First lesson free, children under six free, passes for free admission

- *Prizes.* Free T-shirts, door prizes, contests, giveaways

- *Celebrities.* Local or national celebrities used as spokespersons or available at events or for autograph signings

Sales promotions and incentives are most often used to introduce new programs by offering free trials, attract new clients to programs, stimulate more frequent use through

## 2016 Top Sports Celebrity Endorsements

Sports celebrities have always been used to endorse products. Here is a list of the top 10 athletes and their total endorsements in 2016. Six of the top 10 athletes are either in golf or tennis, and it is not until number 16 on the list that there is a female athlete—Maria Sharapova, of the Women's Tennis Association, earning $20 million. Serena Williams is at number 17, also earning $20 million (Opendorse 2016).

| | |
|---|---|
| 1. Roger Federer ATP | $60 million |
| 2. LeBron James NBA | $54 million |
| 3. Phil Mickelson PGA | $50 million |
| 4. Tiger Woods PGA | $45 million |
| 5. Kevin Durant NBA | $36 million |
| 6. Rory McIlroy PGA | $35 million |
| 7. Novak Djokovic ATP | $34 million |
| 8. Rafael Nadal ATP | $32 million |
| 9. Jordan Spieth PGA | $32 million |
| 10. Cristiano Ronaldo La Liga | $32 million |

such offers as buy five and get the sixth free, and stabilize fluctuations in demand by offering discounts for off-peak times such as inexpensive indoor tennis-court time in the summer. Keep in mind that managers should be careful not to overuse sales promotions and incentives because they may lower the consumer's reference price.

### Personal Selling

**personal selling—** Use of direct, face-to-face discussions to promote a product or service.

Direct, face-to-face communication with the intention of creating an exchange is considered **personal selling**. Although many customers dislike the idea of salespeople, personal selling is an everyday part of many jobs in the leisure services industry. Some people will be involved in hard-core selling such as being a part of the sales staff at a major hotel with the job of bringing in large conferences and meetings. Other jobs in the field focus less on sales and more on providing information that leads to sales. For example, the youth sport coordinator at the YMCA may talk daily to parents whose children are interested in learning a new sport. The coordinator discusses the benefits of the program as well as details on how to register. Although it may not seem like direct selling, that is what the program coordinator is doing: using face-to-face communication with the intention of convincing the parent to register the child for the program.

### Public Relations

Public relations is designed to promote and protect the company or product image by performing five functions (Kotler and Keller 2016, 629):

- *Media relations.* Communicating positive information about the organization to the media

- *Product publicity.* Sponsoring efforts to publicize specific products
- *Corporate communications.* Promoting an understanding of the organization both externally and internally
- *Lobbying.* Dealing with legislators at the state and federal level to support or defeat legislation
- *Counseling.* Advising management about public issues and company position during good and bad times

Given these functions, **public relations** (PR) is a multifaceted form of communication for internal and external publics. Internal publics include staff, board members, and volunteers, whereas external publics include such groups as users, residents, and community members. PR has expanded its scope over the last several years. What once was considered just publicity has expanded from free exposure in the media to a more holistic effort to promote the agency in a positive light.

**public relations**— Programs and activities designed to promote and protect the company or product image.

**Media Relations**   The media play a prominent role in shaping public opinion. As such, positive **media relations** are an important part of public relations. Organizations can take three approaches to the media: the reactive approach, the proactive approach, and the interactive approach.

A reactive approach is used to respond to requests from the media for interviews, queries, and so on. In sport, this may include requests for interviews with coaches or players, photo sessions, or profiles (Mullin and Hardy 2014). A proactive approach occurs when the organization gives the media information in advance of an event or activity. In the hotel industry, for instance, if a new hotel is about to open, a press kit containing information about the property, the grand opening, and interesting amenities is sent to the media in hope of gaining publicity. An interactive approach involves developing partnerships and relationships that are mutually beneficial to the agency and the media. For example, a local park and recreation department holds a major event each summer. An interactive approach with a local radio station creates a partnership where the station promotes the event on air and then is given a role in the event with a tent on site, logos on shirts, and on-air personalities serving as MCs for the event or as judges for a contest. In this situation, both the media and the event benefit from the relationship.

**media relations** —An established relationship between an agency and the media with which the agency works.

**Product Publicity**   Product publicity involves outreach programs to the public to gain support for a product or the organization. These programs create goodwill within the community, generate publicity and media attention, and help create a positive market position for the organization. Organizations participate in community events, sponsor activities and facilities, and raise money for charities in order to be associated with a good cause. Professional sport uses community relations extremely well to generate support that can ultimately lead to ticket sales. For example, Peyton Manning, retired Denver Broncos and Indianapolis Colts quarterback, established the PeyBack Foundation to provide leadership and growth programs for at-risk children (PeyBack Foundation 2017). The WNBA Seattle Storm established Storm Cares to give back to the community that has supported them since the inception of the team. Storm Cares focuses specifically on youth development. In 2016, players and coaches attended 24 community events, provided 365 community service hours, and directly affected 4,265 youth. More than 17,000 people were reached, and more than 9,000 Storm tickets were donated. Storm Cares provides more than 350 items per year for charity auctions, holds free youth basketball clinics, and supports a long-standing summer reading program, among other programs (Storm Cares 2017).

**Corporate Communications** External and internal communication promotes understanding and acceptance of the organization. It cannot be assumed that just because people work for the company they understand what the company does or support company causes, programs, and business practices. Internal communication such as newsletters, weekly reports, or email lists serve to heighten employees' knowledge about the organization.

External public relations provides information to increase knowledge about what the company does. It is not to be confused with advertising that focuses on just one event or program. Corporate communication consists of information that is more general and addresses the branding of the organization as a whole. Communication pieces for this group may include newsletters, annual reports, brochures, social media, and informational DVDs.

**Lobbying** Our jobs as leisure services managers often require that we speak with legislators at the local, state, and federal levels. There are many pieces of legislation that affect parks and recreation, and the profession must have a voice so that important programs continue, budgets remain intact, and laws are not changed that will harm parks and recreation. For example, each year recreation managers work on behalf of the Land and Water Conservation Fund to ensure that the funding remains within the federal budget. At the local level, managers may talk with local state representatives to help them understand the impact of legislation such as the increase in the minimum wage. Effective lobbying efforts are enhanced when a relationship is built with legislators, so they begin to understand the organization and trust those who speak for it.

**Counseling** In addition to positive publicity, negative publicity can also occur. Obviously an agency would not seek negative publicity, but certain events occur that are reported in the newspaper or through other media outlets. This may include such things as a death on the river with a white-water rafting company, a staff member arrested on child pornography charges, or unsafe practices at an ice rink. Agencies must learn to deal with these situations and be as proactive as possible in dealing with the media. Carefully handling these situations can help the market position and branding remain intact.

## Promotions Plan

The promotions mix is complex and must be planned out thoroughly in order to best utilize the resources available. Not all programs, events, and attractions will be promoted in the same way since they have different target markets, have different message needs, and are at different places in the life cycle. A well-thought-out promotions campaign can go a long way in ensuring a successful product, especially if that plan follows the AIDA approach using a balanced mix of promotions to move the consumer from awareness to action.

For example, let's say you are running a special event: the world's largest musical chairs fund-raiser. A minimum of 5,000 people will play musical chairs over 24 hours to raise money for a local playground for people with disabilities.

The objectives of the event are as follows:

- Attract 5,000 players and 200 volunteers to the event.
- Attract community members to watch the game as well as enjoy other entertainment and activities at the event.

Table 7.2 demonstrates how an event can use the promotions mix to create awareness.

**Table 7.2**  Sample Promotions Plan

| Promotions Mix | Weeks from Event | Task | Budget |
|---|---|---|---|
| Personal selling | 1–16 | Planning committee presentations to local service clubs, major employers, fraternities and sororities, and university service clubs | — |
| Publicity | 8 | News releases to area newspapers announcing the event | — |
| | 8 | Public service announcements to area television and radio stations announcing the event | — |
| | 1 | News releases to area newspapers announcing event setup and arrival of 5,000 chairs for a photo opportunity | — |
| | 1 | Public service announcements to area television and radio stations announcing event setup and arrival of 5,000 chairs for coverage | — |
| | 1 | Chalked sidewalks at the university | $10 |
| Sales promotions and incentives | — | T-shirt giveaways to first 500 game participants | $5,000 |
| | — | T-shirts to all volunteers | $2,000 |
| | — | Two airline tickets to the game winner | $600 |
| | <1 | Local celebrity chairs the game to start the event | — |
| Advertising | 4 | Billboards | $2,000 |
| | 4 | Bus boards | $2,000 |
| | 8 | Flyers | $100 |
| | 6 | Posters | $300 |
| | 6 | Radio ads | $2,000 |
| | 6 | Newspaper ads | $2,000 |
| | 6 | Television ads | $4,000 |

Programming note: This promotions mix is budgeted at more than $17,000. Since this event is a fund-raiser, sponsors would most likely be used to offset a portion of these costs.

# SOCIAL MEDIA

Social media offers ways of communicating electronically to share information, ideas, beliefs, and created content. Social media gives organizations a new outlet to build relationships with their target market while also providing a space for consumer-to-consumer communication to take place. Social media incorporates advertising, public relations, and media relations. This requires an understanding of all of these aspects of marketing to effectively use social media as a marketing tool.

## Social Media Presence

A presence on social media sites is critical as many people turn to social media for information about products and services offered. A presence requires more than just presenting information. Social media presence will include three elements: engagement, information, and sales.

- *Engagement.* Social media opens up a channel of communication that does not always focus on promoting a product or service, but instead promotes the brand as a whole and the brand identity. Social media managers will be faced with the task of creating a social media personality that is unique but also aligns with the brand or agency's overall identity. Engagement on social media may not be about anything specific to the agency but focuses on the bonding between consumer and brand. A social media post asking members of a community what their favorite summertime park activity is will engage people with the brand in a more personal manner than a post promoting soccer practices, or a billboard on the side of a highway about a new product.

- *Information.* Social media allows information that may normally be shared in a program brochure or flyer to be shared instantly, without the cost that comes from printing. Not only does posting on a social media platform eliminate cost, it makes it easier for users to share the information with the people who follow them. A post may contain information about a service being offered by a park and recreation agency, which incorporates sales into the message.

- *Sales.* Promotion of goods and services takes place on social media, as seen above. This happens in two main ways: general posts and advertisements through the platform. General posts fall under engagement and information as well. Every post made on a platform is promoting the agency being represented, which is why each message that goes out needs to be crafted to the target audience. Many platforms have ways of allowing brands to create advertisements to be posted throughout the site. Social media ads are a great example of this. A business can craft a message, select a target audience, and create a budget where the agency pays per click, expediting the process of a traditional newspaper, radio, or television advertisement.

## Consumer-to-Consumer Communication

Social media is inherently social, meaning people interact with each other on different platforms. This aspect of social media is a mixture of marketing/public relations and customer service as customers have the ability to speak out about an experience they have had with a brand, opening a door to discussion.

If a customer had a positive experience at a golf lesson, she could post a review on the agency's social media page. This review can spark a conversation on the page about other peoples' experiences, different golf instructors, and golf in general. Managers need to be prepared to interact with customers on social media, especially those who comment negatively about their experience. These interactions appear to be customer service, but since they are on a public site for others to see, these interactions also fall under public relations. Plans must be in place to handle positive and negative discussions happening in an online sphere.

Social media can be an inventive and useful tool in the world of marketing if used effectively. The goal of social media is to create relationships, share information, and promote goods and services along with the brand as a whole. To do this effectively, it may take time to learn how your target audience interacts with your social media pages. Changing how messages are presented, the time of day posts go out, incorporating appropriate images, and how you interact with consumers are all aspects that may need to be adjusted based on who follows your brand. Social media managers must be prepared to actively follow and monitor social media to bring this tool to its optimal potential.

 Check out the web study guide for additional material, including learning activities, sample documents, interactive case studies, web links, CPRP exam connections, and more.

# Conclusion

Marketing is the purposeful planning and execution of the pricing, place, and promotion of ideas, goods, and services to create an exchange of time and resources that results in the satisfaction of individual needs and organizational objectives. Marketing is far more complicated than running an advertisement in the local paper or creating a flyer to hand out. It involves developing programs for the target market, making complex distribution decisions, setting prices, and establishing the right promotions mix to attract people.

Marketing is not just for the commercial sector. It is an important part of any organization and requires managers who are knowledgeable in marketing principles. A well-developed marketing plan will enable the agency to see the big picture of how resources for marketing efforts are being used. Knowledge of marketing also allows managers to market their own programs or work cooperatively with a marketing staff.

# Review Questions

1. Describe how marketing has changed from the Industrial Revolution to today.
2. Discuss the differences between market segmentation and target marketing. Why should managers care about these concepts?
3. Explain the various ways to segment a market.
4. What is the difference between a product and a service?
5. Define the marketing mix and how each component can be used to market a product or service in recreation.
6. Describe the steps of the product life cycle. What strategies can extend the product in the decline stage?
7. Differentiate among the three levels of distribution intensity. Use an example not included in the book to explain each level.
8. Explain the promotions mix and give examples of each element.
9. Describe social media and how it fits into marketing.

# 8

# Communication and Customers

## Learning Outcomes

- Explain what communication is and why it is a critical competency for leisure services managers.

- Understand the process of communication and be able to identify potential communication breakdowns.

- Apply the various uses for communication, including management communication (internal), marketing communication (internal and external), and positioning and repositioning strategies (external).

## Key Terms

communication, encoding, communication channels, decoding, feedback, communication noise, external noise, internal noise, external–internal noise, sociocultural noise, downward communication, rumors, upward communication, horizontal communication, informal communication, grapevines, social networks, crisis, external communication, persuasion, information richness, dynamic websites, positioning, repositioning

## Competency Check

Refer to table 1.6 to see how you assessed these related competencies.

   6. Clearly communicate with staff, customers, and the public.

   7. Possess effective written and oral communication skills.

   36. Network within and outside the profession.

## A Day in the Life

I am the associate athletic director for event management at the University of New Hampshire. No two days are the same in this line of work. During the week I spend a majority of my time preparing for upcoming games. This includes scheduling staff and officials, communication with other agencies on and off campus—such as transportation, facilities, housekeeping, and emergency services—in addition to supporting the coaches of the sports programs I work with. On game days, I typically arrive several hours before the game to prepare the facility. This is generally followed by greeting visiting teams and officials upon arrival, and checking game-day staff and instructing them on their roles and responsibilities. As the game administrator, once the game has begun I am responsible for any issues that arise such as weather delays, customer service concerns, or other problems that may affect play of the game. My favorite part of my job is working with and cheering on our student-athletes.

Kate McAfee
Associate Athletic Director, Event Management
University of New Hampshire
Durham, New Hampshire

Communication is a critical competency for leisure services managers. Successful communication can provide information, coordinate efforts, motivate employees, educate customers, and express organizational values. Communication is about more than just talking. It is an ongoing, dynamic process that involves multiple levels of action, including strategy, message design, message delivery, interpretation, and response. Communication is also about exchange. It is a give-and-take-and-give relationship shaped by the dynamics of the shared process. It is difficult to underestimate the importance of effective communication for leisure services managers; most studies of organizational behavior rate communication as the key competency of effective management. This chapter focuses on the processes of communication and how managers communicate effectively.

# FUNCTIONS OF COMMUNICATION

**Communication** is the process of exchanging information between people or groups to achieve mutual understanding (George and Jones 2011). Two distinct functions underlie the communication process: conveying information and achieving mutual understanding. Merely conveying information is not enough. To communicate effectively, the parties involved in the communication process must understand the information that is conveyed. When information is misunderstood or misinterpreted, the communication process breaks down.

**communication**— The process of exchanging information between people or groups to achieve mutual understanding.

## Conveying Information

Suppose a leisure services organization has a distinct dress code for all frontline service employees—khaki pants and a staff polo shirt with the logo of the organization on the front. Let's also suppose that the organization makes all new employees aware of the dress code as a component of orientation and provides written information on the dress code in an employee handbook. In this case, the organization has informed employees of certain standards through both verbal and written forms. On the surface, communication appears to be a one-way process—the organization is conveying information to new employees. Although conveying information is important, the communication process must go further in order to be effective.

## Achieving Mutual Understanding

Deeper examination of the previous example shows a more dynamic process at work. The employees receive the message about the dress code by attending the orientation session, reading the handbook, and interpreting the messages that they contain. Let us assume that they respond to the request by asking questions about the policy, and they receive clarification from their manager on the importance of a unified agency image for good external communication. The new employees demonstrate their understanding of the message through their compliance with the standards. In this case, the communication process has achieved mutual understanding—a true exchange, or a two-way relationship. This is the second function and the critical component of effective communication. This simple example demonstrates how the basic communication process works. It is both a process of conveying information and arriving at a mutual understanding.

# COMMUNICATION PROCESS

Communication is an active process. It requires individuals and groups to make sense of information and to respond to this information. Communication is also a dynamic process. Effective communicators often adapt their message or delivery to achieve the understanding that they seek. Consider the example of the dress code. Suppose that the new employees did not comply with the various standards that the organization had outlined in orientation and in the employee handbook. Communication occurred, but the results did not yield mutual understanding. The organization would need to examine its communication process, including the message, the delivery of the message, and other factors that may have prevented mutual understanding.

**encoding**—Turning ideas into written or spoken words and communicating information through the use of signs, symbols, or images.

The active and dynamic nature of the communication process often confuses managers. The organization might be convinced that it clearly communicated the dress code and why it was important. How could such plainly spoken and written words not be understood? Understanding the communication process requires breaking down and analyzing the various layers of the process. The communication process involves senders and audiences, and it includes message design, message delivery, message interpretation, and feedback mechanisms.

The communication process (figure 8.1) starts with senders, the individuals or groups who begin the communication process. They take the information they intend to convey and encode it by finding ways to make it easy to understand. **Encoding** can involve turning ideas into written or spoken words, or it can involve representing information through the use of other signs, symbols, or images. Senders also need to deliver the information through an appropriate communication channel. **Communication channels** can involve personal contact, such as presentations, orientations, training, and one-on-one conversations; they can involve print media, such as an employee handbook; or they can involve broadcast media, such as radio, television, email, and other electronic forms of communication.

**communication channels**—Methods for delivering messages, including personal contact or print, broadcast, or electronic mediums.

**decoding**—The process of interpreting a message; how the audience makes sense of the signs, symbols, or images associated with a message.

After the message is received, audiences must decode the information. The **decoding** process focuses on how the message is interpreted, or how the audience makes sense of the signs, symbols, and images associated with the message. After the message is decoded, the audience responds to the message via **feedback**, or providing information and message evaluation to the sender. The feedback process demonstrates the dynamic nature of communication. If the audience does not respond in the manner intended, the sender must evaluate the message strategy. Perhaps the initial message design was encoded inappropriately or the communication channels were inadequate in reaching the intended audience. The audience reaction to the message conveys valuable information to the sender. Managers who ignore the two-way nature of communication miss important information that can be used to refine existing messages or craft new ones.

**feedback**—A dynamic process of providing information and message evaluation back to a sender.

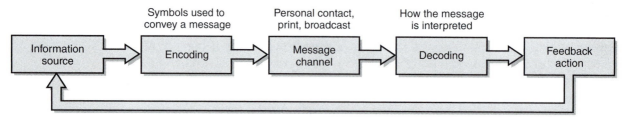

**Figure 8.1** Communication process.

# COMMUNICATION BREAKDOWNS

Sometimes communication breaks down despite our best efforts. Messages go unheard or get misinterpreted. Think of the game Telephone, where a message is whispered to one person, who then whispers the message to the next person. This sequence repeats itself over and over, and the last person who receives the message must repeat it to the group. Invariably, the final message gets distorted to such an extent that it is unrecognizable from the original message. This game gives us insight into how messages get distorted. Recognizing the sources of **communication noise**—the internal and external factors that affect the communication process—can help managers craft communication strategies to minimize message distortion.

**communication noise**—The internal and external factors that affect the communication process.

## External Noise

A number of external distractions can interfere with the communication process. For example, when playing the game of Telephone, perhaps an actual telephone was ringing while the initial message was being delivered, or perhaps the person who was delivering the message had a thick accent and was difficult to understand. Factors that interfere with the interpretation of the message and are external to the intended audience are **external noise**. Managers should be especially careful when communicating in the presence of external noise. For example, managers should be aware of their surroundings when giving instructions or feedback to employees. Providing information in a busy work environment with several other distractions might lead to misinterpretation or misunderstanding not because of the message itself, but because of the manner and context in which the message was communicated.

**external noise**—Factors that interfere with the interpretation of a communicated message and are external to the intended audience.

## Internal Noise

Internal distractions are also responsible for misinterpretation. **Internal noise** refers to those factors that are internal to the message recipient that cause misunderstanding. For example, an employee who is under considerable stress, such as an illness in the family or a sudden change in a child care schedule, might not be in the best position to receive a message regarding job performance. Managers should consider the timing of a message to allow it to resonate and have the most positive impact on the receiver.

**internal noise**—Factors that are internal to the message recipient and cause misunderstanding.

Multiple methods of communication can be helpful in minimizing internal noise. Written communication may be misinterpreted because an employee might focus on certain parts of the message to the exclusion of others. For example, an employee might focus only on the positives of a written performance review and minimize or disregard the manager's concerns. Combining a written review with face-to-face contact can help a manager reinforce the key components of the message, and it can allow for personal feedback to ensure that the message was properly received.

## External–Internal Noise

**External–internal noise** refers to miscommunication that occurs due to the social context in which a message is delivered, or how external factors affect internal interpretations of a message (Hersey, Blanchard, and Johnson 2012). The social context in which a message is delivered can amplify, blunt, or fundamentally alter a message. Consider the employee dress code discussed earlier in the chapter. The organization may have felt that it clearly communicated the dress code in both the

**external–internal noise**—Miscommunication that occurs because of the social context in which a message is delivered; how external factors can affect internal interpretations of a message.

orientation process and the employee handbook. However, perhaps veteran employees suggested to their rookie counterparts that although the dress code is official policy, it is rarely enforced. This might alter the new employees' perception of the message and its importance. Managers must be aware of the social context and culture of the organization when attempting to communicate with employees because messages are often interpreted by the larger group as well as the individual employee.

## Sociocultural Noise

**sociocultural noise**—
Miscommunication that occurs due to differences in cultural interpretations of communication strategy.

Many times noise comes from the message itself. **Sociocultural noise** sometimes occurs because of cultural misunderstandings. For instance, an organization that tries to engage in team building by adopting certain Native American symbols and terminology might have a specific communication strategy in mind, but that strategy might be lost on team members who view the use of such imagery as offensive (George and Jones 2011). The meaning of events is often misinterpreted because of the loose coupling between activity and meaning (Bolman and Deal 2013). People have different perceptions and are likely to assign different meanings to the same events. A manager who holds a staff picnic on a weekend might intend to build esprit de corps, yet an overworked staff might interpret this message as an infringement on valuable weekend family time.

## Language Choices

Finally, language choices such as the specific words or phrases that are used to represent ideas are sometimes vague and open to multiple meanings. When a city manager talks about accountability, what does that mean? When the governor tells the state parks director that the system needs to be more efficient, how should that efficiency be interpreted? When a campus recreation director talks about organizational effectiveness, how should that effectiveness be measured? Each of these terms—accountability, efficiency, and effectiveness—has multiple meanings and can be interpreted in many ways. After all, efficiency can mean cutting staff, or it can mean using less paper in the office. Using specific, descriptive language that is commonly understood is critical for effective communication. Developing shared understanding with employees and constituencies about what words mean, such as clearly defining what efficiency, effectiveness, or accountability mean within the context of your organization, can reduce confusion and misinterpretation.

## STRATEGIC APPROACH TO COMMUNICATION

A strategic approach to communication can reduce the impact of noise and facilitate an exchange of information that develops mutual understanding. Managers can employ this strategic approach to communication by doing the following:

- Identifying the intended audience
- Understanding the needs and information capacity of the audience
- Encoding information in a way that is as clear and unambiguous as possible
- Choosing communication channels likely to be effective in distributing and reinforcing the message
- Surveying the communication landscape to determine whether the message has been adequately received

- Developing a system for multiple levels of feedback
- Adjusting, reinforcing, or changing the message accordingly

Ultimately, avoiding noise is about creating a good feedback system. At its simplest, good communication comes from recognizing that communication is an active, dynamic, multiparty process. Communication should also be multidirectional—it should be an upward, downward, and horizontal process. Renowned management scholar Peter Drucker once said, "The harder the superior tries to say something to his subordinate, the more likely is it that the subordinate will mishear. He will hear what he expects to hear rather than what is being said" (2001, 214). The functions of communication include opportunities for multiparty dialogue and feedback. Effective communication aimed at both internal and external customers must be an ongoing, dynamic process.

## Downward Communication

Providing information to employees is typically accomplished through **downward communication**, characterized by the movement of information from superior to subordinate on an organizational chart. One strength of downward communication is that it allows organizations to convey information that is important for employees and constituents to know. Organizations control the flow of information in this system, so messages are often carefully disseminated to serve particular strategic goals. Ultimately, all forms of communication should enhance organizational effectiveness. Downward communication that is clear, concise, synthesized, and easily understood can help organizations achieve message consistency and keep employees and constituents on the same page.

> **downward communication**—The movement of information from superior to subordinate on an organizational chart; used to convey information.

Certain difficulties are associated with this method of communication, however. In this system, employees are placed in passive roles as recipients of information. They may not have access to complete information, and they may feel as if they are lacking some of the information they need to do their jobs effectively.

In the bigger picture, employees want to know that what they are doing in their jobs is contributing to a larger goal of organizational effectiveness—in other words, that they are making a difference. Employees may need access to a wide range of information to be able to see how they fit within the larger organizational system. In his book *Stewardship*, Peter Block (2013) suggests that all employees should have access to information related to how they, their unit, and their organization are doing. They need to be connected to the larger organizational system in order to effectively contribute to it. Imperfect or incomplete information can lead to **rumors**, or unofficial information that is often distorted, inaccurate, or damaging to people or the organization.

> **rumors**—Unofficial information that is often distorted, inaccurate, or damaging to individuals or the organization.

In many cases, managers have access to a tremendous amount of information relating to organizational practices. As you may recall from chapter 1, Peter Senge developed the concept of the learning organization. Adequate information flow is critical for organizational learning. That said, managers are often bombarded with so much information that paying attention to all of it would waste time, create inefficiencies, and lead to confusion. Rather than overloading employees, managers need to be able to organize and synthesize this vast amount of information and communicate it in a way that sheds light on important issues. Determining what information is important for employees to have in order to do their jobs effectively and to help groups or teams develop shared understanding is a key competency of effective communicators (Senge 1994).

Senge is not suggesting that managers withhold information or engage in situational communication; rather, they should decide which variables enable employees to contribute to effectiveness and which ones just contribute to noise and distract employees from their intended goals. Part of the manager's role is to be a monitor, and monitoring information flows is not in itself bad for the organization (Hersey, Blanchard, and Johnson 2012). Managers must exercise judgment in this area since any information that is withheld can lead to confusion, disconnect, or rumors. Thinking about how information can help employees do their jobs more effectively, communicate with customers, and connect to the larger goals of the organization can be useful when attempting to organize and synthesize information for consumption.

## Upward Communication

**upward communication—**
The movement of information from subordinate to superior on an organizational chart; helps to create shared values.

Whereas downward communication is effective for conveying information to subordinates, **upward communication** allows for information to go up from subordinate to superior. Strong upward communication systems help to build shared values. The basic idea behind upward communication is that there is a considerable distance both in physical and experiential terms between upper-level management and frontline or support staff. It is difficult to develop a system of shared values when there is such distance between members of an organization.

Managers can enable upward communication by providing systems that allow employees to share information, provide insights and perspectives, and give feedback on organizational goals. Upward communication needs to go beyond the employee suggestion box where employees drop their ideas into what often resembles a black hole—the information goes in but almost never comes back out in the form of recognition or organizational improvement. Upward communication can take place in many forms, including team meetings, task forces, network structures, and other mechanisms that allow for significant input from the people in the organization who are most affected by organizational policy or management practices.

Upward communication systems can act as a bridge and provide useful information for managers. Honesty and trust are hallmarks of this communication system; employees must trust that the manager will recognize and address information that is provided. Creating a system where employees are encouraged to speak the truth to people in positions of power is a key characteristic of upward communication. That does not necessarily mean that all upward communication will be acted upon; that still lies in the hands of the decision makers. However, a system that requests information yet does not acknowledge the information that is generated will eventually lose credibility.

## Horizontal Communication

**horizontal communication—**
The movement of information across an organizational chart between peers or managers in different organizational units.

**Horizontal communication** is communication between peers or between managers in different units. It is communication across the organizational chart. Much like upward communication, horizontal systems can be formalized through meetings, task forces, or networks (see chapter 5). The key distinction is the goal of the communication process. Horizontal communication is often used to coordinate efforts between units or individual employees and build on knowledge or resource gaps that cannot be filled without some form of cooperation.

It should be noted that downward communication systems can also be used to coordinate work processes. Providing information on employee roles, demonstrating relationships among jobs, and articulating performance standards are all types of communication that can be distributed in a downward system. However, downward systems are not as effective when units are fairly autonomous yet work processes are highly interdependent. In these cases, horizontal systems are also needed to achieve effective communication.

For example, a large municipal park and recreation department might have a facilities unit and a programming unit, both of which have their own hierarchies, supervisors, employees, and jobs. Both units perform their own job functions, yet what they do has an effect on each other. Communication needs to flow both downward (providing information on roles, scope of responsibility, reporting lines, and quality standards) and horizontally in order to effectively coordinate the efforts of various units. Poor communication could lead to the wrong facilities being prepared for a weekend soccer tournament or the destruction of outdoor facilities because games were played in inclement conditions.

Horizontal communication can also be informal. Strong working relationships can enhance the exchange of information. Conversely, managers must guard against the tendency of semiautonomous units to become insular and closed. Even within the same unit, employees may form cliques or subgroups that can become impediments to the fast and accurate transfer of information.

## Informal Communication

**Informal communication** passes unofficial information through unofficial communication channels. These systems are characterized by grapevines and social networks. **Grapevines** grow naturally, consist of diverse organizational members, and flourish in environments where there is little access to information. They pass along unofficial information such as rumors or falsehoods.

**Social networks** consist of the relationships among specific organizational members. Networks may pass along unofficial information, but they can also be used as part of an official communication strategy. For example, if the boundaries of a social network can be defined and the network consists of opinion leaders, a manager might test a message to see how it plays among employees. In this way, the manager is able to both communicate information and get feedback about how the message was received.

# INTERNAL COMMUNICATION

As noted earlier, managers must ensure that employees operate in an environment where there is ample access to information. Good internal communication is a key leadership competency. Successful communication strategies that allow information to move freely up, down, and across the organizational chart help to create and strengthen organizational culture.

Internal communication functions include

- providing, synthesizing, and organizing information,
- expressing values,
- coordinating and controlling organizational systems, and
- crisis communication.

**informal communication—** The movement of information through unofficial communication channels.

**grapevines—** Informal communication systems composed of organizational members; used to pass along unofficial information, such as rumors or falsehoods.

**social networks—** Social relationships that exist between specific organizational members; can be used to transmit both unofficial and official information.

## Providing, Synthesizing, and Organizing Information

At a basic level, employees need enough information to be able to perform their jobs effectively. For example, employees need information to understand

- how to perform job tasks,
- how job roles relate to one another,
- policies and procedures of the organization, and
- whether their performance meets organizational standards.

Such information might be communicated in a variety of ways, including orientation and training sessions, employee manuals, regularly scheduled meetings, organizational charts and other documents, and frequent performance reviews. Employees also need continual access to information to understand changes in organizational structure or practice, trends, and potential issues that might affect their ability to perform their jobs. Continual access to information can be accommodated through team meetings, written memos, email, continuing education and training, and organizational networks.

## Expressing Values

In addition to providing information, communication can help organizations define themselves. As discussed in chapter 2, values help the organization and its members know what it stands for. In large, complex organizations, clear expressions of values can assist employees in understanding how their daily tasks add to the organization. For example, a maintenance worker in a public park system needs to understand what safe, clean, accessible parks mean to the overall quality of life in the community. In this way, communication can be motivating—it can strengthen the feeling that employees are part of something bigger than themselves.

An organization communicates its values through writing, speaking, signs, symbols, and rituals. It is also important for organizations to develop a system of shared values, or values that are common to the leaders, employees, and external constituents of the organization. Creating a system of shared values requires more than downward communication. It practically begs for a system that is dynamic, provides feedback, and allows an organization to respond to changes.

## Coordinating and Controlling Organizational Systems

Communication is also used for coordinating and controlling complex organizational systems. As organizations increase in size and scope, they become more complex, and as complexity increases, the need for coordination increases. Effective communication and efficient information flow can help coordinate and control various organizational efforts. Good communication between disparate and somewhat autonomous units, for example, can increase efficiency by eliminating duplicated efforts and streamlining work processes. Communication among group members can increase access to critical information without having to rely on third parties to distribute the message. When work tasks are highly interdependent—when the work of one member or group affects the work of another member or group—communication that helps to coordinate and control efforts becomes more important (George and Jones 2011).

# Crisis Communication

An important component of communication for coordination and control is crisis management. Recreation facilities and programs can be fertile ground for crises. A **crisis** is any incident that has the potential to negatively influence public perceptions of the organization. Imagine the impact that the following crises might have on an organization:

- A lost child at a summer day camp
- A drowning incident in a public swimming pool
- The theft of money and valuables from the locker room of a commercial fitness facility
- An injury resulting from violence in a youth sport contest
- A bus accident that happens during a Special Olympics basketball team's road trip
- A major natural disaster that strikes during a group tour

The key to successful crisis communication is for the organization to immediately gather as many facts related to the incident as possible. Good management procedures in other areas of the organization can help this process immeasurably. For example, consider a bus accident that occurs during an athletic team's road trip. If the athletic organization has effective policies for team travel, including knowing itineraries, bus assignments, and schedules, it will be easier to handle difficult questions regarding the impact of the incident and who was affected.

In the immediate aftermath of a crisis, the organization should focus on fact gathering, and this focus should be clearly communicated to the media. Having a designated organizational representative clearly state that facts are being gathered and that the organization will issue a response by a certain date can help manage the critical time right after a crisis occurs. Being truthful, honest, and upfront, as well as not jumping to conclusions or offering unsupported opinions, is critical. "Don't go where you don't know" is the gold standard for crisis communication in the initial stages.

Once a crisis occurs, the organization needs to involve upper-level management, legal counsel, and the marketing or media relations team in reviewing the facts. The crisis team's responsibility is to coordinate a communication strategy and decide on a clear and consistent position related to the cause of the crisis incident. After reviewing the facts, the organization may come to the conclusion that the crisis incident was caused by any number of factors, including human or clerical errors, the use of unauthorized procedures, inadequate supervision, lack of quality control, judgment errors, or inadequate implementation of standard operating procedures (Clawson Freeo 2007).

In addition to communicating effectively to external constituents such as the media or general public, it is also important for managers to provide adequate information and instructions for their own employees to ensure that everyone in the organization is on the same page.

**crisis**—Any incident that has the potential to negatively affect the public's perceptions of the leisure services organization.

---

### Dealing with the Media in a Crisis

- Coordinate media coverage and know exactly what is being released to the media.
- Always be honest. State the facts that can be released and no more. Never speculate on the situation.
- Prepare a written statement and read it. Look for sound bites of 5 to 10 seconds that could be pulled out by the media in the editing process and take extra care to make sure these are well constructed.
- Never say "No comment." It implies guilt and dishonesty.
- Return phone calls from the media and understand that they have the right to ask questions.
- Prepare for interviews and try to anticipate what questions reporters may ask. It may be beneficial to do a mock interview with another staff member.

---

# EXTERNAL COMMUNICATION

**external communication—** Communication that is targeted primarily to external constituencies: customers, the general public, policy makers, or other stakeholders.

Communication that is targeted primarily to external constituencies, including customers, the general public, policy makers, and other stakeholders, is **external communication**. It is important to recognize the connection between internal communication and the ability of an organization to communicate with its public. Consider the previous crisis communication examples. Frontline service staff and staff with high customer contact must possess accurate and up-to-date information, be consistent in delivering message content to both users and nonusers of leisure services, and understand the scope of their positions and how far they are able to go in their communication with customers.

External communication generally comprises two areas: marketing communications and positioning and repositioning strategies. These areas are related; positioning and repositioning efforts are both components of overall marketing and communication efforts. However, each area is discussed separately in the sections that follow.

## Marketing Communication

A manager's ability to communicate effectively to external constituents can be seen as a component of marketing (see chapter 7). At the most basic level, consumption of leisure services cannot happen if a consumer does not know what services are offered, when they occur, where they take place, or why they should be important to the consumer in the first place. Marketing communication can help a leisure services organization answer those questions and encourage and direct customer behavior (Janes 2006). Effective marketing communication gets constituents to consume the leisure services offered by the organization. Communication efforts—informing, educating, persuading, reminding, and continuing contact—are designed to move constituents from stages of increased awareness through repeated initiated action.

Organizations must ensure that their external communication strategy is linked to their overall marketing efforts. A leisure services organization that invests time and energy in developing a new program targeting a new market demographic will find it difficult to get the program off the ground if inadequate information is available to customers or if customers do not readily understand its benefits. New services, distribution strategies, pricing strategies, and promotions will fail unless there is a strong communication effort to inform, educate, persuade, remind, and maintain contact with new, existing, and potential customers (Wirtz and Lovelock 2016).

## Information

At a basic level, managers need to provide information to their customers about the programs, services, and resources they provide. Without access to adequate information, customers cannot begin the consumption process. A good information campaign will provide customers and potential customers with information about the following:

- What services are available
- Where services occur
- How to access services (including registration options, transportation information, and so on)
- When services take place
- What cost, if any, is involved
- What choices and options are available
- How to follow up or obtain additional information

Research on constraints to leisure participation (or why people do not participate in leisure) often reveals that unawareness of the programs and services that are available is one of the strongest reasons given for nonparticipation. Without access to information on the services offered, consumption of those services cannot occur.

## Education

Closely related to information, a good communication strategy will educate consumers about the potential benefits of participating in leisure services. For example, cardiorespiratory activities and other types of fitness activities are often strenuous, and this can dissuade consumers of fitness services from regularly taking advantage of the opportunities available to them. A communication strategy that educates consumers about the benefits of regular physical activity can help provide a more tangible set of outcomes than the ones that they immediately experience following a difficult workout (e.g., weight control versus fatigue; cardiovascular health versus boredom). This also helps consumers more effectively evaluate the service, especially when the positive attributes of the service are not easily discernable.

Education can also be used to direct consumer behavior. For instance, it is easy to see how members of a health club who engage in the same workouts day after day might become bored with their daily fitness routines. An education campaign that directs the club members to different services that yield the same fitness results (for example, varying workouts by running on a treadmill on day 1, swimming on day 2, and taking a group fitness class on day 3) can help prevent boredom and at the same time enhance the demand for other services that the agency offers.

## Persuasion

**persuasion**—
Convincing customers to purchase or use an organization's services rather than not using them at all or using the services of a competitor.

**Persuasion** is convincing customers to purchase the services of an organization rather than not using them at all or using the services of a competitor (Wirtz and Lovelock 2016). The point of marketing communication is to convince consumers and potential consumers to use the services of a specific organization. McCarville (2002) suggests that persuasion takes place via two types of routes:

- Deliberative routes appeal to consumers' logic by providing them with sufficient information to make a sound decision about the attributes of potential services relative to their needs.
- Nondeliberative routes are less rational, more emotional, and based more on the trustworthiness of the message source than the quality of information that is provided.

It is easy to see the importance of having a frontline staff that is properly trained to provide the up-to-date information necessary to help persuade a potential consumer to take action. Frontline staff also must be able to connect with potential consumers on an emotional level because quality information by itself might not be enough. Ultimately, persuasion is about communicating the value of a service and highlighting its benefits to the customer.

## Reminders

In order to close the consumption loop and keep customers coming back, communication must remind consumers about their past experiences and encourage them to use the same services in the future. Customer assessment of the service experience is a critical component in encouraging repeat participation. Because services are intangible and often difficult for consumers to evaluate, communication efforts must provide tangible evidence that reminds consumers of their experience. For example, a women's triathlon event might contract with a photography service to take pictures of triathletes at various stages of participation, such as getting out of the water, getting off the bike, and finishing the run. They might send proofs of these pictures to participants to remind them of their experience, along with an opportunity to purchase the pictures. They might also include information related to the past event (e.g., standings, times), as well as information for future participation opportunities (e.g., save-the-date reminders, online registration information).

Leisure services organizations might also have participants formally evaluate their experience and gauge future intentions to participate. Participants in a 5K road race designed to raise money for charity may be asked to evaluate their experience and provide the following information:

- Participants' demographic profiles (age, running level, household income)
- Participants' evaluation of event organization (registration, cost, check-in, volunteers, course, prizes, sponsors, the overall event)
- How participants learned of the event
- Past participation in the event and intent to participate in the future

By analyzing the information provided by participants, the race organizers are able to modify the event to enhance the race experience. The evaluations also provided valuable market segmentation information and feedback on how the marketing message was received.

## Maintaining Contact

Marketing communication should not only remind participants of their experience, it should also include ongoing contact to help guide consumers to other services based on their past participation behavior. Social media platforms are effective means of keeping in touch with customers and potential customers. Seven out of 10 Americans use some type of social media, and social media use continues to rise for almost all sociodemographic groups (Pew Research Center 2017). Online video streaming websites can also be used to engage customers. Wilson (2016) suggests several ways that social media can be used to maintain contact with customers, including promotion, event documentation, customer engagement, and getting feedback. Table 8.1 shows the trends in social media use.

Databases can be effective tools for keeping track of past consumption patterns and providing tailored information that can directly appeal to a consumer's needs. Disaggregating data by targeting individual consumers can be advantageous because customers are generally more responsive to services that meet their specific needs. Online book retailers such as Amazon have mastered this technique by developing database software that tracks individual purchases and makes individual recommendations to customers based on past consumption. This level of sophistication need not be prohibitive for leisure services organizations. Suppose an adventure organization has a flat-water kayaking program and offers trips for beginner, intermediate, and advanced paddlers. A database containing contact information for the customers who went on the beginning kayaking trip can be harvested and personal reminders sent out with information on upcoming intermediate kayaking trips. By maintaining contact and tailoring the message based on past consumption patterns, the organization can be more effective at meeting individual consumers' needs.

## Communication Mix for Leisure Services

In many cases, leisure services organizations only rely on a few communication strategies to get their messages out to their consumers. Municipal recreation agencies in particular often rely on print messages, such as seasonal program brochures, as their primary promotional communication tactic (Tew, Havitz, and McCarville 1999). This might be an effective method for delivering certain types of messages, but employing a range of communication strategies and tactics can help extend both the reach and depth of the message.

Chapter 7 discussed the traditional promotion mix for communicating benefits to customers, including advertising, personal selling, sales promotions and incentives, and publicity. These four areas are part of a larger communication mix that

## Table 8.1 Social Media Trends

| Social Media Platform | Percent Use | Percent Growth Since 2012 |
|---|---|---|
| Facebook | 68% | +14% |
| Instagram | 28% | +19% |
| LinkedIn | 25% | +9% |
| Pinterest | 26% | +16% |
| Twitter | 25% | +8% |

Data from Pew Research Center (2017). *Social Media Fact Sheet.* Available: www.pewinternet.org /fact-sheet/social-media/.

can help drive communication strategy by highlighting a variety of strategic elements and specific communication tactics. Strategic elements of the communication mix include the following (Lovelock and Wirtz 2016):

- Advertising
- Sales promotion
- Personal communications
- Publicity and public relations
- Service delivery points
- Corporate design

Figure 8.2 suggests communication tools and tactics that can be used for the six strategic elements of the communication mix. For example, Planet Fitness, a large commercial fitness organization, uses multiple methods of communication to reach its customers. To attract new customers, the organization uses staff to help sell new memberships (personal communications), buys ad space in the local newspaper (advertising), offers discounted membership options during certain times (sales promotions and incentives), runs open houses at facilities to increase customer traffic (publicity and public relations), prints brochures (service delivery points), and communicates its mission through its corporate logos and facility design (corporate design). Each technique broadens customer recruitment efforts, and the overall communication strategy is integrated so that each technique delivers a cohesive message.

**information richness**—The breadth and depth of information that a communication method can carry and the extent to which it enables a common understanding.

Different communication choices vary in their **information richness**, or the breadth and depth of information that a communication method can carry and the extent to which it enables a common understanding (George and Jones 2011). Information richness can be plotted on a continuum from high to low. A ranking of communication media from high to low based on information richness follows:

- Face-to-face communication (frontline staff, personal selling, personal conversations)
- Personalized verbal communication (telephone, voice mail)
- Personalized written communication (letters, emails, interactive websites)
- Broadcast communication (brochures, flyers, websites)

**Face-to-Face Communication**  Face-to-face communication, such as information passed from frontline service staff to the customer, has the potential to yield a much higher level of information richness than impersonal information designed for a mass audience, such as a brochure that details available programs and services. Face-to-face communication allows for feedback and a two-way exchange of information. Both parties can ask questions and provide responses. Face-to-face communication is not particularly effective when an organization needs to communicate on a mass scale. Also, this communication method relies on staff members having access to a wide range of information so that they can respond to consumer needs and requests.

**Personalized Verbal Communication**  Personalized verbal communication, such as information that is given over the phone, can also be high in information richness. Live phone conversations provide immediate feedback, and messages can be changed or altered depending on the dynamics of the conversation. The

| Strategic Communication Element | How many of these specific tools and tactics does your organization use? What are some other examples? | Checklist |
|---|---|---|
| Advertising | Advertisements in broadcast media<br>Advertisements in print media<br>Indoor or outdoor billboards or signs<br>Advertisements in online media | |
| Sales promotion | Rebates<br>Coupons<br>Giveaways<br>Product samples | |
| Personal communication | Dedicated sales staff or personal selling<br>Social media posting<br>Database marketing<br>Telemarketing<br>Attending conferences and trade shows<br>Use of word-of-mouth marketing | |
| Publicity and public relations | Press releases<br>Special events<br>Corporate sponsorship<br>Brand coverage in online media (stories, features)<br>Brand coverage in traditional media (stories, features) | |
| Service delivery points | Websites<br>Web-based apps<br>Brochures or flyers<br>Information kiosks | |
| Corporate design | Interior design<br>Corporate signage<br>Company uniforms<br>Corporate logo | |

**Figure 8.2** A general communications mix.

major drawback of phone conversations is that they are one-dimensional—they focus solely on verbal communication. It is difficult to gauge body language or other forms of nonverbal communication, which detracts from the information richness of the medium and minimizes the personal aspect of the communication experience. Remember, persuasion can be as much about trusting the source of the information as the information itself!

Another drawback of phone conversations is again a matter of scale—most leisure services organizations do not have the resources to phone bank or telemarket. The use of automated voice-mail services solves this dilemma. For example, a college intramural sport program might post daily schedules of intramural games, including matchups, game times, and game locations, on a voice-mail system. The message can be updated based on program factors such as weather, forfeits, and other contingencies. The voice-mail system can provide up-to-the-minute information for participants, and anyone can access the system by simply dialing a phone number. In this system, the problem of scale is solved, but the feedback loop is closed—there is no way for customers to respond to an automated message, and questions about information in the message would need to be directed elsewhere. While many leisure services organizations still use voice phone technology, customers are frequently more likely to get their information through online channels, such as websites, social media, and mobile devices such as phones and tablets. Almost all Americans own cell phones of some kind and more than three-fourths of Americans own smartphones (Pew Research Center 2017). Worldwide, there are almost 5 billion mobile phone users—approximately 66 percent of the world's population (We Are Social 2017). Using mobile phone technology for both verbal and written communication has become a necessary component of communication strategy for leisure services managers.

**Personalized Written Communication**   Written information that is personally addressed allows an organization to tailor a message to the needs of a particular customer. Using databases with information on past consumption patterns can help generate personalized messages inviting customers to participate in upcoming programs or to take advantage of certain services. With a good database of information and the right technological system in place, this communication medium can be effective at reaching a large number of customers while still being perceived as a more personal form of communication than a standard brochure or flyer.

A drawback of personalized written communication is that it can be difficult for leisure services organizations to develop the sophisticated data management and tracking system that is required to generate such information. Another drawback is the lack of feedback potential, although the use of electronic and online media, such as email, social media, or dynamic websites, can provide mechanisms for immediate response to these written communication forms. **Dynamic websites** change content frequently, usually as a result of user choices and preferences. Such sites allow user feedback and permit interaction between the customer and the organization. For example, an organization might send a personal email to a parent whose child took beginning swimming lessons inviting the child to participate in upcoming intermediate swimming lessons. The email might include a link to the website of the organization and its online registration system for easy payment and sign-up.

Likewise, organizations can use social media platforms to provide links to registration portals and allow for customer engagement with social media posts, including "likes" and comments. Providing opportunities for peer-to-peer interaction and user-generated content are features of what is known as Web 2.0 technology. Wirtz and Lovelock suggest that organizations use Web 2.0 technology for various reasons: market research, reaching potential customers, creating buzz about their services, and shaping customer behavior (Wirtz and Lovelock 2016). Of course, such a system is contingent on widespread Internet access and usage patterns. Internet access has increased dramatically over the last decade. Approximately 75 percent of American adults and 83 percent of Canadian adults have access to the Internet at home (U.S. Census Bureau 2016; Statistics Canada 2012). However, racial minorities, rural residents, and those with lower levels of education and income are less likely to have Internet access, creating a digital divide between those who can benefit from such a system and those who cannot (U.S. Census Bureau 2016).

**dynamic websites**—Websites that change content frequently, usually as a result of user choices and preferences; they allow user feedback and interaction between the customer and the organization.

One further note on personal written communication—it is important that customers perceive these messages as personalized. Form letters with standardized information that only pretends to be personalized by using word-processing software to change the address field, for example, do not count as personalized written information.

**Broadcast Communication**   Broadcast communication is the lowest in information richness. This communication method relies on moving information to as many customers as possible. The advantage of broadcast communication is that an organization can communicate with a large number of constituents with relatively little effort. Most mass-media strategies fall into this category, including the use of broadcast, print, outdoor, and electronic media. In some cases, these communication media are limited by the amount of information they can contain. For example, communication through paid television, radio, or print advertisements can be cost prohibitive for many leisure services organizations, especially those operating in the public or nonprofit/voluntary sectors. Even if organizations can afford the cost, they are limited in how much information they can communicate by either time (television, radio) or space (print, outdoor media). Websites and social media platforms, however, can communicate a large amount of information at a relatively low cost. Encouraging customer engagement with an organization's online content through comment systems, shares, and likes can add a level of interactivity that also creates an opportunity for feedback.

# Positioning and Repositioning Strategies

Positioning is a component of marketing strategy, but it is critical to understand here because it helps to drive communication efforts. **Positioning** refers to the place of leisure services in the minds of stakeholders relative to their perceptions of competitors. A leisure services agency can position itself based on specific issues that are of fundamental importance to its community. These issues are often related to the larger concerns that a community faces, such as contributing to economic development or alleviating social problems (Crompton 1999). Similarly, an agency might try to position its services and facilities based on strategies that appeal to individual consumers. The set of positioning strategies (McCarville 2002) is listed here, along with corresponding communication implications:

**positioning**—The place that leisure services and programs hold in the minds of stakeholders relative to their perceptions of other services provided by competitors (Crompton 1999).

- *Attributes.* These are the characteristics of the service that are valued by the customer, such as safety, quality, perceived risk, staff competence, and so on. Communication strategies highlight the desired attributes in order to appeal to customer needs.

- *Price.* This strategy focuses on how much the service costs in relationship to competitors. Communication strategies use price as a differentiator and can be based on low-cost provision (community swimming pools) or high-cost luxury (expensive resorts).

- *Comparison with competitors.* This position focuses on services the agency provides that competitors do not. Communication strategies highlight the strengths of the service provided relative to competitors.

- *Product class.* This strategy differentiates the service from a range of other options. For example, a state beach might focus on the desirability of swimming in the ocean versus hiking in the mountains. Communication strategies highlight the differences between the services of the organization and a broad range of competing leisure opportunities.

● *User.* This positioning strategy is based on the interests and needs of particular user groups. Communication strategies demonstrate how the services meet those unique needs and interests.

● *Use-related.* This strategy focuses on how the product is consumed. Communication strategies remind customers about the reasons for their consumption. An example might include focusing on patriotism and national pride as a reason for visiting a national park over the U.S. Independence Day weekend.

Leisure services organizations must effectively communicate with both users and nonusers of their services. This is particularly true for organizations that compete for public tax dollars. Taxpayers in a city are stakeholders in the municipal park and recreation department regardless of whether they use any of its leisure services. Because some stakeholders do not use the services available to them, they are unaware of the benefits that such services provide. For example, citizens might agree that reducing traffic, providing green space, and reducing the amount of energy consumed by residents are important public priorities. However, citizens might not realize how public investment in park and recreation services can achieve these important policy objectives. By using effective communication strategies, organizations can better position their programs and services at a larger level beyond the needs of those who already use their services. In this way, positioning can demonstrate the value of a leisure services organization in relation to other community services that compete for scarce public resources.

Positioning drives communication strategy. Communication efforts should focus on the agency's most salient contributions to important community issues. This can be accomplished through the use of text or verbal descriptions, visuals (pictures, video), statistics, slogans, symbols, sponsorship alignments, and so on. The key is consistency—clearly communicating what the agency does to address the important issues facing the community. Ambiguous positions lead to an unclear organizational identity and cause an agency to get lost in the clutter of competitor organizations, programs, and services. Poorly chosen positions are also dangerous because they miss the mark in connecting with the priorities of stakeholders and do not provide stakeholders with a clear reason for supporting an agency's contribution to pressing community concerns.

## Repositioning

**repositioning—** Changing the frame of reference that stakeholders have about what an agency does and how it aligns with issues that are important to the broader constituency (Crompton 1999).

Sometimes the priorities of a community change and a leisure services organization finds itself in a poor position relative to its competitors on the key issues affecting its stakeholders. In this case, an agency might find that it needs to reposition itself. **Repositioning** means changing its stakeholders' frame of reference about what the agency does and how it aligns with issues that are important to the broader constituency (Crompton 1999). Consider the commercial bowling industry. White Hutchison, a leisure consulting firm, notes that the number of people bowling in leagues has declined by two-thirds since 1980. Traditionally, league bowlers helped to drive the industry. As times have changed and preferences have shifted, bowling alleys have had to reposition themselves as indoor recreation centers catering to families and singles. Successful businesses have repositioned themselves to cater to this shift in the marketplace by eliminating smoking, focusing on customer relations, changing the physical layout and functionality of their facilities, and promoting themselves as indoor recreation and bowling centers rather than bowling alleys. Finding ways to connect to the needs of constituents is the critical piece in this process.

Infographics can help with positioning and repositioning around important constituent needs. Infographics provide information in a visual format in order to convey a message quickly and easily. The National Recreation and Park Association has an infographics library that allows recreation managers to quickly share information with key stakeholders regarding the importance of parks and recreation for individuals and communities (National Recreation and Park Association 2018). Other areas of the leisure services field such as tourism, event management, youth development, outdoor recreation, and recreational therapy have also developed infographics to share important messages about their scope and value. Figure 8.3 shows an example of an infographic related to outdoor recreation priorities in the state of New Hampshire.

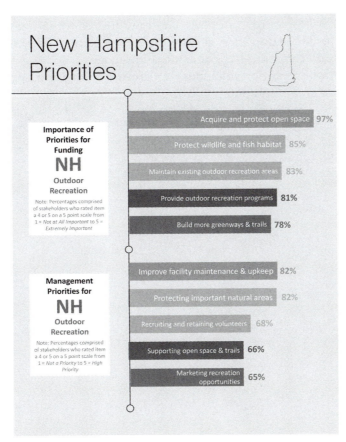

**Figure 8.3** Outdoor recreation priorities in New Hampshire.

Check out the web study guide for additional material, including learning activities, sample documents, interactive case studies, web links, CPRP exam connections, and more.

# Conclusion

Communication is a critical competency for leisure services managers. The ultimate aims of communication are to convey information and achieve mutual understanding. Managers must engage in internal communication within their agency, crafting strategies to communicate with superiors, other managers and organizational units, and staff. Good communication strategies are active and dynamic; they provide feedback and minimize noise. Communication should occur downward, upward, and horizontally within an organization depending on whether the communication is providing information, expressing values, or coordinating and controlling organizational practices.

External communication includes informing, educating, persuading, and reminding consumers and potential consumers about the services that the organization provides. External communication strategies are also designed to position and reposition leisure services in the minds of users and nonusers.

# Review Questions

1. What is communication? Why is effective communication one of the key competencies for leisure services managers?

2. Describe how effective communication works using the communication process model.

3. What are some examples of external, internal, external–internal, and sociocultural noise? How might these examples change or alter the communication process?

4. What are the strengths and weaknesses of downward, upward, and horizontal communication for leisure services managers?

5. Provide an example of how a manager might use informal communication channels (such as social networks) to help amplify an official organizational message.

6. What are some examples of crises in leisure services organizations? How can leisure services managers ensure a clear, consistent organizational message in the face of a crisis incident?

7. Provide some examples of communication strategies that a leisure services organization might use to inform, educate, persuade, and remind their customers about their program and facility offerings. What strategies can be used to maintain contact with customers after they finish the consumption process?

8. Provide an example of a communication tool or tactic related to each of the six communication mix strategies proposed by Wirtz and Lovelock (2016).

9. How can a leisure services organization most effectively use a technology (such as a website) to enhance the communication process?

10. Why are positioning and repositioning important for leisure services managers to understand?

# 9

# Personnel Procedures and Practices

## Learning Outcomes

- Define the concept of human resources and understand it in connection to personnel planning and processes.

- Understand and make connections between modern concepts of personnel management and the philosophies of the behavioral school and human relations era.

- Understand the importance of personnel planning.

- Analyze organizational capacity and organizational needs related to personnel.

- Understand the importance of workplace diversity, federal protected classes, and work processes protected by antidiscrimination laws and statutes.

- Apply the key areas related to the personnel process, including conceptualizing need, candidate recruitment, candidate selection, orientation, training and development, and performance appraisal.

## Key Terms

personnel, Taylorism, law of diminishing returns, human resources capacity, cross-training, cost-of-living adjustments, technical skills, conceptual skills, human relations skills, knowledge, skills, abilities, stage-based screening process, employee training, employee development, high-threshold training, low-threshold training, volunteers

## Competency Check

Refer to table 1.6 to see how you assessed these related competencies.

26. Understand the hiring process.

27. Supervise, discipline, and evaluate a diverse staff.

## A Day in the Life

I am the vice president of operations of a for-profit aerial adventure park with a high ropes aerial adventure challenge course, zip line tours, and team-building programming. My role has evolved since our opening in 2012 from being very involved in the day-to-day of the company to now focusing on the future. Daily I am organizing, developing, and executing team-building programs for clients, sharing marketing responsibilities with my director of operations, networking with local businesses through Chamber of Commerce memberships to educate the community about our programs, and working with employees to ensure their training and skills are up-to-date with industry and company standards. I also work on new program development to expand our offerings to the community and our clients. Every day brings new challenges and adventures!

Sarah Derick
VP of Operations
Take Flight Adventures
Kittery, Maine

In many ways, the lifeblood of an organization is the human resources that it employs. Service organizations, especially those with high customer contact such as parks, recreation, and leisure services enterprises, are judged by the knowledge, skills, and abilities of their personnel as much as they are by the size and scope of their physical or fiscal resources. Finding the right employees and providing them with the tools and resources necessary for their continual development is one of the fundamental traits of great organizations.

Much of what managers do revolves around personnel. One of the four functions of management—leading—focuses on encouraging personnel to contribute to the success of an organization. However, as we have seen in other aspects of management, the other three functions play a critical role in personnel procedures and practices as well. Managers must be able to plan for personnel needs based on the capacity of the agency and its needs for particular sets of knowledge, skills, and abilities. They must be able to organize and coordinate the work output of staff members to avoid inefficiencies and maximize the talents of the staff. Finally, managers must be able to control the process by evaluating the contributions of staff and providing feedback to keep the organization on track to achieve its goals.

What we now think of as accepted practice in personnel or human resources management began with behavioral school theorists, such as Elton Mayo, Mary Parker Follett, and Chester Barnard, and continued with thinkers of the human relations era, such as Abraham Maslow, Frederick Herzberg, and Douglas McGregor (see chapter 1). Chapter 9 deals with the processes and procedures of personnel management.

## HUMAN RESOURCES PERSPECTIVES

In general, the term **personnel** refers to the people employed within an organization, agency, or institution. Personnel may also be referred to as *human resources*, a term that stems from the ideas of the behavioral school and human relations era by emphasizing the fact that personnel are, first and foremost, human. Contrast this thinking with that of classical era thinkers such as Frederick Taylor. **Taylorism** was a principle based on the notion that people could be managed as if they were machines. According to Taylorism, through the application of scientific principles (known as *scientific management*), personnel could function similar to the physical machinery of an assembly line or factory. Specific job tasks could be managed, deskilled, and routinized to such an extent as to render the individual employee as little more than a cog in a large machine controlled and supervised by a group of top-level managers.

The problem with this approach is that people are not machines. Unlike machines, employees have needs that may not be directly linked to the specific job they are attempting to perform. Consider the following examples. What are the consequences to the organization if these needs are not met?

- A single, working mother who has to balance her job with the after-school activities of her children might have a real need for a flexible work schedule.
- An entry-level employee working in an area with a high cost of living needs to be paid enough to cover basic living expenses.
- A facilities manager who has a job that contains physical risk needs a safe work environment to minimize the chance of injury.
- A new father needs to spend time with his family upon the birth of his first child.

**personnel**—People employed within an organization.

**Taylorism**—Based on the notion that through the application of scientific principles, personnel can function in a manner similar to the physical machinery of a factory.

- A middle manager has a need for organizational advancement and building new knowledge and skills through continuing education and professional development.

# Repercussions on Effectiveness

Human needs are powerful motivators. When not addressed, they also can be significant demotivators and can have repercussions on effectiveness in the following ways.

## Underperformance

When certain employee needs go unmet, underperformance in terms of work quantity and quality may increase. Underperformance also can have a ripple effect on other employees or units within the organization. Disgruntled employees require more attention—time that would be better spent on key management tasks.

## Increased Employee Attrition

Poor work environments and employee dissatisfaction can lead to higher rates of employee attrition (leaving the organization). As the conventional wisdom goes, it is most efficient for an organization to do what it can to minimize employee attrition, and especially to retain its best employees. Job searches, staff development, orientation, and training are inefficient when they have to be repeated over and over for the same position. It is in the best interest of an organization to hire the right people and do its best to keep them.

## Underutilization of Employee Capacities

In some cases, an organization may underuse its employees' knowledge, skills, and abilities. If employees' talents have value, then it stands to reason that a manager would want to maximize that value by using those talents. Just as managers would be wasting organizational resources by buying an expensive computer program and only using part of its capabilities, so too are managers inefficient when they only use a portion of an employee's abilities. Tapping into the knowledge and talents of all employees in an organization can improve product quality and organizational efficiency and effectiveness, and thus it is a major goal of management.

# Process and Philosophy

Human resources management has been created to help organizations meet employees' needs and prevent minor situations from becoming significant problems or draining effectiveness later on. Human resources management is both a process and a philosophy. Bolman and Deal (2013) lay out the core assumptions of a human resources philosophy:

- Organizations exist to serve human needs rather than the reverse.
- People and organizations need each other—organizations need the talents and energies of people, and people need careers, salaries, and professional opportunities.
- When the fit between individuals and organizations is poor, one or both suffer.
- Good fits benefit both the employee and the organization. A relationship of mutual exchange is created that benefits both.

Ultimately, human resources management is about understanding the human side of organizations. Human resources management is a process that helps to determine how both individual and organizational needs can be managed in a system that is clear, unambiguous, fair, and legal.

# PERSONNEL PLANNING

As with virtually every other aspect of management, managing human resources requires significant planning. Adding human resources without a clear plan for what to do with them is counterproductive. The **law of diminishing returns** from basic economics theory says that when we add additional variable inputs (for example, new employees) while keeping fixed inputs constant (for example, numbers of supervisory or administrative staff), each new input will contribute less and less after a certain point. Consider some of the fixed inputs of the youth unit in a commercial resort (e.g., fiscal resources, activity space, office areas, support services, supervisory contact). Given these conditions, adding additional staff may continue to increase unit effectiveness up to a point. Lacking adequate supervision, pay, office space, scope of responsibility, or administrative support, new staff members are likely to become dissatisfied. At the same time, the organization may find itself overstaffed given the size and scope of its programming efforts and wasting scarce resources.

**law of diminishing returns**—When new variable inputs (for example, new employees) are added while fixed inputs remain constant, each new input will contribute less and less.

Figure 9.1 illustrates this law. The ideal number of program staff for this organization given its existing resources is probably four. Adding a fifth staff member may not contribute to overall productivity, and overall productivity may actually decrease due to the strains that come with managing and supervising this additional human resource.

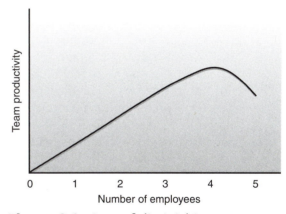

**Figure 9.1** Law of diminishing returns.

## Organizational Capacity

Understanding the capacity of an organization to meet the needs of additional staff members is an important first step in human resources planning. **Human resources capacity** refers to the resources, supervision, and systems that an organization has in place to meet its human resources needs. Adding human resources without addressing the capacity to manage them can result in inefficiency, as described previously. In addressing organizational capacity, the following areas should be considered:

**human resources capacity**—Resources and systems that an organization has in place to meet its human resources needs.

- Existing staff levels
- Fiscal resources
- Supervisory resources
- Physical resources and administrative support systems

### Existing Staffing Levels

One of the first steps in assessing capacity is analyzing current staffing levels of the organization. Managers must ask themselves whether current organizational tasks and functions can be met by existing staff resources. Arriving at the answer to this question can be more complex than it appears, and a definitive yes-or-no answer does not necessarily lead to a particular course of action. For example, suppose the recreation director of a midsized department is conducting a human resources analysis of the aquatics unit. In consultation with the aquatics coordinator and assistant coordinator, the director comes to the conclusion that the tasks of the aquatics unit—pool operations, lifeguarding, and swimming instruction—are not adequately met by existing personnel resources. The next step is to examine why this is the case.

**Numbers**  It is possible that the existing number of staff is inadequate to meet the needs of the program. For example, the number of lifeguards needed during the summer when both outdoor and indoor pools are in operation means that more lifeguards need to be hired when demand increases. The decision to add staff in this case would be an appropriate response. Of course, the decision to add staff must take into consideration the capacity of the organization to accommodate the needs of new employees.

**Expertise**  It could be that existing staff are not able to meet unit goals because they lack the expertise to carry out their job duties. For example, the aquatics unit might lack enough certified pool operators or staff with specialized expertise in aquatics facilities management. In this case, a course of action might be to recruit and hire additional staff with the needed expertise. Another solution would be to cross-train present personnel in the specialized skills needed to accomplish the tasks. **Cross-training** refers to preparing staff to perform the tasks associated with various jobs in an organization. In this example, the assistant aquatics coordinator could be trained as a certified pool operator and given responsibilities for pool operations and maintenance. Or entire job categories could be cross-trained to handle varying responsibilities—for instance, lifeguards might be certified as water safety instructors so that they could provide swim lessons.

**cross-training**— Preparing staff to perform the skills and tasks associated with different jobs within an organization.

By cross-training existing staff, the size of the workforce may not need to change and problems with capacity are diminished. This solution is most effective when there is room to add responsibilities to existing workloads, when the required expertise is fairly easy to obtain, and when combining job functions (job enlargement) makes sense. Adding new staff to address gaps in expertise makes more sense when the needed skill sets are highly specialized or when the nature of the work makes job enlargement impractical.

**Work Allocation**  Sometimes staff members are not able to meet their goals because work is not allocated in a way that maximizes efficiency and effectiveness. This indicates that there might be a structural problem that requires personnel reorganization. Let's continue with the aquatics example. Suppose that the assistant aquatics manager's job duties were largely redundant with the supervisor's and that there was room for subordinate staff to take on additional responsibilities. If the organization eliminated the assistant aquatics coordinator's position, it might be able to reallocate its personnel resources by hiring additional lifeguards (or swim instructors, or pool maintenance staff) to address current demands.

Or suppose that the aquatics unit was overstaffed in one area and understaffed in another. Reorganizing pool maintenance staff by eliminating or downsizing full-time positions could help supplement personnel resources in another program area. It might be that only a small crew of full-time pool maintenance staff is needed year-round with additional part-time help needed in the summer, whereas swim instructors are in high demand year-round. Assessing the organization and allocation of personnel resources is a critical component of human resources planning.

## Fiscal Resources

When resources are limited, as is commonly the case with leisure services organizations, fiscal and budgetary realities often dictate personnel decisions. Decisions to add personnel may be constrained by tight budgets and, particularly in public or nonprofit organizations, by strict approval processes for adding personnel. Even when additional personnel resources are clearly needed in response to increasing demand or gaps in existing expertise, decision makers may be reluctant to commit financial resources to permanent benefits-eligible positions. This may be due to political realities related to taxation in the public sector, constraints on spending decisions in the nonprofit sector, or a concern that future demand may not be strong enough to justify increasing personnel costs in the commercial sector. In all of these cases, fiscal and budgetary realities are the driving force behind personnel decisions, especially when staff additions are being considered. The result is that existing staff are often asked to shoulder the burden of doing more with less.

Conducting a careful analysis of fiscal resources is an important step in determining the capacity of an organization for adding personnel. Before determining the capacity to invest in new personnel, managers and decision makers must consider the types of positions that are needed. Different job types will require different investments of fiscal resources. For example, many staff positions in leisure services organizations are part-time, hourly wage, seasonal, and benefits exempt. Lifeguards, sports officials, front-desk attendants, camp counselors, coaches, and group fitness instructors can be hired with less financial investment and generally less financial risk than program, management, executive, and certain support and technical staff positions. Not only do part-time and seasonal positions cost less, they are also more easily eliminated during times of lower demand.

Full-time, permanent, salaried, and benefits-eligible positions require a greater fiscal commitment. This commitment extends beyond the increased salary that such positions are likely to command. The commitment begins during the search process, where the organization may be required to lay out thousands of dollars recruiting qualified candidates. Salaries must be competitive in order to attract the best candidates, especially for positions that are in high demand or that require specialized skill sets. Benefits, including health care, retirement savings, life insurance, and paid vacation time, can cost employers up to 40 percent on top of the employee's salary, meaning a $40,000 entry-level position could cost an organization more than $55,000 in total compensation.

Organizations must also consider fluctuations in the larger economy, including increases in cost of living—the cost of goods and services that a household is expected to be able to purchase at an average level of consumption. In order to ensure that employees are able to keep up with the cost of inflation, many organizations provide annual **cost-of-living adjustments**. Such salary adjustments help ensure that employees continue to be adequately compensated even as the price of goods and services in the larger economy increase. Finally, ongoing training costs and professional development that are required for employees to do their jobs effectively must also be considered as part of the employee's cost to the organization. Much like other assets, human resources are investments that organizations must carefully consider in order to maximize efficiency and effectiveness.

**cost-of-living adjustments**—Salary increases for employees in order to offset losses in purchasing power due to inflation.

## Supervisory Resources

When assessing the capacity of an agency to accommodate additional personnel resources, managers must take into account the level of supervision that is needed to manage new employees. An assessment of supervisory resources is important because coordination is needed to ensure efficient work processes. Employees also need adequate access to their supervisors to enhance communication and avoid misunderstandings.

**Coordination and Control**    As organizations grow, they become more complex, creating structural dilemmas and questions regarding how best to coordinate and control staff activities. Recall that in chapter 5 we discussed how increasing the number of supervisors (decreasing spans of control) generally leads to greater coordination. When adding new personnel, managers must assess whether current supervisory resources are adequate to achieve the proper balance between coordinating staff and providing enough autonomy for staff to demonstrate expertise and tap into their potential.

This assessment will depend on the nature of the position that is being considered. Some staff positions may require increased supervision and narrower spans of control, whereas other positions may be better served by creating autonomous structures that allow for more individual freedom and greater accountability. Sales positions, for example, might benefit from such freedom, with quotas serving as the principal accountability mechanism for ensuring adequate job performance. Additional sales staff might not require additional supervisory resources; salespeople often work independently and overcoordination can hinder such flexibility.

However, hiring additional maintenance staff might also require a new maintenance supervisor, because maintenance tasks are often highly interdependent with other organizational functions (such as programming, facilities management, or even marketing). Because of this interdependence, there is a greater need to coordinate and control maintenance efforts. Failing to plan for the integration of new maintenance staff could lead to structural dilemmas.

**Supervisor–Employee Relationships**    Employees look to their supervisors for guidance, feedback, and resources so they can do their jobs effectively. In highly interdependent positions where the actions of one person greatly affect the actions of others, staff must be able to rely on their supervisors to frame their job roles, coordinate the activities of their unit, and advocate for them in times of conflict. When considering organizational capacity to handle new personnel, managers must ask whether existing supervisor–staff relationships will be adversely affected by the addition of new positions. Noneconomic costs are involved in adding new staff, especially with respect to the time that is spent orienting, training, coordinating, and managing their efforts. Failing to account for these noneconomic costs may create new inefficiencies, especially if management feels strained in the ability to handle new staff or if new staff members feel that their needs are not being met by their supervisors.

## Physical Resources and Administrative Support Systems

Organizations also need to provide employees with the tools to do their jobs effectively. For some positions, this means providing adequate office space, computing resources, and communication systems. Other positions may have specialized equipment or specific physical space needs. Without access to the proper resources, employees may find it difficult to accomplish their tasks. Before adding new staff, managers must be sure that the organization has the physical resources to accommodate job-related needs.

In addition to physical resources, employees need administrative support systems that help them navigate their often-complex job roles. Administrative support means assisting staff in areas that may or may not be directly related to their everyday tasks. For example, some staff positions may require administrative support consisting of typing letters, making copies, organizing office systems, scheduling meetings, taking registrations or payments, answering phones, handling employee payroll, or responding to emails. Administrative support can also mean assisting employees with more general personnel needs, including assistance with benefits or questions regarding organizational policy. Questions related to capacity must consider whether staff levels can be provided with the administrative support needed to effectively perform necessary job functions.

# Organizational Needs

In addition to considering their capacity, organizations must also think about their personnel needs. One of the classic personnel dilemmas is whether to think about personnel needs in terms of specific positions and technical skill sets or whether to think about such needs more broadly by considering the qualities that an organization wants its employees to possess. Although this dilemma does not necessarily present itself as an either–or proposition—a candidate can be both technically skilled and possess the qualities that the organization is seeking—sometimes finding the right combination of conceptual, human, and technical skills can be a daunting task. In the process of assessing human resources needs, organizations should clearly define the qualities that they most value in their employees. These qualities should fit the vision, values, mission, and culture of the organization. Remember one of the propositions of human resources philosophy—when the fit between employee and organization is a good one, both tend to benefit.

## Personnel Needs Based on Position

Often, personnel needs come in the form of specific expertise. In this model, personnel decisions stem from the vision and strategic planning efforts of an agency. When a position becomes vacant in a specific unit, the organization often seeks a replacement with the same technical skill sets as the previous employee. For example, if a fitness organization needs to replace a personal trainer, management may seek qualified candidates who possess the competencies, certifications, and experiences that best meet the fitness and personal training needs of the clients.

The specialized nature of many jobs in leisure services organizations, especially at the program level, may lead managers to think in terms of position needs first. Organizations may have a need for aquatics coordinators, sport programmers, fitness directors, turf maintenance specialists, youth development professionals, or marketing managers. Each of these positions requires a specialized set of skills. If the organization needs an aquatics coordinator, it needs someone with proper certifications, training, competencies, and experience in lifeguarding, swim instruction, and pool operations and maintenance.

Though it is important for managers to consider the job-related competencies that they expect their employees to possess, it is equally important to remember that skill sets extend beyond the technical. **Technical skills,** which include the job-specific knowledge and techniques that enable an employee to do a job effectively, are important, but so are conceptual skills and human skills. **Conceptual skills** include the ability to analyze situations, determine causes and effects, come up with solutions to programming or organizational challenges, and see the big picture. **Human relations skills** include the ability to work with, lead, and understand other people, including both individuals and groups. Each of these skill sets should be considered

**technical skills—**Job-specific knowledge and techniques that enable employees to do their job effectively.

**conceptual skills—**Ability to analyze situations from multiple perspectives, determine cause and effect, and come up with solutions to challenges.

**human relations skills—**Ability to work with, lead, and understand other people, including both individuals and groups.

when analyzing the personnel needs of the organization, and, as we consider in the next section, sometimes the best candidate for the organization may not be the candidate who possesses the highest level of technical expertise at the time of the hire.

Considering personnel needs primarily based on position and technical qualifications is appropriate under the following conditions:

- When a particular job function requires highly specialized skill sets
- When the acquisition of the required technical skills is difficult or costly to obtain
- When recruiting efforts yield a deep enough pool of candidates who possess the technical, conceptual, and human relations skills to meet the needs of the organization
- When the organization is required by law or policy to justify hiring decisions based on an objective set of criteria such as certification, licensure, specific academic degrees, or specific technical expertise

Because many of the jobs in leisure services organizations are highly specialized, considering personnel needs primarily based on the qualifications needed for a specific job is often the most pragmatic means for personnel planning. However, it is important to go beyond the technical requirements for the position and consider a broad range of competencies that often are not skill specific. In chapter 2, we discussed the importance of competencies that cut across many of the job types found in leisure services organizations. Many of these competencies are not job or skill specific yet are still considered to be vital for employees to possess. Although some competencies, such as technical skills, can be obtained through training and education, many interpersonal competencies, such as conceptual or human relations skills, can only be obtained through experience and professional perspective.

## Personnel Needs Based on Qualities

What if the best fit for the organization is not the candidate with the highest level of technical skill but the candidate who possesses the right mix of conceptual and human relations skills? What if the best fit is the candidate who possesses the qualities that the organization values the most? Some organizations focus on getting the best people first—they think about specific jobs later.

The general concept that underlies this idea is that people who possess the right mix of qualities that are valued by the organization (e.g., robust work ethic, commitment to team, strong communication ability) can be trained in the technical skills that a specific job requires. For instance, employees with a strong work ethic can be trained in a variety of job-related tasks, but it is difficult to train someone to have a strong work ethic.

This method is admittedly difficult to implement for leisure services organizations. Training and employee development, especially in specific programming areas that require specialized skills or certifications, may be too difficult, expensive, or time consuming for the organization. For example, it takes years of study and experience to be a turf maintenance specialist. It may also be difficult for organizations to justify hiring decisions based on criteria that are difficult to measure, such as values, work ethic, or team focus. Hiring based primarily on an employee's perceived qualities can also open the door to various forms of discrimination or abuse. However, considering the personnel qualities that are most important to the organization and significantly weighing those qualities during a job search is a critical step in the personnel planning process.

# Employee Diversity

Part of the personnel planning process includes thinking about the diversity of a workforce. Beyond being the right thing to do, developing and maintaining a diverse workforce makes good business sense. Demographic trends show a changing workforce in the United States. Racial and ethnic minorities have increased their participation in the labor force since the early 2000s and are expected to continue to increase their presence in both the population and labor force through 2060. Hispanics, in particular, are projected to increase their participation in the labor force. Likewise, the percentage of foreign-born residents is expected to grow faster than the native-born population. While women's participation has been declining since its peak in 1999, almost 60 percent of women are in the U.S. labor force. The median age of the labor force is expected to continue to increase as the baby boomers age and approach retirement. However, the percentage of young workers (aged 16–24) is expected to decrease through at least 2060 due to declining birthrates (Toosi 2016). All residents of California, Hawaii, New Mexico, and Texas are technically members of a minority group since the percentage of non-Hispanic whites as a proportion of the population is less than 50 percent in those states. Further, the U.S. population as a whole is expected to become majority-minority by 2044. (U.S. Census Bureau 2015).

Similar demographic trends can be seen in Canada as well. More than 7.6 million Canadians identify as a visible minority (non-Caucasian). Figures show that visible minorities now make up 22.3 percent of the population—up almost 10 percent since 2007 (Press 2017). Indigenous people continue to make up a sizable portion of the population in the north and west, even holding a majority in the Northwest Territories and Nunavut. Further, the proportion of seniors in the Canadian population is growing, as life expectancy continues to climb (Statistics Canada 2017).

The labor force in the United States and Canada is clearly growing more diverse. Leisure services organizations must continue to focus on the diversity of their workforces, both to reflect the diversity of their constituents and to benefit from the skills of the broadest array of potential job seekers.

It is important for organizations to recognize the moral imperative and good business practices behind workforce diversity, but it is also important to recognize that federal, state, and provincial laws in the United States and Canada prohibit organizations from discriminating against employees and job seekers. For example, in the United States, it is unlawful for employers to discriminate against employees or job seekers based on race, color, religion, sex, national origin, disability, genetic information, or age. Many states broaden these areas through their own laws and statutes, barring discrimination based on sexual orientation, marital status, or status as a veteran. Many individual organizations have also adopted antidiscrimination policy that goes beyond the legal requirements.

Federal legislation in the United States forbids discrimination in the following areas:

- Hiring and firing
- Compensation, assignment, or classification of employees
- Transfer, promotion, layoff, or recall
- Job advertisements
- Recruitment
- Testing

- Use of company facilities
- Training and apprenticeship programs
- Fringe benefits
- Pay, retirement plans, and disability leave
- Other terms and conditions of employment

Similar rights are extended to workers in Canada. The Canadian Human Rights Act prohibits federally regulated employers or service providers from discriminating against employees or potential employees based on race, national or ethnic origin, color, religion, age, sex, sexual orientation, marital status, family status, disability, and conviction for which a pardon has been granted. Provincial and territorial legislation offers similar protection for most employees who are not federally regulated.

Discriminatory practices covered by the Canadian Human Rights Act are numerous, and leisure services managers are encouraged to familiarize themselves with the provisions of the act, including exceptions. Provisions of the act related to discrimination in the workplace include the following:

- Employment
- Employment applications or advertisements
- Employee organizations
- Discriminatory policy or practice
- Equal wages
- Assessment of the value of work
- Harassment and sexual harassment
- Workplace accommodations

Legislation involving human resources is complex and extensive. As such, the discussion here is a general overview focused specifically on employment discrimination and equal opportunity laws. Recall that we discussed many of the key employment laws in chapter 3 (see table 3.1). You can also refer to figure 9.2 and the sidebar on major discrimination laws for a brief discussion of important equal opportunity legislation in the United States and Canada.

# PERSONNEL PROCESSES

A considerable amount of planning is required before actually addressing the personnel needs of an organization. Consideration of organizational capacity, needs, and legal requirements is the necessary first step. After the organization and its management team carefully consider these factors, they need to develop a process for staffing the organization. In general, personnel processes follow these steps:

1. Development of the job description
2. Creation of the job announcement
3. Candidate recruitment
4. Candidate selection
5. Orientation, training, and employee development
6. Performance appraisal

# Equal Employment Opportunity is

# THE LAW

## Employers Holding Federal Contracts or Subcontracts

Applicants to and employees of companies with a Federal government contract or subcontract are protected under the following Federal authorities:

**RACE, COLOR, RELIGION, SEX, NATIONAL ORIGIN**

Executive Order 11246, as amended, prohibits job discrimination on the basis of race, color, religion, sex or national origin, and requires affirmative action to ensure equality of opportunity in all aspects of employment.

**INDIVIDUALS WITH DISABILITIES**

Section 503 of the Rehabilitation Act of 1973, as amended, prohibits job discrimination because of disability and requires affirmative action to employ and advance in employment qualified individuals with disabilities who, with reasonable accommodation, can perform the essential functions of a job.

**VIETNAM ERA, SPECIAL DISABLED, RECENTLY SEPARATED, AND OTHER PROTECTED VETERANS**

38 U.S.C. 4212 of the Vietnam Era Veterans' Readjustment Assistance Act of 1974, as amended, prohibits job discrimination and requires affirmative action to employ and advance in employment qualified Vietnam era veterans, qualified special disabled veterans, recently separated veterans, and other protected veterans.

Any person who believes a contractor has violated its nondiscrimination or affirmative action obligations under the authorities above should contact immediately:

The Office of Federal Contract Compliance Programs (OFCCP), Employment Standards Administration, U.S. Department of Labor, 200 Constitution Avenue, N.W., Washington, D.C. 20210 or call (202) 693-0101, or an OFCCP regional or district office, listed in most telephone directories under U.S. Government, Department of Labor.

## Private Employment, State and Local Governments, Educational Institutions

Applicants to and employees of most private employers, state and local governments, educational institutions, employment agencies and labor organizations are protected under the following Federal laws:

**RACE, COLOR, RELIGION, SEX, NATIONAL ORIGIN**

Title VII of the Civil Rights Act of 1964, as amended, prohibits discrimination in hiring, promotion, discharge, pay, fringe benefits, job training, classification, referral, and other aspects of employment, on the basis of race, color, religion, sex or national origin.

**DISABILITY**

The Americans with Disabilities Act of 1990, as amended, protects qualified applicants and employees with disabilities from discrimination in hiring, promotion, discharge, pay, job training, fringe benefits, classification, referral, and other aspects of employment on the basis of disability. The law also requires that covered entities provide qualified applicants and employees with disabilities with reasonable accommodations that do not impose undue hardship.

**AGE**

The Age Discrimination in Employment Act of 1967, as amended, protects applicants and employees 40 years of age or older from discrimination on the basis of age in hiring, promotion, discharge, compensation, terms, conditions or privileges of employment.

**SEX (WAGES)**

In addition to sex discrimination prohibited by Title VII of the Civil Rights Act of 1964, as amended (see above), the Equal Pay Act of 1963, as amended, prohibits sex discrimination in payment of wages to women and men performing substantially equal work in the same establishment.

Retaliation against a person who files a charge of discrimination, participates in an investigation, or opposes an unlawful employment practice is prohibited by all of these Federal laws.

If you believe that you have been discriminated against under any of the above laws, you should contact immediately:

The U.S. Equal Employment Opportunity Commission (EEOC), 1801 L Street, N.W., Washington, D.C. 20507 or an EEOC field office by calling toll free (800) 669-4000. For individuals with hearing impairments, EEOC's toll free TDD number is (800) 669-6820.

## Programs or Activities Receiving Federal Financial Assistance

**RACE, COLOR, RELIGION, NATIONAL ORIGIN, SEX**

In addition to the protection of Title VII of the Civil Rights Act of 1964, as amended, Title VI of the Civil Rights Act prohibits discrimination on the basis of race, color or national origin in programs or activities receiving Federal financial assistance. Employment discrimination is covered by Title VI if the primary objective of the financial assistance is provision of employment, or where employment discrimination causes or may cause discrimination in providing services under such programs. Title IX of the Education Amendments of 1972 prohibits employment discrimination on the basis of sex in educational programs or activities which receive Federal assistance.

**INDIVIDUALS WITH DISABILITIES**

Sections 501, 504 and 505 of the Rehabilitation Act of 1973, as amended, prohibits employment discrimination on the basis of disability in any program or activity which receives Federal financial assistance in the federal government. Discrimination is prohibited in all aspects of employment against persons with disabilities who, with reasonable accommodation, can perform the essential functions of a job.

If you believe you have been discriminated against in a program of any institution which receives Federal assistance, you should contact immediately the Federal agency providing such assistance.

Publication OFCCP 1420
Revised 2004

**Figure 9.2** Equal employment opportunity poster.

Reprinted from The Office of Federal Contract Compliance Programs (OFCCP), Employment Standards Administration, U.S. Department of Labor.

# Major Discrimination Laws in the United States and Canada

The following federal laws provide general guidelines for employee rights and discrimination in the United States and Canada. Leisure services managers should make the effort to understand each of these laws and should consult appropriate legal authorities if questions arise.

## United States

- Equal Pay Act of 1963: Prohibits sex discrimination in payment of wages to women and men performing substantially equal work in the same establishment.

- Title VII of the Civil Rights Act of 1964: Prohibits discrimination in hiring, promotion, discharge, pay, fringe benefits, job training, classification, referral, and other aspects of employment on the basis of race, color, religion, sex, or national origin.

- Pregnancy Discrimination Act: Amended Title VII to make it illegal to discriminate against a woman because of pregnancy, childbirth, or medical condition related to childbirth, or to retaliate against a person because of a discrimination claim.

- Age Discrimination in Employment Act (ADEA) of 1967: Protects applicants and employees 40 years of age or older from discrimination on the basis of age in hiring, promotion, discharge, compensation, terms, conditions, or privileges of employment.

- Rehabilitation Act of 1973: Prohibits job discrimination because of disability and requires affirmative action to employ and advance in employment qualified people with disabilities who, with reasonable accommodation, can perform the essential functions of a job.

- Title I and Title V of the Americans with Disabilities Act (ADA) of 1990: Protects qualified applicants and employees with disabilities from discrimination in hiring, promotion, discharge, pay, job training, fringe benefits, classification, referral, and other aspects of employment on the basis of disability. The law also requires that covered entities provide qualified applicants and employees with disabilities with reasonable accommodations that do not impose undue hardship.

Each of these laws prohibits retaliation by an employer against an employee who files a charge of discrimination, participates in an investigation, or opposes unlawful employment practice.

For more information, visit the United States EEOC website at www.eeoc.gov/laws/statutes/

## Canada

- Canadian Charter of Rights and Freedoms: Requires employers to ensure that equal employment opportunities exist for both job applicants and current employees; guarantees the rights of aboriginal peoples, the right to equality for men and women, and the right to use either of Canada's official languages (French and English).

*(continued)*

> **Major Discrimination Laws in the United States and Canada**  *(continued)*
>
> - Canadian Human Rights Act: Requires employers to ensure that equal employment opportunities exist for both job applicants and current employees. Prohibits discrimination based on the following protected classes: race, national or ethnic origin, color, religion, age, sex, sexual orientation, marital status, family status, disability, and conviction for which a pardon has been granted.
> - Employment Equity Act: Requires that employers identify and eliminate employment barriers for designated group members that result from the employer's employment systems, policies, and practices; designated groups include women, aboriginal peoples, people with disabilities, and visible minorities.
>
> For more information, visit Employment and Social Development Canada at www.canada.ca/en/employment-social-development.html www.hrsdc.gc.ca/en/labour/index.shtml.

Developing a specific plan to navigate through each step can help an organization be purposeful about its personnel decisions, and it provides a blueprint to guide personnel decisions.

# Developing the Job Description

Developing a written job description is the culminating act of the various planning steps discussed previously. The job description is the formal, written definition of the essential functions of a job, as well as its required qualifications and competencies. The job description is the basis for personnel recruitment, candidate selection, training, and performance appraisal. A well-written, thorough description clearly communicates the scope of responsibilities associated with a particular job. It sets the expectations for employment and provides a framework for personnel supervision.

At a minimum, a job description should list the essential functions and competencies required to perform the duties associated with the job. Even the best job descriptions cannot capture every responsibility assigned to a particular job; thus, a job description should be an overall summary of the duties assigned to a particular position and should leave room for additional assignments as needed. Different agencies may have unique formats for job descriptions. However, the following sections are usually included:

- *Salary range.* Job descriptions may include a salary range that represents the minimum and maximum salaries that can be earned by an employee in a specific job class. This is particularly important in public and nonprofit organizations, where organizational or political mandates require specific salary ranges.

- *General definition.* This is a general definition of the job and its overall scope of responsibility within the organization.

- *Supervision.* This statement details the supervision the position receives and exercises.

- *Job segments and functions.* Most job descriptions provide a detailed list of the essential job functions that the position is responsible for within the organization. Job segments might include program planning, personnel supervision, budgeting, accounting, marketing, policy making, and so on. Job descriptions should go beyond just listing broad job segments, however. They should be fairly descriptive in specifying the functions that are associated with each particular segment. For example, instead of merely listing *marketing* as a job segment, a job description might also state that the position is responsible for all aspects of marketing and publicity for recreation programs, including developing and distributing brochures and press releases, updating the program websites, customer service, and communicating with the media.

● *Working conditions.* Some job descriptions include a statement regarding the conditions that the employee is expected to work under. This is particularly important for jobs that require specific physical or manual labor or that require the employee to work in somewhat dangerous settings.

● *Qualifications.* Job descriptions must outline the minimal qualifications necessary for the particular job, including both the level of formal education and the length and type of experience. If there are any additional qualifications for the position, such as specific licensure requirements, certifications, background checks, or physical abilities, they should be listed here as well.

● *Competencies.* This section focuses on the specific attributes that are needed to fulfill the essential functions of the job. They generally derive from a combination of education and experience. Some job descriptions will focus on general competencies, whereas others will focus on specific knowledge, skills, and abilities (KSAs) associated with the job. In general, **knowledge** refers to the body of information that directly applies to specific job functions, such as knowledge of the recreation needs of a particular community or understanding of program evaluation techniques. **Skills** are physical or psychomotor competencies required for a particular job, such as operating certain types of machinery or typing on a keyboard. Finally, **abilities** are the aptitudes for a position, or if and how well a person is able to perform a certain task. Examples of abilities might be communicating effectively with the public or establishing effective interpersonal working relationships.

Job descriptions are not static documents. Jobs evolve over time, and as organizational needs change, new knowledge, skills, and abilities are required. Organizations should conduct regular job reviews, especially if position descriptions are out of date and incongruent with the actual job duties being performed.

## Creating the Job Announcement

Following the personnel planning process and the development of the job description, the leisure services organization should have a clear idea of its personnel needs. The first step in the candidate selection process is the development of an open job announcement. Job announcements serve several purposes:

● They provide notification of available positions to potential job seekers.

● They provide a template for organizational decision making in candidate selection.

● They act as a marketing tool for the organization.

The job announcement sets the tone for the hiring process. As such, it plays an important role in communicating what the organization wants in an employee and what the organization is about. The job announcement should be viewed as a two-way communication tool. It should clearly delineate the employment need of the

---

**knowledge**—Information required to perform a job.

**skills**—Physical or psychomotor competencies, such as operating certain types of machinery or typing on a keyboard.

**abilities**—The aptitudes for a position; if and how well a person is able to perform a certain task.

organization but should also be developed to attract the best candidates. In this way, the job announcement can be seen as part of marketing and communication efforts. Poorly written job announcements reflect negatively on the organization.

Many organizations have standard formats for job announcements or require that certain information be included. An example of this might include statements affirming the commitment of the organization to equal employment opportunity and workforce diversity. Leisure services managers should first consult with their human resources division, if one exists, to ensure that job announcements conform to whatever standard formats might exist. When developing a job announcement from the beginning, consider including the following components.

## Title of the Position

Job announcements should include the title of the open position. In some cases, organizations may have an official position title that corresponds with specific employment classifications within the larger organization but is not representative of common job titles in the field. For example, for human resources purposes, a city or municipality might generically categorize all agency heads as unit managers, but their working titles might be more specific (e.g., chief of police, director of housing, director of parks and recreation). In these cases, it is wise to include both the official title and the more common working title for the position. Remember, the job announcement is a communication tool, and job titles often help communicate the scope of responsibility.

It is also important to remember that job titles may differ from organization to organization. This is especially true of organizations in different leisure services settings. For example, campus recreation organizations often use titles such as director, associate director, assistant director, and program coordinator to designate scope of responsibility. Municipal recreation departments may use titles such as recreation director, recreation superintendent, assistant superintendent, and program manager. Using titles that are common in the institutional setting of the organization helps prospective job seekers understand the scope of the position.

## Overview of the Organization

Job announcements should include basic details about the organization that have relevance for the scope of responsibility. Consider briefly describing the mission, structure, facilities, personnel, or other areas of potential interest to prospective candidates. In many cases, this is the first contact that a prospective job seeker will have with the organization, so a brief overview can help create interest in potential candidates.

## Brief Overview of the Position

In addition to the position title, the announcement should include a general description of the position and its scope of responsibilities. This information could be similar to the general definition of the position discussed earlier. For example, a brief overview of the position might state the following: "Under the direction of the recreation director, the youth sport program supervisor is responsible for all phases of the design and delivery of a comprehensive community recreational sport program for young people, including but not limited to program design, facility management, tournament administration, supervision of coaches and officials, communication with parents, program evaluation, budgeting and accounting, risk management, and program evaluation."

## Academic and Professional Qualifications

Job announcements should clearly state both the required and preferred academic and professional qualifications for the job. In general, academic qualifications include education levels, degrees, and areas of study. Professional qualifications include requirements for licensure, certification, or other credentials. A rule of thumb to consider is that as requirements become more specific, the potential applicant pool shrinks. For example, requiring an undergraduate degree in a specific academic area or requiring an advanced graduate degree may limit the pool of applicants. A benefit to this is that it can discourage underqualified applicants from applying, and it eliminates them from consideration early in the process if they do decide to apply. A drawback is that stringent qualifications may prevent good candidates from applying because of their inability to meet the specific requirements for the position. Another potential drawback is that stringent qualifications may reinforce existing inequities in employment based on sex, race, or other areas. For example, if certain racial or ethnic minorities are underrepresented in graduate degree programs in leisure services management, then requiring an advanced degree may further limit the pool of otherwise qualified minority candidates.

In figure 9.3, the position of recreation superintendent responsible for community sport and special events requires candidates to possess a bachelor's degree in recreation management, sport management, or a related field. This obviously limits the applicant pool to candidates who possess academic qualifications in the general field while still allowing a search committee some flexibility in deciding if a degree in a different but related academic area (such as physical education or public administration) could be substituted. The position announcement also states that the organization prefers candidates to possess a master's degree in recreation administration, sport administration, or a related field. Such a statement might give weight to an advanced degree during the selection process but does not completely eliminate otherwise qualified candidates who might not hold a graduate degree. Discussing the required and preferred academic qualifications for the position during the personnel planning process can provide insight into the benefits and costs to the organization when making these decisions.

## Required and Preferred Competencies

Similar to academic qualifications, job announcements should list the competencies that are both required and preferred for the position. When listing required competencies, consider the base level that the position requires. Preferred competencies are those that the organization desires but are not absolutely critical.

## Compensation

Some organizations list salary ranges and other forms of compensation on the job announcement, especially for entry-level and middle-management positions. Others merely state that compensation is "commensurate with experience and qualifications." The decision on whether to list compensation on the job announcement is tricky. By providing specific information on salary and benefits, organizations may be either attracting or discouraging job seekers from applying for the position. Providing specific compensation information also means that the organization goes public with its salary structure, which it may be reluctant to do for any number of reasons. In general, if an organization believes its salary structure is competitive with other organizations or believes that providing specific compensation

## Position Announcement: Recreation Superintendent for Community Sports and Special Events, Any Town, USA

Any Town, USA, seeks a qualified and enthusiastic individual for the position of recreation superintendent for community sports and special events. The Parks and Recreation Department offers a wide range of programs and facilities servicing the tri-town area, including New Town, Young Town, and Old Town. The Any Town Parks and Recreation Department sponsors youth and adult sports, special events, community festivals, art, music, drama, after-school programming, summer camps, senior recreation, and inclusive recreation for persons with disabilities. The Parks and Recreation Department operates the new $10 million Any Town Community Center, as well as the Any Town Outdoor Sports Complex and Tennis Facility. In addition, the Parks and Recreation Department oversees numerous outdoor recreation areas, parks, and hiking/walking/biking trails that serve residents of the tri-town area.

- *Position overview.* Under the direction of the recreation director, the recreation superintendent for community sports and special events is responsible for all phases of the design and delivery of a comprehensive community recreational sport program for youth, adolescents, adults, and seniors in the tri-town area. Programs under the direct supervision of this position include recreational and travel youth sports, Camp Fun in the Sun, and adult sports and special events. Facilities under the direct supervision of the recreation superintendent include the Community Center, the Outdoor Sports Complex, and the Tennis Facility. The position oversees a full-time program supervisor, as well as numerous part-time and volunteer staff.

- *Academic and professional qualifications.* A bachelor's degree in recreation management, sport management, or a related field is required, and a master's degree in recreation administration, sport administration, or a related field is preferred. The position requires 1 to 3 years of demonstrated experience in recreation program design and supervision. More than 3 years of experience is strongly preferred.

- *Certifications and other credentials.* Certification in CPR and standard first aid from a reputable national certification agency (i.e., American Red Cross) is required. Preferred credentials include certified park and recreation professional (CPRP) and certified youth sports administrator (CYSA).

- *Competencies.* The successful candidate will have demonstrated experience in the following areas: policy development, tournament design and administration, program design and delivery, staff supervision (including both paid staff and volunteers), risk management, facility maintenance and management, budget development and financial accounting, marketing and publicity, program evaluation, personal computing, and web publishing. In addition, the successful candidate must have the ability to provide high levels of customer service, to speak in front of large audiences, to connect personally with the

**Figure 9.3** Position announcement for recreation superintendent. *(continued)*

public and fellow staff, and to communicate effectively in written reports and other forms of written communication. Experience supervising full-time staff is strongly preferred.

- *Compensation.* $53,472 to $67,345, depending on experience and qualifications. A full benefits package, including paid vacations; health, dental, and life insurance; and 401(k) contributions are included.
- *Application deadline.* Completed applications received before November 1, 2019, will be given priority. Applications that are received after November 1 may be considered.
- *Application process.* Submit a cover letter expressing qualifications and interest in the position, along with a résumé and the names, addresses, and phone numbers of three professional references, to: Human Resources Director, PO Box 1234, Any Town, USA 55555. For questions about the application process or about the position, contact Recreation Director Jane Smith at (603) 555-5555, or by email at jane.smith@anytown.us. You can also visit the Any Town Parks and Recreation Department website at www.anytownrec.org.

The Any Town Parks and Recreation Department welcomes females and minority applicants to apply.

The Any Town Parks and Recreation Department is an equal opportunity employer.

**Figure 9.3**   *(continued)*

information may help attract good candidates, then it makes sense to provide that information. If an organization does not want salary to be the deciding factor in whether a job seeker applies for the position, or if it has the flexibility to negotiate salary with a successful candidate, then it may make sense to limit the information provided in this section.

## Application Process

The job announcement should be extremely clear about the process that candidates must follow to apply for the position. This section should include the contact person to send application materials to, the materials required to apply (e.g., cover letter, résumé, references), specific formatting requirements for application materials, and the deadline for receipt of materials.

Deadlines may be hard (all application materials must be received by a specific date), soft (application materials are encouraged by a specific date, but applications received after the date may still be considered), or open (application materials will be considered until the job is filled). Advantages of hard deadlines are that they encourage job seekers to get their applications in early, they make organization of the application process easier, they help to achieve fairness in the process, and they help to limit large applicant pools. Soft and open deadlines allow greater flexibility on the part of the organization and potential job seekers, but they can also be more difficult to manage, especially with large numbers of applicants for a given position.

## Additional Information

Job announcements should include contact names, phone numbers, physical and email addresses, and Internet links for candidates to obtain more information about the position. If the organization has specific requirements for candidates to follow (e.g., no phone calls), this information should be clearly stated. For professional or career positions, many organizations include information pertaining to lifestyle interests, including information about the area, local amenities, access to cultural events, and other areas of interest to potential job seekers. This can also be helpful in attracting the best candidates for a particular position.

# Recruitment

The job announcement might be seen as the first step in recruiting qualified candidates. The recruitment process is about finding the best possible candidate for the position. Recruitment strategies should be proactive—that is, organizations should invest both time and resources in the candidate search process. Organizations are generally best served when their applicant pools for open searches are wide and deep, because this puts them in the best position to choose the best fit among qualified candidates.

When open positions arise, organizations are faced with two recruitment options: Fill the position with an internal candidate (an existing employee), or fill the position with an external candidate (someone from outside the organization). The decision whether to recruit internally or externally depends on the specifics of the situation, and there are trade-offs when choosing either approach.

The following are benefits of internal recruitment:

- Provides in-depth knowledge of existing employee skills, abilities, and work habits
- Less time and fewer resources designated for candidate recruitment
- Creates a performance incentive for existing employees and may increase motivation
- Less time and fewer resources devoted to getting new employees oriented and trained
- Creates long-term attachments to the organization and deepens organizational loyalty

There are also benefits to attracting candidates from outside the organization:

- Allows organizations to choose from a wider range of qualified candidates to achieve the best fit for the position
- Adds skills and abilities that may not be present in existing employees
- Fresh ideas and perspectives brought in from outside the organization
- Can help change the existing organizational culture
- Can promote diversity in the existing workforce

If the organization chooses to recruit externally, it should employ a range of strategies to attract potential candidates. Keep in mind that an external job search does not exclude internal candidates from applying for the position. Recruitment strategies may be extremely targeted, such as the use of personal and professional networks, or they may be more wide ranging, such as the use of newspaper advertisements or generic web-based job sites. Both targeted and wide-ranging approaches to recruitment can be advantageous. For example, using trusted personal or professional networks to seek candidates for an open position can increase confidence that the candidate will be a successful hire. Wider recruitment strategies can help extend communications beyond traditional search boundaries and may yield candidates with skills and expertise that might have gone unnoticed.

Overreliance on any one strategy can have negative consequences for the organization. Focusing on personal or professional networks to identify potential candidates can create an insular search and can perpetuate existing hiring biases and patterns. Relying on newspaper advertisements or generic job search websites can be cost prohibitive and creates a passive approach to candidate recruitment. A mix of recruitment strategies provides multiple advantages to the organization.

Possible methods for candidate recruitment from the most targeted to the least include the following:

- Using personal and professional networks
- Posting the job announcement on the website or through the internal human resources system of the organization
- Utilizing a services search or other third-party firms
- Posting positions at career fairs or using career services through professional organizations
- Disseminating job announcements over email distribution lists affiliated with professional organizations
- Placing advertisements in professional publications or websites
- Placing advertisements in relevant newspapers or other print sources
- Advertising the position on generic job websites

Organizations should also reach out to traditionally underrepresented groups through networks and professional organizations to capitalize on diverse talents and expertise that might go undetected through traditional recruitment strategies.

# Selection

The job search is about selecting the right candidate for the job. If the organization does a thorough job identifying its needs, articulating them in a formal job announcement, and recruiting a large pool of prospective candidates, it stands a better chance of bringing the right candidate on board. To select the right candidate from among the pool of prospective applicants, the organization must develop a selection process, screen applicants, interview top candidates, and make an official offer to the top candidate. Although the specifics might differ, the general steps in candidate selection are usually the same regardless of whether an organization is filling positions at the entry, middle, or upper levels.

## Developing a Process

One of the first steps in developing a candidate selection process is deciding who will be responsible for making the hiring decision. In most cases that involve professional staff positions, a search and screen committee is put together to narrow the candidate field. Organizations may take different approaches to putting together the search and screen committee. A typical model for committee development includes a committee chair, who is usually the person responsible for supervising the position, along with approximately three to five committee members who represent various interests that intersect with the open position. It can be advantageous to allow broad organizational input on candidates, especially where other employees might be affected by the hire; however, large search and screen committees with too many decision makers are difficult to manage and can become unwieldy.

The search and screen committee should agree upon a reasonable time frame for candidate selection. It is important for committees to have enough time to identify the ideal candidate and make the proper hire. However, taking too much time can lead to losing good candidates because other organizations may move more quickly in making them an offer.

## Screening Candidates

One of the roles of the search and screen committee is to narrow a large group of applicants to a more manageable number of candidates that the organization would like to examine more closely. The committee should develop a process for screening applicants that is unambiguous and fair. Being purposeful about the screening process and avoiding arbitrary decision making can help to avoid potential conflict over specific candidates. One method for narrowing an applicant pool is through the use of a **stage-based screening process**. Stage-based processes set specific benchmarks for applicants to meet based on their qualifications for the position. Each stage sets more stringent benchmarks, narrowing the applicant pool as the process moves along. Figure 9.4 shows the benchmarks set for the first two stages of a search and screen process.

Committee members evaluate applicants based on their application materials (e.g., cover letter, résumé, letters of reference, written application). All committee members score a candidate based on their impression of the candidate's qualifications. When the committee convenes, the group identifies areas where they have consensus to pass an applicant to the next stage and can discuss disagreements about particular candidates. How disagreements are settled is based on the committee process. Some methods could include averaging committee members' scores, attempting to come to a general agreement about an applicant, or putting the final decision to a vote.

**stage-based screening process**—Candidate screening process that sets specific benchmarks for applicants to meet based on their qualifications for the position. Each stage sets more stringent benchmarks, narrowing the applicant pool as the process continues.

## Interviewing Candidates

After the applicant pool has been narrowed to the top group of promising candidates, the process should include some formal contact between the organization and the top candidates. Usually this contact comes in the form of an official job interview, where both the organization and candidate are able to formally evaluate the potential employment opportunity in a deeper way. As with other forms of management communication, interviews are two-way processes. While the organization evaluates the candidates, the candidates should also evaluate the fit between themselves and the organization. Just as some job applicants look better on paper than they do upon closer scrutiny, so do some organizations.

The number of candidates that an organization decides to interview will depend on various factors, including the nature of the position, the number of qualified candidates left in the applicant pool, and the time and financial costs of the interview process. There are three specific types of interviews: screening interviews, phone interviews, and face-to-face interviews. Each type usually takes place at different times during the search process and involves different numbers of potential candidates.

**Screening Interviews**  Screening interviews typically occur at the beginning of the search process and are used when organizations have easy access to applicants. For example, a city park and recreation department might use the NRPA National

# Search and Screen Committee: Recreation Superintendent

## CANDIDATE SCORE SHEET

Name:

### Stage I: Initial Screen

For yes-or-no questions: Indicate whether the candidate meets the criteria and place the point total assigned to the yes or no value in the last column.

| Criteria | Evaluation | Total |
|---|---|---|
| Bachelor's degree in recreation management, sport management, or related field | Yes (50)  No (0) | |
| 1–3 years demonstrated experience in recreation program design and supervision | Yes (50)  No (0) | |

**Total points needed to pass to stage II = 100 points: (circle)   Pass   Does not pass**

### Stage II: Secondary Screen

For yes-or-no questions: Indicate whether the candidate meets the criteria and place the point total assigned to the yes or no value in the last column.

For rating questions, use the following as a guide:

5 = Candidate has superior experience or ability in competency area.

3 = Candidate has some experience or ability in competency area.

1 = Candidate has no experience or ability in competency area.

| Criteria | Evaluation | Total |
|---|---|---|
| Experience supervising full-time staff | Yes (15)  No (0) | |
| More than 3 years of experience | Yes (15)  No (0) | |
| Master's degree in recreation administration, sport administration, or related field | Yes (10)  No (0) | |
| Certified park and recreation professional | Yes (5)   No (0) | |
| Demonstrated experience in policy development | 1  2  3  4  5 | |
| Demonstrated experience in tournament design and administration | 1  2  3  4  5 | |
| Demonstrated experience in program design and delivery | 1  2  3  4  5 | |
| Demonstrated experience in staff supervision for part-time and volunteer staff | 1  2  3  4  5 | |
| Demonstrated experience with risk management protocols | 1  2  3  4  5 | |
| Demonstrated experience with facility maintenance and management | 1  2  3  4  5 | |
| Demonstrated experience in budget development and accounting | 1  2  3  4  5 | |
| Demonstrated experience in marketing and publicity | 1  2  3  4  5 | |
| Demonstrated experience in program evaluation | 1  2  3  4  5 | |
| Demonstrated experience working with personal computers and web design | 1  2  3  4  5 | |
| Demonstrated ability to communicate effectively in written form | 1  2  3  4  5 | |
| | **Total** | |

**Total points needed to pass to stage III = 55 points:  (circle)    Pass    Does not pass**

**Figure 9.4**   Search and screen committee score sheet.

Congress to meet briefly with delegates who might be interested in an available position. Screening interviews allow organizations to talk more about themselves and their job openings, and they allow applicants to ask questions. Screening interviews may be informal discussions with prospective candidates, or they may use formal questions designed to elicit specific responses.

Screening interviews can be informal (face to face) or they can be a written response to specific questions, a phone interview (see the next section), or a video interview where candidates submit recorded responses to predetermined questions. During screening interviews, the organization can get a sense of the human skills that potential applicants possess, and the applicants can get a sense of the people they might work with someday. Screening interviews may not be possible unless the organization can obtain access to potential job applicants in one location. For positions that require a national search, this is obviously a difficult task.

**Phone Interviews** Phone interviews typically occur before bringing the final list of candidates in for face-to-face interviews. Phone interviews usually involve 5 to 10 candidates, with the intent of narrowing the final field to 3 to 5 candidates. These interviews may be conducted as conference calls with all members of the search committee taking part, or they may be conducted with smaller subsets or individual members of the committee.

In some cases, phone interviews may not be necessary. For example, part-time or seasonal staff positions, such as lifeguards, youth coaches, group fitness instructors, and similar positions where candidates are easily accessed might not require this step. For professional positions, national searches, and searches where organizations do not have easy access to candidates or where time and money are obstacles to hosting more than two or three top candidates, phone interviews can be useful in narrowing lists of potential candidates. Phone interviews can also allow an organization to more deeply evaluate candidates beyond their written application materials.

Advantages of phone interviews include the following:

- They allow organizations to follow up on questions related to application materials.
- They provide a two-way exchange of information between the candidate and the committee.
- They are less expensive than face-to-face interviews.
- They can eliminate poor fits without wasting time and money by bringing candidates in for a face-to-face interview.
- They are more flexible and require less commitment on the part of the organization and candidate than face-to-face interviews.

Disadvantages of phone interviews include the following:

- They are limited to verbal communication between candidates and the search committee.
- The committee is unable to evaluate other aspects of a candidate's communication ability (e.g., nonverbal communication) or other sets of desired skills (e.g., person-to-person interaction).
- Technology limitations can create confusion with multiple-party dialogue over phone lines.

**Face-to-Face Interviews** The last step before arriving at a final ranking of top candidates is the face-to-face interview. As with other job interviews, face-to-face interviews provide an opportunity for an exchange of information and should be seen as a chance for both organization and candidate to get to know one another. At this point, candidate qualifications should be well known from their application materials, screening interview, and phone interview. Face-to-face interviews are as much trial runs as they are fact-gathering forums. In other words, during the interview experience, both the organization and the candidate will be finding out whether a good fit exists.

Face-to-face interviews can be categorized into three types: individual interviews, group interviews, and assessment centers. These formats do not necessarily need to be mutually exclusive. Organizations may find it useful to combine interview formats to assess the suitability of a candidate for the position.

The standard format is the individual interview. The individual, in this case, is the candidate. One or more people from the organization interview the candidate regarding the job. Individual interviews generally use standard question-and-answer formats. The types of questions that are asked during an interview will vary depending on the position. However, questions should go beyond asking candidates to restate the technical qualifications that are already listed in their application materials. Many interview questions seek deeper insight into an employee's potential work behavior or various skills they have that might not easily translate onto a résumé or job application. For example, interview questions should attempt to illuminate the candidate's conceptual or human relations skills through scenario or application formats. Consider the differences between these two questions:

- What are your experiences with budget preparation and financial management?
- Following your first budget approval process, you have been told that appropriated funds toward your operating budget for programs and services will be cut by 5 percent. What ideas do you have for recovering the lost revenue or balancing your budget?

Both questions attempt to understand the candidate's experience with budgeting and financial management. The first question focuses solely on the technical experiences of the candidate. Although this is important, these experiences should be apparent from reading the candidate's application materials. The second question attempts to more deeply understand the candidate's approach to budgeting and financial decision making, and it delves into the candidate's competencies. To answer the question, candidates will still need to speak to their technical skills in this area, yet they have an opportunity to reveal more insight into their actual work behavior and decision-making ability. This approach can be used to reformulate almost all standard interview questions and provide greater insight into the competencies that candidates possess relative to the job. Keep in mind that interview questions should be based on the job description.

The second major type of face-to-face interview is group interviews, which are conducted with a number of candidates answering questions in the same interview session at the same time. In a group interview, an interviewer or panel of interviewers asks the same set of questions to each candidate in some random order, and candidates provide answers to the questions in the presence of each other. Each candidate gets to hear the answers of every other candidate, and the interviewers

## Ordering Interview Questions

When deciding on an order for interview questions, start with general questions about education and experience to put the candidate at ease. As the interview goes along, make the questions increasingly more specific and challenging. At the end, always ask if they have any questions for you.

can evaluate answers in relation to the other answers provided. Group interviews can be advantageous because they can reveal candidates' ability to adjust their approach based on what others have already said. Group interviews work well in situations where there are a number of highly qualified candidates for the position, when the position requires candidates to think outside the box and come up with different solutions to challenges, or when candidates are relatively similar and there is a desire to see how they differentiate themselves from one another. However, group interviews are high-stakes endeavors. As such, they can be overly stressful on candidates and may lead to highly competitive exchanges or place candidates and interviewers in uncomfortable positions.

The third major type of face-to-face interview is the assessment center. Often the traditional candidate evaluation and selection process is conducted away from the context of the position. The assessment center is a response to the critique of the traditional question-and-answer interview format that focuses more on a candidate's knowledge than on the candidate's actual work behavior and processes. As noted, standard interview questions can be reformulated to gain insight into the latter, but the assessment center takes this a step further. The assessment center attempts to understand a candidate's work behavior in context. It utilizes a mix of evaluation approaches that can provide more understanding of a candidate's work behavior within the context of the job that is being hired. Some of these approaches include the following:

- *In-box exercises.* A simulated in-box is put together by interview teams with a variety of tasks that are associated with the day-to-day duties required of the position. The candidate is given a set amount of time to respond to the various tasks contained in the in-box. The candidate is then evaluated on criteria such as the quality of the work performed, the decision making behind the tasks selected, and the ability to prioritize tasks in a limited time frame.

- *Team project.* A simulated team project asks the candidate to function as part of a group with the intent of producing a piece of work within a given time frame. The simulated team could comprise other candidates for the position, similar to a group interview, or it could comprise members of the organization who might be required to work with the person who is hired. Through simulated team projects, the organization can gain insight into the candidate's leadership skills, ability to listen to others' ideas, personal relationship skills, ability to handle conflict, and ability to produce under a deadline.

- *Demonstrations.* Candidates may be asked to perform various tasks associated with the position, including mock budget hearings, staff trainings, presentations, or demonstrations of specific skills or abilities (e.g., fitness instruction, sport officiating skills, outdoor adventure leadership). Through these demonstrations, the organization can more accurately evaluate the candidate's competence related to the requirements of the position.

All three of these assessment center techniques can be used together to enhance candidate evaluation. Each technique should be used to understand the candidate's competencies within the context of the job. The goal of this process is to select the candidate with the best skill set (technical, human, and conceptual) for the position, as well as the best fit for the organization.

### Making an Offer

At the conclusion of the interview process, it is time for the organization to make an offer to its top candidate. This process can be more complicated than it seems because the top candidate may not accept the job offer. At the end of the process, the search committee should have a clear sense of who would fit with the organization and who would not. For example, among the three finalists for a position, which of the three would be the best hire? If the top candidate does not accept the offer, is the second candidate an acceptable choice? If the second and third candidates would not be acceptable, the organization needs a contingency plan in case the top candidate refuses the job offer. This contingency plan often includes regrouping and starting the search over again.

The organization needs to make some decisions before making an offer to its top candidate. For example, what parts of the offer are open for negotiation? Is there room to negotiate compensation, such as starting salary or fringe benefits? Is there room to negotiate moving expenses? Start date? Vacation time? To a large extent, the answers to these questions will depend on the position that is being hired. Top-level executives may have more leeway to negotiate than entry-level employees, and full-time employees may have more room to negotiate than part-time employees. Negotiation of compensation might be more acceptable in the commercial sector than in the public or nonprofit sector, where salary levels may be regulated by policy or statute. Positions where there is a scarcity of qualified employees may require more flexibility in reaching a final offer. Organizational planning is critical before making a job offer. The organization needs to fully understand the ramifications behind its decisions both in terms of landing the ideal employee and the implications for existing staff.

## Orientation and Training

Orientation and training are critical steps in employee development. Organizations that do not invest in training and development waste human potential. New employees who are not properly oriented to the policies, rules, and culture of the organization can feel anxious, out of place, or undervalued. Poorly trained or unprepared employees can lead to poor work performance, waste of organizational resources, and could even create dangerous situations for customers or other staff members depending on the position. In organizations where employee orientation and training are shortchanged, supervisors may need to spend more time teaching and correcting performance errors. In short, investing in employee development through orientation and training can help to maximize potential more quickly, create greater job satisfaction, create a sense of organizational stewardship, and reduce the need for constant supervision by management.

# What Can I Ask?

Not all interview questions that an employer may ask are appropriate or legal. The critical question for employers to ask themselves is, "What do I really need to know about these candidates to judge their competence to do the job in question?" Interview questions must be directly applicable to the job vacancy. Some examples of legal and illegal interview questions follow. These are just guidelines; individual states or provinces may expand this list. Be sure to refer all questions about legality to the legal counsel of your organization.

**Age**

Illegal: How old are you?

Legal: Are you over the age of 18?

**Disabilities**

Illegal: Do you have any disabilities?

Legal: Are you able to perform the functions of the job with or without reasonable accommodations?

**Nationality**

Illegal: Where are you from? Where were your parents born? What is your native language?

Legal: Are you authorized to work in the United States?

**Armed Forces**

Illegal: Which branch of the military did you serve in? Were you honorably discharged?

Legal: What type of experiences did you gain in the military? What type of training did you receive?

**Height and Weight**

Illegal: How tall are you? How much do you weigh?

Legal: Can you lift 60 pounds (27 kilograms)? Do you need any special accommodations for the job? (Questions about ability need to be related to the job.)

**Marital Status and Dependents**

Illegal: Are you married? Do you have children? Do you plan to have children? Whom do you live with?

Legal: Are you willing to relocate for this job? Are you willing to travel? Are you able to work weekends? (Again, questions need to be related to the job.)

No legal questions may be asked about the following categories:

- Race
- Religion (except whether one can work on a specific day, if it is related to the job)
- Sex

Hiring the best person is only the beginning of the staff development process. Regardless of how well new employees fit with the organization, they will most certainly have questions related to policies, rules, culture, values, and the nature of their job in relation to others. For new employees, orientation provides an introduction to the organization and is often focused on two areas: general orientation and job-specific orientation. For some positions, new employees may need training in specific technical skills to perform their jobs effectively. Regardless of their tenure with the organization, all employees need ongoing support, knowledge, and skills development in order to maximize their talents as professionals. Thus, training can be broken down into two categories: skills training and ongoing learning and development.

## Orientation

The purpose of most orientation programs can be seen as helping new employees fit into their new organizations. Orientation programs should provide employees with information about the organization and the job that the employee has been hired to do. They should also integrate new employees into the social fabric of the organization by building esprit de corps.

The following components should be included in a general organizational orientation program for new employees:

• *Organizational values.* Although new employees should already be aware of organizational values from the application process, orientation programs are opportunities to further articulate the areas that the organization cares deeply about (e.g., history, tradition, excellence, community development, customer service, safety). These areas also contribute to organizational culture.

• *Organizational structure.* Orientation programs are good places to educate new employees on organizational structure and layout, including reporting lines. New employees should also become aware of how their position relates to other positions up, down, and across the organizational chart.

• *Work-related policies, procedures, and rules.* Orientation programs should clearly articulate the major policy areas that employees should understand. If the organization has an employee manual or handbook—and it should—orientation programs are good opportunities to share and discuss the critical content areas.

• *Facility tours.* To understand the scope of the organization, new employees should be given tours of the facilities. These tours can also be an opportunity to provide keys or other forms of access to secure facilities. This is particularly important for organizations with large or multiple facilities.

• *Compensation and benefits.* New employees will need to spend some time with a benefits counselor or other human resources expert to discuss options for health and life insurance, retirement plans, tax withholding, and other aspects of employee compensation. See the sidebar for examples of employee benefits.

• *Bonding.* Orientation programs should provide opportunities for staff to become acquainted with one another and should attempt to quickly integrate new employees into the organization. Adding a social component to the orientation either on- or off-site can help build relationships and can ease the transition of new employees into the organization.

In addition to a general orientation, new employees need information related to the basic functions of a particular job. The following components should be included in a job-specific orientation for new employees:

---

### Examples of Employee Benefits

- Vacation and holiday pay
- Domestic partner benefits
- Pension plans
- Use of agency facilities
- Paid education fees
- Childcare services

---

● *Supervisor.* New employees should have significant time to meet with their direct supervisor to discuss the boss–employee relationship. This is a time for supervisors to discuss their management philosophy and their approach to running their unit, including any unit-specific policies, procedures, guidelines, or protocols.

● *Scope and duties.* New employees need to be sure that they adequately understand the duties of their position. This can include areas of responsibility, supervisory capacity, and day-to-day job functions.

● *Office space and resources.* Employees need the proper resources to do their jobs effectively. One of the areas that new employees tend to get most excited about is their office space and the resources available to them. Orientation programs should introduce new employees to their office space, computing resources, storage files, and other office resources.

● *Staff introductions.* As mentioned, orientation programs are opportunities to form relationships and build esprit de corps among staff. Job-specific orientation programs should also include meetings between the new employee and fellow unit coworkers. If the position has supervisory responsibility, the new supervisor should be able to spend time getting to know staff members.

Orientation programs are critical in easing the transition for new employees into an organization. As such, orientation should not be shortchanged. Sometimes organizations try to provide too much information in a compressed amount of time. Too much information can lead to overload and may create more anxiety for the new employee. Mixing methods for delivering orientation programs, including formal presentations, workshops, one-on-one meetings, social gatherings, and alone time for new employees to reflect and digest information, can help keep the process interesting and effective. Some information presented during orientation will not be retained, so to reinforce critical information, ongoing training and development programs are also needed.

## Training and Development

**Employee training** refers to the process of preparing employees for the work that they do. **Employee development** is a broader concept and implies an ongoing process of learning and improvement. Block (2013) differentiates between the two concepts by stating that training tends to be management imposed and focused on organizational concerns, whereas learning and development should be employee initiated and focused on the concerns of the employees or their unit.

**employee training**—Process of preparing employees for their responsibilities.

**employee development**—Ongoing process of learning, improvement, and change for workers in an organization.

Training and development programs may focus on the following:

- Preparing employees to operate within specific organizational protocols or systems
- Providing employees with specific technical skills to do their jobs effectively
- Developing competencies that address key organizational concerns (e.g., team building, handling conflict, diversity)
- Preparing employees, managers, and units to navigate significant organizational change
- Providing employees with the resources and opportunities to continually learn, grow, and develop as both individuals and organizational actors

The goals of employee training and development will differ depending on the situation. New employees may need to focus on learning how the organization does business or building specific technical skills to do their jobs effectively. All employees may need to gain more knowledge on diversity or how to manage conflict in the workplace. Managers may need to spend time understanding larger organizational challenges and preparing their units to handle significant change. Individual employees may desire to take on greater challenges in their jobs or broaden their knowledge for their own self-improvement.

Investing time and resources in employee training and development is a necessary step in preparing employees to do their jobs effectively and to help their organizations meet their performance mandates. Employee training and development programs can be either high- or low-threshold investments. **High-threshold training**, which involves a considerable investment of time, expertise, or resources, includes

**high-threshold training**—Training methods that involve a considerable investment of time, expertise, or resources.

- workshops,
- retreats,
- clinics,
- formal education programs (colleges or universities), and
- professional certification or licensure programs.

**low-threshold training**—Training methods that can achieve results through modest investments of time or resources.

**Low-threshold training**, which can achieve results through modest investments of time or resources, includes

- meetings,
- job shadowing (observation),
- job coaching (observation, practice, and feedback),
- employee mentoring programs,
- providing access to professional resources (trade magazines, Internet and intranet access),
- professional association involvement and conference attendance,
- networking,
- job enrichment (adding responsibilities that provide opportunities for professional growth),
- job rotation (providing opportunities to work in different positions or units), and
- committee or task-force assignments.

# Performance Appraisal

Performance appraisal, also referred to as *employee evaluation*, is used by managers to achieve several goals:

- Provide feedback on performance
- Provide opportunities for ongoing learning and education
- Stimulate employee motivation
- Help make decisions related to commendation, promotion, discipline, or termination
- Draw connections between an employee's individual job performance and unit or organizational goals

Employees need information related to their job performance in order to effectively fulfill the responsibilities of their position. Without access to this information, employees may continue to repeat mistakes, waste resources, or underserve customers. Managers may find it difficult to make decisions about pay increases or promotions without documented information related to an employee's job performance. Absent such information, these decisions may be perceived as arbitrary or unfair. Employees also cannot seek out opportunities for further development if they are unaware of their strengths and weaknesses. In some situations, employees who are terminated or disciplined without regular, documented performance reviews may legitimately perceive that they have been denied due process or, worse, discriminated against. Regular performance assessment benefits both the employee and the employer, and it can be used as an employee development tool as well as a framework for managerial decision making (George and Jones 2011).

Performance appraisal can be formal, informal, or a mix of both. Examples of informal performance reviews include frequent meetings to discuss progress, pats on the back, constructive criticism, short handwritten notes, and emails for jobs well done or a performance that missed the mark. In some cases, informal performance reviews can be documented—copies of handwritten notes can be placed in employees' files, emails can be saved and copied, and meetings can be noted. However, the purpose of these informal reviews is to keep lines of communication open and to be sure that expectations are clearly articulated, problems are addressed, and good performance is recognized. Informal methods are useful because they provide immediate feedback for employees and allow flexibility in adjusting to the information that is exchanged.

Formal performance appraisal takes place less frequently and typically relies on specific methods of measurement and feedback. For example, an organization may conduct formal performance reviews twice per year, or perhaps more frequently during an employee's introductory probation (if one exists). Formal performance reviews rely on either objective or subjective measures of performance. Objective measures are used when performance is determined by specific numeric results, such as participation counts, dollars raised, or new members signed up. Subjective measures are used when performance cannot be objectively measured. They rely on an evaluator's interpretation of performance based on preestablished criteria.

One of the main challenges of formal performance appraisal, especially when subjective measures are used, is the accuracy of the assessment. Different people have different perceptions of performance, and bias is possible unless there are multiple measures of assessment. One way to help prevent bias is to develop a process that adds a variety of voices to the assessment process, a method George and Jones

(2011) call *360-degree appraisal.* In this process, performance appraisal is conducted by those who come in contact with the employee or are in a position to assess performance. This includes peers, superiors, subordinates, and customers. It may also make sense to include the employee's perspective through self-appraisal. By providing multiple measures of assessment, supervisors can look for patterns in the results, as well as note where there might be areas of disagreement among assessors.

As part of performance appraisal, employees should have the opportunity to discuss the results with their supervisors, ask questions, request resources to help them improve performance, and set goals with the supervisor to be achieved by the next appraisal. Supervisors should be sure to document questions, requests, and future performance goals in writing and have the employee sign off on the process.

When performance appraisals reveal that employees have failed to live up to job expectations, or in cases where employee performance puts the organization at risk in some way, managers must take action. This could range from documenting the problem and providing suggestions for improvement to disciplinary action or, in extreme cases, termination. It is important to understand your own organization's process and policies regarding employee discipline. However, it is also important to employ a system of progressive discipline. Progressive discipline seeks to help an employee change his or her behavior or performance by using the least severe action that can accomplish the goal (Barcelona, Wells, and Arthur-Banning 2016). Progressive discipline typically involves four steps:

1. *Counseling.* This can include verbal or written feedback for the employee that documents the issue and provides suggestions for improving performance. Counseling is intended to be developmental and not punitive. Feedback should be used to clarify expectations and should help the employee understand standards of performance.

2. *Written warning.* In cases where counseling feedback is not heeded, or where performance has not improved, a written warning may be necessary. Warnings should clearly document the issue, provide clear expectations for improvement, and document the consequences of further poor performance. Written warnings generally provide a time frame for corrective action.

3. *Suspension (usually without pay).* When employee behavior puts the organization or any individual in the organization at risk, or when performance levels continue to fall short of expectations, it may be necessary to suspend an employee without pay. In some cases, employees may receive compensation while they are suspended, particularly in cases where an active investigation is underway, but the organization cannot take the risk of having the employee continue on the job. The parameters of the suspension (e.g., length, compensation status, conditions for return) must be documented in writing, as well as any corrective action required upon the employee's return.

4. *Termination.* In extreme cases, a manager may need to terminate an employee for repeated poor performance or for actions that put the organization or other individuals at risk. Employees have a right to know the reason for termination, and decisions to terminate an employment must be well researched and documented. It is true that termination can be a difficult process in many organizations. However, if the steps above are taken, employees are clear on their performance expectations, and they are aware of the consequences of their actions, it is possible to terminate employment. The key is to use a

progressive process, clearly communicate with the affected employee along the way, and document each step.

The personnel process is time consuming but one of the most important management functions in any agency. The value of human resources has been demonstrated throughout the entire text and should be understood by all professionals for the sake of agency efficiency and effectiveness.

# MANAGING VOLUNTEERS

**Volunteers** are people who provide labor or services for the benefit of the community through their own free will and without monetary reward. A recent study in Canada revealed that approximately 12.7 million Canadians over the age of 15 engage in close to 2 billion volunteer hours (Volunteer Canada 2015). In the United States, more than 62.6 million people over the age of 16, or about 24.9 percent of the total population, volunteer for an organization (U.S. Bureau of Labor Statistics 2016).

**volunteers**—People who provide labor or services for the benefit of the community through their own free will and without monetary reward.

For many leisure services organizations, volunteers are important staff members. Volunteers provide critical functions, including program delivery, administration, logistics, and advisory roles. It is difficult to discuss specific volunteer positions in leisure services because responsibilities are so different from organization to organization and from community to community. However, volunteer management is not much different from other forms of personnel management. Leisure services managers should think in terms of four broad areas regarding volunteers: recruitment, training, supervision, and retention.

## Volunteer Recruitment

Leisure services organizations need to ask two key questions when thinking about recruiting possible volunteers. The answers to these questions will help guide the organization in developing a sound volunteer recruitment strategy:

• What types of volunteer positions are needed? Different organizations have different volunteer needs. For example, some organizations with limited full-time staff may rely on volunteers to take on significant administrative or program responsibilities. Other organizations may rely on volunteers for logistical or support purposes, such as coordinating travel, fund-raising, publicity, or maintenance. Still others may use volunteers as board members or on policy-making teams. As with full-time staff, volunteers may serve different clientele or program areas. For example, volunteers may work specifically with youth, the elderly, or people with disabilities. They may serve as sport coaches, program leaders, or personal care attendants. Carefully considering the types of volunteer positions that are needed will help the organization search for the volunteers who are best suited to the jobs.

• What competencies and skills are needed for the position? Developing competency sets for volunteer positions is just as important as identifying needed competencies for full-time staff. As we have noted, volunteers can fulfill a range of roles within the organization, and many of these roles require specific competencies. Depending on the position, it may not be enough to settle for anyone who is willing to do the job. Certain volunteer positions require specific competencies, such as the ability to teach sport skills, write grant proposals, speak effectively in public, or drive a 15-passenger van. Considering the necessary competencies associated with each volunteer position is critical in attempting to recruit the right person for the position. Furthermore, having a job description for volunteer positions can better match the volunteer and the job.

Each of these questions is important because the answers help to create strong matches between position and volunteer. There are a variety of motivations for volunteering, including personal satisfaction, sharing knowledge with others, making a difference in the community, connecting with other people, accomplishing goals, and strengthening neighborhoods and communities (Corporation for National and Community Service n.d.). Volunteering is often a key part of an individual's identity. Finding volunteers who are committed to the role they are about to fulfill is an important consideration in the recruitment process.

In answering these two questions, leisure services organizations need to decide whether it is appropriate to narrowly target or broadly advertise for volunteers. Some positions are best suited to a careful, individualized, tailored recruitment process. Recruiting an advisory board member, for example, might best be accomplished by talking individually to program leaders who have established track records as friends of recreation. On the other end of the spectrum, recruiting volunteers for a 5K road race might include advertising in newspapers, connecting with the local school district, and engaging the local business community.

Depending on the position and the role that the volunteer is expected to fulfill, it might be prudent to conduct some form of background screening, such as checking work references, conducting criminal background checks, verifying physical addresses and Social Security numbers, drug testing, and checking the public sexual offender registry. The National Recreation and Park Association recommends that all volunteers who are working with vulnerable populations (e.g., youth, elderly, people with disabilities) should be subject to background screening. Despite this recommendation, at least one study has shown that only 40 percent of recreational sport organizations required background checks of their volunteer coaches, and less than 25 percent required coaches to go through a mandatory coach training program (Barcelona and Young 2010).

## Training and Supervision

Too often, volunteers are left without proper training to fulfill their roles effectively. For example, it has been estimated that up to 90 percent of volunteer youth sport coaches have not gone through a formalized coach training program (Ewing, Gano-Overway, Branta, and Seefeldt 2002). This is a concern in the broader field of youth development; volunteers often report feeling unprepared to work effectively with children and adolescents (Huebner, Walker, and McFarland 2003). Other groups of volunteers, including those working with the elderly, with participants with disabilities, and in administrative positions, often experience the same lack of training support.

Once volunteers are recruited and selected, the leisure services organization is responsible for orienting and training them for the role they are going to perform. The type of training provided for volunteers is going to depend on the nature and scope of the position. For example, event volunteers working a 5K road race will need a basic orientation and training for the duties that they will perform on the day of the race. Volunteers who have more frequent contact with participants, work with vulnerable populations, or perform roles that require significant responsibility will need more in-depth training. The following can be helpful guides to structuring a volunteer training program:

- Provide volunteers with information on the agency, including the mission, vision, goals, and objectives.
- Develop volunteer job descriptions that list specific job roles and scope of responsibilities.
- Develop a set of expectations for the position, including estimated time commitment, meeting requirements, and behavior and ethical standards.
- Provide a list of policies and procedures applicable to the position, including purchasing guidelines, communication protocols, and risk management plans.
- Develop a system for communication, including one-on-one meetings to clarify expectations and provide feedback.
- Where applicable, require or encourage attendance at a training program that is applicable to the volunteer position (e.g., youth coach training, inclusion training, first aid and CPR training).
- Provide support for attendance at relevant professional conferences or workshops that are applicable to the position.

It is important to provide the support and resources to help volunteers do their jobs. Many volunteers want access to training and development resources, and developing these systems can maximize the volunteer experience and lead to higher levels of volunteer retention.

## Retention

Keeping a solid core of volunteers is important for leisure services organizations so the organization doesn't need to start over with new volunteers each year. This is especially important for programs that require continuity or that focus on building and maintaining relationships with participants. To a large extent, retention is dependent on sound recruiting, access to training and development, and effective supervision. If significant resources are devoted to these areas of volunteer management, then the organization is well on its way to a successful retention strategy. In addition, volunteer-recognition programs that recognize the effort and importance of volunteers can aid in the retention process.

Volunteer recognition can take many forms and can include both large-scale events and small tokens of appreciation. Some examples to consider for a volunteer-recognition program include the following:

- Thank-you letters
- Certificates
- Appreciation plaques
- Volunteer awards
- Staff apparel
- Dinners and banquets
- Appreciation weeks

Public recognition also plays a valuable role in increasing awareness of the volunteer opportunities that are available through an agency. This process can thus be a valuable recruiting tool for future volunteers.

Check out the web study guide for additional material, including learning activities, sample documents, interactive case studies, web links, CPRP exam connections, and more.

## Conclusion

Much of what leisure services managers do on a daily basis involves planning, organizing, controlling, and leading personnel. Successful personnel management addresses the needs of the organization and the employee and involves both planning and processes. Personnel planning includes considering the capacity of an organization for accommodating staff. This requires analyzing existing staffing levels, fiscal resources, supervisory resources, physical resources, and administrative support systems. Personnel planning also includes considering the personnel needs of an organization. Organizations must consider the composition of their staff and commit to ensuring a diverse workforce.

Personnel processes involve developing a system for staffing and employee training and development. This system includes conceptualizing organizational needs; developing job announcements; recruiting qualified applicants; selecting and hiring the best candidate; creating orientation, training, and development processes; and providing feedback on employee performance through formal and informal appraisal.

## Review Questions

1. What is the difference between the terms *personnel* and *human resources*? What are the core assumptions of Bolman and Deal's human resources philosophy?

2. What are the organizational capacity factors that leisure services managers need to consider before adding additional staff?

3. What are the differences between technical skills, human relations skills, and conceptual skills?

4. What are some of the key diversity trends in the United States and Canada? Why is increasing diversity in society an issue for leisure services managers to consider?

5. What are the key federal and state/provincial discrimination laws in the United States and Canada? What is the impact of each of these laws on the hiring process?

6. What are the key components of a job description?

7. What is a job announcement used for? What content areas should it include?

8. What are the advantages and disadvantages of hiring from inside and outside the organization?

9. What is a competency-based interview question?

10. What are the three main forms of candidate interviews?

11. What should be included in a general orientation program for employees? What about a job-specific orientation program? Why are orientation programs necessary in the first place?

12. What are the main differences between the concepts of training and development?

13. What are some examples of high- and low-threshold training or development programs?

14. What are the key decisions involved in the performance appraisal process?

15. How is volunteer management similar to yet different from managing paid staff members?

# 10

# Motivation, Rewards, and Discipline

## Learning Outcomes

- Understand foundational and current thinking on motivation in leisure services organizations.

- Understand how to develop and grow employees in leisure services organizations.

- Explain ways to recognize and reward employees in leisure services organizations.

- Define the concept of self-care in a management capacity.

- Discuss the effective use of discipline in leisure services organizations.

- Understand the steps to take when hiring and terminating employees.

## Key Words

engagement, motivation, three needs theory, equity theory, expectancy theory, recognition, rewards, extrinsic rewards, intrinsic rewards, monetary rewards, nonmonetary rewards, performance-based rewards, membership-based rewards, progressive discipline

## Competency Check

Refer to table 1.6 to see how you assessed these related competencies.

10. Communicate the organization's values, vision, and mission.

16. Be creative and innovative.

23. Take initiative.

27. Supervise, discipline, and evaluate a diverse staff.

28. Motivate employees.

29. Have leadership skills and abilities.

30. Be able to work in a team.

## A Day in the Life

My areas of responsibility include fitness, aquatics, the sport shop, kids' programs and camps, and acting as a liaison between our three racquet sports. My days begin with checking emails and voicemails and reviewing my calendar for any upcoming meetings or appointments. Usually, my to-do lists are long, so prioritizing tasks becomes integral to make the most of my days. Next, I make my rounds. I try my best to set foot in each area of the club that I'm responsible for at least once a day. Private clubs are unique in that you are always dealing with the same people over and over again. It means that my team and I have to work even harder to ensure we are creating and maintaining a variety of recreation programs that will keep our captive audience engaged for a lifetime. My days are long, and there's always more work to be done. It would be easy for me to say my job is too busy—and that's because it is. I'm busy creating memories of summer camp and fitness programs that help seniors squeeze more enjoyment out of life. I'm busy improving the process of registration so that parents can easily sign their kids up for sports programs that might lead to a lifelong love of physical activity. I'm busy handling the details of a tournament that showcases teamwork and commitment, and I'm busy recognizing staff members who go the extra mile. But most of all, I'm just really busy loving the dynamic, challenging, and immeasurably rewarding tasks that I get to call my job.

Heather Nivison
Programs Manager
Vancouver Lawn Tennis and Badminton Club
Vancouver, British Columbia

Throughout this text you have learned the important skills and knowledge you need to effectively manage a leisure services organization. However, organizations do not accomplish goals, satisfy client needs, or create active and involved communities—people do. Employees are the most critical resource in meeting goals and fulfilling the mission of an organization. This chapter gives you a deeper understanding of how to engage employees in a meaningful way to contribute to the success of the organization.

In this chapter we discuss employees; however, many organizations involved with leisure, sport, and recreation have not only paid staff but volunteer staff as well. The principles for managing, motivating, and rewarding volunteers are similar to those for paid employees. Volunteers are working members of an organization who require motivating, managing, leading, and evaluation, just like paid employees. The term *employee* will be used throughout most of the chapter; however, in most instances the general principles of rewards and motivation apply to both.

This chapter explores employee **engagement** and motivation, from getting the right people into your organization, providing opportunities for them to develop and grow, to recognizing and rewarding their contributions. Finally, an important part of managing human resources is the effective use of discipline and, less frequently, dismissing employees. This chapter provides an overview of this challenging area of management.

**engagement**—
Commitment the employee has to the organization and its goals.

# EMPLOYEE ENGAGEMENT AND DEVELOPMENT

In simple terms, employee development is the strategic investment of an organization in its people. Many organizations spend time and money selecting the appropriate technology or equipment for a facility but neglect a similar investment in their people. Developing employees is a critical management task that begins with the initial stages of recruiting, hiring, and orientation, and continues with ongoing training. Thoughtful planning and implementation in the early stages helps to create and grow the initial spark of motivation the employee has toward working in the organization.

## Get the Right People on the Bus

Recruiting and hiring the right people into an organization is the most important step in ensuring employees are a good fit. When recruiting, interviewing, and hiring new employees, an organization communicates what it values, what it expects, and how it recognizes and rewards its employees. This can be done intentionally through carefully orchestrated recruitment and new-employee socialization, or it can be more haphazard if an organization fails to pay attention to the details at this critical juncture in the employee's tenure. Investing time and effort in orientation for new employees often pays future dividends by avoiding misunderstandings and developing employees who will be motivated and self-reliant in the future.

Recruiting and hiring new staff takes considerable resources. Once an agency has chosen wisely and hired the best available candidates, it is the agency's responsibility to provide the new employees with the information they need to be motivated and successful. This may include the following:

- Explain and model the organization's vision, values, and mission
- Have new employees learn from the organization's high performers

- Have new employees' supervisors observe, monitor, and evaluate employee development and performance; ensure that there are probationary performance reviews for all new employees
- Provide regular in-service training opportunities
- Where practical, provide access to relevant employer training opportunities

This initial process from recruiting to orienting new employees is a vital part of engaging and motivating new employees.

In his work as a manager in aquatic and arena services, Dave McBride believes that employees are an organization's most valuable asset. Especially in recreation, where the majority of workers are front-line staff who facilitate community participation in a wide variety of programs and services. Employees are the faces and voices of the organization, and their actions and commitment to customer service excellence often have the highest impact on the quality of the guest experiences. Recreation front-line staff are often teenagers and young adults who work on a casual or part-time basis while completing high school or postsecondary education. These employees often have many competing interests in their lives—studies, sports, activities, relationships, and family expectations. Most of these employees may not be employed long term in recreation. They need to work to cover their tuition, car expenses, and so on while moving toward their future career choices and ambitions. These young employees typically start their employment full of enthusiasm and with an open mind. They intrinsically want to do a good job and make a positive difference. The challenge for all employers is to encourage and sustain this enthusiasm, and provide opportunities for that initial high job motivation to continue and not wane with time. Motivated employees are happier employees and, as a result, are often more committed and dedicated to quality customer service, teamwork, and job performance. It should come as no surprise, then, that highly motivated employees are often the best employees.

## Create an Environment for Employees to Grow

Employee motivation comes from understanding what is required in their jobs and being given room and freedom to grow. Although people are motivated by different factors, as we will see further in this chapter, there is a consistent baseline required for growth. According to Maslow's hierarchy of needs (covered in chapter 1), employees need safety, security, and a sense of belonging in order to achieve. Providing employees with a fair and competitive salary connects to this need for security, and providing a safe, inclusive work environment creates a sense of belonging and a solid foundation for employees to contribute in a meaningful way to the organization. It is important to note that your actions and inactions as a manager can have a direct effect on the motivation of your employees. Clearly communicated expectations of the job and a sense of security for your employees provide a framework where they can grow.

Peter Senge's concept of the learning organization, which you read about in chapter 1, is another key part of creating opportunities for employees to be engaged in their work, be part of a team learning atmosphere, and have a shared vision for the organization that engages intrinsic motivation. In a learning organization, learning and education are encouraged among staff because increasing one person's competence strengthens the organization so that it is better able to respond to changes.

Daniel Pink talks about creating an environment at work based on understanding humans' need for self-determination, a powerful intrinsic motivator. In his book *Drive: The Surprising Truth About What Motivates People,* he says that people have an innate drive to be autonomous, self-determined, and connected to one another, and that today's work environment has moved beyond "factory worker" style roles, which requires managers to rethink what motivates their staff. He argues that people want to make a meaningful contribution to their organizations (Pink 2009). Managers should create opportunities that support the human needs to direct their lives, learn new things, and contribute to the organization and the world.

A working group of managers in the North Vancouver Recreation and Culture Commission offer this:

> *The field of recreation is an intrinsically motivated work environment. We like the idea of "take money off the table"—pay a wage that people are reasonably satisfied with and then focus on purpose.*
>
> *We think that this aligns with Aristotle's' concept of eudaimonia—a good human life, living well and faring well, flourishing. Recreation gives us the opportunity to help others live at the top end of the hierarchy of needs, where they are self-actualizing. Many of us in the field are motivated by knowing that we are a part of something significant and special that changes people's lives for the better.*

It is the manager's responsibility to create an environment for employees to feel safe, secure, and have a sense of belonging to the organization. This lays the groundwork for motivating employees through opportunities for learning, growth, and connecting to their intrinsic motivation in their work.

For Allyson Friesen, director of Abbotsford Parks, Recreation and Culture in British Columbia, the most successful teams she has worked with have grown from a clear vision and guiding philosophical framework and expectations.

> *As a leader, I spend a considerable amount of time at the beginning of an initiative or the forming of a new team discussing the vision to ensure there is a solid understanding of what we are trying to achieve, why it is important, and each of our roles in moving toward the vision. The philosophical framework provides the guiding principles that prescribe how the vision will be achieved and the expectations or level to which it is to be completed (how do you know when you are there?). The framework also acts as a criteria or checklist to give the team autonomy to use their skills and creativity to achieve the vision. The intention is that when a team member is faced with a situation where they need to make a decision and there is no one available with whom to confer or they try a different approach, they can be confident their decision will be supported if it meets the criteria from the framework.*

## Connect to the Purpose of Your Organization

Many people are attracted to work in leisure services organizations because they believe in contributing to the health and wellness of people, families, and communities. Acknowledging the value of this intrinsic motivation is important to engaging employees in their roles. Although many employees come with a desire to do good work, it is up to the manager to understand and share how their specific role is important to the purpose of the organization and to help them see a larger picture and deeper meaning of how they contribute to the goals of the organization.

For example, a swimming instructor might see her role as limited to teaching people how to swim, with a focus on technical skills. A manager could help that swim instructor see a bigger picture that increases her motivation—she is not just teaching swimming lessons, she is increasing physical literacy, developing leadership, encouraging a potential lifelong passion, and enhancing self-sufficiency, social skills, and confidence. Seeing a bigger picture of how the swim instructor is contributing in her work stimulates motivation. Sharing this deeper understanding of connection to the organization and the community motivates the manager too.

In his book *Start with Why*, Simon Sinek says, "People don't buy what you do, they buy why you do it" (Sinek 2009). Most of us know what we do in our work and how we do it, but understanding why we do it provides a deeper connection to meaningful work and motivation, inspiring ourselves and those around us. Managers need to help their employees see beyond the "how" and "what" of their work to a bigger picture of why their work is important to people. Managers who share their "why" help employees to articulate their own "why" based on their core values and the values of the organization.

For example, the YMCA (now known simply as "The Y") shares personal essays called "My Y Story" on their website for the general public, but managers can also share them with their employees to show the impact their work has on people in their community.

City Centre Community Centre in Richmond, British Columbia, hosts an exhibit that features photographs of seniors in the community, highlighting their stories and individual histories and how belonging to that community center has affected their lives. Walking through this exhibit is motivating for staff, as it helps them understand the roles they play in people's lives in the community. It gives them a bigger picture than what they may see in their individual parts of the work. The exhibit promotes the benefits of recreation as well as bringing the mission of the organization alive. Storytelling is a compelling way to share the impact recreation and leisure service work has on people.

At the North Vancouver Recreation and Culture Commission, managers make it a point to talk to staff about the purpose and intention behind different pieces of the work, and appreciate and celebrate the staff in all positions that support this happening. Recognizing the building services person who shovels a pathway through the remnants of a freak hailstorm directly to a senior participant's waiting car, taking her by the arm and helping her into her car to ensure she doesn't slip, will help all staff see how their actions can make a great impact. Or recognizing the front office person who took the time to build a relationship with a participant, noticing when the participant hadn't been in for a while and calling to let him know they were thinking of him. Or explaining to the team the importance of the front office staff who sell the labor-intensive play passes, because they know they are helping to make the community a healthier, more active place. They can take satisfaction in knowing that they are playing a role in helping young people actively participate in community center activities instead of playing video games or watching TV. It is about connecting the impact of mundane daily tasks to the great good they are trying to achieve.

## Build Positive Relationships with Staff

A this point in the chapter, you should notice how important the manager's relationship is to an employee's motivation and engagement in the organization. Building positive relationships with your staff and having them feel they have a good boss who cares is one of the most significant factors that engage people in their jobs.

There is a saying that might ring true for you in your own work experience: "People don't leave their jobs, they leave their managers." Not only does relationship building motivate staff, it also motivates the manager. Many managers feel that creating opportunities to develop and grow their staff is motivating for them. Managers who spent time talking to their employees, asking them questions about what they like about their work, understanding what motivates them and how they want to move forward, and then creating training opportunities felt that this was an important part of their job that kept them engaged in the organization.

The Cameron Recreation Centre in Burnaby, British Columbia, has a collaborative model to provide recreation services. In this model, staff work with senior volunteers to lead most activities. The major focus of the staff is facilitating the volunteers to provide excellent recreational activities and experiences.

The following things are key motivators to both the staff and the volunteers:

- *Purpose and impact.* Knowing that what they do makes a positive impact in the community, both on others and in their own lives
- *Shared values.* Wellness, inclusion, security, accessibility, kindness—benchmarks as well as rewards
- *Community support.* Informal mentoring, authentic appreciation, material and moral support from the seniors' society and the city, all aimed at the same focus of excellent activities and experiences

The center's working relationships are codified in terms of reference created collaboratively with the four seniors' societies many years ago, but the real motivation is not captured in a policy manual or procedures list anywhere. It's organic and attracts staff and volunteers who find it to be a good fit, and it keeps people involved and contributing for many years.

# MOTIVATION

Organizations need employees who are willing and skilled. Training and developing competencies is essential; however, without motivation, the willingness to perform may not be present. **Motivation** is one of the most studied areas in organizational behavior, and we have come to view employee motivation in several ways.

A number of foundational theories have laid the groundwork for an understanding of motivation. As you will recall from chapter 1, Maslow's hierarchy of needs, McGregor's theory X and theory Y, and Herzberg's motivation-hygiene theory are all early theories that attempted to explain motivation within the workplace. Maslow suggested that unless people have basic needs fulfilled, they will be unable to progress to the higher-level needs that drive the behavior most organizations expect from employees. McGregor focused on whether the manager views employees as inherently lazy and in need of coercion (theory X) or wanting to contribute and gain personal fulfillment from their work (theory Y). Finally, Herzberg's work focused more on reward systems. He suggested that some benefits, such as pay, are hygiene factors—necessary but not sufficient to motivate employees. Motivators, on the other hand, could have a positive influence on behavior. These early motivation theories have been a springboard to several current approaches that have received significant support. Three of the most prevalent modern theories are the three needs theory, equity theory, and expectancy theory.

**motivation**—Internal or external factors that affect the direction, intensity, and persistence of behavior.

## Three Needs Theory

You may notice that some people are strongly driven to achieve whereas others are more concerned with things such as friendship or being in control. David McClelland and his colleagues at Harvard University spent more than a quarter of a century

**three needs theory**—Motivation theory proposing that people are motivated by three needs: the need for achievement, the need for power, and the need for affiliation.

investigating this phenomenon. McClelland's **three needs theory** (McClelland 1961) proposes that in most work situations, there are three relevant needs or motives for employee behavior: the need for achievement, the need for power, and the need for affiliation.

The need for achievement is the desire to strive for excellence, to meet goals, and to do things better. People with this need seek tasks in which they can be successful and in which they feel they contributed to that success. As such they often avoid extreme tasks—those that are very easy and those that are extremely difficult. The need for power is the need to influence the behavior of others. People with this need focus on being influential; they enjoy being in charge and tend to prosper in situations that are status oriented or competitive. Finally, the need for affiliation is a desire for close relationships and a friendly place to work. People with this need seek to be liked and accepted by others. Not surprisingly, they are more likely to seek out cooperative settings and situations where they can have a high level of mutual understanding. This particular need is the least studied of the three.

Let's look at three hypothetical employees working in a marketing role for a minor league baseball team. Bill is in charge of game-day preparations. He is meticulous in making sure everything is right and often exceeds the standard that management has set for the facility. Bill loves it when his manager recognizes the quality of his work and his commitment to excellence. In the three needs theory, Bill would be driven by a need to achieve.

Jillian, on the other hand, is the corporate sales leader for the team's marketing department. Her job is to sell the corporate boxes at the stadium and develop effective marketing strategies to attract the support of the local corporate community. Jillian loves the public attention and status of this position. She is driven by increased sales numbers and keeping her corporate clients coming back year after year. She has a knack for getting others to help her make the wishes of her corporate clients come true, such as meeting with players, throwing out the first pitch, and even on one occasion having a company bring its employees and families to sleep on the field and watch movies after a ball game. Jillian reflects a need for power.

Finally, Mario is the team's community and public relations coordinator. He is all about relationships and loves the social nature of his job. He helps bring together the needs of the club and the community. Mario's rewards are the strong friendships he has developed and the focus on cooperation that his job demands. Mario would be a prime example of the need for affiliation.

## Equity Theory

Most people want to be treated fairly, and when they feel that they are not receiving fair treatment, they may act in some way to change the situation. For example, if you worked long and hard developing a new program for your local recreation department and received little positive feedback, whereas a colleague quickly threw together a new program idea in a couple of hours and then received a promotion for that work, you might not feel that the promotion was fair. This notion of fairness is what led John Stacey Adams to develop the **equity theory** of motivation (1963).

Equity theory looks at employees' comparison of their inputs (what they put into a job) and their perceived outcomes (what they get out of it). This input–output ratio is then compared with what Adams (1963) called *relevant others*. In simple terms, employees look at their effort and what they get back, whether it is something tangible such as a promotion or intangible such as praise or recognition. They then compare this ratio with someone who matters to them, such as a coworker or a

**equity theory**—Proposes that employee motivation is based on the comparison of employee inputs to perceived outcomes of a particular action.

friend in another organization. Adams calls this person a *referent*. A referent can be a system, another, or oneself (self-referent). Other referents are people with similar roles, such as other lifeguards at the pool and other lifeguards at another facility across town. System referents are a comparison of the situation with the policies and procedures of the organization, such as pay or promotion. Lastly, a self-referent is a unique comparison based on a person's own contacts and experience. For example, an employee may have put in less effort in a previous job and been paid more than at her current job.

If employees assess their situation as inequitable, they can see it as underrewarded or overrewarded. Feeling underrewarded, where the employee gives more than she receives, may be the most common perception. However, overrewarded perceptions are also common. For example, a person who loves tennis, works summers at a tennis club, and gets to play most of the day may perceive this situation as overrewarded. Someone who feels underqualified for a position, such as a new graduate who gets a great job, may perceive an inequity based on greater output than input.

When inputs match outputs, a balance, or equity, is achieved. The theory suggests that this is the desired state and that employees will act in ways to return to a perception of equity if an inequity exists. Employees who are overrewarded may increase their output in order to correct the inequity, whereas employees who are underrewarded may do the opposite and reduce their output. Employees may also change their perceptions of the situation to rectify the inequity.

## Expectancy Theory

**Expectancy theory** builds on the idea of fairness and holds that people expect certain results from their actions. For example, a runner who trains hard may expect a certain time improvement. The actual behavior (training hard) will be more likely to occur if achieving the fastest route time is something that the runner values. Victor Vroom's expectancy theory addresses these issues and may be the most supported motivation theory. Vroom suggests that the expectation of how a behavior will influence a given outcome and how attractive that outcome is to a person is the best way to understand employee motivation (Vroom 1964).

Expectancy theory has three parts:

1. The effort–performance link refers to the expectation or probability that a given effort will result in a given outcome.

2. The performance–reward link is the degree to which a person believes that performance at a certain level will lead to the attainment of a desired outcome.

3. Attractiveness refers to the importance a person places on a potential reward or outcome.

> **expectancy theory**—Assumes that motivation is based on employees' comparison of how hard they have to work, what the reward will be, and how attractive that reward is to the person.

For example, say you are a salesperson for a professional sport franchise. You believe that if you work hard, you will perform well. The more calls you make, the more tickets you will sell. You also believe that if you sell a lot of tickets (i.e., perform well), you will be rewarded financially through salary and bonuses and also through a promotion to your dream job of sales manager for the team. This process shows that individual effort leads to performance, which leads to organizational rewards and finally achievement of an attractive individual award.

Conversely, if your actions do not seem linked to performance, you may have reduced motivation. Say you are a student in a leisure management course. You start the course highly motivated and put in a great deal of effort, but when you take the midterm, you score much lower than expected. You may find your motivation lacking in the second part of the term, and you miss more classes and just skim the textbook. What happened? Expectancy theory would suggest that the link between effort and performance was broken with the midterm. You may have perceived the midterm as unfair because trivial questions were weighted too heavily or because it was an essay exam and you felt the instructor's grading was off base. If the link between effort, performance, and outcome is broken, motivation may be reduced. If, however, you felt the exam was fair, then you may have increased your motivation knowing that more effort was required to reach your goal.

Expectancy theory offers several practical applications for managers looking to motivate employees. First, the theory emphasizes rewards and outcomes that an employee values; therefore, managers must provide rewards that employees want, and they must ensure that employees understand what they need to do in order to get the performance and in turn the rewards they desire. Second, expectancy theory is about perceptions, not actual behavior. This requires continual feedback on performance to help employees align their perceptions with the reality of what is required. Looking again at the classroom example, the instructor could sit down with you and explain the expectations for getting a desired grade in the class. The instructor would want to understand the reward that you desired and what effort you felt was necessary to achieve it. The instructor could then help to clarify what was needed and get you on track for a successful second half of the course.

# EMPLOYEE RECOGNITION

**recognition**—
Recognizing and rewarding the contributions of employees.

Recognizing employees for their work is an important and exciting part of a manager's role. There are many ways to recognize employees for their contributions: intrinsic, extrinsic, formal, and informal. Sincere **recognition** generates a feeling of commitment and belonging, which can encourage employee motivation and engagement in their work. Even if managers are not solely responsible for financial rewards, they can use a number of tools to increase the effectiveness of their organization. Employee recognition and reward systems can address several important managerial objectives as they relate to employee motivation. A solid reward system requires concerted attention in its development. The following sections provide a basis for a well-constructed reward system.

## Purposes of Reward Systems

Reward systems serve several purposes in organizations. Effective reward systems help an organization be more competitive, retain key employees, and reduce turnover. Reward systems also can enhance employee motivation and reinforce the image of an organization among key stakeholders or future employees.

People are the most important resource for organizational competitiveness, and keeping them on the job is a key task for any manager. Competition to attract and keep the best employees is intense. For people looking for a career opportunity, that's great news, but as a manager of an organization needing to keep the best and brightest, it is a challenge. It may be even harder in the nonprofit and public sectors where flexibility in providing financial rewards may be more limited than in a commercial context. Retaining employees saves money on retraining costs, improves the consistency of services, and allows for relationships to develop between clients and the organization. In addition, proper reward systems can reduce absences. Absences cause innumerable headaches for managers. Instructors who don't show up, too few staff members at busy times, and the lack of a cleanup crew can all increase work-place stress. Absences affect not only the manager but also fellow employees who need to pick up the slack and clients who feel the brunt of too few employees on site.

As suggested earlier, understanding who, what, and when to reward can improve employees' performance. However, the improper use of **rewards** can have a debili-tating effect on employee performance. Managers need to understand their employ-ees' perceptions of the importance and fairness of the reward and then clearly communicate what needs to be done to receive the reward.

**rewards**—The return one receives for engaging in a particu-lar behavior.

Effective use of rewards can encourage employees to gain the skills that are nec-essary to help them and the organization grow. This can also increase their desire to continue being part of the organization. For example, an organization can pay and provide time off for employees who want to take advanced courses in an area that is valuable for the organization. Some organizations may even provide time off or support to help employees advance their own personal goals or skill sets.

Ideally, an organization wants employees who not only show up to work but are excited about being there as well. This passion for work has been referred to as *affec-tive commitment*. Although research is somewhat preliminary, there is some indica-tion that affective commitment can be strengthened by rewards that enhance employee perceptions of being supported and having control of their work situation.

Finally, reward systems can also help with recruiting efforts. Just as happy custom-ers may be the best advertisement for a particular product, happy employees are often a great tool for recruiting new employees and making the organization a workplace of choice. Think about the kind of job you want. Often you will easily be able to iden-tify an organization that stands above the others as a great place to work. As a conse-quence of this, the organization can attract the best and brightest, creating a virtuous circle whereby it becomes an even more attractive workplace. Hopefully you can see that establishing the right reward structure for an organization is critical to its suc-cess. The following sections delve into the details of various reward structures.

## Types of Rewards

Understanding how each employee perceives and values different rewards is an essential part of management. Managers need to grasp an understanding of extrin-sic and intrinsic rewards.

**Extrinsic rewards** are external rewards tied to certain employee behaviors, skills, time, or roles in an organization. How employees perceive these rewards relevant to their performance and the rewards given to others will ultimately determine the effectiveness of the rewards. Managers also need to understand how much value each employee places on specific extrinsic rewards. For example, a well-paid but overworked employee may value additional vacation time or a reduced workload more than a few extra dollars. Money, praise, awards, and incentive prizes such as tickets to a concert or a game are all examples of extrinsic motivators. Whatever motivator the manager chooses, the employee must see the reward as a motivator for it to be effective. For example, if the extrinsic reward is tickets to the opera, an employee who hates the opera likely would not be motivated by the tickets. On the other hand, if the employee is a football fan and the extrinsic reward is tickets to a major game, the motivator might be more effective.

**extrinsic rewards**—Tangible rewards such as pay, bonuses, benefits, or extra time off.

It is simpler to explain what intrinsic rewards are by discussing what they are not. **Intrinsic rewards** do not have an obvious external incentive; that is, people are not acting to get a tangible reward, be it time off or money. Instead, they act because it feels good or provides some form of internal satisfaction. Intrinsic rewards are often more highly valued and more effective over time, yet using them is a difficult

**intrinsic rewards**—Intangible rewards based on feelings of accomplishment or personal satisfaction.

managerial task. Intrinsic rewards derive from employees feeling good about the job they have done, the effort they have put forward, or the role they played in a team project. Intrinsic rewards in the workplace come from the job itself, so to provide intrinsic reinforcement, a manager should enrich the job. Job enrichment involves improving work processes and environments so they are more satisfying for employees, such as eliminating dysfunctional elements or enlarging jobs (increasing the duties and responsibilities of a job).

Developing an effective reward system can be a difficult task. The following sections provide some guidance on the basics of an effective reward system. These sections focus almost exclusively on extrinsic rewards, but intrinsic rewards should also be considered when developing each employee's job.

## Monetary Versus Nonmonetary Rewards

**monetary rewards**—Rewards that have a direct financial price, such as a salary or performance bonus.

**Monetary rewards** are most commonly given in the form of pay increases, bonuses, or increases in benefits, such as pension or health care premiums. Such rewards can be divided into two categories: direct and indirect compensation (table 10.1). Both contribute to the financial betterment of an employee. Direct compensation is relatively straightforward and consists of increases in hourly pay, increases in hours (for nonsalaried employees), increases in salary, merit pay based on performance, seniority pay based on time with an organization, and bonuses based on the achievement of individual, group, or organizational objectives.

Indirect monetary compensation includes increases to benefits or the addition of benefits such as a dental plan. It can also include paid leave in the form of vacation days, days off for training, or longer time off such as a sabbatical, as well as paid leave for illness, caring for a child, or caring for an elderly parent. Additionally, some organizations may offer services as part of an indirect compensation package, such as on-site child care, an elder care program, an on-site cafeteria, a games room or gym, and confidential counseling services for employees and their families. Again, indirect compensation should be valuable to employees and ideally should offer choices from a range of services.

**nonmonetary rewards**—Rewards without a financial price attached to them, such as praise, providing the best equipment and tools, or the promise of a better office.

**Nonmonetary rewards** cost the organization but do not directly improve the employee's financial position (table 10.1). Supplying employees with the best tools possible to do their job is an example, such as providing a new high-end laptop or having an excellent training facility for coaches at a university. A good office location,

**Table 10.1** Direct Monetary Rewards, Indirect Monetary Rewards, and Nonmonetary Rewards

| Direct Monetary Compensation | Indirect Monetary Compensation | Nonmonetary Compensation |
|---|---|---|
| Base salary | Pension contributions | Use of recreation facilities |
| Hourly wages | 401(k) (U.S.) RRSP (Canada) Regulated Complying Superannuation Funds (Australia) | On-site cafeteria |
| Merit pay | Paid leave | Learning and advancement opportunities |
| Bonuses | Various forms of insurance | Flexible work hours; work-at-home days |

## Creative Low- or No-Cost Ideas

Rewarding employees doesn't need to be expensive, nor should it be boring! Following are some ideas for employee rewards ranging from the simple to the more creative.

- Write employees a thank-you note.
- Surprise them with coffee from the best local coffee shop.
- Hold a staff meeting at an afternoon ball game.
- Give an afternoon-off pass to be used whenever they want to do something fun.
- Have the staff develop their own lists of great gifts for under $20 and choose from the lists to reward them.
- Give gift cards, which are easy and always welcome.
- Give away team pedometers and count steps as the team walks across the country, state, or province. Have special lunches celebrating the places reached.
- Bring a dunk tank in for dunk-the-boss day.
- Have a treasure hunt.
- Turn an office into a miniature golf course.
- Arrange for a boss several levels up to stop by to say thanks.
- Give them a new challenging assignment to show your trust in their performance.

choice of furnishings, or special parking place can all be nonmonetary rewards. Employees may not know the full details of pay and other monetary benefits of coworkers, but nonmonetary rewards are often visible and can create perceptions of inequity in an organization. In some cases, this may be the intent of managers who want employees to strive to achieve the stereotypical corner office, but often it may also unintentionally encourage feelings of inequity. That inequity may have positive implications for an organization if employees strive to increase performance, or it can result in turnover and reduced performance. As with any reward, nonmonetary rewards need to be carefully thought out before being implemented Appreciation rewards can be a valuable part of this category such as a thank-you note, a specific acknowledgement about what is appreciated and noticing when things are done well

**performance-based rewards**—Individual or group rewards based on the accomplishment of a certain goal or level of performance, such as a performance bonus for high levels of client service.

## Performance-Based Versus Membership-Based Rewards

One of the most difficult challenges for managers is to decide what to base rewards on. A common distinction is performance-based versus membership-based rewards. As the name implies, **performance-based rewards** are tied to the ability of an individual, team, group, or organization to meet some previously agreed-upon standard of performance. Performance rewards are based on an evaluation of contribution, and awards are allocated based on that evaluation.

**membership-based rewards**—Rewards received for being the member of a specific group rather than for individual performance, such as an annual cost-of-living pay raise.

**Membership-based rewards** are allocated solely for being part of a group within an organization. These rewards commonly include annual cost-of-living increases to a base salary or support for an equity policy. For example, if a parks and department was looking to encourage staff to have master's degrees or obtain certification, they might offer pay incentives for having either or both. Membership-based rewards are also often tied to length of time with an organization. For instance, after a certain length of service with an organization, employees may receive a certain percentage increase to their pay or be eligible for additional benefits. In a unionized environment, many of these rewards are spelled out in a labor agreement.

To illustrate the difference between the two structures, let's look at annual raises. A performance-based structure means that each employee's performance is evaluated and raises are based on performance, with the highest performers getting the most money. A membership-based structure means that all employees receive the same raise regardless of performance. Membership structures can be demotivating to high performers because they get the same rewards despite working harder.

# Nontraditional Rewards

As more and more managers understand the importance of individualizing reward systems, the use of nontraditional rewards will continue to grow. Time is often a key constraint, and for many people work is a major time commitment. Ways in which employees can individualize their work schedule are becoming increasingly important rewards. Four methods of individualization are reduced workweeks, staggered daily schedules, flextime, and working from home.

## Reduced Workweek

A reduced workweek often sees employees working a four-day week instead of five days. In return for that extra day, employees work longer on their four days in the office. For example, in a 40-hour workweek from Monday through Friday, employees would work eight-hour days, but the reduced workweek would see hours increase to 10 hours a day for four days. The benefits to the employees are longer blocks of time to take care of their personal lives, less frequent and often less busy commutes, and ultimately more useful time for themselves. The organization has no additional expenses, and evidence suggests that absenteeism and time lost for personal reasons decrease.

However, there are also downsides for both employees and the organization. Parents, for example, may find it difficult to find child care that is open late or early enough to accommodate the longer work schedule. The longer workday may also be a constraint to people who are involved in weekly evening activities, be it coaching a team or attending an art class. Some jobs may also not lend themselves to longer days. A lifeguard or sport instructor may be considerably less effective in those last two hours, which can lead to decreased performance and in some cases safety risks. Also, the hours and timing of work may affect service to clients. Even if an organization maintains its regular schedule, clients expecting to reach a particular person during traditional business hours may find the new schedule frustrating. Finally, reduced workweeks seem to be most effective when employees themselves are involved in creating the schedule. Understand that employees participating in reduced workweeks need to be scheduled so that the entire organization is not gone on Friday!

## Staggered Daily Schedule

An alternative to a reduced workweek may be a staggered daily schedule. Employees still work their designated weekly hours but can allocate those hours in different ways. For example, one employee may want to come in late and leave later to accommodate dropping off children. Someone else may prefer being in the office an hour earlier and leaving an hour earlier. These schedules may even be adapted weekly or monthly to accommodate changing employee needs. This idea meets employees' individual needs but can often be difficult to manage. Again, a staggered daily schedule may not be appropriate in all settings and must consider not only employee needs but also organizational requirements and client desires.

## Flextime

Flextime allows some employee freedom while still meeting client and organizational needs. Employees are expected to be in the office during a certain time frame, usually ranging from four to six hours, such as 9:30 a.m. to 3:30 p.m. Flextime emphasizes productivity and allows the employee some leeway in that flexibility zone (before 9:30 a.m. and after 3:30 p.m.).

For example, take Pat, an aquatics programmer. Pat has two school-aged children and requires some flexibility to drop them off and pick them up at school. Pat has worked with the employer and agreed that he will be at the pool between the hours of 9:30 and 3:30 but will complete the rest of his work elsewhere. This ensures that Pat's coworkers and clients can reach him at predictable times while still allowing him the personal flexibility he requires at this point in his life. This type of arrangement has been effective for many organizations and employees, although obviously it won't work in all situations.

Flextime also allows a staff person more control over their hours. For example, a special events coordinator works five hours over the weekend. The following week, the coordinator comes in an hour later than usual each day.

## Working From Home

As technology has advanced, the option of working at home for some or all of the workday is becoming increasingly possible. A high-speed Internet connection and a laptop computer connected to the workplace network provide many people with everything they need to do their job. Obviously this arrangement is more suited to some positions than others. A job developing programs for a municipal recreation department would be more suited to a work-at-home plan as opposed to the job of instructing the programs. Working for some or all of the workweek at home can offer fewer workplace distractions, allow employees time to concentrate on projects that are important to the organization, and make more effective use of the day by eliminating the need to commute as well as the usual time killers present in most offices.

However, working from home is not for everyone. The distractions of the home require discipline, and for those who consistently work at home the blurred distinction between home and office can be unsettling. Additionally, monitoring employees at home is nearly impossible. Evaluation needs to be performance based, and work-at-home schemes do not work for organizations that want to monitor how employees spend their time. Allowing employees to work at home part of the time, however, may be an excellent compromise for both employees and the organization.

# Four Options for Rewards

So far we have discussed the purposes and types of rewards. This section addresses four options on which managers can base rewards: job, skill, seniority, and performance.

## Job-Based Rewards

Traditionally, rewards were based on position or the roles employees hold in an organization. A manager evaluates one job in relation to another and gives rewards based on those evaluations. A programming position may be evaluated as more valuable than an instructor and the instructor position as more valuable than the front-desk clerk. Jobs that are more valuable tend to have greater responsibility, but they also may be more intrinsically appealing and offer greater opportunities for achievement and autonomy.

## Skill-Based Rewards

Using skills as a basis essentially rewards employees for what they know and do that helps meet the needs of the organization. As employees gain more skills, they can do many more things in the workplace, which can also improve their satisfaction and overall organizational efficiency and effectiveness, much as described in systems theory (see chapter 2). However, paying for skills can be expensive. An employee may continue to add skills that are above and beyond the requirements of a job, which can make the cost to the organization more expensive than is reasonable. It could be argued that the job-based approach already accounts for skills needed; when allocating the work to positions, a manager is paying for skills the jobs require rather than the employees for every skill they have whether those skills are needed or not.

One context where a skills-based reward system may be optimal is where employee flexibility is key, as often occurs in smaller organizations that don't require full-time employees for all the roles that need filling. Nonprofit organizations or small sport organizations are examples where staff with experience in marketing, fund-raising, accounting, and event management may be highly desired rather than specialists in any one of those areas.

## Seniority-Based Rewards

Seniority-based reward systems pay people for their tenure in a job or with an organization. This approach is often justified with the argument that time on the job leads to mastery and enhanced skills. Seniority-based systems do not account for changes in technology or best practices that may not always be learned on the job, nor do they account for individual effort in improving skills or performance on the job. Furthermore, seniority-based systems may create inequities between newer and more senior employees. A new employee may be the best fitness instructor yet receive 60 percent of the pay of a longer-serving employee who has much lower ratings. This can reduce motivation, reinforce behaviors that do not enhance organizational effectiveness, and increase workplace conflict.

## Performance-Based Rewards

The example in the previous section may work better with a performance-based system where fitness instructors are rewarded based on how well they deliver programs to clients. Higher ratings, more returning clients, and fewer complaints may all be bases upon which to evaluate performance, and the better the rating, the greater the reward. However, this may not always work as planned. Better instructors may face more challenging classes where ratings are lower, or they may be personable and get good ratings but not be as effective at teaching the skills clients desire in the long run. This is not to say that performance rewards do not lead to organizational effectiveness but rather that careful attention must be paid to choosing how to measure performance (these ideas are discussed in more depth in chapters 9 and 13).

## Putting It All Together

It may have become evident by this point that no one reward system is effective under all conditions. The most effective systems provide a mix of rewards that are meaningful to employees. For example, a fitness club may give annual salary increases to all employees on a job basis, giving similar increases to each grouping of job. In addition, it may give a small annual increase for seniority to demonstrate a value in staying with an organization over time. Individual or groups of employees may also receive increases based on courses they have taken that year as well as performance ratings on elements deemed important to their jobs.

This mix includes all four categories of reward bases. It could be further individualized to take into account individual values and desires. Rewards could be distributed through cafeteria-style benefits where employees get to choose how their individual increases will be applied. For instance, take an employee who is expecting a $1,500 increase from the four reward bases. Rather than dictating where that money will go, the organization can let the employee choose. Some may go to annual salary, some to an enhanced dental plan, and some to increased medical coverage. An employee's life circumstances, personal preferences, and life stage all are taken into account in a cafeteria-style approach to benefits.

## REWARDING VOLUNTEERS

As stated in the beginning of this chapter, the principles of managing, leading, and motivating volunteers are similar to those for nonvolunteers. Managers must understand volunteers' commitment to the organization and convey their expectations to volunteers. Volunteers often come to an organization with a passion or some intrinsic interest in the organization that is their main reward for participation. However, managers should not forget that understanding what a volunteer values is just as important as it is for a paid employee. Volunteer roles require careful attention to job enrichment to help sustain the volunteer's intrinsic motivation. Volunteers' passion for the mission of the organization can also rub off on paid employees, and ensuring that passion remains can be a useful management tool.

Even though volunteers rarely receive monetary rewards, other extrinsic rewards should not be discounted. Providing the appropriate tools for volunteers to do the job required, such as office space, a place to park, or anything else relevant to a particular context, should be considered. An organization can often unintentionally convey low status to volunteers by making them pay for their own parking, giving them no space to work, or having them borrow an employee's computer or phone. If volunteers are important to your organization, you must treat them that way and ensure that their value is felt throughout the organization.

## REWARDING YOURSELF

The previous sections have been devoted to creating a caring and motivating environment for employees. Even though the leisure services profession focuses on health and well-being, a commonly neglected area of human resources management is caring for yourself, the manager. We can go back to early motivation theorists

## Ideas Contest

It is important to recognize the valuable information that staff can provide to improve facility operations. Each employee deals directly with the public every shift they work. Customers (especially regulars) often share details with staff about the quality of their facility visit. Not surprisingly, managers often only hear the very best or worst of what patrons and staff have to say about the operations.

In order to try and glean meaningful information from the staff team, I would periodically hold a "Dave Wants Your Ideas" contest. A contest form was provided to each employee, asking them to identify the three most common suggestions, concerns, or complaints they hear from patrons. The employees were also asked to list three things that would make their job easier, more enjoyable, or more efficient. Employees were asked to be realistic and serious—for example, installing a retractable roof over the indoor pool for warm, sunny days wasn't practical, but purchasing more size 6 rental ice skates or revising an outdated procedure was easily doable. Every employee who submitted their "Ideas" form had their name entered into random draws for gift cards.

The first time I tried this initiative, I was really impressed with the quality of the suggestions but disappointed with the low percentage of staff who took the time to complete and return the form. The next time I ran the contest, I was determined to find a way to motivate more staff to buy in and participate. Upon reflection, I realized that my accountability as manager, and that of the leadership team, was the key to success. I committed to staff that the information on every form would be compiled and reviewed by me and the leadership team. I also committed that a summary document would be prepared by the leadership team with a list of all suggestions received, along with an explanation for each suggestion indicating why it was accepted, deferred, or not supported. I also improved the contest prizes with a combination of random prize draws and prizes for the top suggestions received.

As I hoped, the number of submissions significantly increased, as did the quality of the suggestions. Reviewing the 200-plus forms and preparing the summary document explanations was very time consuming, but also very illuminating for the leadership team. We were surprised at how practical, simple, and inexpensive many of the suggestions were, and I am pleased to say that the majority of the suggestions were successfully implemented over a relatively short period of time. Some of the more expensive initiatives were included in the next year's budget.

When the employees saw the sincerity, effort, and outcomes supported by the leadership team, there was a noticeable improvement in staff motivation and morale. The staff felt listened to, and they appreciated that the leadership team was committed to improving both working conditions and customer service. They recognized that their input was important and meaningful. There was increased trust in the leadership team, and the employees began to realize how valuable their suggestions were. They also gained a deeper understanding of the importance of good communication and how they can personally make a positive difference by sharing information, ideas, and suggestions.

Employees began to contribute more personal suggestions without prompting because they understood that their input would be seriously considered. I repeated this initiative periodically over my career, and

*(continued)*

**Ideas Contest** *(continued)*

learned that the best results came when there was a gap of about three years between contests. There wasn't enough new information received to warrant the time involved on an annual basis. Also, since the recreation workforce includes a lot of students who may only work with your organization for a few years, a periodic approach to the contest had the advantage of reaching newer employees and developing a stronger culture of motivated employees.

Dave McBride

Manager, Aquatic and Arena Services

Richmond Parks Recreation and Culture, Richmond, British Columbia

such as Maslow and Herzberg to understand that if base needs are not met, we are less likely to be high performers. The best thing you can do for your employees is to model the behavior of a high performer.

According to Dr. Jim Loehr and Tony Schwartz in their article "The Making of a Corporate Athlete" (2001), high performers not only focus on the work at hand but also take care of themselves by taking breaks throughout the day, committing to exercise and good nutrition, and remaining connected with family and community. You must be engaged with the workplace if you want your employees to be engaged. Encourage healthy behavior at work by inviting employees to hold meetings during a walk, making sure lunches at the office have healthy options, and offering a fruit basket or healthy whole-grain baked items instead of Friday doughnuts.

Loehr and Schwartz suggest that we need to oscillate throughout the day. We can't run day after day at 110 percent. Instead, you should work like a professional athlete, totally focusing on the task at hand when you are working on it but taking breaks every hour or so to walk around the office, stretch, or grab a healthy snack. Caring for yourself is the best reward you can give your employees. You will find that your energy is more balanced throughout the day, your emotions are more in control, and your productivity is increased.

If this is how you want your employees to behave, you need to walk the walk. Particularly in leisure services it is essential for us to demonstrate that we believe in and act on the benefits that a healthy, active life has to offer both professionally and personally.

# DISCIPLINE

Of course, not all employees are going to be stellar. Those who are not can have a major impact on the agency. They consume a lot of the supervisor's time because the supervisor must deal with the issue. Also, a poor employee probably has lower productivity and morale than a good employee and can cause these same symptoms in average employees through their attitude alone.

Disciplining employees requires that a systematic process be put in place. This system will detail the guidelines all managers are to follow and will also create the documentation needed in case the employee is eventually terminated. A progressive discipline process is outlined along with an improvement plan in this section. Keep in mind that agencies will have the discipline process detailed in their policy manual. However, most will follow a similar process.

# Progressive Discipline

**progressive discipline**—A process of addressing undesirable employee work behaviors in a systematic way with increasing efforts to correct the problem.

**Progressive discipline** is used when disciplinary action is needed because of attendance problems, safety issues, poor performance, or undesirable behaviors. Managers typically follow this progression model:

1. Verbal warning
2. Written warning
3. Intervention
4. Termination

This model becomes more serious with each step, culminating in dismissal from a position. Keep in mind that some infractions may require the manager to skip one or more steps based on the actions of the employee. For example, an employee caught drinking alcohol on the job may automatically be dismissed if this course of action is detailed in the policy manual. There are behaviors such as this for which the policy manual will dictate how the situation is to be handled, and therefore the policy will supersede the progressive discipline model.

## Verbal Warning

When a situation arises that requires the manager to begin disciplinary action, the first step is usually a verbal warning. The manager should set up a meeting with the employee to have a non-confrontational conversation about the incident. The manager must communicate what is acceptable behavior and then set consequences for further incidents. Although this is a verbal warning, many managers will keep notes on what the situation is, what transpired, and how it was handled. The notes are usually not put in the employee's personnel file but kept by the manager for future reference if the situation escalates.

## Written Warning

If the situation occurs again or a similar situation arises, the next step for the employee is a written warning. The manager will formally document the incident, mention the verbal warning, and again discuss acceptable behavior and consequences. A written warning should be discussed in person with the employee, much like the verbal warning. At the end of the meeting, the employee will be asked to sign the written warning to acknowledge that the matter was discussed. If the employee refuses to sign the written warning, a note will be made on the warning that the employee refused to sign. Additionally, the employee is given an opportunity to respond to the warning. The response is then attached to the warning, and all documents are placed in the employee's personnel file.

## Intervention

The next step in the progressive discipline model is an intervention, which results in an employee improvement plan. Intervention requires the completion of a five-step process. To illustrate the model in action, consider the following situation:

*Erin works at the front desk of a fitness service as a customer service representative. She has been there for three years. Recently Erin's behavior has grown increasingly difficult. She fluctuates between apathy, complaining, and exhibiting disdain toward the organization. On several occasions, she has been seen moping around the front desk. Little work gets done on those days. At other times, she complains how nothing is ever right or how others are to blame for mistakes. Erin's work productivity has diminished and is half of what it was six months ago. Her errors are increasing, and she sometimes handles conversations with callers discourteously. Furthermore, a recent project had numerous mistakes that required correction by coworkers, causing a deadline to be missed.*

**Step 1: Identify and Define the Performance Problem**   Determine what the issues and problems are. Are they attendance problems, safety issues, poor performance, or undesirable behaviors?

The case: Erin is apathetic and complaining; her productivity has diminished; she blames others for mistakes; and she is rude to customers.

**Step 2: Explain the Impact of the Problem**   Tell the employee how this problem is affecting others both internally and externally to the organization.

The case: Erin is upsetting customers with her attitude; coworkers have to redo her work; this situation requires additional attention from the supervisor; her diminished productivity reduces the organization's productivity.

**Step 3: Define the Expected Performance Standard**   At this point the manager needs to bring the employee in to talk about the situation and define expectation standards. During this meeting it is imperative to define the level of performance expected in clear and measurable terms. Managers sometimes make the mistake of assuming that the employee knows what is expected. This step is to initially establish performance goals.

The case: Erin is expected to raise productivity to an acceptable level, decrease errors in work completed, and treat customers with respect.

**Step 4: Explore Ideas for a Solution**   The manager and employee need to explore how to solve this problem together. They should generate ideas and discuss each option as it pertains to each performance standard.

The case: Erin and her manager have determined the best course of action is a change in job tasks for Erin; the manager will set deadlines for projects; Erin will develop customer service skills through training; and Erin will strive to reduce errors.

**Step 5: Write an Improvement Plan**   An improvement plan is a roadmap aimed at eliminating employee problems and weaknesses. It takes the information gathered in the previous steps and puts it in writing for the employee. An improvement plan will have four elements: the goal or area that needs improvement (step 3), the step-by-step action plans (step 4), positive and negative consequences, and follow-up time.

The case: Here is one example to include in Erin's improvement plan.

**Treat customers with respect (goal):**

- Attend customer service training through XYZ corporation within the next two months. (action plan)
- Implement five new practices learned in the customer service program within one week of attending the training.
- Always be courteous with all customers calling the company or walking into the facility.
- These tasks will be reviewed at the end of 30 days. (follow-up)
- If these tasks are not met, a two-week suspension is in order. (consequences)

### Termination

If all attempts at an intervention are unsuccessful, then termination may be necessary. When firing an employee, a manager can never have too much documentation. Details of the progressive disciplinary action should be in the employee's personnel file. Prior to terminating an employee, the manager needs to prepare for the meeting by discussing the situation with the necessary parties, including human resources staff and the agency attorney. Personnel policies will dictate who should be notified.

Selecting the location for the termination should be given careful consideration. The manager may want to go to the employee's office so that the person fired does not have to walk by other employees if they are visibly upset. It can be in a neutral setting such as a boardroom. If the firing could be confrontational, the manager may want to choose a room that has multiple doors for escape or sit near the door so they can get out easily. Although these situations are rare, they can occur.

During the termination meeting, keep the following tips in mind:

- Have a witness in the meeting. It could be a higher supervisor or someone from human resources.

- Be direct in telling the employee why he is being terminated. Give facts, but do not elaborate too much and belabor points. Answer all questions honestly and to the point.

- Let the employee know the termination is a final decision and that it is not up for debate or negotiation.

- Present the employee with a termination letter. This letter should state the facts and reasons for termination. It should also detail the progressive disciplinary steps that were taken. List the effective termination date and any financial details, including any severance package, the final paycheck, and the date when health benefits will end. A copy of the letter should be signed by the terminated employee, acknowledging that he received the letter.

- Once the employee has been terminated, give him the opportunity to clean out his own office or offer to have two staff members (for witness purposes) clean out the office and send his belongings to the terminated employee. All company property must be returned, including keys.

- During the termination meeting, all access to such things as the computer system or security systems should be stopped. For instance, password changes should be made for the computer to deny access to important company information.

Terminating an employee is arguably one of the most difficult things a manager will have to do. However, sometimes it is the only remaining option. Since employee termination can be a legal issue, agencies will have detailed policies that must be followed. The information presented here is merely an example of what you might expect to find in an agency.

## Discipline and Dismissal of Volunteers

As noted earlier, volunteers are critical to many leisure services organizations. Just as managers must reward volunteers and treat them as valuable staff members, managers may also need to use principles of discipline and dismissal with volunteers. An ineffective volunteer can cause an organization as much trouble as an ineffective paid employee. For instance, take a nonprofit agency where a volunteer answers the phone and is the first point of contact with clients and key stakeholders. This person is in a critical role that requires certain behavior. Just as with any employee, managers should work with volunteers to develop behaviors and skills that meet the demands of their role.

Volunteers differ from paid employees in that they are freely giving their time, and dismissing a volunteer may have negative repercussions on how other volunteers perceive the organization. A manager's task may be to find volunteers an opportunity that best fits their desires and their skill set even if that opportunity is not within the organization. A proactive, professional, and empathetic approach will go a long way to ensure success in working with volunteers.

 Check out the web study guide for additional material, including learning activities, sample documents, interactive case studies, web links, CPRP exam connections, and more.

# Conclusion

Understanding how to motivate, reward, and discipline employees and volunteers is a critical task for managers. As discussed at the outset of this chapter, employees are the key resource in accomplishing organizational goals. Motivation and organizational rewards are topics most people have an opinion on; however, impressions of the topic are often based on incomplete information. A solid understanding of the current thinking in these areas can be valuable for anyone working in a leisure services organization. Equally important is understanding how to effectively use discipline and when to use dismissal. Although they are among a manager's toughest tasks, effective discipline and dismissal are essential to a productive workplace.

# Review Questions

1. Differentiate between performance-based and membership-based rewards.
2. Describe nontraditional forms of rewards and give an example.
3. What are the four primary bases of organizational rewards?
4. What is the cafeteria-style approach to benefits and why might a manager use it?
5. Describe the purposes of reward systems.
6. Compare and contrast rewards for volunteers and paid staff.
7. Describe how you might go about addressing tardiness with an employee who is often late for work.
8. Explain how to use discipline effectively in a leisure services setting you are familiar with.
9. What steps would you take if you needed to dismiss an employee?

# 11

# Sources and Methods of Financing

## Learning Outcomes

- Identify the five sources of revenue and their applicability to each sector.
- Differentiate between operating and capital expenditures.
- Understand how to price programs using fixed and variable costs, contingency, and demand.
- Demonstrate knowledge of indirect cost allocation.
- Apply the concept of program subsidy to pricing.

## Key Terms

revenues, compulsory income, real property taxes, personal property taxes, excise tax, gratuitous income, matching grants, earned income, operating expenditures, capital expenditures, subsidy rate, differential pricing

## Competency Check

Refer to table 1.6 to see how you assessed these related competencies.

1. Understand financial processes (i.e., purchasing, budget).
2. Develop, monitor, and stay within a budget.

## A Day in the Life

I start the day checking my calendar to confirm any last-minute changes to any appointments for the day. Then I check and respond to any urgent emails that require my attention. Once that is complete, I check in with my staff and supervisor on our work program. One of our strategic park plans is currently under public exhibition with the community, and on this particular day the team's discussion is centered around whether the plan has reached the community with the right messages. The group concludes from reviewing the media monitor that an extra community session is required, and one staff member is assigned to plan and prepare for five events in five towns within three weeks. After the staff meeting I rush off to a workshop we arranged with the environmental science team to undertake an environmental risk assessment of recreational activities occurring at a park for which we are currently developing a new strategic plan. Each park has different issues due to its unique geographical location, historical use, community interest, and any emerging use issues that need to be resolved and needs to be considered. The workshop went on for three hours, but the outcome was all great information. During a short break, I notice two missed calls from our Traditional Owner Management board representatives. On checking my email, I see they have requested my team's assistance to review their current version of the joint management plan. I call them back to discuss how much time we need to review the plans. I check my other phone messages and email and call them back or respond to them, respectively. Tomorrow we have a workshop on developing visitor experience strategies with regional staff, and we pack all materials required as the venue is in a different town and it will be an early morning start. Ensuring transparent, well-informed decision making with stakeholders and communities, and collaboration among all park managers, are crucial in park management success.

Joshua Chikuse
Manager, Park Planning
Parks Victoria
Melbourne, Australia

Financial management is "the process of planning, acquiring, and using funds to achieve pre-determined organization goals and objectives" (Gladwell, Bouton, and Elder-White 2016, 525). Regardless of whether the leisure service is in the public, nonprofit, or commercial sector, sound financial management is paramount to the success of the agency. Although each sector has unique financial concerns and regulations, certain basic tenets of financial management are consistent across the sectors. To be a good financial manager, it is not necessary to be an accountant. A basic knowledge of accounting principles as well as revenue streams and expenditures will form the foundation of budgeting. It is these elements that are the focus of the next two chapters. Financial topics to be covered include revenues, expenditures, program pricing, budgeting, and financial analysis.

# SOURCES OF REVENUE

Fundamental to any recreation product is the budgeting process. However, budgeting is complex and it takes experience to become adept at it. Before discussing budgeting (covered in chapter 12), it is necessary to understand the concepts of revenues, expenditures, and basic program pricing.

**Revenues**, or income, are the monies coming into an organization. All organizations have some sort of income, and these sources vary by sector as well as agency type. Brayley and McLean (2008) identified five common sources of revenue—compulsory, gratuitous, earned, investment, and contractual—and outlined what sources are most important to each sector.

**revenues**—Money coming into the organization from such sources as fees, charges, and taxes.

## Compulsory Income

Taxes at different levels of government, from the local to the federal, provide **compulsory income**. In both the United States and Canada, public agencies generate most of their revenue from taxes. This tax revenue comes in many different forms, including real property taxes, personal property taxes, sales taxes, and excise taxes.

**compulsory income**—Revenue generated from taxes at the local, state or provincial, and federal levels.

### Real Property Taxes

The most common taxes used by public providers of leisure services are **real property taxes**. In the United States, 96 percent of all property taxes stay at the local level. Local residents are taxed on their property, and this tax stays within the community to fund local programs. Property taxes are to local government as personal and corporate income taxes are to federal government—major revenue streams (Howard and Crompton 2005).

**real property taxes**—Taxes levied on real estate, including the land, crops growing on the land, and structures built on the land.

In Canada, property taxes are typically divided among the municipality, the county or region, and local school boards. Although organizations such as police departments, fire departments, and libraries can receive property taxes directly, it is more common that they would fall within one of the three taxing entities (Havitz and Glover 2001). Many provinces in Canada levy property tax on real estate based upon the current use and value of the land. Although property tax levels vary among municipalities, usually common property assessment or valuation criteria are laid out in provincial legislation. A current trend in most provinces is using a market value standard with varying reevaluation cycles. A number of provinces have established an annual reassessment cycle as market activity warrants; others have more time between valuations.

Real property that is taxable includes any land owned and whatever is built or growing on that land, including homes, barns, and crops. However, land owned by churches, charitable organizations, governmental entities, and educational institutions are exempt from real property taxes in both the United States and Canada (Crompton 1999). Cities with major universities miss out on a large amount of revenue because the university is exempt from property taxes. In addition to these exemptions, there are also tax abatements, which are tax exemptions given to businesses for a short amount of time. Tax abatements are often used to attract new businesses to a community. For example, a large discount store may choose to build its newest store in one town over another because the chosen town has given the company a five-year tax abatement during which it does not have to pay taxes on land and structures. Most often this type of tax abatement is worth millions of dollars to the company and incentive enough to influence location decisions.

Property tax owed to the government is based on the type of property, such as residential property, farmland, or open space, as well as the assessed valuation of that property. The valuation of land is determined by a tax assessor and is generally reassessed every three to five years, depending on the community. Assessed value is the taxable worth of the property and is different from fair market value (Brayley and McLean 2008). Fair market value is the price the property would be sold for if it was put on the real estate market. In most areas the assessed value is less than the fair market value. Ideally, a homeowner would want a high fair market value and a low assessed valuation. This would ensure a high selling price for the home and lower property taxes. However, in reality there is a direct relationship—the higher the fair market value, the higher the assessed value.

The taxing of all applicable property in a given county, city, or region makes up the tax base for the area. The monies composing the tax base are distributed to local governmental agencies. The higher the assessed value of property in a designated area, the larger the tax base and the more money that local governments have to work with.

Similar to any organization, local government units have budgets they must work within. Once the annual budget is determined, the local government knows how much revenue is needed to operate during the upcoming budget year. Property is then taxed at a rate that will generate the needed revenue. This rate is called the *tax rate*. This is not to say that a municipality can determine that its needs have tripled within a year and charge the property owners a sharply increased rate. Laws set maximum tax rates that local governments cannot exceed without voter approval. Figure 11.1 depicts how all of these tax pieces fit together.

To determine the tax rate, use the following formula:

Tax rate = required taxes / net assessed valuation

Required taxes are the total expenditures outlined in the city or agency budget after subtracting the revenue received from nontax sources (i.e., fees and charges). The remaining expenditures must be covered by tax money. The *net assessed valuation* is the total assessed value of the property after all tax exemptions and tax abatements have been subtracted out.

The basic unit of taxation is the mill rate. The mill rate is the fraction of the net assessed valuation paid as tax. The tax rate is the mill rate expressed as a percentage.

**Figure 11.1** Property tax system.

Example: Consider a community with $7,000,000 in required taxes; that is, it needs $7,000,000 in tax money to cover its expenditures after all other sources of revenue have been accounted for. Suppose the assessed valuation of the property in the community is $520,500,000 with $12,500,000 in tax exemptions. The net assessed valuation is therefore $520,500,000 − $12,500,000, or $508,000,000. The mill rate and tax rate are calculated as follows:

$$\text{Mill rate} = \$7,000,000 / (\$520,500,000 - \$12,500,000)$$

$$= \$700,000,000 / \$508,000,000$$

$$= 0.0138$$

$$\text{Tax rate} = 1.38\%$$

The mill rate expresses the amount of tax paid per dollar of assessed valuation. Since this amount of tax is usually a small number, it is commonly reported in terms of mills, a *mill* simply being a tenth of a penny. The tax rate expresses the amount of tax paid per hundred dollars of assessed valuation.

Example: Continuing from above, the mill rate of 0.0138 indicates that a homeowner would pay $0.0138 in taxes for every dollar of valuation. Since a dollar contains 1,000 mills—there are 100 pennies in a dollar and 10 mills in a penny—the homeowner would pay 13.8 mills ($0.0138 \times 1,000$) for each dollar of valuation. The tax rate of 1.38 percent indicates that a property owner would pay $1.38 for every $100 of assessed value.

$$\text{Taxes paid} = \$0.0138 \text{ per dollar of valuation}$$

$$= 13.8 \text{ mills per dollar of valuation}$$

$$= \$1.38 \text{ per } \$100 \text{ dollars of valuation}$$

To compute the property tax, multiply the mill rate by the assessed valuation. For example, a homeowner with a home assessed at $100,000 would pay $1,380 in property tax ($1,380 = \$100,000 \times 0.0138$).

The general formulas are as follows:

$$\text{Required taxes} = \text{Total expenditures} - \text{nontax revenue}$$

$$\text{Net assessed valuation} = \text{Total assessed valuation} - \text{tax exemptions}$$

$$\text{Mill rate} = \text{Required taxes} / \text{net assessed valuation}$$

$$\text{Mills} = \text{Mill rate} \times 1,000$$

$$\text{Tax rate} = (\text{Mill rate} \times 100)\%$$

and

$$\text{Taxes paid} = \text{In dollars: Mill rate per dollar of valuation}$$

$$= \text{In mills: } (1,000 \times \text{mill rate}) \text{ per dollar of valuation}$$

$$= \text{In dollars: Tax rate per } \$100 \text{ of valuation}$$

*Tax rates can be expressed in terms of mills per dollar, dollar or cents per $100 of assessed valuation, or dollars per $1,000 of assessed valuation. Tax rates have traditionally been* *expressed in terms of mills. One dollar equals 1,000 mills. The following are examples of the conversion of monetary units:*

*1.00 = one dollar (1,000 mills)*
*0.10 = one dime (100 mills)*
*.01 = one cent (10 mills)*
*.001 = one mill*

(Gladwell, Bruton, and Elder-White 2016, 538)

Tax rates vary each year depending on the amount of taxes needed and the assessed valuation of property within a community. If the amount of taxes needed stays fairly consistent over a few years and assessed value increases significantly, property taxes may actually decrease. New homeowners buy a house knowing what the property taxes are for the current year, but they do not know exactly what the taxes will be in the upcoming years.

Local recreation agencies are typically established in two ways. First, the park and recreation agency can be part of city or county government. This means that it is a department within the city or county much like police, fire, and sanitation. This is the only way parks and recreation is established at the local level in Canada. These agencies rely on money distributed via the city or county council. Kaczynski and Crompton (2006) found that parks and recreation typically receives 2.2 to 2.6 percent of the tax revenue of a municipality, which ranked seventh of the nine city services compared; only corrections and libraries ranked lower. Because of the lower-than-desired rankings and the importance of the services provided, park and recreation organizations need to rely on other revenue sources. However, as discussed later in the chapter, such organizations are fortunate that they have more opportunities to generate revenue from sources than do departments such as fire, police, and education.

A second public park and recreation structure in the United States is the special district. Special districts "are established to provide only one or a limited number of designated functions and having sufficient administrative and fiscal autonomy to qualify as independent governments" (U.S. Census Bureau 2006).

Park and recreation districts have their own taxing authority and receive tax money directly from property taxes without having to receive their allocation through the city or county council. They set their own tax rate, but they also have legal limits set by the city. Special districts for parks and recreation do not exist in Canada.

## Personal Property Taxes

**personal property taxes**—Taxes assessed on personal items owned, including intangible property, tangible household property, and tangible business property.

In addition to real property taxes, there are several other taxes that affect leisure services. Some states (but no provinces) have **personal property taxes** in addition to real property taxes. Real property is not easily moved, such as land or barns, whereas personal property is portable, such as furniture. Personal property taxes are divided into three categories:

- *Intangible property.* Money markets, bonds, loans, stocks; in Canada, these taxes would come in the form of provincial and federal capital gains tax through personal income tax.
- *Tangible household property.* Boats, cars, recreational vehicles such as snowmobiles and campers; in Canada, these taxes come in the form of goods and

services taxes (GST) and provincial sales tax (PST), which are discussed under sales taxes.

- *Tangible business property.* Equipment, fixtures, furniture, computers, software; in Canada, these taxes come in the form of GST and PST.

Not all states tax personal property. These states rely on other types of taxes such as increased real property taxes to make up revenue that would normally be incurred from personal property.

## Tax-Increment Financing

Tax-increment financing (TIF) is used by municipalities in the United States to fund redevelopment such as parks, sidewalks, landscaping, or shopping. It is hoped that the redevelopment will attract new business and retain those currently in an area. The premise behind TIF funding is that when an area is redeveloped, its current tax rate increases. When the TIF is approved for a project, the current tax rate is set as the base rate. Once the redevelopment is complete, the base tax rate continues to be assessed with the funds going to the same taxing bodies as before. The increased taxes due to the redevelopment are then used to fund the redevelopment.

Municipalities do not have the freedom to use TIF money whenever they would like; instead there are specified TIF districts where this funding option is available. Many municipalities have TIF districts in their downtown areas. For example, a University North Park TIF district in Norman, Oklahoma, is proposing to spend $90.75 million from TIF funds on a new arena and entertainment district (Burke, 2017).

TIF financing does not occur in Canada. Improvements to areas can be made by the municipality if the municipality itself buys the land, improves it, and then resells it. Essentially the city invests in itself and receives a return on the investment (Havitz and Glover 2001).

## Sales Taxes in the United States

Statewide sales tax is collected in all but five states: Alaska, Delaware, Montana, New Hampshire, and Oregon. In addition, residents in 38 states also face local sales tax (Walczak and Drenkard 2017).

Sales tax is a combination of both local and state taxes. In 2017, combined sales tax ranged from a low of 1.76 percent (Alaska) to a high of 9.98 percent (Louisiana) (Walczak and Drenkard 2017). Regardless, only 1 to 2 percent of the total stays with the local government and the rest goes to the state government. Sales tax is assessed on products and not services, and some states have tax exemptions on such things as groceries and prescription drugs.

Some states and municipalities dedicate a portion of sales tax directly to parks and recreation. For example, in Texas, the legislature voted to dedicate 94 percent of the state sales tax attributed to sporting goods to Texas Parks and Wildlife Department (TPWD) with the provision that each session the legislature may still appropriate all or only part of the amount to TPWD to spend (Texas Parks and Wildlife Department 2017b). Sales tax increases have also been used for funding sporting venues, such as renovating the Green Bay Packers Stadium and building Bank One Ballpark for the Arizona Diamondbacks and Coors Field for the Colorado Rockies (Howard and Crompton 2005).

Sales tax is exceptionally beneficial in tourism-oriented cities since tourists will visit local restaurants, bars, and businesses buying meals, drinks, and souvenirs.

The revenue generated from these sales comes from people living outside the community but benefits residents.

## Sales Taxes in Canada

Canada has three sources of sales taxes. First, the goods and services tax (GST) is a federal tax on goods and services such as sporting goods, event tickets, and greens fees. GST is not charged on many necessary goods and services such as groceries, rent, and medical services. The United States does not have a GST; however, many other countries have something similar in value-added taxes (VAT). These tax rates tend to change and are used politically.

Second, provincial sales taxes (PST) are assessed on the sale of goods and services in all provinces except Alberta. As in the United States, the rate varies from province to province. The third means of sales tax in Canada is a merging of GST and PST into the harmonized sales tax (HST). Currently there is a flat percentage HST in the provinces of New Brunswick, Newfoundland, Nova Scotia, and Prince Edward Island (Cherniak 2017).

## Excise Taxes

**excise tax**—Tax placed on select goods and services in addition to the standard sales tax.

**Excise tax** is assigned to select goods and services in addition to the standard sales tax. There is often a hotel–motel tax, or bed tax, on hotel rooms, as well as car rental taxes in many municipalities. So-called sin taxes are imposed on cigarettes and alcohol. The revenue from excise tax has been used to develop sport stadiums and promote tourism. For example, Las Vegas Stadium, the new home of the Oakland Raiders as of 2020, will be funded by $750 million in excise taxes generated from Hotel Taxes (Stadiums of Pro Football 2018). Furthermore, Wayne County, Pennsylvania, imposed a 3 percent hotel room excise tax in 2005. The revenue is used to fund the Pocono Mountain Vacation Bureau, the official county tourist promotion agency, as well as Wayne County tourism promotion and tourist destination improvement (Wayne County, PA, 2018). Federal tax on gasoline is funneled to the

---

### Alberta Lottery Fund

The Alberta Lottery Fund in Canada oversees money generated from provincial lotteries, including video lottery terminals, slot machines, and ticket lotteries. The revenue generated is allocated to 11 specific ministries in support of public initiatives. In 2015–16 it was estimated that more than $1.548 billion dollars would be distributed to worthwhile community initiatives. Sport, arts, and recreation were major recipients of these funds (Alberta Lottery Fund 2017):

| | |
|---|---|
| Community facility enhancement program | $38 million |
| Hosting of major athletic events | $0.5 million |
| Alberta Foundation for the Arts | $26.6 million |
| Alberta Historical Resources Foundation | $8.2 million |
| Alberta Sport, Recreation, Parks, and Wildlife Foundation | $22 million |
| Parks operations | $10 million |

Federal Highway Administration, which funds trail programs (Jensen and Guthrie 2006). In Canada, excise taxes are charged on fuel-inefficient vehicles, automobile air conditioners, and certain petroleum products (Canada Revenue Agency 2017).

Although it is easy to equate taxes with organizations in the public sector since much of their funding comes from this source, the nonprofit and commercial sectors indirectly benefit from the funding of such things as convention and visitors bureaus and sport stadiums.

## Gratuitous Income

**Gratuitous income** is money that an agency does not have to pay back, and this income often results from fund-raising. It can also come in the form of federal grants, such as the Land and Water Conservation Fund or Open Space Land Acquisition and Development, or from private foundations, such as the Ford Foundation or the Lilly Endowment Inc.

Gratuitous income also comes from corporate sponsorships of programs, events, and facilities; individual donations of land, money, equipment, stocks, and bonds; and bequests from wills or money left from life insurance policies. The nonprofit sector relies heavily on gratuitous income, and the public sector is increasingly using it, especially from grants and sponsorships. The commercial sector is more likely to give away gratuitous income. For example, since 1976 REI, an outdoor equipment store, has invested more than $87 million in organizations across the United States that have a goal of creating, improving and sustaining access to inspiring outdoor places. They give 70 percent of their profits back to the outdoors community; in 2017, that came to nearly $9 million. (REI Stewardship 2017).

Gratuitous income from fund-raising may be directed toward daily operations to offset the cost of programs or events, buy new equipment, or fund special projects. Funds can also be raised in an annual campaign or a capital campaign. In an annual campaign, the agency sets a fund-raising goal for the year and pursues donors to give to this fund. The United Way runs an annual campaign where communities set goals for the amount of money they want to raise and then encourage people to

**gratuitous income**—Money obtained through such means as fund-raising and grants that the agency does not have to pay back to the giver.

---

### Grants for Parks and Recreation

The North Carolina Parks and Recreation Trust Fund (PARTF), established in 1994, provides **matching grants** to fund capital projects for state and local parks and recreation and to increase public access to state beaches. Since its inception, more than 400 local governments across the state have used the program to establish or improve parks for their citizens (North Carolina State Parks 2017). PARTF is funded by taxes on real estate deed transfers, a form of excise tax (Gladwell, Anderson, and Sellers 2003).

Since 2006, the Steve Nash Foundation, founded by professional basketball player Steve Nash, awards grants to child-focused nonprofits that provide direct benefit to under-served youth in British Columbia, Canada. Money from the foundation comes from fund-raisers such as the Steve Nash Foundation Charity Shield (Steve Nash Foundation 2017).

**matching grants**— Allocations of money from a foundation or other granting agency that is to be equaled by the receiving agency so that the total money for a project is double what the granting agency gives.

give to the campaign, which will ultimately fund such programs and agencies as the YWCA and Boys & Girls Clubs.

Capital campaigns are longer term. The goal for this type of campaign is usually much larger and may include establishing a foundation that operates off the interest from the account, building a new facility, or making major renovations to existing facilities. Although all amounts of donations are accepted in capital campaigns, a special emphasis is usually placed on larger or long-term donations.

---

## Planned Giving

Planned giving is an emerging means of fund-raising in parks and recreation. This method of donation focuses on long-term giving over the course of a lifetime or upon the death of the donor. Following are a few examples of planned giving.

### Securities

Donors may give stocks and bonds to agencies to use as they see fit. Agencies may hold on to the securities in hopes that their value will increase or sell them and use the revenue from the sale.

### Real Estate

Donation of land is common and is especially prevalent in public agencies where families donate land for use as a park or natural area. However, mortgaged land often is not accepted until the mortgage is fully paid.

### Life Insurance

An organization can be named as the beneficiary of life insurance policies. Once the purchaser dies, the life insurance turns over to the organization. This is one way a person can give a substantial amount of money while only paying a small annual premium.

### Personal Property

Tangible personal property such as jewelry, cars, or artwork may be donated to an organization that can then use the property as is or sell it. Nonprofit organizations occasionally are given automobiles for use or resale. Public agencies have been given such things as houses and valuable collections.

### Life Income Gifts

The main purpose of life income gifts is to provide a fixed income for an organization for the life of the donor. Although there are numerous ways to set up life income gifts, one of the most common is the charitable gift annuity where the donor gives cash, securities, or real estate to an organization and the organization then gives the donor and up to two beneficiaries an annual payment for the life of the donor. This payment is generally accrued from interest made on the invested gift.

From selected text in B.L. Ciconte and J.C. Jacobs, *Fundraising Basics: A Complete Guide*, 2nd ed. (Gaithersburg, MD: Aspen Publishers, 2001).

# Earned Income

Revenue generated from fees and charges is the main element of **earned income**. The commercial sector relies heavily on earned income by selling its services. Both the nonprofit and public sectors rely on earned income to supplement their fundraising efforts and/or compulsory income. The main classifications of earned income include entrance and admission fees, rental fees, user or program fees, sales revenue, license and permit fees, and special fees (Brayley and McLean 2008).

**earned income**— Revenue generated from fees and charges for services, programs, and products.

## Entrance and Admission Fees

Entrance and admission fees are paid either at the door or gate of a facility, through ticket sales or gate receipts, or in the parking lot. Many state, provincial, and national parks in Canada and the United States have entrance fees that are paid at the gate. Individual states and the National Park Service also offer annual passes for frequent users of parks. Four states do not have state park entrance fees, but California generated more than $132,000,000 in FY 2014-15 (Pew Charitable Trust 2016). Parking fees in place of gate fees are also popular. For example, the Lincoln Park Zoo in Illinois has free admission to the zoo but charges visitors to park.

## Rental Fees

Rental fees are charged in all types of leisure services. In the public sector, pavilions, pools, and other facilities can be rented for reunions, parties, and meetings. At the University of Arkansas, the Outdoor Adventure Program rents outdoor equipment from tents to kayaks at low prices to students, faculty, staff, and the community. In the nonprofit sector, places such as the YMCA rent out their pools, meeting rooms, or gymnasiums. For example, the Howard County Historical Society in Kokomo, Indiana, rents the Seiberling Mansion house, kitchen, and grounds for meetings, weddings, and other events (Howard County Museum 2017). The commercial sector also may be in the rental business. Special-event companies rent equipment such as tables, chairs, and sound equipment. Sporting goods stores can rent equipment, such as Bike and Roll Chicago, which rents bikes and offers bike, Segway, and food tours to Navy Pier and other Miracle Mile attractions (Bike and Roll Chicago 2017).

## User or Program Fees

User or program fees are assessed to people who use services or programs. Personal trainers and specialized fitness classes at health clubs; leadership and self-esteem programs through the Girl Scouts; and youth and adult softball at the local park and recreation department are all examples of programs collecting user and program fees. These fees make up varying percentages of revenue depending on the type and philosophy of the agency. A commercial agency will generate a much higher percentage of revenue versus expenses than the other two sectors, and the variances within these two sectors will fluctuate considerably based on the organizational philosophy regarding how much of the program cost should be recovered. As tax money becomes tighter, many public agencies are being pushed to cover an ever-increasing percentage of operating expenses—including staff, benefits, and insurance—with program fees and charges. For example, 100 percent of the 2018 operating budget for the Woodlands Township Recreation Division is expected to come from a combination of program fees, rentals, sponsorship, boat rental fees, and concession revenue (Woodlands Township 2017).

### Sales Revenue

Sales revenue is acquired from the sale of goods and services. The commercial sector comes to mind first in terms of revenue generation through sales, especially businesses such as sporting goods stores, restaurants, and hotels. However, the public and nonprofit sectors have their own share of sales revenue through concession stands and snack bars, pro shops in places such as golf courses and ice arenas, gift shops in museums and zoos, and souvenir shops at national and state park visitor centers. For instance, Texas Parks and Wildlife Department generated more than $51 million in FY 2017 from sales (Texas Parks and Wildlife Department 2017b). Keep in mind that sales revenue is different from sales taxes. All sectors directly benefit from the sales of their products whereas the tax assessed on the item is diverted to the local and state government and may not necessarily be a source of revenue for parks and recreation.

### License and Permit Fees

Outdoor recreation agencies often receive funding from license and permit fees for snowmobiles, hunting, all-terrain vehicles, special environmental license plates, and so on. The sport industry also capitalizes on revenue generated through licenses. This lucrative revenue source derives from the organization selling the rights to its name or logo for use on apparel, collectibles, and other novelties that are then sold to the public (Sawyer, Hypes, and Gimbert 2017). For instance, North Carolina has special vehicle license plates with proceeds supporting the Blue Ridge Parkway Foundation, Friends of Great Smoky Mountains, Friends of the Appalachian Trail, and North Carolina State Parks (North Carolina Department of Transportation 2017).

### Special Fees

Special fees are assessed for out-of-the-ordinary services. For example, ticket brokers such as Ticketmaster charge a special fee for using their service, universities may charge special technology fees to students for computer services, and the sport industry charges personal seat license (PSL) fees to generate large amounts of money. With PSLs, people pay a one-time fee for the right to buy season tickets for a specific seat during a defined time frame. The primary purpose of PSLs is to reduce the debt incurred from major facility renovations or building a new facility. The Green Bay Packers, for example, charge between $600 and $1,400 per seat, a fee that is considered well below market value.

## Investment Income

All three sectors have the opportunity to generate revenue by investing some of their assets into money-market certificates, stocks, and mutual funds. Revenue from these investments supplements income from other sources. Although it is easy to associate investment income with the commercial sector, it is used frequently in the other two sectors as well. For example, the NRPA, a nonprofit organization, earned $138,006 in 2016 from investments, which contributed 2 percent of its overall budget that year (National Recreation and Park Association 2017).

## Contractual Receipts

A major source of revenue for all three sectors, contractual receipts are agreements with outside organizations that provide services and monetary resources. These contracts can come in many forms, but some of the more common ones include con-

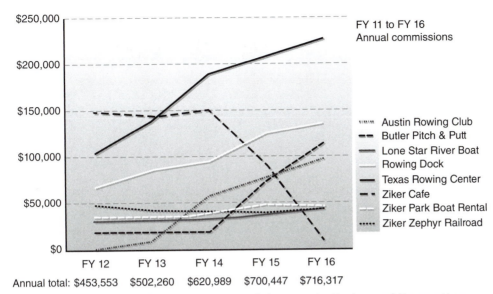

**Figure 11.2** Revenue from contracts of the Austin Parks and Recreation Department.

Data from Austin Parks and Recreation Department.

tracting with an outside agency to operate concession stands, golf and tennis pro shops, and ice arenas. The Austin Parks and Recreation Department in Texas brings in more than $500,000 each year in commissions paid to the city from contracts for various concessionaires in the parks (figure 11.2).

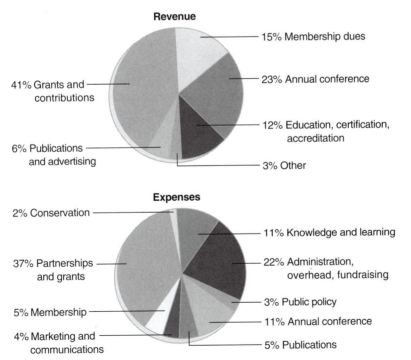

**Figure 11.3** NRPA generates 6 percent of its income from publications and advertising and 38 percent from trainings and conferences.

Reprinted by permission from National Recreation and Park Association (NRPA), *2016 Annual Report* (Ashburn, VA: NRPA, 2017).

**Table 11.1**   Revenue Sources for the YMCA of Austin

| 2015 Audited | | 2016 Unaudited |
|---|---|---|
| REVENUES | | |
| Contributions | $1,807,712 | $2,356,271 |
| Membership fees | 18,442,289 | 18,370,131 |
| Less financial assistance to members | (1,742,659) | (1,592,047) |
| Program service fees | 7,396,957 | 8,770,835 |
| Less financial assistance to participants | (738,233) | (848,223) |
| Investments | (105,437) | 175,611 |
| Other | 274,322 | 362,003 |
| Total revenue and other support | $25,334,951 | $27,594,581 |
| EXPENSES | | |
| Salaries and related payroll costs | $13,358,217 | $14,596,016 |
| Outside Services | 1,359,607 | 1,341,367 |
| Occupancy | 2,744,885 | 3,334,329 |
| Other operating costs | 3,256,306 | 3,823,568 |
| National YMCA support | 285,387 | 328,643 |
| Other Expenses | 625,486 | 763,496 |
| Total Expenses | $21,629,888 | $24,187,419 |
| Sub-Total Net | $3,705,063 | $3,407,162 |
| LESS | | |
| Interest Expense | $337,836 | $279,405 |
| Depreciation | 2,221,552 | 2,384,200 |
| Change in net assets | 1,145,675 | 743,557 |
| Net assets at beginning of year | 34,028,944 | 35,174,619 |
| Net Assets—End of Year | $35,174,619 | $35,918,176 |

From YMCA of Austin Annual Report (2016).

## Summary of Revenue Sources

Agencies use a variety of the discussed revenue sources. Some sectors are more prone to use one source than another. Take a look at figure 11.3 to see the breakdown of revenue sources for the NRPA, a nonprofit professional association. The YMCA of Austin, on the other hand, counts on revenue from earned income (membership fees and program fees), gratuitous income (contributions), and investment income. (table 11.1).

## EXPENDITURES

All organizations have expenditures, or money going out of the organization to pay for staff, facilities, program needs, and so on. Expenditures fall into two broad categories: operating expenditures and capital expenditures.

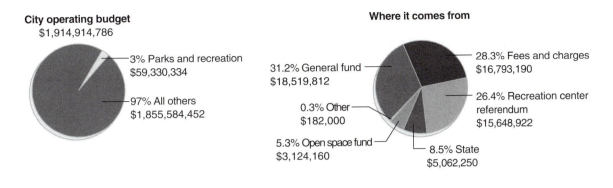

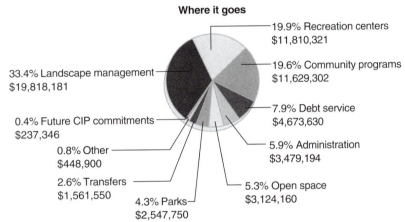

**Figure 11.4** Virginia Beach Parks and Recreation Department expenditure sources for fiscal year 2017. Note: Figures do not add up to 100 percent due to rounding.

Reprinted by permission from Virginia Beach Parks & Recreation Department, *Virginia Beach Parks & Recreation Department 2017 Annual Report* (Virginia Beach, VA, 2017).

## Operating Expenditures

**Operating expenditures**, also called operating costs, are recurring costs associated with doing business. Operating costs include personnel, utilities, office supplies, equipment, and program supplies, which can be divided into fixed and variable costs (see figure 11.4). Fixed costs are incurred regardless of the volume or number of participants. For example, if a youth basketball league is canceled due to low enrollment, there are still costs associated with the program, such as utility costs for the unused facility or staff salary for those directly or indirectly involved in planning the program. Variable costs, on the other hand, change based on volume. If the youth basketball program actually runs, there are several variable costs, including referees, team jerseys, and basketballs. All of these costs will change based on the number of players and teams in the league. Fixed and variable costs are important when determining the cost of a program, as is discussed later in the chapter.

**operating expenditures—** Recurring costs associated with doing business.

## Capital Expenditures

**Capital expenditures** are costs incurred by large-scale purchases, such as playground equipment, updates to a facility to meet ADA standards, new facilities, or park land. The previously discussed streams of revenues will more likely be used

**capital expenditures—** Costs incurred by large-scale purchases such as land, facilities, or expensive equipment.

## General Obligation Bonds

The City of Albuquerque, New Mexico, routinely places park and recreation general obligation bond questions on the ballot for voter consideration. They prepare a general obligation bond program every two years, including a variety of public works from streets to community centers to information technology to parks and recreation. In 2017, city residents voted to fund more than $17,000,000 in park and recreation projects, including a park irrigation system, golf equipment, park improvements, and recreation center renovations. (City of Albuquerque 2017).

to cover the cost of operating expenses and maybe some capital expenditures. Large-scale capital expenditures in the nonprofit sector must rely on fund-raising efforts, and this is often when capital campaigns are instituted.

In the public sector, exceptionally large capital expenditures reach beyond what the tax base and other revenue streams can cover. These expenditures are financed most commonly through bonds. Although several types of bonds are available, two in particular are used to fund capital projects such as a new golf course or minor league baseball stadium: general obligation bonds and revenue bonds.

General obligation bonds (United States) and debenture bonds (Canada) allow a public agency to borrow large amounts of money over a longer length of time, even as long as 30 years, with the intention of paying back the principal and interest. Payments are budgeted for and paid annually; however, because these bonds impose a burden on taxpayers via a temporary increase in property taxes to pay for the bond, general obligation bonds require voter approval through a bond referendum. In addition, there are state limitations on the amount of debt a local governmental agency can assume. See figure 11.5 for an example.

In the United States, revenue bonds are issued for projects where the revenue generated from the completion of the facility will be sufficient to pay back the debt. Since the project itself generates the revenue rather than taxpayers, no bond referendum is needed.

In Canada, general revenue bonds are called debentures and operate in much the same way as revenue bonds in the United States. However, there are three types of debentures. The serial debenture has a fixed schedule to repay the debt and accrued interest. Serial debenture is the most common type, but there are also sinking fund debentures. Sinking fund debentures require no payment until the final year of the loan, and then the entire amount is due in one payment. In order to meet this obligation, the agency will set aside the annual amount owed so the money is available when the payment is due. Lastly, balloon issue debentures require a set payment for a certain length of time, then a balloon payment or extra-large amount may be due in the last year. This sort of debenture is the least common for financing municipal entities (Glossaire National Bank Financial 2017).

Capital improvements in the commercial sector rely on investors or the business owners themselves for funding. They can also use corporate bonds where a loan is secured with the expectation that the lender will receive a fixed rate of return on investment. The bonds are sold with different maturity dates indicating when the

## Bond Election Results in the State of Texas

2016–2017

| | | | |
|---|---|---|---|
| City of Arlington | $45,000,000 | Adult Activity Center | Approved 5/6/2017 |
| City of Plano | $78,850,000 | Park Improvements | Approved 5/6/2017 |
| City of Plano | $12,500,000 | Recreation Centers | Approved 5/6/2017 |
| City of San Antonio | $187,313,000 | Parks and Recreation | Approved 5/6/2017 |
| City of Lavon | $9,200,000 | Sports and Recreation Complex | Defeated 5/6/2017 |
| City of Llano | $500,000 | Parks and Recreation | Approved 5/6/2017 |
| City of Amarillo | $22,247,485 | Parks | Defeated 11/8/2016 |
| City of Amarillo | $66,627,253 | Athletic Facilities | Defeated 11/8/2016 |
| City of Allen | $27,000,000 | Parks and Recreation | Approved 5/7/2016 |
| City of Leander | $26,274,000 | Parks and Recreation | Approved 5/7/2016 |
| City of Leander | $4,185,400 | Senior Center | Approved 5/7/2016 |
| City of Leander | $18,000,000 | Recreation Center | Approved 5/7/2016 |
| City of Portland | $25,200,000 | Parks and Recreation | Approved 5/7/2016 |
| City of Red Oak | $17,255,000 | Parks and Recreation | Defeated 5/7/2016 |

**Figure 11.5** Here is an example of the 2016–2017 referenda results for park and recreation departments in Texas. Ten of the fourteen listed were approved by voters.

Data from State of Texas Comptroller Office (2017).

lender can expect payment. Corporate bonds can either be mortgage bonds, where real estate is used as collateral; equipment trust certificates, where the corporation pays off the loan and is issued a clear title; or income bonds, where interest is only paid if it is earned. Income bonds are usually issued to corporations in bankruptcy (Brayley and McLean 2008).

# PRICING

Pricing has several marketing implications, as previously discussed, and it also drives the fiscal processes of an organization. Pricing of programs and services is done for several reasons. The list below contains examples of why agencies might charge a fee. These are known as pricing objectives (DeGraaf, Jordan, and DeGraaf 2010):

- *Cost recovery.* Pricing may recover the costs of offering programs and services.

- *Create new resources.* Programs can generate additional resources that could be used to fund other programs or simply serve as the profit margin for commercial agencies.

- *Establish value.* Price is the first indicator to a consumer about the value of a program or service (see chapter 8).

● *Influence behavior.* Pricing can influence behavior through damage deposits on rental facilities, late fees for rental equipment returns, early-bird registration opportunities that give discounts for registering by a predetermined date, and so on.

● *Promote efficiency.* Prices can shift demand from peak times to off-peak hours. For example, in the summer, Northstar-at-Tahoe Resort Golf Course offers four different greens fees based upon when you tee off. The highest price is charged for a tee time before 11:00 a.m. There is a $10 discount for golfers teeing off between 11:00 a.m. and 12:50 p.m., a $25 discount between 1:00 p.m. and 4:00 p.m., and a $35 discount after 4:00 p.m. (Northstar-at-Tahoe Resort 2017). Resorts and tourist destinations offer less expensive room rates during the off-peak season to draw people to the area during less busy times. Pricing for efficiency is also used by membership-driven agencies, such as tennis or yacht clubs. Members are given monthly discounts for signing annual contracts and paying through direct withdrawal from a bank account. This method ensures long-term program revenue and saves staff time collecting and processing monthly on-site payments. Sport organizations sell season tickets for the same reasons—to ensure a revenue stream while simultaneously reducing staff costs for selling individual tickets.

## Approaches to Pricing

Price setting can be approached in different ways. Prices can be set arbitrarily because the programmer thinks the price sounds right. They can also be set based on what the competition is charging or what the market will bear. However, the most sound and logical approach is cost recovery, which is "based on the principle of seeking a return from the consumers that represents a predetermined portion of resources that are required to provide the sport or leisure service to them" (Brayley and McLean 2008, 104).

## Pricing a Program

Cost recovery requires understanding how to price a program. A program or service can be priced using a three-step process:

1. Determine pricing variables.
2. Determine the cost of one unit of production.
3. Determine the subsidy rate.

### Step 1: Determine Pricing Variables

Pricing a program is similar to solving a word problem in math class. Several variables and their values are needed before solving the final equation. In terms of pricing programs, information is needed on demand, contingency costs, fixed and variable costs, and direct and indirect costs.

Program demand is an estimate of how many people will attend a program. Most programs have minimum and maximum enrollment figures that determine when to cancel a class as well as when to stop taking more participants. For example, a program with a minimum of eight participants would be canceled if only five people registered. Conversely, if a theater only had 500 seats, that would be the set maximum. The maximum number of participants for programs such as plays, sporting events, or trips using buses is fairly simple to set because it is based on seating. Other programs may set maximums based on room capacity, the amount of equipment or gym space available, or the maximum number of people an instructor can handle. Setting minimum numbers is not any easier than setting maximum numbers. Part of this decision will come from determining a break-even cost where revenues and expenditures are equal, which is discussed later. Many programs determine the break-even point and set the minimum at that point so that any people above that level will be added revenue.

In addition to demand, decisions on contingency costs need to be made. Contingency costs are included in programs in order to cover unexpected costs. This may mean replacing a broken backboard for the basketball program, making unexpected major repairs to the Zamboni machine used at the ice rink, or replacing nets that were vandalized on the tennis courts. Contingency costs can be assessed on a per-person basis, such as $1 per registrant, or added into the cost of the program on a percentage basis, such as 5 to 10 percent of expenditures.

Variable costs are those costs that change in proportion to a change in volume. Thus, each person registering for a program will increase the cost of expenditures such as supplies that are allocated per person. For example, a soccer clinic would have such variable costs as team t-shirts, soccer balls, and a booklet with drills and exercises, because these items are given to participants. As each person registers for the clinic, these costs increase proportionately per person.

Fixed costs, on the other hand, do not change with volume. They remain steady regardless of the number of participants. For the soccer clinic, fixed costs include such things as facility rental and field maintenance. With some programs there are also changing fixed costs. These costs can increase but not proportionately to the volume. For example, this soccer clinic exceeded projected registration. In order to accommodate those on the waiting list, additional instructors must be hired so that the ratio of instructors to players remains at 1:10. So, while the wage for the instructor is fixed, the change in this fixed cost occurs after every eleventh soccer player is added.

Determining price variables requires understanding the fixed and variable costs of a program. These fixed and variable costs include both direct and indirect costs of a program. A direct cost results from actual operation of a particular program. For example, a direct cost for a tennis program would be tennis balls. The tennis program needs this equipment to operate, so the tennis ball cost is directly attributed to its operation. A direct cost can be both fixed and variable, depending on what the item is. A direct fixed cost for tennis would be the tennis professional's salary, whereas a direct variable cost may be the t-shirts for each participant.

Indirect costs are attributable to the program, but indirectly. A tennis pro will directly oversee the tennis programs; however, most likely a supervisor will oversee the tennis pro. Although this supervisor does not directly work with tennis programs, some of her salary and fringe benefits will be attributed to all tennis programs. Another common indirect cost is marketing. The marketing staff is responsible for marketing all programs, including developing a seasonal program brochure listing all available programs and services. Each tennis program must include a portion of the cost of the marketing department, including staff, supplies, and printing of brochures, when calculating the total cost of operating the program. These additional costs are considered indirect costs, sometimes referred to as *overhead costs*. As with direct costs, indirect costs can be either fixed or variable. The indirect cost of the supervisor may be fixed if 5 percent of her salary is assigned to the tennis center. However, it may be variable if $1 is added to all program registrants to cover her salary.

**Table 11.2** Cost Allocations of a $100,000 Salary

| Allocation Method | Tennis | Golf | Fitness | Bowling |
|---|---|---|---|---|
| Equal share | $25,000 | $25,000 | $25,000 | $25,000 |
| Percentage of budget | 40%<br>$40,000 | 25%<br>$25,000 | 30%<br>$30,000 | 5%<br>$5,000 |
| Time-budget study | 10%<br>$10,000 | 25%<br>$25,000 | 45%<br>$45,000 | 20%<br>$20,000 |

Deciding how to allocate indirect costs is a complicated process. Rossman and Schlatter (2015) outlined several methods for this decision making, but three are used more than others in the field: equal share, percentage of budget, and time-budget study.

The first method is equal-share allocation of indirect expenses. With this approach, the indirect costs are equally split among all the departments. To demonstrate allocation costs, assume a sport club has a general manager who oversees the supervisors in each of the four program areas—tennis, golf, fitness, and bowling. If the sport club is using equal-share allocation, then each of the four areas would assume 25 percent of the general manager's salary into their budgets and must account for this indirect cost in the programs offered. This method would be used if all four units were similar in size and ability to generate revenue.

A second allocation method is percentage of budget. If the units are exceptionally unequal in size, cost, or the ability to generate revenue, this approach may be better than the equal-share system. With percentage of budget, each program is assigned a percentage based on their share of the budget. This same percentage is used to divide the indirect costs. In our example, because tennis has 40 percent of the budget, it must account for 40 percent of indirect costs, or $40,000.

A more accurate method of cost allocation may be a time-budget study where time spent on tasks is measured and then assigned to that unit. This process assumes that some units require more attention than others. Though this system may be a better reflection of what the general manager actually does, it takes considerable money and time to complete the study, and it will no longer be accurate as job responsibilities and requirements change over time. Furthermore, this method of allocation works well with salaries but can get more complicated with some other indirect costs such as equipment or utilities.

Looking at the comparisons of the three methods in table 11.2, you can see how determining cost allocation could be tumultuous. The tennis unit would prefer the time-budget study because it is the least expensive to them, fitness would prefer equal share, bowling would prefer percentage of budget, and golf would not see a difference with any of the methods. This is where it is a management decision to determine which method is best for the organization.

## Step 2: Determine the Cost of One Unit

Once the variables are identified, the cost of one unit of production can be determined. This unit might be cost per hour, cost per person, cost per park, and so on. Cost per unit is determined using the following formulas, where

$UC$ = unit cost

$F$ = fixed costs

$V$ = variable costs

$C$ = contingency costs

$N$ = demand (or number of participants expected)

If there is no contingency cost, the following formula should be used:

$$UC = (F + V) / N.$$

The data in the tennis center cost summary (table 11.3) can be used to determine the cost of operating the facility without any programs, reflecting the number of hours the facility will be open rather than the number of people participating in programs. At this point in the pricing process, we are trying to determine how much it costs to keep the facility open rather than looking at individual programs. The individual programs will be accounted for in the budgeting process.

## Table 11.3 Tennis Center Cost Summary

| | Cost | Months or Hours | Subtotal | Total |
|---|---|---|---|---|
| FIXED COSTS | | | | |
| General obligation bond payment | $3,500 | 12 | $42,000 | |
| Facility maintenance | $1,700 | 12 | $20,400 | |
| Head professional | $50,000 | 1 | $50,000 | |
| Administrative overhead | $1,200 | 12 | $14,400 | |
| Total fixed costs | | | | $126,800 |
| VARIABLE COSTS | | | | |
| Utilities | $15 | 5,600 | $84,000 | |
| Front-desk staff | $7 | 5,600 | $39,200 | |
| Custodial staff | $8 | 5,600 | $44,800 | |
| Total variable costs | | | | $168,000 |
| Total fixed and variable costs | | | | $294,800 |

For this example, the facility will be open 350 days a year, 16 hours a day—or 5,600 hours per year. In this example, 5,600 hours is the program demand. Calculating the unit cost using these figures results in a cost of $52.64 per hour to open the doors of the tennis center.

$$UC = (126,800 + 168,000) / 5,600$$

$$UC = \$52.64$$

Next, assume a 5 percent contingency cost is associated with the facility. Calculating contingency costs modifies the formula.

With contingency cost,

$$UC = (F + V + C[F + V]) / N$$

**Table 11.4** Youth Clinic Unit Cost

| | Cost | Months or Hours | Subtotal | Total |
|---|---|---|---|---|
| FIXED COSTS | | | | |
| Tennis balls (1 case) | $60.00 | 1 | $60.00 | |
| Court time | $55.28 | 2 | $110.56 | |
| Total fixed costs | | | | $170.56 |
| VARIABLE COSTS | | | | |
| Supplies | $25.00 | 1 | $25.00 | |
| Four instructors | $25.00 | 4 | $100.00 | |
| Total variable costs | | | | $125.00 |
| Total costs | | | | $295.56 |
| Cost per person | | | | $9.85 |

Demand: 30 kids on 6 courts.

The per-hour facility cost now changes to the following:

$$UC = (126{,}800 + 168{,}000) + .05(126{,}800 + 168{,}000) / 5{,}600$$

$$UC = 294{,}800 + 14{,}740 / 5{,}600$$

$$UC = \$55.28$$

For every hour the tennis center is open, it will cost the organization a base rate of $55.28. So each program that is offered on the courts will need to generate $55.28 on top of the program costs in order to break even. Table 11.4 outlines a youth tennis clinic for 30 people that will be held for two hours. The clinic would be priced at $9.85 to break even, including the per-hour court rate.

$$UC = (\$170.56 + \$125.00) / 30$$

$$UC = \$9.85.$$

Take this example one step further and assume there is an additional $1 charge per person that will be used as a program contingency fee for unexpected program-related occurrences. With this $1 program surcharge, each participant would pay $10.85.

## Step 3: Determine the Subsidy Rate

**subsidy rate**—
Percentage of the program, service, or product cost that will be covered by sources other than the consumer.

The **subsidy rate** is the percentage of unit cost that will be covered by sources other than the consumer (Brayley and McLean 2008). For the public sector, costs may be subsidized using tax dollars or sponsorships; nonprofit organizations may use money from fund-raising or sponsors; and the commercial sector can use cross-subsidization. In cross-subsidization, revenue generated from other programs off-sets the expenses of a program that will not break even. Assume that the tennis center is going to offer the youth tennis clinic free of charge in order to get more people interested in playing the sport. As such, the program needs to be subsidized

**Table 11.5** Subsidy Levels and Hourly Rates

| Program | Program Type | Subsidy Rate | Court Price |
|---|---|---|---|
| Open court time | Public | 100% | Free |
| Adult team tennis | Private | –25% | $69.10 |
| Youth beginner lessons | Merit | 60% | $22.11 |
| Teen traveling team | Private | –20% | $66.34 |
| Youth intermediate league | Private | 0% | $55.28 |

by $295.56 without the $1 contingency fee in order to break even. If cross-subsidization is used, money generated from a program such as an adult tennis tournament that had a $1,000 profit could subsidize the clinic.

Subsidy rates are usually based on the type of program being offered—public, merit, or private. A public service is offered to the public at large and benefits everyone, such as parks, sidewalks, or walking trails. These services benefit both users and nonusers; both users and nonusers see increased property value, community aesthetics, and overall health of residents. Public services are usually free and totally subsidized with tax dollars.

Merit services, on the other hand, usually see a partial cost recovery as well as a partial subsidization. These types of services directly benefit the people who use them, but they also indirectly benefit the community as a whole. For example, an after-school program benefits participants by providing structured programs, help with homework, and a safe place to stay until parents finish their workday. Indirect benefits come from decreases in vandalism or criminal activity that results when children do not have after-school supervision or decreases in public funding needed if parents can take full-time jobs knowing their children are adequately cared for.

Private services see at least a full cost recovery, and many times they turn a profit. These programs mostly benefit the person who is participating in the program. An all-inclusive weekend getaway to Mexico benefits the person taking the trip but not the rest of the community. This trip is a luxury rather than filling a need for the good of the entire community and should be paid for by the person benefiting.

Classifying all programs and services that an organization offers helps establish their subsidy rate. A commercial agency may see that all of its programs are private and must make a profit; its conundrum is deciding how much of a profit to make. Conversely, the public and nonprofit sectors must first determine which programs to subsidize and then decide how much to subsidize them.

Table 11.5 demonstrates subsidy levels for tennis programs as well as hourly rates for the courts. A 0 percent subsidy is the break-even price since no portion of the fee is subsidized whereas a 100 percent subsidy means the entire cost is subsidized and the program is free.

In table 11.5 some of the programs list a negative subsidization rate. This means that a profit will be made. For example, the teen traveling team has a –20 percent subsidy rate. Rather than paying a break-even cost of $55.28 per hour, the program would actually cost $66.34. There are two ways to calculate this cost ($S$ = subsidy rate).

**Method 1:**

$$P = (1 - S)(F + V + C[F + V]) / N)$$

$$P = (1 - S)(294{,}800 + .05[294{,}800]) / 5{,}600$$

$$P = (1 - S) \times 55.28$$

$$P = 1.20 \times 55.28$$

$$P = \$66.34$$

**Method 2:**

$$P = \text{Unit cost} \times (1 - S)$$

$$P = \$55.28 \times 1 - (-20)$$

$$P = \$55.28 \times 1.20$$

$$P = \$66.34$$

Both methods will give the same end result within a few cents because of rounding the prices.

# PRICING TRENDS AND ISSUES

Pricing can be a sensitive subject for many park and recreation agencies. Each agency has its own philosophy on cost recovery, who should be charged what, and how to increase revenues and decrease costs. Here are a couple of issues regarding pricing in leisure services organizations.

## Subsidies and Double Taxation

For public and nonprofit agencies in particular, subsidy rates can be complex. Subsidies have been a point of discussion in the field for many years because public and nonprofit recreation agencies are expected to continue to increase services to their constituents. It is unrealistic to think that park and recreation services should be free. If all programs and services are free, then their quality and quantity are limited.

In order to provide the services needed, fees and charges must be assessed for some programs. The downside of fees and charges is twofold. First, they can eliminate some groups from participating, such as low-income community members. Second, fees and charges are sometimes viewed as double taxation because property taxes are used to fund many of the services.

To avoid eliminating people from participating, fees charged for some programs can either generate revenue for funding free or low-cost programs or tax dollars can be used for the same purpose. Termed *cross-subsidization*, this method of shifting resources allows for increased service provision for all people.

The double taxation perception is actually inaccurate. For most public agencies, tax dollars are used to provide basic public services such as parks and special events. As discussed previously with public, merit, and private services, a portion of merit programs are paid with taxes to represent the benefit to the community as a whole, and the remaining portion of the fee is paid by the person who most directly benefits.

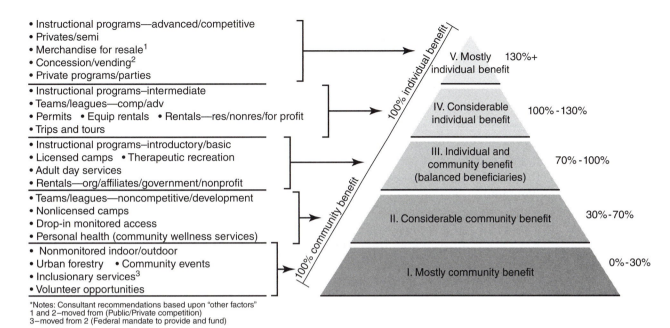

* Instructional programs—advanced/competitive
* Privates/semi
* Merchandise for resale[1]
* Concession/vending[2]
* Private programs/parties

* Instructional programs–intermediate
* Teams/leagues—comp/adv
* Permits  • Equip rentals  • Rentals—res/nonres/for profit
* Trips and tours

* Instructional programs–introductory/basic
* Licensed camps  • Therapeutic recreation
* Adult day services
* Rentals—org/affiliates/government/nonprofit

* Teams/leagues—noncompetitive/development
* Nonlicensed camps
* Drop-in monitored access
* Personal health (community wellness services)

* Nonmonitored indoor/outdoor
* Urban forestry  • Community events
* Inclusionary services[3]
* Volunteer opportunities

*Notes: Consultant recommendations based upon "other factors"
1 and 2–moved from (Public/Private competition)
3–moved from 2 (Federal mandate to provide and fund)

100% individual benefit

V. Mostly individual benefit    130%+

IV. Considerable individual benefit    100% - 130%

III. Individual and community benefit (balanced beneficiaries)    70% - 100%

II. Considerable community benefit    30% - 70%

I. Mostly community benefit    0% - 30%

100% community benefit

**Figure 11.6**  This cost recovery model illustrates five levels of benefits from a community benefit up to a complete individual benefit. The more of a community benefit a service has, the more it will be subsidized with tax dollars.

Reprinted by permission from City of Spokane (2010).

More and more agencies are examining how fees and charges are assessed and how subsidies are used. For example, in 2010, the City of Spokane Parks and Recreation Department developed a comprehensive financial resource allocation philosophy which they use to determine how much cost recovery different types of programs will be expected to generate (figure 11.6).

In Spokane's version of the cost-recovery pyramid, the basic services that have up to 30 percent recovery of direct costs are at the base of the pyramid. They are seen as the foundation of the agency and serve the largest portion of the community. They include such things as special events and inclusion services. Moving up the pyramid means that an increased portion of direct costs are assessed to the user. For example, the remaining four levels have established cost recovery of 30 to 70 percent, 70 to 100 percent, 100 to 130 percent, and 130+ percent. Each additional level of programs is only implemented when the previous level is well established and meeting the needs of the community. Displaying cost recovery in this manner aids the community in understanding the need for fees as well as where tax dollars are spent. Although this specific example cannot be implemented in every organization, it is a sound model to use when pricing programs.

## Differential Pricing

**Differential pricing** is charging a different price to different populations for the same service. *Customer characteristics* are one means for instituting differential pricing and include age, income, intensity of consumption, and so on. Age is arguably the most common way to differentiate prices. For example, the Chelsea Piers Sports and Entertainment Complex in Manhattan is home to a multiuse recreation area. The area includes a bowling alley, field house, golf driving range, roller rink and

**differential pricing**—Pricing a service differently for different populations based on customer characteristics, product level, distribution, and so on.

skate park, health club, and ice rink. The roller rink charges $7 for children and $8 for adults, and the ice rink charges less for children and seniors than adults. In addition, skaters can buy discounted tickets for 10 admissions to the rink, a savings of $10.

*Product level* can also serve as a distinguishing variable for pricing. A rock-climbing class may be priced differently based on experience—beginning climbers would most likely pay the lowest fee whereas the advanced climbers would pay the most. The low fee for beginners is sometimes used as a promotional strategy with the idea that people are more inclined to try a new activity if the cost is lower. Once they begin to enjoy the activity and take more lessons, they're hooked and willing to pay more for it.

*Distribution* is also a common means of assigning differential pricing, including location of the program, seats in a venue, or time of day. At the Chelsea Piers bowling alley, it is least expensive to bowl Monday through Friday until 5:00 p.m., and it is most expensive to bowl Wednesday through Sunday evenings. Program location can have an impact on pricing, especially for the public sector. The location of a facility such as a pool may dictate the price of programs; an underused facility may charge less in order to stimulate use.

Pricing programs is just one step in the financial management process. It is the impetus to budgeting and reaches to the core of recreation programming. It is far more complicated than simply pulling a price out of the air. It has marketing implications in terms of stimulating demand, and it has the ability to cross-subsidize worthy programs that would not otherwise be offered because of funding.

## Creative Financing

Financial constraints often require organizations to be creative in their financing. Agencies do many things to bring in revenue, including the following:

- Reexamine the return on investment of monies invested.
- Use creative programming to attract a multitude of target markets. These programs are designed as cost centers to generate profits.
- Lease space for cell phone towers, which can generate anywhere from $12,000 to $22,000 per year.
- Corporate sponsorships and grants are on the rise. They often require the hiring of development staff to raise funds.
- Partnerships with local agencies enable the joint provision of services or joint use of spaces. These partnerships reduce the need to duplicate services and/or facilities in the community.
- Attracting national sporting and cultural events to communities brings in needed revenue through tourism dollars.
- Minor and major league sport teams often have variable pricing options where they charge higher prices for tickets to premier games such as opening day, rivalries, and weekend games.
- Eliminate inefficiencies in operations.
- Reexamine the core mission of the agency and eliminate services that do not meet the mission.
- Establish nonprofit foundations so that people may make tax-deductible donations to the organization.

Check out the web study guide for additional material, including learning activities, sample documents, interactive case studies, web links, CPRP exam connections, and more.

# Conclusion

This chapter presented an overview of financial management in park and recreation services. Regardless of your job in the field, finance will be a major part of it. The foundation and most basic unit of finance is program pricing. Establishing prices means understanding revenue streams as well as expenditures since both influence the ultimate price. The steps outlined here move a manager from philosophical topics such as indirect cost allocations and whether to label services as public, merit, or private to more concrete elements such as fixed and variable costs, subsidy rates, and differential pricing.

The pricing piece of the financial picture intimately involves programs, events, and services within the jurisdiction of each programmer. The next chapter looks at the big picture by bringing all of the pricing elements together to form the budget, and it is the budget that drives the entire organization.

# Review Questions

1. Define the five types of income. Indicate which sector is most likely and least likely to use each one.
2. Differentiate between real property taxes and personal property taxes.
3. Compare and contrast operating and capital expenditures.
4. Describe the four approaches to pricing.
5. Define the following terms: contingency costs, fixed and variable costs, and direct and indirect costs.
6. Explain subsidy rates and how private, merit, and public services affect subsidy rates.
7. Describe three ways to allocate indirect costs for leisure services agencies.

# 12

# Budgets and Financial Cost Analysis

## Learning Outcomes

- Demonstrate an understanding of the budget process.

- Differentiate between capital and operating budgets.

- Compare and contrast the most prevalent types of budgets used in leisure services.

- Identify the most common financial analysis methods used in leisure services.

## Key Terms

budgets, budget cycle, work plan, cutback management, capital budget, capital improvement plan (CIP), operating budget, allocated funds, petty cash, purchase requisition, purchase order, invoice, invitation for bid (IFB), request for proposal (RFP), request for quotation (RFQ), financial analysis, balance sheet

## Competency Check

Refer to table 1.6 to see how you assessed these related competencies.
1. Understand financial processes (i.e., purchasing, budget).
2. Develop, monitor, and stay within a budget.

## A Day in the Life

Leading a midsized agency (100 full-time employees), my typical day can involve anything. Typically, in the morning we work on resolving outstanding issues from our evening and weekend crews. This includes items such as parking problems at a special event, people swimming in a non-swimming lake, and how profitable our boathouses were from the previous day or weekend. Also in the morning, I have discussions with my operational units—parks, aquatics, and construction—to discuss with them the status of capital projects or residents' issues and projects that might be three to four months out. In the afternoon, I will talk or meet with my assistant directors to review with them where we are in terms of our current budget—revenues and expenses, what large capital projects are coming up, issues that might be brought to our city manager, our board, and our residents. In the afternoon, I will generally catch up on emails, work on spreadsheets and contracts, and make calls back to residents. In the evening, I become a park user with my children as they play lacrosse. There I am able to see how they and other community members use the park on a daily basis.

Chris Nunes, CPRE
Director of Parks and Recreation
The Woodlands Township, Texas

The previous chapter laid the groundwork for financial management. A thorough understanding of revenues, expenditures, pricing, and subsidy are the small pieces of the larger financial plan—the budget. This chapter focuses on the budget process from the development of the budget cycle and preparation to implementation, monitoring, and evaluation.

It is easy to think of the budget as a summary of the revenues and expenditures for a year, but it is much more than that. A budget has political, managerial, short- and long-term planning, communication, and financial implications (National Advisory Council on State and Local Budgeting 1999). Financial management and budgeting serve several important functions in the organization, thus requiring extended discussion throughout this book.

## DEFINING BUDGETS

**Budgets** are the financial plan for the year. They outline revenues and expenditures, and this outline drives decision making for the organization. Any decision that has financial implications must be examined based on the financial resources available, thus allowing managers to make informed choices. For example, assume the Cincinnati Recreation Commission plans to change its registration system. This requires the purchase of new computers and software for the 31 recreation centers and 41 swimming pools in the city—a large expenditure that can either be phased in over several fiscal years or done within one. Analyzing the budget will determine what options are available and what the best financial decision is for the department.

**budgets**—Financial plans detailing revenues and expenditures of an organization for a fiscal year.

Budgets also reflect the priorities of an agency. These priorities are a result of organizational goals, objectives, and strategic plans, and they are reinforced by the financial resources allocated to priority projects. For example, Camp Fire USA is a nonprofit program whose mission is youth development, including leadership, self-reliance, inclusion, and the reduction of sex-role, racial, and cultural stereotypes. The budget from the parent organization reflects this mission, with 68 percent allocated to programs for young people and to councils that provide these programs (Camp Fire USA 2016).

In addition, budgets reflect the effectiveness and efficiency of resources, including how resources are spent and acquired. The effectiveness of resources demonstrates what programs and services achieve the goals and priorities of the organization, and efficiency relates to minimizing the waste of resources. In an ideal financial situation, programs are funded based on whether they are congruent with the mission of the organization and whether they meet its goals. Then these programs are operated so they are most efficient. This may mean that thorough planning is done so that the right number of staff members is hired, sufficient sponsors are sought, and participant demand is correctly projected.

As you will see, financial management is far more complex than a spreadsheet of expenditures and revenues—it guides processes and decision making throughout the entire organization. Without a solid understanding of budgeting, a manager can quickly face a multitude of problems because of poor decision making, inaccurate revenue or expenditure projections, or inefficient service provision. The following sections build an understanding of the budgeting process, different types of budgets, and means of tracking and analyzing financial activities.

# BUDGET CYCLE

**budget cycle**—Steps associated with the budgeting process, from preparation to approval to implementation to closing of the budget at the end of the fiscal year.

Developing a budget is a long process with several steps. These steps are called the **budget cycle** and are prevalent within all sectors of leisure services. Some organizations may modify the process or order of the steps, but the budget cycle remains relatively consistent throughout the profession.

## Step 1: Develop a Budget Calendar

A budget calendar is a time line of tasks to be completed, including when budget preparation begins, when the budget is due from each level of administration, when the budget is presented to and approved by a governing body, and when the fiscal year begins. A budget runs on a fiscal year and consists of the 12 months during which a financial cycle runs. A fiscal year does not have to start on January 1 and follow a calendar year. For example, the City of Columbia Parks and Recreation Department in Missouri has a fiscal year of October 1 to September 30, and the National Recreation and Park Association (NRPA) has a fiscal year of July 1 to June 30. The budget calendar is based on the start of the fiscal year, and all proposed budgets must be completed, approved, and ready for implementation before the new fiscal year starts.

A budget cycle can require working with the budget for more than one fiscal year. For example, in the United States, the National Park Service (NPS) began the creation of the FY 2018 (October 1, 2017 to September 30, 2018) budget in October of FY 2015 with the NPS Servicewide Comprehensive Call. The budget was completed in February 2017 when they submitted the information to Congress. With any luck, they will have an enacted appropriation before the start of the new fiscal year on October 1. The entire budget process in the NPS takes two or more years (table 12.1), with that time frame expanding if a new presidential administration takes office (National Park Service 2017).

## Step 2: Develop a Departmental Work Plan

**work plan**—Outline of what programs and services will be offered or what products will be produced.

A **work plan** outlines what programs and services will be offered or what products will be produced. In essence, the work plan forecasts service volume. It also allows for evaluation and opportunities to eliminate unsuccessful programs, services, and products, as well as add new ones. The work plan will drive the budgeting process since the budget should account for the products in the work plan.

**Table 12.1**   The National Park Service Federal Budget Timeline for Fiscal Year 2018

| Servicewide Comprehensive Call | WASO Budget Formulation | DOI Review | OMB Review | Greenbook Production | Congressional Review and Enhancement |
| --- | --- | --- | --- | --- | --- |
| October 2015 | May 2016 | September 2016 | November 2016 | February 2017 | February–October 2017 |

The budget cycle takes more than two years to complete; three different budgets are active at one time.
Reprinted from National Park Service (2015).

## Step 3: Develop an Expense Budget

Once the products, services, and programs are outlined in the work plan, it is time to develop the expenses to produce them. A major part of the expense budget is salaries and related employee expenses such as fringe benefits. Salaried employees receive a set annual wage that is broken evenly into the designated pay periods for the agency, and most agencies pay weekly, biweekly, or monthly. This salary, as well as any anticipated raises, should be included. An employee making $40,000 per year and anticipating a 3 percent raise at the beginning of the fiscal year would have $41,200 budgeted for salary.

Hourly employees are different only in that you need to calculate for each position individually. Assume a facility supervisor is working 20 hours per week at $12 per hour. Wages would be calculated as

$$20 \text{ hours per week} \times 52 \text{ weeks a year} \times \$12 \text{ per hour} = \$12{,}480.$$

In addition to wages and salaries, all other operating expenditures need to be accounted for, including facility maintenance, equipment, and supplies. Although managers have a tendency to overestimate expenditures in their budgets, this is not good practice. Ideally, a manager will attempt to account for all anticipated expenses fairly accurately knowing that if enrollment is low, they will need to cut spending.

## Step 4: Develop a Revenue Budget

Sources of revenues for organizations in the public, nonprofit, and commercial sectors were discussed in chapter 11. It is during this step in the budgeting process that revenue is accounted for, whether it is fees and charges, taxes, or investment income. Many managers are conservative in their revenue projections. It is better to bring in more revenue than projected than to have a shortfall. If the projected revenues do not come in, then the expenses will need to be adjusted in the middle of the fiscal year to account for the change in circumstances.

## Step 5: Modify and Finalize the Budget

With the revenues and expenditures in place, it is necessary to analyze whether the budget meets the goals, objectives, and priorities of the organization. This includes ensuring that all subsidy projections are met and that products meant to be subsidized, break even, and turn a profit actually do. This step reviews whether the expenditures are too high or revenues too low. In this step managers are sometimes asked to make budget cuts. They may be told to cut a percentage of money from the budget or given a flat amount to cut, either from reducing expenditures or increasing revenues. If revenues are increased, there should be a justification for doing so. Once revenues are projected, they are expected to actually materialize.

## Step 6: Present, Defend, and Seek Approval for the Budget

The finalized budget will go through a review process with the administrative board for public and nonprofit agencies and larger commercial agencies. Small commercial agencies, such as partnerships and sole proprietorships, need only the approval of the owners. Budgets that are presented in front of a board will demonstrate the overall financial picture as well as explain any major increases or decreases in revenues and expenditures. The board usually asks numerous questions seeking justification for some areas. At this point in the process, the board may approve the budget or ask for revisions. Once approved, the budget is set and ready to begin the fiscal year.

## Summary of the Budget Cycle

Budget preparation requires involvement from all levels of the organization. Any staff members who are involved in spending money or bringing in revenues should be part of the process. This helps get commitment from staff who must work within the financial parameters set in the budget. In addition, these employees know the inner workings of their programs, services, and products. They will be well versed in what expenditures to expect as well as better able to project revenues than someone higher in the organization who does not work directly with the services, programs, or products.

# CUTBACK MANAGEMENT

Developing a budget requires a great deal of time, fortitude, and foresight. However, sometimes it is necessary to cut budgets due to unforeseen circumstances such as a declining economy, as happened after the terrorist attacks of September 11, 2001, or unplanned expenses, such as a major facility falling short of revenues by thousands of dollars.

## How Cuts Are Made

**cutback management**—The process of determining what expenditures to reduce within a budget.

When such unforeseen events occur, it is necessary for the organization to implement **cutback management**, where the agency must cut projected expenses from the budget. Determining what to cut is a difficult task and can become political in nature. Cutback management has long-term effects and cannot be done quickly or without a plethora of information. Thus, cuts should be made with the involvement of stakeholders, as much information as possible, and the guidance of the strategic plan. When deciding what to cut, it is important to look at several aspects of the agency to see where cuts are possible. In terms of parks and recreation, managers should examine core values, vision, and mission; the vision for the future and how cuts will affect that vision; how well the organization is performing; what outcomes result from the programs and services; and what would happen if the programs and services were no longer offered (Thomas 2002).

Cuts can be made in three areas: workforce reduction, where staff numbers are reduced; work redesign, where the work itself is the focus; and systematic change requiring a change in the culture, values, and tradition of the organization (Cameron 1994). Workforce reduction means that staffing levels are reduced through such methods as attrition, where staff members who leave are not replaced; hiring freezes; elimination of positions currently held by employees; layoffs; and early retirements or buy-outs, where people are given a sum of money if they leave or retire from the company at a specified time. The workforce is often the first place managers look during cutbacks since staff is usually the single largest expenditure in the budget of a leisure services organization. The result of workforce reduction is often low morale. When staff is cut, it is logical to assume that the remaining employees will not trust the organization, they will be worried about their own job security, and they will be less committed to the organization (Thomas 2002). It is a challenge for managers to clearly communicate why cutbacks were made and what it means for the rest of the organization. It is imperative to be honest with employees in order to aid morale.

Work redesign changes the products and services offered. Services may be eliminated altogether, phased out, or changed. At first glance, work redesign seems to be a negative concept. However, true work redesign requires the agency to look at what programs it is offering and determine which are the most important for meeting the needs of the constituency. It can identify labor-saving approaches to staffing and technology; eliminate duplication of services within the agency or with other agencies in the community; and eliminate organizational layers in staffing, giving the organization a larger span of control (see chapter 4) with fewer managers and layers of bureaucracy (Cameron 1994).

Systematic changes in culture, values, and attitudes can be difficult. Such changes require the organization to operate more efficiently and effectively through streamlined processes, and they result in doing fewer things better. Streamlining processes requires reducing resource waste and hidden costs.

Staff can influence how cutbacks are managed within an agency. A good manager will strive to be transparent about what needs to happen and ask staff for ideas and input on how to achieve the desired result. Rather than focusing on one idea or area from the outset, managers need to have an open mind about what changes can and should be made. Staff have detailed knowledge about how their programs operate and should be ready to share how proposed cutbacks will affect those programs and services—both negatively and positively. Not all cutbacks are bad; in fact, some cutbacks ultimately result in even better programs and services for the constituents.

## Politics of Cutback Management

Cutback management can result in agency politics, especially in the public sector. The political aspects of the budget process can include special interest groups, board or city council reelection, or city priorities. It is not uncommon for special interest groups to become involved and fight for their particular service if cuts are looming. These special interest groups may be very vocal, but that should not dictate whether their budget area is cut. Their programs must be evaluated just as those of less vocal interests are. With special interest groups, much information and misinformation will be presented. It is the job of the manager to acquire as much accurate information as possible and listen to these groups so their interests can be considered. Special interest groups may be able to present outcomes of programs and services that are unknown to the staff.

The election cycle also affects cutback management. If city council or board members are coming up for reelection, they may be more likely to make the popular decision for reelection purposes rather than making decisions in the best interest of the agency. Typically, politicians do not like to have bad publicity or controversies arise near a campaign season, and it is during this time that the special interest groups can become even more vocal.

Finally, understanding and negotiating the priorities of elected officials can be key to reducing cutbacks for specific departments. Let's use a Midwestern city as an example. This city recently built a new coliseum despite the fact that the community voted in a nonbinding resolution not to build it. The city council made the decision to build the coliseum anyway and in its first year of business it lost over $2 million. Even though the city council members who voted to build the coliseum in the first place were not reelected, the current council has the task of covering the $2 million loss from the current year and in the future since upcoming fiscal years look only slightly better. This city council has decided that cutback management is needed rather than raised taxes. The council has also set as its priorities basic city services such as police and fire. However, it does not see parks and recreation as a basic service and is devaluing its effects on the community. This has caused the council to make major cuts to the park and recreation budget while leaving other city services intact. Now the challenge for the park and recreation department is to reposition itself as a vital service to the community in hopes of changing the priorities of the council (see chapter 8).

Cutback management is never easy. It is difficult to identify areas to cut and it makes staff uneasy. It also brings out the political aspects of budgeting. However, it is something that managers face regardless of whether they are in the public, nonprofit, or commercial sectors. When it happens, the manager has many options, with the priority being to work with staff and other stakeholders to reach the best solution possible under difficult circumstances.

# TYPES OF BUDGETS

The previous steps outlined the process for developing the budget; now it's time to consider the types of budgets available to managers. Budgets typically come in two forms: capital budgets and operating budgets. Both types go through the same process but are considered separate budgets.

## Capital Budgets

**capital budget—**
Financial plan for large-scale purchases within an agency.

**Capital budgets** are developed for big projects such as land acquisition, facility development, or major equipment purchases with a useful life of more than five years (Zimmermann and Davidson 2016). Capital budgets are a result of long-term planning and careful research. Organizations do not just decide to build a new facility, put it in the budget, and open it the next year. Because of the cost and unique funding sources needed for these projects, organizations should develop "a plan, processes, and criteria to ensure the strategic and cost-effective acquisition, replacement, and retirement of capital resources" (Zimmermann and Davidson 2016, 615). With proper planning and research, it is much more likely that the right decisions will be made and that project priorities are in the best interest of the organization.

**capital improvement plan (CIP)—**
Plan outlining capital projects to be completed; guides budget decisions related to the projects.

**Capital improvement plans (CIPs)** contain "all the individual capital projects, equipment purchases, and major studies for a local government; in conjunction with construction and completion schedules, and in consort with financing plans. The plan provides a working blueprint for sustaining and improving the community's infrastructures" (Francis 2016). The CIP is reviewed annually, and the order of projects can change over time. For example, Vancouver Parks and Recreation in British Columbia developed a CIP that proposed a $154.5 million investment over the next four years to maintain and upgrade city facilities and infrastructure (Vancouver Parks and Recreation 2017). CIPs are regularly evaluated and priorities adjusted as the community changes

An advantage of the long-term CIP is that many projects require phases of development that will not happen within a fiscal year. The CIP outlines the phases so that funds are available when needed for the project. For example, the Park District of Oak Park created a table in their capital improvement plan so that it is easy to see when money is needed and for what projects (table 12.2)

The capital budget is the financial plan for major resource investment, but the operating budget is also affected because daily operating costs such as staff, maintenance,

**Table 12.2** Park District of Oak Park Capital Improvement Plan Expenditures by Location from 2017–2021

| Park | 2016 | 2017 | 2018 | 2019 | 2020 | 2021 | Total |
|---|---|---|---|---|---|---|---|
| Andersen Park and Center | | | $150,000 | | $500,000 | | $650,000 |
| Austin Gardens | | | | | | | $0 |
| Barrie Park and Center | | | | $115,000 | $1,000,000 | | $1,115,000 |
| Carroll Park and Center | | | | $250,000 | | | $250,000 |
| Elizabeth F. Cheney Mansion | | | | | | | $0 |
| Dole Center | | | | | | | $0 |
| Euclid Square Park | | $1,300,000 | | | | | $1,300,000 |
| Field Park and Center | | $175,000 | | $400,000 | | | $575,000 |
| Fox Park and Center | | $320,000 | $105,000 | | | | $425,000 |
| Gymnastic and Recreation Center | | | | | | | $0 |
| John L. Hedges Admin Center | | | | | | | $0 |
| Lindberg Park | | | | | | | $0 |
| Longfellow Park and Center | $500,000 | $85,000 | | | | | $585,000 |
| Maple Park | $1,200,000 | | | | | | $1,200,000 |
| Mills Park | | | | | | | $0 |
| Oak Park Conservatory | $100,000 | $200,000 | | | | | $300,000 |
| Pleasant Home | | | $500,000 | | | | $500,000 |
| Rehm Park | | | | | | | $0 |
| Rehm Pool | $150,000 | | $540,000 | | | | $690,000 |
| Ridgeland Common Recreation Complex | | | | | | | $0 |
| Scoville Park | | | | | | | $0 |
| Stevenson Park and Center | | $115,000 | | $800,000 | | | $915,000 |
| Taylor Park | | $25,000 | | | | | $25,000 |
| Wenonah Park | | | | | | | $0 |
| Randolph Park | | | | | | | $0 |
| Nonsite Specific | | | | | | $2,100,000 | $2,100,00 |
| Vehicles/Technology/Repairs/Nonsite | $90,000 | $60,000 | $125,000 | $130,000 | $85,000 | $120,000 | $610,000 |
| ADA/Surveys | $125,000 | $50,000 | $50,000 | $50,000 | $50,000 | $50,000 | $375,000 |
| Reserve for Turf Replacement | $100,000 | $100,000 | $100,000 | $100,000 | $100,000 | $100,000 | $600,000 |
| Reserve for Property Acquisition | $200,000 | $200,000 | $200,000 | $200,000 | $200,000 | $200,000 | $1,200,000 |
| **Project Costs** | **$2,465,000** | **$2,630,000** | **$1,770,000** | **$2,045,000** | **$1,935,000** | **$2,570,000** | **$13,415,000** |
| **Debt Service** | **$1,997, 969** | **$2,000,194** | **$2,002,119** | **$1,998,744** | **$1,998,944** | **$1,998,644** | **11,996,614** |
| **Total CIP Costs** | **$4,462,969** | **$4,630,194** | **$3,772,119** | **$4,043,744** | **$3,933,944** | **$4,568,644** | **$25,411,614** |

Adapted by permission from Park District of Oak Park, Illinois.

and utilities are in the general operating budget and not the capital budget. So, although the two types of budgets are separate, they are very much intertwined in the management of the organization.

## Operating Budgets

**operating budget—** Budget containing revenues and expenditures associated with day-to-day operations of the organization.

**Operating budgets** affect managers at all levels of an organization. Managers exercise most control with these budgets because they outline and implement the expenditures and revenues for their departments or areas within the fiscal year. Keep in mind that although a 12-month fiscal year is most common, some agencies operate on a two- or three-year budget cycle as well.

Operating budgets can come in several different formats. Each organization will differ, but a general understanding of the most common types will be beneficial to a manager new to the organization.

### Line-Item and Object Classification Budgets

Line-item and object classification budgets are the most common budget formats in leisure services. They are similar in format and function. The line-item budget is a listing of expenditures, or items, and their dollar amounts. These expenditures are then placed in a line so they can all be viewed at once (table 12.3). This type of budget is best for small programs or agencies. With a line-item budget, it is easy to leave out expenditures since line items are not consistent from program to program. This also makes it difficult to compare budgets across programs if they do not have the same expenditures.

The object classification budget takes the line-item budget one step further in that it categorizes, or classifies, line items. There may be major classifications such

**Table 12.3** Sample Line-Item Budget

| Line Items | Total |
| --- | --- |
| REVENUES | |
| Ticket sales | $1,875 |
| Reserve (carryover from previous budget) | $36 |
| Total revenue | $1,911 |
| EXPENDITURES | |
| Meal | $900 |
| Appetizers | $132 |
| Damage deposit | $50 |
| Facility rental fee | $75 |
| DJ | $300 |
| Mailings | $55 |
| Printing—invitations | $15 |
| Printing—information sheets | $60 |
| Envelopes | $60 |
| Total expenditures | $1,647 |

as personnel services and contractual services, and within these categories there are often subcategories and objects. In table 12.4, personnel services does not have a subcategory, but contractual services has numerous subcategories, such as communication and transportation and utilities. Personnel services moves directly to the objects with contractual employees and wages. The totals from each object line item are summarized in the subcategory totals, which are then totaled in the category column.

The predetermined categories are used by all managers within an organization, although not all managers will use all of the categories or line items. In order for these categories to be effective, each needs a standardized definition. For table 12.4, the definitions could be the following:

- Personnel services: Full- and part-time salaries and hourly wages paid to staff employed at the organization
- Contractual services: Products purchased on contract or services obtained through a contractual agreement between the agency and another party

Creating an object classification budget means assigning the appropriate monetary amounts to each object or line item. A manager is then allowed to spend the allocated amount in the budget. **Allocated funds** are those that are approved by the governing body to be spent on a specific line item. As money in this line item is spent, it needs to be tracked by the manager, and will often be double-checked using a purchasing approval process to ensure the money expended does not exceed the allocated amount and go over budget.

Object classification budgets are popular because of their ease and flexibility. The objects are predetermined so it is easy to see if any expenditures were omitted from the budget. The object classification budget also is relatively easy for all levels of employees to learn and use. It is flexible in that categories, subcategories, and objects can change as needed. However, for consistency purposes they remain relatively stable unless a major change occurs such as adding cemeteries or libraries to the local park and recreation agency. These units would need some of their own classifications since they most likely will not fit neatly into a park and recreation budget.

This budget format has some weaknesses as well. The most prevalent problem is that an object classification budget does not identify how budget figures were obtained, so a separate document outlining this information is needed. Second, with predetermined categories it is sometimes difficult to find an object for unusual expenditures. This means they get placed wherever seems the most logical to the manager. Object classification budgets have also been criticized for not being goal driven. They focus solely on how much the program costs and not how it fits with the goals of the organization. Finally, object classification can perpetuate a status quo approach to budgeting. "In many agencies the assumption is that existing programs will continue at some increased or reduced level and that proposed new programs will only be developed if additional money becomes available" (Zimmermann and Davidson 2016, 603). With this budget format, the benefits and costs of the services are not evaluated (Zimmermann and Davidson 2016). However, this weakness can be ameliorated by following the work plan that reviews programs and services.

**allocated funds**— Money that has been approved by the authoritative body to be spent on specific line items within the budget.

## Program Budgets

As mentioned, a weakness of object classification budgets is that they are driven more by expenditures and less by the value of the program to consumers. Program

**Table 12.4** Sample Object Classification Categories

| | Object Total | Subcategory Total | Category Total |
|---|---|---|---|
| **1000: Personnel services** | | | $2,037,000 |
| 1100: Salaries, regular (full-time) | $1,500,000 | | |
| 1200: Salaries, temporary (part-time) | $25,000 | | |
| 1300: Wages, regular (hourly, full-time) | $250,000 | | |
| 1400: Wages, temporary (hourly, part-time) | $175,000 | | |
| 1500: Contractual employees | $75,000 | | |
| 1600: Other compensations | $12,000 | | |
| **2000: Contractual services** | | | $641,252 |
| 2100: Communication and transportation | | $183,252 | |
| 2110: Postage | $5,002 | | |
| 2120: Telephone | $23,000 | | |
| 2130: Freight and express | $10,000 | | |
| 2140: Travel and lodging | $70,000 | | |
| 2150: Vehicles | $32,000 | | |
| 2160: Gasoline, oils, and lubricants | $43,250 | | |
| 2300: Printing, binding, and advertising | | $16,475 | |
| 2310: Printing and photocopying | $12,000 | | |
| 2320: Typewriting and word processing | $500 | | |
| 2330: Binding | $500 | | |
| 2340: Photocopying and blueprinting | $250 | | |
| 2350: Advertising and publication of notices | $3,225 | | |
| 2400: Utilities | | $396,375 | |
| 2410: Heating service | $54,500 | | |
| 2420: Interior lighting service | $65,000 | | |
| 2430: Street lighting service | $76,525 | | |
| 2440: Power (electricity and gas) | $102,350 | | |
| 2450: Water service | $98,000 | | |
| 2500: Repairs | | $17,700 | |
| 2510: Repairs to equipment | $2,350 | | |
| 2520: Repairs to buildings and other structures | $15,350 | | |
| 2600: Janitorial, cleaning, waste removal, and other services | | $27,450 | |
| 2610: Park trash removal | $12,000 | | |
| 2620: Outdoor facility cleaning | $15,450 | | |
| **Totals** | | | **$2,678,252** |

budgets focus more on results, benefits, beneficiaries of services, and how programs interconnect with the mission, goals, and objectives of the agency (Zimmermann and Davidson 2016).

Program budgets are outcome driven. Outcomes are the benefits received from participation in the program, such as changes in behavior, skill, knowledge, attitudes, or fitness levels. These outcomes, discussed in detail in chapter 1, tie directly to the benefits discussed in chapter 8 and are often used to market the programs.

The format of the program budget requires program information be solidified before the budget process begins. Each program must have goals, objectives, a description, and a budget (figure 12.1). The goals and objectives demonstrate the value and results of the program rather than simply presenting budget figures. The emphasis is on effectiveness rather than efficiency. In program budgets, the programs are grouped together based on their outcomes or type. For example, program areas may include special events, aquatics, sports, and teens. The programs are then budgeted as a group with a manager overseeing and being accountable for the program area. These groupings of programs are called *cost centers*.

In addition to program budgets being outcome driven, they also account for all costs associated with a program, including indirect costs. This budget format provides a more realistic picture of what the program actually costs. A negative aspect of program budgeting has to do with overemphasizing the outcomes of a program. Objectives that are inflated or overly lofty can be used to sell the value of the program to those who have final approval of the budget. Another weakness of this budget format is that it requires another system such as the object classification budget to present the data (Kelsey, Gray, and McLean 1992). Many agencies that use program budgets combine them with the object classification budget to demonstrate revenues and expenditures. The combination of these two formats minimizes the identified weaknesses of both budgets.

Table 12.5 shows an object classification budget and program budget combined. The classifications, subclassifications, and objects are still present, but within each object is the program area or cost center (e.g., membership or marketing). This level of detail allows comparisons across program areas and within classifications.

## Performance Budgets

Performance budgets focus on results rather than money spent, and they are based on the principles of accountability and previous funding decisions. This budget format was first implemented by the U.S. government in 1997 in order to focus on results-oriented management, increase visibility of outputs to the public, improve decision making, offer effective programs, maximize performance, and achieve accountability. Performance budgeting encourages policy makers to reconsider how they prioritize projects rather than focusing on incremental changes in detailed categories of expenditures (National Conference of State Legislatures 2017). It is assumed that performance measures improve budget decisions and support requests for resources from the final approving body.

This budget format links inputs (funding and other resources used) and outputs (volume of work produced or the number of people served) to outcomes (the extent to which results have been achieved relative to customer or program goals and objectives). Inputs are the resources dedicated to programs and services, such as money, staff, time, equipment, and facility space. Outputs are the volume of work produced or the number of people served, such as the number of canoes sold or the number of people served in a soccer league. Outputs, or performance indicators,

**Agency Name**: Backroads Bike Tours

**Name of Program**: New York Wine Country Bike Tour

**Target Market:** (age group) Adults

**Staff:Participant Ratio:** 1:4

**MAX Number of Participants:** 20

**Program Description**: This bike tour starts in Skaneateles, New York, and tours the wine country in the Finger Lake area. Riders stay at unique inns and bed-and-breakfasts along the 300-mile (483-kilometer) route. Trip fee includes 5 nights' lodging, 10 meals, beverages and snacks, van support, and 5 experienced guides.

### Program Goals and Objectives

Goal 1: To gain appreciation of the wine country in the Finger Lakes area.

Objective 1.1: Staff will give each rider a cue sheet describing the attractions and points of interest along the bike route each day.

Goal 2: To meet and interact with riders from all over the country.

Objective 2.1: The agency will advertise the trip nationally beginning at least six months in advance.

Objective 2.2: Tour guides will facilitate social interaction opportunities for riders.

Goal 3: To attract beginner, intermediate, and advanced riders.

Objective 3.1: Tour guides will offer two or three distance options to choose from to meet the needs of all riders.

### Budget Summary

| Revenue | |
|---|---|
| Registration fee | |
| $1,350×20 participants | |
| **Total revenue** | **$27,000** |
| Expenses | |
| Payroll | $6,000 |
| Meals | $4,316 |
| Lodging | $9,750 |
| Supplies | $2,600 |
| Vehicles | $500 |
| **Total expenses** | **$23,166** |
| **Net** | **$3,834** |

**Figure 12.1**  Sample program budget.

**Table 12.5** Combination of Program Budget and Object Classification Budget

| | Object Total | Subcategory Total | Category Total |
|---|---|---|---|
| 1000: Personnel services | | | $802,100 |
| 1100: Salaries, regular (full-time) | | $600,000 | |
| (12) Membership | $160,000 | | |
| (13) Marketing | $80,000 | | |
| (14) Meeting planning | $120,000 | | |
| (15) Special events | $240,000 | | |
| 1200: Salaries, temporary (part-time) | | $190,300 | |
| (12) Membership | $50,000 | | |
| (13) Marketing | $45,000 | | |
| (14) Meeting planning | $72,300 | | |
| (15) Special events | $23,000 | | |
| 1300: Wages, regular (hourly, full-time) | | $11,800 | |
| (12) Membership | $1,200 | | |
| (13) Marketing | $2,400 | | |
| (14) Meeting planning | $3,200 | | |
| (15) Special events | $5,000 | | |
| **2000: Contractual services** | | | $91,970 |
| 2100: Communication and transportation | | | |
| 2110: Postage | | $38,970 | |
| (12) Membership | $10,000 | | |
| (13) Marketing | $9,000 | | |
| (14) Meeting planning | $9,870 | | |
| (15) Special events | $10,100 | | |
| 2120: Telephone | | $8,000 | |
| (12) Membership | $2,000 | | |
| (13) Marketing | $2,000 | | |
| (14) Meeting planning | $2,000 | | |
| (15) Special events | $2,000 | | |
| 2300: Printing, binding, and advertising | | $45,000 | |
| 2350: Advertising and publication of notices | | | |
| (12) Membership | $5,000 | | |
| (13) Marketing | $25,000 | | |
| (14) Meeting planning | $6,000 | | |
| (15) Special events | $9,000 | | |
| **Total budget** | | | **$894,070** |

**Table 12.6** Sample Performance Budget

| AFTER-SCHOOL PROGRAM (40 WEEKS) | | | |
|---|---|---|---|
| | Last Year | This Year | Next Year |
| **INPUT** | | | |
| Number of permanent, full-time staff members | 1 | 1 | 2 |
| Number of part-time staff members | 9 | 9 | 12 |
| After-school general fund budget | $60,000 | $62,000 | $75,000 |
| **OUTPUT** | | | |
| Total revenue | $144,000 | $144,000 | $216,000 |
| Total number of participants | 90 | 90 | 120 |
| Number of after-school sites | 3 | 3 | 4 |
| **EFFICIENCY** | | | |
| Percentage of expenditures covered by revenue | 58% | 57% | 65% |
| Estimated cost per participant | $40/week | $40/week | $45/week |
| **EFFECTIVENESS** | | | |
| Percent satisfied on participant survey | 92% | 91% | 93% |

Reprinted by permission from A. Hurd and D.M. Anderson, *The Park and Recreation Professional's Handbook* (Champaign, IL: Human Kinetics, 2011), 151.

can be divided into three types: workload outputs, efficiency measures, and effectiveness measures.

- Workload outputs include number of parks managed, number of conferences held, number of worker hours, and so on.
- Efficiency measures include the cost per person served, hotel capacity rates, and so on.
- Effectiveness measures resemble outcomes in that they look at how satisfied people were with a program and how well it met its goals and objectives (Crompton 1999).

Agencies such as the U.S. Fish and Wildlife Service use performance budgets that outline goals, objectives, and budget figures allocated to achieve goals and objectives (Tynan 2005). Table 12.6 is an example of a performance budget for an after-school program, identifying performance in light of budgetary figures.

Although budget formats will be unique to an organization, most will be some derivation of the object classification budget, program budget, or performance budget. Some agencies may even use a combination of one or more formats to outline their financial plan for the fiscal year.

## APPROACHES TO BUDGETING

There are many approaches to developing a budget regardless of the format used. Organizations may adopt zero-based budgeting, incremental budgeting, or activity-based costing. Each has its strengths and weaknesses.

# Zero-Based Budgeting

With zero-based budgeting, managers supervise groups of programs or perhaps an entire department, which are then referred to as decision units or cost centers. These cost centers develop program budgets from scratch regardless of whether the program was offered in previous years. This requires managers to evaluate all programs and services based upon future relevance, contribution to agency goals, and cost effectiveness rather than on historical precedence (Zimmermann and Davidson 2016). Managers then prepare decision packages, which are one-page summaries describing program objectives, outputs, outcomes, consequences of not funding the program, and money needed (Mayers 2004). The decision packages (figure 12.2) are then ranked by decision unit and moved up the hierarchy of the budget process for review. A clear advantage of zero-based budgeting is that it allows employees at all levels of the organization to get involved in the budget process and to establish

---

### Priority Rank

3

### Program

Friday Night Teen Dance

### Objective

To provide structured and supervised activities for teens in the community to serve as alternatives to less positive behavior

### Outcomes

Reduced arrest rates of teens on Friday evenings in the area; reduced number of teens hanging out in local parks after closing hours; supervised place provided where teens feel comfortable

### Consequences of Not Approving

Increased teen arrest rates for minor crimes; increased need for park police to patrol park areas to control behavior of teens

### Workload

| | |
|---|---|
| 1. Number of teens served | 500 |
| 2. Unit cost of service | $5 |
| 3. Staff positions required | 4 |
| 4. Personnel costs | $2,000 |
| 5. Other expenses | $500 |
| 6. Total income | $0 |
| Total funding requested: | $2,500 |

---

**Figure 12.2**  Zero-based budget decision package.

their own priorities for programs rather than higher levels of management with less intimate knowledge of the programs establishing priorities.

Once the programs have been prioritized by units, all agency programs are prioritized, creating an overall ranking of programs. The available resources are determined and the programs are accepted in priority order as long as funds remain. For example, an organization has $5,000,000 for programs and services. This is enough money to fund 23 of the 37 programs on the list. Programs ranked 24 through 37 will not be funded because they were rated as less important.

An advantage of zero-based budgeting is that all programs are treated equally and expected to demonstrate how they meet the goals and objectives of the agencies and why they should be higher priorities. Programs that are stagnant will be replaced by more effective programs. However, zero-based budgeting is time consuming, especially for a large agency. In addition, the process lends itself to politicking, or trying to influence decision makers by overselling the outcomes of programs.

## Incremental Budgeting

Unlike zero-based budgeting, incremental budgeting is based only on past budgets. Proposed budgets are increased or decreased by a determined increment, usually a percentage each fiscal year. For example, a budget may increase by 3 percent for the next fiscal year, decrease by 2 percent, or see no increase or decrease.

Incremental budgeting is firmly entrenched in the history rather than the value of programs. Furthermore, program outcomes are not reviewed. They simply remain in the budget and are seldom, if ever, evaluated for relevancy, contribution, or cost-effectiveness. With this philosophy it is difficult to incorporate new programs or large-scale change because previous budget decisions and priorities strongly affect current and future budgets.

Incremental budgeting is a fairly simple process to learn. A manager rarely makes adjustments line by line in a budget but usually by program or service. Incremental budgeting also makes defending and approving the budget simple. Programs that remain at the same funding level are approved without scrutiny and those that are increased are reviewed to ensure they were only increased by the designated increment (Crompton 1999).

Depending on the agency, however, things are changing. Especially in a tough economy, policy makers are less inclined to simply approve a budget that has only been changed using incremental budgeting. Most are now seeking additional justification. Some agencies give staff guidelines as to how much specific expenses are allowed to increase and may in some cases require a percentage decrease in some or all expense categories.

## Activity-Based Costing

Activity-based costing (ABC) emerged in the commercial sector because of the difficulty in accounting for indirect costs, and it has since been adopted in the public and nonprofit sectors as well. This costing approach more accurately identifies the true costs of providing a service. It eliminates arbitrarily assigning indirect costs or leaving some indirect costs unaccounted for, and it identifies what a unit of production actually costs, taking into consideration administrative costs, facilities, technology, and so on. ABC links total production costs to outputs. It focuses on inputs and outputs and not so much on outcomes. However, the outputs must be measurable or quantifiable for this system to work effectively. Because of this, commercial organizations that produce tangible products, sell memberships, or have other units of production may be more likely to use ABC than those that are service based, since quantifying services is more challenging.

## Multiyear Budgeting

Multiyear budgeting is becoming increasingly popular among state, provincial, and local entities. Multiyear budgets extend beyond the annual budget to three and even five years. The two-year, or biennial, budget is the most common form of multiyear budgeting. The biennial budget is implemented one of three ways. First, the biennial financial plan uses an annual budget with an appended financial plan that serves as the tentative budget for the second year. Since the second part of the budget is a financial plan, it is not adopted by the governing body and is subject to change. A second form of biennial budgeting is the traditional biennial budget. This budget details revenues and expenditures for two years as one complete budget. The third form is the rolling biennial budget. With this format, two annual budgets are created simultaneously but are adopted each year rather than as one budget covering two years (Jackson 2002).

There are several advantages to the multiyear budget. First, there is a decrease in staff time dedicated to budgeting. Although this time is increased during the first year, the second year requires little time; the only task is to review and revise the second year of the budget. Second, multiyear budgeting integrates and improves financial and strategic planning by requiring staff to think beyond a single year. They must focus on what is to be accomplished in the long term and build it into the budget. The Government Finance Officers Association (GFOA) rewards agencies that prepare multiyear projections of revenues and other resources. A third advantage is that multiyear budgeting requires the agency to reduce incrementalism where the annual budgets are simply increased a certain percentage each year. Instead, goals and objectives are linked with finance and planning, which require an agency to improve program monitoring and evaluation processes (Blom and Guajardo 2000; Jackson 2002; Oakland County, MI, n.d.). Finally, five-year budget planning helps with understanding what an agency can afford, as it provides transparency, accountability, flexibility, visibility, and discipline (Solomon, Mason, and Scarbrough 2012).

Multiyear budgeting also has disadvantages. First, it is difficult to project long-term expenditures and revenues. In particular it is difficult to project staff needs and current staff who will receive raises such as cost of living and merit pay. Since revenues are tightly tied to the economy in a given year, they can also be tricky to predict at times. A second disadvantage is that it is time consuming to put together a new budget for the upcoming fiscal years (Blom and Guajardo 2000; Jackson 2002). Regardless of its disadvantages, multiyear budgeting is increasingly popular in the public sector.

## BUDGET IMPLEMENTATION

Once budgets are approved and the new fiscal year begins, they are implemented. This means that the revenue generated goes into the accounts represented in the budget and expended money goes out to pay bills.

The largest expenditure items in a budget are most often personnel, including salaries, hourly wages, and employee benefits. A payroll staff member within the accounting or bookkeeping department will have the responsibility of paying employees. Salaried employees are automatically paid the allotted amount, and hourly employees submit time cards designating how many hours were worked and at what rate. The second largest expenditure items in a budget are regular operating expenditures such as equipment, supplies, and advertising. These items must be purchased by the manager in charge of each particular program or service.

All agencies have policies and procedures that guide purchasing. These guidelines vary too extensively to cover in depth here. However, purchasing can be categorized as petty cash purchasing, normal purchasing procedures, and the formal bidding process (Gladwell, Bruton, and Elder-White 2016).

## Petty Cash

**petty cash**—Cash on hand that is used for small purchases where it is inefficient to write a check.

Many organizations keep actual cash on hand for purchases that are too small to be worth submitting to the more rigorous purchase or reimbursement procedures of a company or institution (Investopedia 2017). This cash, perhaps $25 to $100, is called **petty cash**. This system allows managers to forgo normal purchasing procedures (described next), but it has its own processes, which usually require cash receipts for items purchased. An employee making a purchase with petty cash often does so with his own money. The employee would then submit the receipt and a completed request form in order to be reimbursed. See figure 12.3 for a sample petty cash form from American University. The petty cash fund must be reconciled on a regular basis like other funds within an agency or organization. Increasingly, however, agencies are moving away from keeping cash on hand and are instead using a purchasing card, sometimes referred to as a P-card. These cards also come with a number of rules for usage and may be constrained as to what types of products may be purchased using it.

## Normal Purchasing Procedures

When purchasing equipment and supplies, each organization will follow its own process. However, most processes will include these basic steps.

### Step 1: Complete a Purchase Requisition

**purchase requisition**—Form used to request and detail items to be purchased.

A **purchase requisition** is a listing of the items to be purchased and a description of each item. The manager in charge of the program completes this requisition after reviewing the budget to ensure adequate funds exist.

### Step 2: Request Quotations

Larger purchases require a manager to get quotes from vendors who sell the items. Purchasing policies and procedures will determine benchmarks for the minimum dollar amount that requires a quote. The same policies and procedures will identify the minimum number of quotes to be received. For example, an agency may require two quotes for purchases of $500 to $1,000 and three quotes for purchases of $1,000 to $2,500.

### Step 3: Issue a Purchase Order

**purchase order**—Purchase agreement detailing the specifics of a purchase, including the brand, number, and what program the purchase is for.

A **purchase order** is a purchase agreement from the agency with the specifics of the purchase. The vendor accepts this as an order for the products.

## American University Club Sports
## Petty Cash Form

Original receipts must be submitted taped to a sheet of paper within 14 days of trip/purchase.

Date: _____     Club: _____

Name: _____     AU ID #: _____

Phone: _____     Email: _____

Address: _____

City: _____     State: _____     Zip: _____

Signature: _____

| Description | Price |
|---|---|
|  |  |
|  |  |
|  |  |
|  |  |
| Total | $ |

Reason for purchase or trip: _____

_____

_____

_____     _____     _____
Club treasurer signature             Name                 Date

Contact #: _____

_____     _____
Director of club sports              Date

Budget account number: _____

Entered into tracking: _____

**Figure 12.3**  American University petty cash form.

Reprinted by permission from American University Recreational Sports and Fitness.

### Step 4: Invoice When Products Are Received

**invoice**—Receipt of sale and delivery of products purchased; serves as a bill for the products.

Once products are received, they are accompanied by an **invoice** that serves as a receipt. The receipt is given to the accounts payable department so it may disperse funds to the vendors.

## Formal Bidding Process

Many organizations have policies outlining a formal bidding process. Purchases over a predetermined amount require a formal bid. For example, the County of Franklin (North Carolina) has a policy where goods and services costing more than $10,000 but less than $30,000 require a written quote from at least three vendors (County of Franklin 2017).

A formal bidding procedure is similar to receiving quotes but more structured. The bids are acquired either through an **invitation for bid (IFB)**, **request for proposal (RFP)**, or **request for quotation (RFQ)**.

**invitation for bid (IFB)**—Advertised contract, or sealed bid, where specifications are detailed for the product or service and bids are submitted by competing agencies.

### Invitation for Bid

An IFB is an advertised contract, or sealed bid, where the specifications are detailed for the product or service. The bids are submitted by vendors in a sealed envelope to ensure the contents remain confidential until the predetermined opening. The low bidder is usually awarded the contract per the specifications in the bid.

### Request for Proposal

**request for proposal (RFP)**—Binding, negotiated contract for services where both parties determine what work will be done for what price.

An RFP is a negotiated contract. Specifications are outlined for the service or product and companies submit proposals detailing what they will do for what price. Proposals are discussed, and the bidder may have the opportunity to change bid pricing, procedures, and so on. Pricing and other factors such as work to be done will determine the winner of the contract. The contract is binding once both parties reach a signed agreement.

### Request for Quotation

**request for quotation (RFQ)**—Nonbinding, negotiated contract for services where both parties determine what work will be done for what price.

An RFQ is similar to an RFP except it is not a binding contract. An RFQ seeks information and prices and is negotiable after discussion of the details obtained from the quotations.

## FINANCIAL ANALYSIS AND REPORTING

**financial analysis**—Methods to monitor the fiscal status of the organization over a period of time.

Once the budget is complete, approved, and implemented, the financial analysis phase of the process begins. **Financial analysis** is done through records of revenues, expenditures, and other financial activity over a given time frame, usually monthly, quarterly, or annually depending on the analysis or report used. It monitors activity through several methods, including a break-even analysis, balance sheets, income statements, cash-flow statements, and budget statements. Although some of these reports are most likely prepared by accountants, it is important to understand what they are and what they mean for the organization.

## Break-Even Analysis

Break-even analysis determines how many units of a product must be sold in order to cover all costs of producing that unit. This analysis uses fixed and variable costs to determine profit levels; profit occurs after enough units are sold to cover all of the fixed and variable costs. There are two formulas managers can use to calculate the break-even point depending upon the situation.

Formula 1 determines how many units (registrations, rentals, etc.) are needed to break even:

$$BE = F / (P - V), \text{ where}$$

$$BE = \text{break-even point}$$

$$F = \text{fixed costs}$$

$$P = \text{selling price per unit}$$

$$V = \text{variable costs per unit}$$

For example, a bike rental shop is located in a tourism town on a boardwalk, and they rent bikes for $50 per day. Fixed costs for the month total $8,000, and variable costs are $10 per bike. This company needs to rent 200 bikes per month to break even:

$$BE = \$8,000 / (\$50 - \$10)$$

$$BE = 200 \text{ bikes per month}$$

Notice in figure 12.4 that each rental above the break-even point is considered profit. The total costs keep going up in $10-per-bike increments because of the variable costs, so for every bike rented above 200, the company sees a $40 profit. If 350 bikes were rented for the month, the company would realize a $6,000 profit.

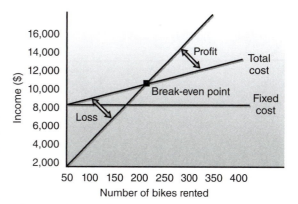

**Figure 12.4** Break-even analysis.

Formula 2 determines how much to charge per person to cover expenses for a program:

$$\text{Price} = \frac{\text{direct (fixed and variable)} + \text{indirect costs}}{\text{number of participants}}$$

Let's go back to the example above. The bike shop manager is now doing the budget for next year, and the following changes have occurred: Fixed costs have risen to $10,000, and variable costs are now $12 per bike rental. Assuming they meet the historical rental average of 300 per year, how much do they need to charge to break even?

$$\text{Price} = \frac{(10,000 + (12 \times 300))}{300}$$

$$\text{Price} = \$45.33$$

# Balance Sheets

The **balance sheet,** sometimes called the *statement of financial position*, is a record of the accounting equation:

$$\text{Assets} = \text{liabilities} + \text{equity}$$

**balance sheet—** Accounting report demonstrating the financial condition of an organization, including assets, liabilities, and equity.

**Table 12.7** Sample Balance Sheet

Clear Water Rafting Company

Balance Sheet as of July 31, 2017

| ASSETS | | LIABILITIES | |
|---|---|---|---|
| **Current assets** | | **Current liabilities** | |
| Cash and investments | $3,546,975 | Accounts payable | $25,729 |
| Accounts receivable | $1,243,785 | *Long-term debt* | |
| Total current assets | $4,790,760 | Mortgage | $376,971 |
| **Fixed assets** | | **Total liabilities** | **$402,700** |
| Store fixtures | $243,876 | | |
| Office equipment | $7,659 | Equity | $5,175,923 |
| Rafting inventory | $543,987 | | |
| Total fixed assets | $787,863 | | |
| Total assets | $5,578,623 | Total liabilities and equities | $5,578,623 |

The balance statement is divided in half, with assets on the left and liabilities and equity on the right (table 12.7). It depicts the financial position of an organization at a given point in time (Fried, DeSchriver, and Mondello 2013).

Assets are the things owned by the organization, such as cash, land, and equipment. The assets can be divided into current and fixed assets. Current assets can be converted into cash within a year whereas fixed assets cannot be quickly converted to cash (Brayley and McLean 2008).

On the liabilities side of the balance sheet, the different types of liabilities are listed according to when they must be paid. Current liabilities must be paid within a year, whereas long-term liabilities will not be paid within this time. Equity, also on the right side of the balance sheet, is the money invested in the organization by the owners in a commercial organization or the balance in specific funds for public and nonprofit organizations. The bottom line in each column must balance with total assets equal to total liabilities and equity.

## Income Statements

Income statements reflect the profitability of the organization during a certain length of time such as a month, quarter, or fiscal year. It includes revenues, expenses, and net income (table 12.8). The income statement shows whether the organization is making a profit (running in the black) or losing money (running in the red).

In table 12.8, revenues exceed expenditures, so the organization showed a $3,914 profit for the month of July.

## Cash-Flow Statements

A cash-flow statement depicts revenues versus expenditures (table 12.9) and thus reports changes in the company's cash holdings over a specific period of time (Fried, DeSchriver, and Mondello 2013). The statement shows positive and negative cash flow and determines if cash should be borrowed to remain solvent or if excess cash should be invested (Crossley, Jamieson, and Brayley 2018).

**Table 12.8**  Sample Income Statement

Clear Water Rafting Company

Income Statement as of July 31, 2017

| Revenues | |
|---|---|
| Trips | $12,320 |
| Concessions | $2,486 |
| Store receipts | $3,345 |
| Total revenues | $18,151 |
| **Expenditures** | |
| Staff | $9,562 |
| Supplies | $527 |
| Utilities | $452 |
| Mortgage | $2,342 |
| Marketing | $732 |
| Maintenance | $622 |
| Total expenditures | $14,237 |
| Net revenue | $3,914 |

**Table 12.9**  Sample Cash-Flow Statement

Clear Water Rafting Company

Cash-Flow Statement, 1st and 2nd Quarters

| | February | March | April | May | June | July | Total |
|---|---|---|---|---|---|---|---|
| Net revenues | $1,276 | $4,985 | $8,076 | $12,486 | $16,958 | $18,151 | $61,932 |
| Expenses | $4,978 | $6,890 | $7,013 | $9,213 | $11,345 | $14,237 | $53,676 |
| Monthly cash flow | $(3,702) | $(1,905) | $1,063 | $3,273 | $5,613 | $3,914 | |
| Cumulative cash flow | $(3,702) | $(5,607) | $(4,544) | $(1,271) | $4,342 | $8,256 | |
| Cash position at beginning of month | $12,000 | $8,298 | $6,393 | $7,456 | $10,729 | $16,342 | |
| Cash position at end of month | $8,298 | $6,393 | $7,456 | $10,729 | $16,342 | $20,256 | |

Numbers in parentheses indicate a negative balance.

In table 12.9, although expenses are greater than revenues for February and March, the $12,000 at the beginning of February helps carry this seasonal business through the off-peak season.

# Budget Statements

A budget statement reports how much money has been received and spent in comparison to what was allocated in the budget (table 12.10). Revenues and expenses

**Table 12.10** Sample Budget Statement

Clear Water Rafting Company

Budget Statement, 1st and 2nd Quarters

| | Actual | Budget | Committed | % | Balance |
|---|---|---|---|---|---|
| REVENUES | | | | | |
| Trips | $42,113 | $72,500 | $0 | 58.1% | $30,387 |
| Concessions | $8,671 | $14,000 | $0 | 61.9% | $5,329 |
| Store receipts | $11,148 | $20,000 | $0 | 55.7% | $8,852 |
| Total revenues | $61,932 | $106,500 | $0 | 58.2% | $44,568 |
| EXPENDITURES | | | | | |
| Staff | $35,963 | $52,100 | $1,500 | 71.9% | $14,637 |
| Supplies | $2,147 | $3,100 | $0 | 69.3% | $953 |
| Utilities | $1,610 | $2,430 | $0 | 66.3% | $820 |
| Mortgage | $8,051 | $16,000 | $0 | 50.3% | $7,949 |
| Marketing | $2,684 | $4,300 | $500 | 74.0% | $1,116 |
| Maintenance | $3,221 | $4,300 | $0 | 74.9% | $1,079 |
| Total expenditures | $53,676 | $82,230 | $2,000 | 67.7% | $26,554 |

are listed as well as the amount of money that has been committed, the amount of money budgeted, and the amount remaining to be spent.

A manager would be responsible for analyzing the budget to ascertain if it is on track with projected revenues and expenditures for the first two quarters of the fiscal year. In table 12.10, 67.7 percent of the projected expenditures have been realized and 58.2 percent of the projected revenues have been received. The manager will need to monitor expenses for the remaining year so as to stay within the budget. However, since this is a seasonal business, it is not unusual to spend a larger portion of the budget during the peak season. Bear in mind that although the example shown is a monthly statement, if there is a large volume of business you may get budget statements on a weekly, daily, or perhaps even hourly basis.

The reports are a means of analyzing data from several different perspectives, including revenues, expenditures, assets, and equity. Each report provides a different view of financial activity and requires constant management in order to stay within the financial parameters set in the budget. Reports track and monitor revenues and expenditures for analysis, but several other financial analysis indicators are also used in leisure services to determine efficiency of an organization, particularly in the commercial sector. Most of the data needed for the ratio analyses are available from income statements, balance sheets, and other financial reports. See the Financial Indicators sidebar for a brief description of the more common financial indicators used in the field.

 Check out the web study guide for additional material, including learning activities, sample documents, interactive case studies, web links, CPRP exam connections, and more.

# Financial Indicators

Following is a brief description of the more common indicators used in the field (Fried, DeSchriver, and Mondello 2013). Financial indicators are typically classified as liquidity ratios, activity ratios, and profitability ratios. Each has a different purpose in the financial management of the organization. Financial ratios are important as they provide benchmarks in three different ways: they compare against previous company ratios, competitors' ratios, and ratios of other firms of similar size and scope (Fried, DeSchriver, and Mondello 2013).

Listed here is just a sample of those that can be used. Some of them are more applicable to the commercial sector where sales of inventory are more prominent. While it will be typical for the accountant in the organization to prepare the financial indicators, it will be the manager's responsibility to know what they actually mean.

## Liquidity Ratios

Liquidity ratios reflect the ability of the organization to meet its short-term financial obligations. They include the following ratios.

- A current ratio above 1.0 indicates that the company can use its current assets to cover current liabilities.

$$\text{Current ratio} = \text{total current assets / total current liabilities}$$

- A quick ratio indicates whether the organization can meet its short-term liabilities without selling inventory to meet them.

$$\text{Quick ratio} = (\text{total current assets} - \text{inventories}) / \text{current liabilities}$$

## Activity Ratios

Activity ratios, sometimes called *efficiency ratios*, determine the ability of an organization to efficiently manage its resources.

- Inventory turnover ratio indicates how many times during the year the inventory is purchased and sold. Companies want a high ratio because this indicates the inventory is turned over efficiently.

$$\text{Inventory turnover ratio} = \text{cost of goods sold / average inventory}$$

- Assets-to-sales ratio determines how efficiently assets are being used.

$$\text{Assets to sales} = \text{total assets / total sales}$$

- Average collection period is the average time it takes to convert sales to cash. The average collection period is measured in days and is not an actual ratio.

$$\text{Average collection period} = (\text{accounts receivable / sales}) \times 365 \text{ days}$$

## Profitability Ratios

Profitability ratios show how successful a business has been over a certain time frame.

- Net profit margin and gross profit margin demonstrate the ability to turn a profit on sales.

$$\text{Net profit margin} = \text{return on sales} = \text{net income / revenues}$$

$$\text{Gross profit margin} = \text{earnings before interest and taxes / revenues}$$

- Return on assets depicts the effectiveness of investment in assets.

$$\text{Return on assets} = \text{net profit after taxes / total assets}$$

# Conclusion

Sound financial management is required by professionals at all levels of organizations in all three sectors. Revenues and expenditures are a daily part of doing business. Agency budgets are as unique as the agencies themselves, but a clear understanding of the different types of budgets is important. A strong grasp of basic budgeting principles helps lessen the learning curve in terms of financial management for anyone entering a new agency.

In addition to preparing a budget, a manager with strong financial skills will closely monitor and analyze the activity within it. In order to stay within the budget, managers need an understanding of financial reports. Although most organizations will have an accountant prepare the statements, the manager must interpret the statements and handle problems involving cash flow or liabilities.

# Review Questions

1. Describe the budget process and the steps taken to develop a budget.
2. Differentiate between pricing and budgeting.
3. Discuss how capital and operating budgets interrelate.
4. Compare and contrast object classification budgeting, program budgets, and performance budgets.
5. Explain zero-based budgeting, incremental budgeting, and activity-based costing.
6. Describe the three ways bids are acquired.
7. There are several ways to track budgets, revenues, and expenditures. Discuss how each method works.
8. List the three types of financial indicators and discuss why each is important to a manager.

# 13

# Evaluation

## Learning Outcomes

- Understand the rationale for evaluation in leisure services organizations.
- Explain the role of performance measurement.
- Identify and understand different types of evaluation.
- Summarize the steps of the evaluation process.
- Discuss a variety of ways to report evaluation results.

## Key Terms

performance measurement, evaluation process, formative evaluation, summative evaluation, quantitative research, qualitative research, questionnaire, attitude scale, raters, secondary data, case study, sampling, best practices, benchmarking

## Competency Check

Refer to table 1.6 to see how you assessed these related competencies.

- 11. Know the community and its needs.
- 34. Conduct program evaluations.
- 39. Conduct research and evaluation.
- 40. Conduct needs assessments.

## A Day in the Life

Working as a community recreation coordinator is a rewarding, dynamic job that enables me to make a difference in my community. I love that every day is filled with new opportunities to connect with people, solve challenges, and help people live healthy, fulfilled lives. My job is to bring a principled approach to providing recreation services in the community: to ensure that the things we do align with the vision and values of our organization and that we are truly operating in service to the community. Each day brings different challenges: identifying and responding to community needs, ensuring quality customer service, managing facility operations, budgeting, and leading and supervising staff. More importantly, each day is a chance to make a difference and to witness the joy that comes through participation in the programs and services we offer. Through our work we create opportunities for many great things to happen—from taking unassisted steps for the first time after participating in a rehab fitness program and learning to swim, to meeting friends in a fitness class or performing a dance. There is no better field and no better place to work.

Jaimie Brown
Community Recreation Coordinator,
North Vancouver Recreation Commission
North Vancouver, British Columbia

Evaluation is an important part of a manager's role. Managers evaluate many things, from people, programs, and facilities to organizational direction, goals, risk profiles, and fiscal situations. Without evaluation, it is difficult to know how well the organization is performing or if goals are being met. This chapter explains the importance of evaluation and performance measurement, describes types of evaluation, and provides practical information on conducting evaluations in leisure services organizations. In simple terms, evaluation is making a judgment about the value of something (Henderson, Bialeschki, and Browne 2017). This chapter provides practical information on conducting evaluations in leisure services organizations as well as exploring the opportunity that the process of evaluation can have for staff, customer, and stakeholder engagement.

# WHY EVALUATE?

One of the fundamental reasons for evaluation is to determine if what is being evaluated is doing what it is intended to do. Earlier in the text, the notion of goal setting was discussed. Goals provide a basis for evaluation—is the organization actually achieving what it set out to achieve? The reasons for evaluation differ depending on who the user of the information is. For example, a recreation programmer may use evaluation information to guide future programming decisions, an elected official may use evaluation information to demonstrate that a program is serving constituents, and a researcher may use evaluation information to recommend policy change, build on current understanding of leisure behavior, or discover best practices in an area. Understanding the purpose of the information is critical. This understanding guides the evaluation process and should connect to the organization's goals and objectives. Evaluations are a way for managers to collect important information that will give them an informed perspective of the organization and lead to good decision making.

The scope and type of evaluations can vary considerably within leisure services organizations. Skating and swimming instructors provide evaluations to inform participants of their skill development progress. Staff evaluations provide an opportunity for managers to give coaching and feedback to their employees. Evaluations can also tell managers about the appropriateness of program scheduling times, frequencies, and locations. A common use for evaluation in leisure services organizations is the evaluation of community needs through a needs assessment. A needs assessment can look at facility needs, staffing needs, community needs, or any concerns an organization may have related to the effective delivery of leisure services. Application of the concepts in this chapter will provide a strong foundation to develop effective needs assessments.

As you have learned throughout this text, information is the key to helping managers make decisions about the things that are important to their organization. The manager should already understand what those priorities are and then go about collecting information on them. For example, if the main concerns are employee satisfaction, client satisfaction, and facility safety, then develop systematic ways to collect information on those areas. If there is a performance measurement strategy in place in the organization, the manager may be involved in creating performance indicators for specific areas or collecting data that show how the organization is achieving its goals. The manager will be in the best position to determine what to actually measure. Evaluations should connect to the strategic plan, mission, or vision of the organization. Managers in North Vancouver Recreation Commission, for example, say that their strategic plan provides an incredible roadmap in terms of the priorities of the organization, and all reporting and evaluation are tied directly to those strategic directions. This helps them keep focused on outcomes and ensures that programming and service decisions are values- and principles-based.

In leisure services, many times we are asked to evaluate things that are hard to measure, such as experiences of community connectedness or community engagement. In *Thinking in Systems*, Meadows identified a systems wisdom that is important for managers to understand throughout the evaluation process: "Pay attention to what is important, not just what is quantifiable" (Meadows 2008). Some programs and experiences are easier to measure than others. That doesn't mean that they aren't as (or more) important. The process of evaluation involves asking questions and creating tools to measure the important things in the right ways, not just focusing on what is easy to measure.

At the Boys & Girls Club, the single most important outcome of their work is belonging. How do you measure belonging? If you were a manager at the Boys & Girls Club, how could you create an evaluation that measures whether you are achieving that outcome? Knowing if you are accomplishing this is important to employees, participants, and stakeholders in the organization.

Outward Bound Canada recently completed an impact report that assesses their core values as an organization:

*At Outward Bound Canada, it is our mission to cultivate resilience, leadership, connections and compassion through inspiring and challenging journeys of self-discovery in the natural world. But do we really do what we say? Do our wilderness programs actually succeed in cultivating these things in those who actively take part in them? As part of our research for the 2017 Impact Report, our national research coordinator, Nevin Harper, conducted a study to measure whether or not our programs achieve our mission.*

(Outward Bound Canada 2017)

In *Good to Great and the Social Sectors*, Jim Collins acknowledges the challenges of measuring performance within organizations like leisure services, education, and health:

*To throw our hands up and say, "But we cannot measure performance in the social sectors the way you can in a business" is simply lack of discipline. All indicators are flawed, whether qualitative or quantitative. Test scores are flawed, mammograms are flawed, crime data are flawed, customer service data are flawed, patient-outcome data are flawed. What matters is not finding the perfect indicator, but settling upon a consistent and intelligent method of assessing your output results, and then tracking your trajectory with rigor.*

(Collins 2005)

"Not everything that can be counted counts, and not everything that counts can be counted." In leisure services, this adage emphasizes understanding the importance of deciding what to measure and how to measure it. Later in the chapter, you will read examples of creative and evidence-based ways to capture what is happening in your organization and how to report it.

Louise Rusch, program coordinator at Parks, Recreation, and Cultural Services in Burnaby, British Columbia, reflects that we are often challenged to "count" experiences that were meant to end in a concept such as feeling closer to your neighbor,

> ## Live & Local: The Edgemont Village Concert and the Flash Mob
>
> On summer Friday nights in North Vancouver, British Columbia, the North Vancouver Recreation Commission and the Edgemont Merchants Association sponsor the "Live & Local" Edgemont Village Concert. They close one of the streets, and a local live band plays from a small flatbed truck. People bring their lawn chairs and blankets and hang out as a community, enjoying music and dancing. The kids start dancing as soon as the band starts, and by a couple of songs in, there's a gang on the "dance floor."
>
> One night last summer, about four songs into the first set, a bus showed up from one of the local seniors' residences. About 50 seniors poured off the bus, straight onto the street dance floor. When the last person was off the bus, the band started playing "Heatwave" (you know the song—circa 1965 by Martha and the Vandellas). The seniors took over the dance floor, and there was a whole lot of moving and grooving and laughter and fun. At the end of the song, the seniors' flash mob boarded the bus and they were off.
>
> If you were a manager in the North Vancouver Recreation Commission asked to evaluate this special event, what would you measure and how would you measure it? Is the number of people who attended important? The impact of the experience on the participants and the seniors who were in the flash mob? What are some key indicators you would look for to tell the story? Whom would you talk to? Whose perspective would you look for? These questions are important to keep in mind as you read this chapter.

rather than a specific product such as learning how to swim. Sometimes this is done through art (a visual expression of the idea shared), video storybooking, storytelling, and so on. "It is not so much about counting the process. It is more about ensuring the value of the process is just as much a part of the conversation as the product-based services. Complete evaluations are a way for everyone to talk about something—it often connects to something being valued and therefore receiving resources."

## PERFORMANCE MEASUREMENT

The scope and variety of evaluations within leisure services is vast. Evaluations can range from participant progress reports to program evaluations, staff evaluations, facility experience evaluations, and needs assessments. Ideally, evaluations should be tied to the strategic plan, mission, or goals and objectives of the organization, but many times evaluations are done in isolation without a strong sense of how the information fits into the bigger picture of what the organization is trying to achieve. Changing a program or service in one area of an organization can affect another area without a manager realizing it.

**Performance measurement** is a strategy that assesses whether an organization is achieving its objectives and moving forward in its strategic plan. A performance

**performance measurement**—A strategy that assesses whether an organization is achieving its objectives and moving forward in its strategic plan.

measurement system links results to expectations (where you are, where you want to go) and tells a story of the organization's progress based on an intentional process of data collection.

In order to have a successful performance measurement strategy, managers need to clearly identify what is important to measure; performance measurement needs to be connected to the mission, vision, and strategic plan of the organization. The organization should concentrate on a small number of clearly understood performance elements and ensure that each has a specified set of measures.

Organizations should read and discuss their mission and vision statements, asking the following questions: If we were entirely successful, how would we know? What difference are we making in the world? Are there immediate outcomes necessary for ultimate outcomes achievement? Performance measurement is intended to produce objective and relevant information on programs or organizational performance. This information can be used to strengthen management and inform decision making, achieve results, and improve overall performance and increase accountability. It creates an opportunity to bring evaluations into line and develop a clear plan for evaluations, assessment, and data collection in the organization.

Figure 13.1 shows an example of how performance measurement works using the strategic plan of Habuela Springs Swim Club. Notice the vision is the guiding element of the strategy and the strategic objectives of the organization are clearly articulated:

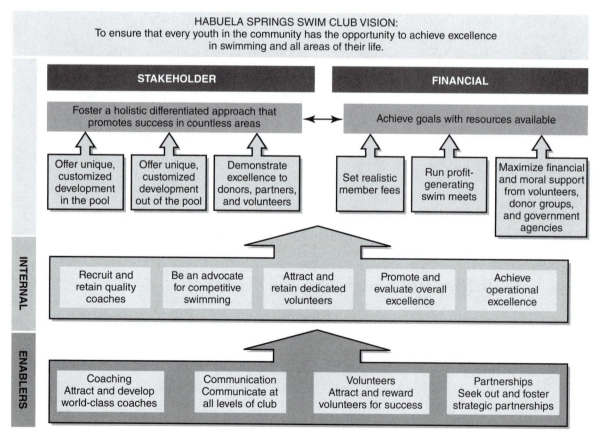

**Figure 13.1** Habuela Springs Swim Club strategy map.

| STAKEHOLDER PERSPECTIVE 30% | | FINANCIAL PERSPECTIVE 20% | |
|---|---|---|---|
| **Objectives** | **Measures** | **Objectives** | **Measures** |
| Maximize member value in the pool | Swim meet results (gold/silver/bronze points system) | Grow operating revenues to add and sustain programs | Annual revenue ($000's) |
| Maximize member value out of the pool | Members' class average and member satisfaction survey | Realize modest earned income level to demonstrate value and plan for growth | Actual realized earned income ($000's) |
| Utilize volunteers efficiently and effectively | Volunteer programs quality and satisfaction | Runs swim meets profitably | Swim meet profits ($000's) |
| Expand and enhance donor relationships | Number of donor agreements and number of donor meetings | Increase donor and fundraising dollars | Actual dollars raised |
| Forge new donor relationships | Number of potential donors profiled and contracted | Efficient use of financial resources | Overhead costs as a % of total revenue |
| INTERNAL PROCESS PERSPECTIVE 25% | | ENABLERS PERSPECTIVE 25% | |
| **Objectives** | **Measures** | **Objectives** | **Measures** |
| Offer world-class coaching programs | Member feedback score Swimmer attendance | Attract and develop world-class coaches | Coaching score and wait list |
| Achieve excellent competitive results | Swimmer performance (local, provincial, national meets–out of 10) | Communicate at all levels of the club | Percentage of HSSC members aware of weekly updates |
| Attract and retain dedicated volunteers | Volunteer turnover ratio (new and departing) | Attract and reward volunteers for efforts and success | Percentage of volunteers affirming intrinsic reward of efforts |
| Promote and evaluate overall excellence | Average member comprehensive score | Seek out and foster strategic partnerships | Number of partners and potential partners profiled and number of partner meetings |
| Achieve operational excellence | Coach to swimmer time ratio | | |
| | Available pool time capacity usage (practices and meets) | | |

**Figure 13.2** Completed Habuela Springs Swim Club balanced scorecard (summary level).

Using a balanced scorecard approach, the strategy map shown in figure 13.1 moves into a performance measurement plan identifying objectives and measures in figure 13.2.

Each objective for the swim club has a measure attached to it. Each measure requires a data collection method, such as an evaluation or an attendance report. A manager looking at this scorecard can clearly see what information is required and make a decision on how best to collect that data. Once the information has been collected for each measure, managers can create a visual dashboard to see how the organization is doing in achieving its objectives and ultimately its mission or vision.

Figure 13.2 reflects a balanced scorecard. A balanced scorecard is a system agencies use to communicate:

- Financial goals; tracks financial performance and resource use
- Customer goals and priorities; satisfaction, service provision
- Internal process goals and objectives or strategic planning strategies
- Knowledge, education, and growth; staff skills, competency development, and plans to enhance these

These four elements are seen as the "legs of the stool" that need to be in balance in order for the stool to remain upright—or for the business to remain vibrant. The balanced scorecard is often presented as a graphic depiction of these elements designed to give internal and external stakeholders a simple understanding of the present and future of the organization.

From a systems theory perspective (see chapter 1), performance measurement provides a clear strategy to connect areas of the organization and create a strategic role for evaluation within the organization. This strategy of performance measurement makes sense, but it requires commitment from managers within the organization to create it and ensure that it works well.

Following are some advantages and challenges to implementing a performance measurement plan.

**Advantages to implementing performance measurement:**

- There is a greater chance of meeting goals if organizations monitor progress by measuring performance.
- When managers and employees clearly understand and contribute to the organizations goals, they are motivated.
- Using that data can help managers make good decisions about resource allocation.
- Effective performance measurement systems provide managers with reliable, valid data to communicate to decision makers.

**Challenges to performance measurement:**

- Too much data may be collected to be easily processed.
- Managers may be unclear about what to measure or what to do with the data collected.
- The results may DRIP (be data rich but information poor).
- The measurements may result in unclear correlations—how can you prove that $x$ is a result of $y$?

**Steps to designing a performance measurement system:**

1. Design a system that will work for all areas of the organization.
2. Identify the services that will be measured.
3. Tie the performance measurement to the intended results.
4. Decide how the data will be collected and managed.
5. Determine how to analyze the data and report the results to the intended audience.
6. Establish a means to ensure that the information is used effectively to assist with decision making.

Performance measurement is an ongoing process, whereas evaluation has a specific time frame. Evaluations are a tool to collect data for areas of the performance measurement plan.

# HOW TO EVALUATE

In this section, there is an eight-step process that outlines how to design and conduct evaluations. Before getting to the "how to" part, it is important to look at the process of evaluation and some opportunities and impacts this can have within the organization. The process of evaluating can be an important part of building social capital, customer service, and staff engagement. It creates an opportunity to focus on a specific part of the organization, ask good questions, listen to employees, and collect information from customers and stakeholders. Evaluations need to be planned in an intentional way and tied to the mission and values of the organization. Managers should be able to share the "why" of the evaluation and connect it to a larger performance measurement plan, which in turn is connected to the goals and objectives or the strategic plan of the organization.

It is important to recognize that an evaluation can be the first step to change in an organization. As a result of an evaluation, a service may be changed or discontinued, or a new policy may be implemented for staff. Managers should be aware that evaluations create change on some level and ensure that the reason for the evaluation is clearly identified as well as how the information will be used. The process of evaluation is bigger than just the evaluation tool itself. Managers should take advantage of the opportunity to build relationships with customers, staff, and stakeholders in the process of evaluation. Evaluations provide an opportunity to get staff on the same page and involved in the process. Evaluations can create and build a shared language within the organization, an understanding of the strategic plan and direction of the organization, and an opportunity to work toward a common goal.

The focus of this chapter is on formal evaluations, but it is worth pointing out that there is a lot of value to informal evaluation. This is what managers can do when they are walking around the facility, talking to patrons and talking to staff. Remember the "Ideas Contest" sidebar in chapter 10? Dave created a way for the frontline staff to report feedback from patrons. This was motivating to the staff, and they felt engaged in the organization, but it also was an excellent way for management to conduct informal evaluations of what patrons were experiencing. Managers should encourage frontline staff and instructors to tune into listening to and reporting feedback from patrons. This provides great customer and staff engagement and gives the manager a solid source of informal evaluation information.

An eight-step evaluation process may sound like a lot of steps, but as you work through them, you will see that each step is important in making sure the evaluation process and results are valuable and connected to organization goals. The **evaluation process** starts by deciding what to evaluate, then reviewing the literature or an environmental scan to find out what information is currently available. It ends with instrument development, data collection and analysis, and reporting with accountability measures (see figure 13.3).

**evaluation process**—The collection and analysis of information in systematic ways to make better decisions or to improve programs, products, or policies.

## Step 1: Decide What to Evaluate

Taking the time to understand what you are going to evaluate and why, and asking the right questions, is critical to the success of the evaluation. How to define the problem will determine what the measures are; do this carefully to make sure you are measuring the right thing. Evaluations connect to change and to building trust within your staff, customers, and the community. If you are asking questions that you do not want the answers to or will not be able to act upon, you will lose credibility and people will stop answering your questions.

Why are you measuring/evaluating? Are you solving a problem? Are you creating a benchmark or assessing a performance measure? At this stage, it is important to consider what you are going to do with the information from your evaluation. If you are going to use it to create positive change, that is great, but if you do not have

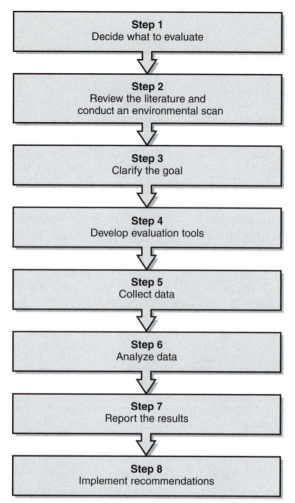

**Figure 13.3** Eight-step evaluation process.

the resources to change anything, consider why you are doing the evaluation. At the Burnaby seniors center, one of the first questions they ask before doing an evaluation is "Do we have capacity to do something additional?" If an organization doesn't have the capacity, is it worth going through the evaluation process to find out that participants want new services that the organization is not in a position to offer them?

In this first step, it is valuable to be willing to question assumptions and ask seemingly simple questions. Ask "What should we be measuring?" not "How can we measure what we do?" Good measures are often the result of thinking outside the box.

## Step 2: Review the Literature and Conduct an Environmental Scan

This step can be interesting and fun and can create an opportunity to expand your knowledge of the evaluation area within your organization and beyond. At this point, do some research about what you are planning to evaluate. Look at best practices or emerging practices from other organizations in your field and outside of your field. How are they measuring what you are planning to evaluate? Research current practices within the organization to see if that information is already being collected in a different way. Managers do not need to do this step themselves; they can set up a working group of staff to take parts of the research and then come together to share it. This provides an opportunity for engagement in the organization and a shared vision for the evaluation.

## Step 3: Clarify the Goal of the Evaluation

This step is essential to ensure that you have looked at various perspectives for measurement and evaluation. At this point, you can look at what you are going to evaluate from a more informed position based on the research and environmental scan that was done. One of the key areas of this step is circling back to the question "What will we do with the information collected?"

Another part of this step is defining the population. Whom do you need to talk to to get the information you need? For example, if you are evaluating volunteer

## Evaluations in Action

In my seniors group of staff and volunteers, we do not do formal, ongoing, or routine general evaluation. Evaluation efforts happen when we have to make a decision about a change of practice or a new activity. It's usually ad hoc and can take a long time or a short time depending on what's at stake. Our most frequent topic for evaluation is "Do we have capacity to do something additional?" Seniors activities tend to be perpetual and expansive. Nothing ends, but new things want to be added. Evaluation is needed to determine if it's a good fit for us, if we have facility space, time, and people power to do it well. Generally, the questions are similar each time. We look for whether or not the program or service:

- Benefits most or all members (although we have taken actions to benefit specific smaller groups that are not being served elsewhere)
- Is within the mandate of our service (we are often asked to take on programs and projects that are not within our mandate)
- Is not already being offered here or somewhere nearby in a way that is identical or very similar
- Has adequate resources available for startup and sustainability

Sue McIntyre

Program Coordinator, Cameron Recreation Complex

Parks, Recreation and Cultural Services

Burnaby, British Columbia

---

programs and experiences in the organization, you would need to talk to current volunteers, volunteer supervisors, and perhaps sample potential volunteers. Identifying your population and sample is covered later in this chapter.

In step 3, you also connect your evaluation to the vision, mission, and objectives of the organization. If you are working within a performance measurement plan, at this point you clearly identify where your evaluation fits into the plan. You should also identify the connection to the strategic plan, the time line, check-in points, and an understanding of how to engage people in the evaluation process. Having a plan ensures accountability for the work to staff, stakeholders, and customers.

## Step 4: Develop Evaluation Tools

In this step, it is useful to know you may need more than one evaluation tool in order to collect the information you need. As you choose and design your evaluation tool(s), consider the question "Does the data we will collect with this tool tell the whole story?" Many times a combination of qualitative and quantitative data gives a fuller picture of what you are measuring. Numbers are important, but they don't always tell the whole story in leisure studies. Another area to look at is if you are going to create a formative or summative evaluation.

## Formative Evaluation

As the name implies, a **formative evaluation** is a way of judging the value of a program as it is happening. For example, when designing a new recreation facility, getting user, community, and staff feedback on architectural plans would be a type of formative evaluation; you are assessing the fit of the building before spending large sums of money on it. Creating a prototype of a product would also be considered formative evaluation, such as if a baseball team invites a group of season-ticket holders to give their perceptions of potential new uniforms. Formative evaluation can include continual feedback from participants throughout a program that is used to make changes as the program continues, such as when a tennis instructor asks participants what they enjoyed most from a lesson and what they would like to do more of. This is an informal yet effective formative evaluation. The instructor can come back to the next lesson with a plan that is even better suited to the students' needs.

## Summative Evaluation

**Summative evaluation** concerns the sum total of activities in a program. It is a way of judging the worth of a program at its conclusion. Using the facility example, a summative evaluation of a recreation facility could assess its impact on the community after it has been built, including economic impact and impact on participation rates in physical activity. A summative evaluation could also look at the results of a program that has been operating in a community for a long time, such as the impact of an ongoing youth club on crime in a community or how the fitness level of participants in a fitness program has changed since they joined.

## Quantitative and Qualitative Research Methods

**Quantitative research** is what many people associate with evaluation because it involves numbers; it includes counts of program participants, program satisfaction, number of injuries per facility hour, or other such indicators. **Qualitative research** uses information in the form of words, pictures, objects, or other visual images. For example, participants' descriptions of how they felt about a program or an instructor would be qualitative impressions.

There is much debate over the appropriateness of these approaches in various situations; however, for managers, one approach is not better than the other. Rather, the question being asked should dictate the approach. If you are looking at questions of how many participants reached a certain standard or the cost–benefit ratio of a particular program or facility, for example, then a quantitative approach may be the way to go. As a general guideline, many process-oriented evaluations can be addressed with quantitative approaches. Conversely, qualitative approaches tend to be well suited to examining many outcomes, particularly questions about attitudes or impressions, such as asking participants what they liked about a program or what features of a facility need improvement. These kinds of questions lend themselves to a more qualitative approach. You may also end up combining approaches, often starting with a quantitative approach to understand a particular situation, then examining it in detail using a qualitative approach to get a deeper understanding of the situation.

Experience will help you adapt methods to get the information necessary to make quality decisions. Within these approaches there are many tools to choose from. Some of the most common tools include questionnaires, observation, interviews, focus groups, secondary data, and case studies.

# Questionnaires

**Questionnaires**, or surveys, may be one of the first things that come to mind when thinking of evaluation. Questionnaires are effective at soliciting opinions, attitudes, and demographic information or providing information about participant or employee behavior. A questionnaire can collect quantitative data through yes-or-no questions or through scales that rate some attitude or element of the evaluation target, or it can collect qualitative data through open-ended questions. Questionnaires can be in paper form handed out to participants or staff, or they can be in electronic form using a specific software program that creates surveys. If you are using survey software for an electronic evaluation, it is important to know in what country the information will be stored and what the software company's privacy policy is on protecting personal information.

> **questionnaire**—Form containing a set of questions that is submitted to people to gain insight into issues of interest or concern.

The length of the questionnaire can increase or decrease the response rate. Participants should be told how long the questionnaire will take to complete, and you should be diligent about creating the best questions in a short framework. Surveys that are too long probably will not be completed well if at all.

In figure 13.4, questions 1 and 2 are two ways of collecting data on participants' thoughts about a program. Question 1 is a quantitative approach and a simple question that does not provide much detail. An improved quantitative approach to this question could be to use a rating or Likert scale (very satisfied, satisfied, neutral, dissatisfied, very dissatisfied), discussed in the section on attitude scales. Question 2 is an open-ended qualitative approach whereby participants supply a response under their own terms. This can result in richer data and a deeper understanding of what is being investigated. For example, consider evaluating someone's satisfaction with an outdoor experience. Rather than a score of very satisfied or unsatisfied, a qualitative question may elicit much more detail on what the participant liked or did not like about the experience. This type of question can provide a lot of information but in doing so it allows participants to choose what they divulge, so responses may have little consistency. Additionally, in some cases input may be limited because the question requires more effort to answer (Babbie 2015).

**Rating Scales**    In figure 13.4, question 3 uses a rating scale to assess participants' impression of an instructor. Rating scales commonly use wording such as *strongly agree, agree, neutral, disagree,* or *strongly agree.* Other terms might include *excellent, good, fair, poor,* or *very poor,* or *always, sometimes,* or *never.* It is important to have balanced rating scales. For example, a form asking customers to rate a restaurant where the rating options are outstanding, excellent, very good, good, and fair is not balanced. Although the owners may be happy that 75 percent of customers see the service as good, the scale biases the results because no negative options are available. A balanced rating scale has an equal number of positive and negative choices.

Another problem with rating scales is that different people may view excellence in different ways. Rating scales can also bias future answers. Once you circle *very good,* you might continue with similar responses throughout rather than carefully reading and responding to each individual question (Babbie 2015).

**Checklists**    In figure 13.4, question 4 is an example of a checklist. This type of question works best to obtain the frequency of an occurrence compared with some standard. It can also be used to better understand customers' or employees' preferences, such as what activities they take part in or what services they would like to see in a new facility. A checklist often includes a line for *other* to give respondents the opportunity to add something that the organization may not have thought of.

## Client Satisfaction Questionnaire

**Q1: Sample Quantitative Question**

Overall I was satisfied with the program. (Please circle the best response.)

    Yes        No        No opinion

**Q2: Sample Qualitative Question**

Please describe your satisfaction level with the program. Tell us what we could improve upon and what you liked about the program.

_____

_____

_____

_____

_____

**Q3: Sample Rating Scale**

The instructor was well prepared for classes. (Please circle the best response.)

    Always        Sometimes        Never

**Q4: Sample Checklist**

How did you learn about our program? (Please check all that apply.)

_____ Local newspaper

_____ TV ad

_____ Leisure magazine

_____ Radio ad

_____ From a friend

_____ Poster in the facility

_____ Other (please list)

**Q5: Sample Likert Attitude Scale**

The program was appropriate for my skill level. (Please circle the best response.)

| 1 | 2 | 3 | 4 | 5 |
|---|---|---|---|---|
| Strongly disagree | Disagree | Neutral | Agree | Strongly agree |

**Figure 13.4**  Sample client satisfaction questionnaire.

---

## Sample Question

Circle the number following each statement that best fits your opinion about that statement, where 1 means you strongly disagree with the statement and 5 means you strongly agree with the statement.

Q1: The instructor for the Saturday evening salsa class comes prepared for each class.

| 1 | 2 | 3 | 4 | 5 |
|---|---|---|---|---|
| Strongly disagree | Disagree | Neutral | Agree | Strongly agree |

---

**Figure 13.5**  Sample Likert scale questionnaire.

**Attitude Scales**  An **attitude scale** uses a rating scale to examine a person's opinion or attitude on a topic of interest. Likert scales are the most frequently used attitude scale. Similar to a rating scale, the Likert scale offers options for a person to respond to some statement. For example, for the evaluation of a dance instructor for a salsa class, a statement may be given such as "The instructor is prepared for each session." Respondents would then answer on a scale of 1 to 5 where 1 is equal to *strongly disagree* and 5 is equal to *strongly agree*. More moderate options include 2 and 4, *disagree* and *agree*, and 3 is neutral, often labeled *undecided* (figure 13.5). Likert scales provide more detail than yes-or-no questions but have more consistent responses than open-ended qualitative questions. As the name implies, attitude scales are great at assessing perceptions and attitudes about some statement provided by the researcher (Babbie 2015).

**attitude scale**— Numeric representation of a person's agreement or disagreement with a statement, often reflected in a Likert scale.

## Observation

Observation is watching someone or something and recording observations in a systematic way. A simple example would be an aquatics director taking a daily walk around the pool to check for safety, risk management, and maintenance concerns. A predetermined list could be used to check off concerns or the manager could simply take a note of anything that needs attention. This can also be done with employees or clients. A formal example might be an evaluation of the employee's customer service skills where you watch (or hire someone to watch) how the employee interacts with clients. A checklist can be used to check for required behaviors, such as whether the employee greeted the client within a predetermined time frame or provided information on some upcoming event.

Observation is also a good way to evaluate and provide feedback to instructors and staff. You (or the observer) can have a checklist tied to the job description, program description, and the mission and values of the organization. For example, if one of the values of the organization is creating an inclusive environment in the program, identify what inclusive would look like and write down examples of how you are observing that. This is an exercise you can also share with the employee before the observation; ask if there is anything they would like you to observe and provide feedback on as part of their own self-evaluation.

**raters**—People who judge or evaluate performance against some set of criteria.

A qualitative approach could also be used for noting negative and positive service behaviors. The effectiveness of this approach often lies in consistency among raters, and even consistency of the same rater from one time to the next. **Raters** are simply the people collecting the information; consistency refers to different people rating the same thing similarly. For example, if two raters said a trail was busy, there should be similar numbers of people on that trail during both their observations. Careful definition of terms and training of raters goes a long way toward increasing consistency.

As a manager, informal behavior observations can be effective if conducted in a thoughtful manner. The idea of management by walking around helps you stay connected to issues in your organization and may help in developing more formal evaluation methods based on informal observations (Patton 2001).

## Interviews

Interviews are a common way to evaluate areas such as employee performance. An interview can range from structured to informal. With a structured approach, the interviewer asks predetermined questions and records the responses, much like a verbal questionnaire. A more informal approach is similar to an open conversation where some topics may be predetermined by the interviewer, who can probe for deeper answers or to clarify responses, but each interview has its own unique direction. This approach also lends itself to discovering information you may not have known or considered important. The disadvantage of the less structured approach is that it often does not provide consistency between interviews and makes the data analysis more difficult. For example, an informal interview may help you learn about an employee's satisfaction level or needs in the workplace, but it may not work as well for assessing the performance of employees compared against a standard or each other (Patton 2001).

## Focus Groups

Focus groups can be thought of as group interviews. They are usually conducted with groups of 8 to 12 people who have been screened in some way before the meeting so that the group is of interest to the evaluator. For example, a group may include people who have attended a Vancouver Canucks hockey game in the past year and who have been gathered to discuss their thoughts on client service at the event. Focus groups are an excellent way to get an impression of a new program or initiative such as changes to a facility. A professional sport organization, for example, may use a focus group to get fans' impressions of a uniform change.

Focus groups can be hard to handle if the moderator is inexperienced, and organizations might also call for outside assistance to get unbiased participant responses. Moderators may encounter one person who dominates the group or people who don't want to speak. In addition, some people may modify their opinions to avoid conflict in the group, and thus focus groups may not be as well suited to highly personal topics where politically correct answers are the norm. However, focus groups can help bring out new ideas or raise issues you may not have thought of, and the group dynamics can enhance creativity and help people think more broadly than they might in a more individual setting.

Following is a simple example of how a focus group could be used in a university athletic department. The athletic director wants to know how season-ticket holders for women's basketball feel about the game-day service, particularly concerning the concessions. He sends a letter out to all season-ticket holders and plans to conduct three focus groups of 10 people each. He feels that community ticket holders, faculty and staff ticket holders, and student ticket holders may have different needs, so he randomly picks 10 people from each type of ticket holder. He brings in a person to facilitate the session so as not to bias the answers. The groups are recorded with their consent.

The focus groups are held before a game, and food is offered as an incentive for the participants. The participants introduce themselves, and the facilitator makes them feel comfortable with some chat about basketball. The facilitator then asks the group what they currently like about the concessions, followed by what they would improve. Group discussion ensues. The food is then provided, and the facilitator mentions that some of this food could be in the concessions. She asks if they would be interested in purchasing it there, what they might pay, and what they might change about it. The discussion continues for an hour or so, and the process is repeated with the three different groups. The value of the focus group is that it provides detailed comments from key customers about current service (summative evaluation) as well as some formative evaluation on future items that might be offered in the concession (Patton 2001).

## Secondary Data

Secondary data is information already available that can be used in an evaluation. It may include census data for understanding changing patterns in a community, as well as program records, employee records, and operational records. Program records may document equipment use, participation numbers in various programs, and so on. Employee records might track attendance and absenteeism, employee turnover, disciplinary notes, client complaints, and compliments directed to specific employees. Operational records may document safety inspections, accident reports from staff and clients, and revenue and expense information, as well as problems with equipment or facilities. Secondary data might also come from previous participant registrations stored in a database. This information can be valuable for learning about registration trends and participant demographics of various programs (Patton 2001). Many process-oriented evaluations can use this type of information.

**secondary data**—Data collected by another person or for another purpose that is used to gain understanding of a topic.

## Case Studies

Case studies are similar to observation but much more involved. A **case study** is an in-depth longitudinal look at a single instance or case. Case studies can combine many of the elements discussed previously. Let's say an evaluation of client service ratings has noted a consistent decrease over the past six months. You know things are not going well, but you don't know why. A case study would use a variety of tools to take an in-depth look at how the organization provides client service. During some informal evaluations of staff–client interactions, interviews with a few staff members, and focus groups with long-term clients, a generally less-happy mood around the facility is discovered due to the desire for an increase in time off.

**case study**—Research method that involves an in-depth examination of a single instance or case.

As you gradually piece together the puzzle, you realize that your success is actually your downfall. Client numbers are up and, correspondingly, staff workloads are also way up. The staff is committed to getting the work done, but it is taking a toll. The fatigue is now resulting in less friendly and attentive client service, something that is essential to the business, so you adjust the staff scheduling to accommodate the new busy times at the facility. Obviously, the case study approach is resource intensive and not for all situations. However, when faced with complex problems that are essential to success, it may well prove to be an effective management tool (Patton 2001).

## Step 5: Collect Data

This step utilizes the evaluation tool(s) to collect data and information. Remember to maintain a focus on the process, creating engagement with customers, staff, and stakeholders and building social capital. Ensure a consistent approach to collecting data to get the best information. If the staff is involved in evaluating—by handing out questionnaires, conducting interviews, or observing—ensure they have training and understand the role and process of the evaluation. Monitor the process to make sure the questions and the overall tools are working as planned.

It is important to create time for the users to complete the evaluation or have staff assist by asking the questions or writing the answers on the form. This can increase the response rate or the number of completed evaluations. If the evaluation is electronic, staff can have tablets to assist in completion. If participants are being asked to complete an electronic evaluation when they get home, think about offering an incentive to them for doing this (like a chance to win a prize). Once the participant has left the facility, they may not remember to fill out the evaluation at home and the response rate may be low.

## Step 6: Analyze the Data

Step 6 involves analysis of the data collected through one or more of the previous methods. Analysis of quantitative data may be more straightforward than qualitative analysis. The use of simple spreadsheet programs such as Microsoft Excel allows you to conduct the necessary analysis through simple statistics, such as averages or the most frequent response to a question. Qualitative data can be analyzed using a coding process that separates responses into themes; these themes can be used to understand the experiences of the participants and can provide valuable information in their own words. This information can be compared to the quantitative data, and together they create a clearer picture of what you are measuring.

When analyzing the data from the evaluations, it is a good time to reevaluate whether you are measuring the right things. What is the data saying? Were you asking the right questions of the right people? What was the response rate—did you choose a good evaluation tool? Even at this point in the process it is important to critically think about what the responses are saying and to look at the context of the information and the evaluation tool.

## Step 7: Report the Results

Evaluation can have many uses and audiences, and the evaluation report must be tailored to each of these constituencies. The challenge managers often face is dealing with more information than they can handle. Two key considerations are the size of the report and the choice of medium. Putting everything in the report may make it cumbersome and not useful to the target audience. In some circumstances, findings may be presented to a board, commission, or council, the staff, or the community. This may require a comprehensive written report as well as a verbal presentation.

The key to preparing an evaluation report is making sure it answers the questions that are important to its audience. For example, a local council may be concerned with the effects of certain programs in the community, so highlighting related findings would be critical. Similarly, at a community meeting people may be interested in access to services, quality ratings, and other concerns that directly affect them. Visual tools such as PowerPoint slides can help present findings. Avoid excessive use of text in such presentations; as the saying goes, a picture is worth a thousand words. Easy-to-understand charts, relevant pictures, or even video and audio clips of actual staff or participant comments can be powerful ways to deliver the message. Be careful not to let the technology make or break the report. Well-thought-out evaluations, a solid collection strategy, and thoughtfully analyzed data should take center stage. The report should be engaging and clearly tied to the strategic values of the organization. There are many ways to report results of an evaluation. Depending on the audience, you can write a report, tell a story, or create a dashboard. It may be useful to share information with the people who participated in the evaluation. In this way, you can thank them for taking the time to share their experiences with you and let them know they were heard and taken seriously.

The example shown in figure 13.6 is a qualitative evaluation of the Urban Weaver Project at the McLean Park Fieldhouse (2012–2015, Vancouver Parks and Recreation). It demonstrates a creative way of reporting key objectives for community-engaged arts through numbers.

## Step 8: Implement Recommendations

Implementation may seem obvious, but for busy managers it is an important step to keep in mind. Evaluations are done for a reason: to address important areas of operation. You must track the implementation of recommendations for change. As you have learned elsewhere in the text, change is often met with resistance, so it is important to continue to monitor the implementation. Finally, remember that evaluation is an ongoing effort, including reassessing the program, improving areas viewed as weak, and reevaluating the program. The credibility of an organization can rest on what they do with the information. Remember that evaluations can be the first step to change, and how the recommendations are implemented can affect the relationship you have with your customers, staff, and stakeholders.

## SELECTING EVALUATION PARTICIPANTS

Even if all eight steps of the evaluation process are successfully completed, the end result may still be evaluation information that does not represent the people you want it to represent. How to choose whom to observe, give questionnaires to, interview, or invite to join focus groups is essential to successful evaluation. In research terms this is often referred to as *sampling*. The following section provides a brief overview of sampling for both qualitative and quantitative evaluation.

## Sampling

**Sampling** is selecting a certain number of cases from a larger set of data that is representative of the larger group. In some cases, managers may collect data from all the people they are interested in evaluating; this is called the *population*. For example, if all employees filled out a questionnaire on job satisfaction, that would not be a sample but rather a survey of the entire population. In many cases, though, surveying an entire population is not feasible. Take a university athletic department

**sampling**—Selecting a certain number of cases from a larger set of data that you believe is similar to or representative of the larger group.

**By the Numbers:**

600 pots of tea made

36 kilos of Folgers coffee consumed

40 darning needles broken or missing

5 new cedar weaver instructors trained

1 package of dental floss used for weaving

1,437 Urban Weaver Cedar Weaving Facebook members

250 cheesy songs sung spontaneously as related conversational segues

1,363 likes for Haida language learners Facebook community

2,010 participants in weekly studio workshops

217 Urban Weaver Facebook members

429 events over a three-year period

1 trip to Haida Gwaii

800 potluck meals

**Over a Period of 19 Months, Five Urban Weaver Artists Spent:**

592 hours doing project administration

2,163 hours in unpaid face time with the public

1,010 hours with the public in paid related projects

231 hours maintaining the project blog and online social media engagement

1,031 hours doing project prep, cleaning the Fieldhouse or making project tools

346 hours having project-related meetings or connecting with other Fieldhouse residencies.

**Skills We Have Learned or Shared:**

Splitting fibers, twining, cordage, coiling, spinning, plying, fiber blending, knitting, crocheting, multiple stitch variations and patterning, crochet and tatted lace edgings, processing invasive species, growing flax, retting, breaking, scutching, rippling, hackling, dressing a distaff, false embroidery, spinning cotton balls, mending socks, knitting socks, darning sweaters, making pin looms, warping peg looms, back strap weaving, simple cloth weaving, loom warping, weaving tea towels, frame loom weaving, fixing spinning wheels, re-homing floor looms, washing fleece, wool hackling, making roving and predrafting using a diz, dying fiber, making solar dyes, woad and indigo baths, crocheting old sheets to bathmats, crocheting hats, drafting a pattern from old clothing, cedar bark harvesting, dancing Scotch broom for fiber, making Scotch broom brooms, weaving ivy bike baskets, wet felting, and sharing recipes for favorite meals.

**Where You Have Seen Us:**

BC Parks and Recreation Annual Conference

Colony Farms Mid-Summer Fete

**Figure 13.6** Urban Weaver Project, McLean Park Fieldhouse (2012–2015)

*(continued)*

Reprinted by permission from EartHand Gleaners Society.

CULTIVATE exhibit at Roundhouse CC

Culture Crawl x 2

Draw Down

Maclean Park Harvest Festival

Makers Faire

Maritime Festival x 3

Oppenheimer Park: Aboriginal Days x 3

Sasquatch Days

Stanley Park Ecology Society invasive removal community events x 30

Strathcona Spring Break environmental art camp for children x 2

Strathcona Sustainability Festival

Sustaining our World Festival: Britannia CC

Trout Lake Aboriginal Days

Trout Lake Days

**Figure 13.6** *(continued)*

that wants to know how its football fans feel about the food service at the game. Several hundred thousand people may attend games over the course of a season, so asking them all, let alone dealing with that amount of data, is impractical. Sampling is simply taking a smaller number of cases from a larger pool and then generalizing that sample to the population (Babbie 2015).

Sampling is done to save time and cost. There are two forms of samples: probability and nonprobability. A probability sample consists of random selection procedures to make sure that each unit of the sample is chosen by chance. All units of the evaluation should have an equal chance (or at least a known chance) of being selected for the sample. For example, if you want a probability sample of participants in fitness classes during the past year, you would need to create a sampling frame that contains the entire population. A sampling frame is simply the list of all the people or cases that could be selected for the evaluation. Most likely the participants can be found through registration data, so such a list could easily be created. Then assign a number or some identifier to each person on that list and put the numbers in a hat or use a random-number generator to select the participants. If at all possible, a random sampling method should be used because it will result in the most accurate data.

A probability sample using a stratified random sample or a systematic sample can also be conducted.

## Stratified Sampling

A stratified random sample involves creating a sampling list for each of several categories of interest and then drawing a random sample from those categories. For example, you might want to sample program participants from the key program areas in an organization, such as fitness, sport, arts, and aquatics. To do so, create four separate sampling frames (one for each area) and then draw a random sample from each (Babbie 2015).

### Systematic Sampling

Systematic sampling is when every *n*th person on a list is selected. To create a sampling frame, randomly choose a starting place and select every seventh person on the list. (Choosing the seventh person is an example; you could choose every third person, every ninth person, or whatever you wish.) Continue to select every seventh person on the list until reaching the appropriate number of people for the evaluation. This may mean going through the list numerous times.

## Sample Size

A common question in creating a probability sample is how large the sample should be. Unfortunately, the best answer is that it depends on the situation. Statistical equations can be used to understand the size of the sample, but they require a statistical discussion that is beyond the focus of this chapter. With statistical equations, researchers make assumptions about the sampling errors and degree of difference or variation in the population. But don't despair—two rules of thumb are helpful in the vast majority of cases, especially in the context of evaluation.

First, the smaller the population is, the larger the sample should be. If you have a relatively small population, you will need to use a larger percentage of that population; however, small increases in sample size produce big gains for all samples. Determine sample size based on

- the accuracy required,
- how diverse or variable the population is, and
- the number of things being evaluated.

Evaluators can get by with a smaller sample when less accuracy is needed, the population is relatively homogenous, or only a few variables are being measured.

Second, methods used to analyze the data also influence the sample size. Generally speaking, you would ideally want at least 50 people for each group to be investigated. For example, to compare males with females, a sample of at least 100 (50 for each group) would be needed. Ultimately, the accuracy of the numbers, the resources available (money, time, and people), and the size of the population will determine the best sample size. As with management, evaluation research is part art, part science, so your understanding of the stakeholder population will be the best guide in ensuring that you select appropriate samples (Henderson, Bialeschki, and Browne 2017).

## Nonprobability Sampling

In many cases it may be impossible to have a complete sampling frame, or a qualitative approach may be desired. Under these conditions, a nonprobability sampling method would be used. This form of sampling often focuses on the relevance to the evaluation topic as opposed to accurately representing the population. Nonprobability sampling is a selection of cases or people based on some factor of importance to the evaluator instead of by random chance.

For example, let's look at how you might create a sample to understand client intentions to renew a fitness club membership. You could select a group of people who have not renewed their membership and invite them to discuss their reasons with you. Rather than randomly selecting from the membership list, you purposely select people who have chosen not to renew their membership. This is nonprobability sampling in action. You could choose from a variety of nonprobability sampling methods when selecting which people to invite, including convenience, quota, purposive, snowball, and deviant-case samples.

## Convenience Sample

A convenience sample involves selecting cases that are convenient, such as talking to participants who happen to be at a facility that day. These samples are easy and cheap, but they can produce ineffective, unrepresentative samples or even misleading information. Selecting a readily available case may create some kind of bias in the response. For example, if the athletics department wanted to know how the students at a university feel about university sports, the staff could talk to groups of students who are tailgating before a big game. These students would be easy to find and the data could be quickly collected with little expense, but it is likely to result in a positive response to university athletics. This sample of convenience could be unrepresentative of all students, since students who don't like university athletics are not likely to attend games.

## Quota Sample

Quota sampling attempts to get a preset number of cases in each of several preselected categories. For example, if campus recreation is looking at client satisfaction in a campus recreation facility, the staff may want to sample a certain number of students, a certain number of faculty and staff members, and a certain number of community members. It may also be beneficial for each group to represent gender and age in those groups. Table 13.1 shows a sample size chart to use for quota sampling in this situation. The numbers in this table are examples; actual numbers would be determined by the specific situation.

## Purposive Sample

A purposive sample (sometimes called a judgmental sample) uses an expert to select cases with a particular purpose in mind. For example, you might want to conduct a focus group with participants who have complained during the year, or you might want to speak with those employees who are deemed the most effective at their jobs in order to gather ideas for improving services. Purposive sampling is ideal for many evaluation efforts, particularly if they are exploratory, meaning you are in the initial stages of understanding what you are evaluating.

## Snowball Sample

A snowball sample is useful for understanding interconnected groups of people or even organizations. Essentially, one person recommends the next as a possible participant in the evaluation. For example, this approach might be helpful in trying to develop a new club for rock climbing and to understand the needs and desires of

**Table 13.1** Sample Size Chart for Quota Sampling

| Gender or Role | Faculty Members or Staff | Students | Community Members |
| --- | --- | --- | --- |
| Male | 20 | 50 | 45 |
| Female | 20 | 50 | 45 |

climbers. You likely would have no data or contact information for creating a list of climbers, but you may know one or two climbers who have been eager to get something started. You can ask those people if they know others who may be interested in speaking with you. Through these connections you can learn more about the local climbing community so you can design a program that will better fit their needs and desires.

### Deviant-Case Sample

A deviant-case sample is a look at extreme cases. When looking at client satisfaction at an aquatics center, you would sample both those who are enthusiastic supporters of the center and those who think the center is the worst facility on the planet. You could also look at employees who are extremely satisfied on the job and those who are not to get a better understanding of the workplace dynamics. Caution must be taken, though, not to assume that all clients or employees hold these extreme values.

# BEST PRACTICES AND BENCHMARKING

Another purpose of evaluation is providing information that can help benchmark best practices and provide information to others in similar organizations in order to enhance the quality of programs, facilities, or personnel practices. Evaluation research of this type can also help develop policies or assess their effectiveness. Often this research is conducted by researchers or people in an academic setting such as a university. Although managers might not conduct this research themselves, the information gained may be helpful in understanding industry trends and best practices. Best practices and benchmarking can be useful tools in many organizations; however, they must be pursued with caution and not seen as a quick fix to problems an organization might be facing.

## Best Practices

**best practices**—A part of a business, process, procedure, or system that is considered the best or superior to other ways of doing something.

A best practice is some aspect of a business, process, or system that is considered superior. **Best practices** have been used extensively in the commercial sector and have more recently been adopted by public and nonprofit organizations. An example of a best practice might be the current standard for software used to register people in leisure programs or a training plan for the best customer service. Because best practices are constantly evolving, staying on top of current industry standards is an important task for managers. This can be done informally by keeping up with journals and professional magazines in the industry and attending seminars or conferences as part of a commitment to lifelong education.

More formal research on best practices would involve researchers studying organizations that are leaders in an area. Often a case study will aid in understanding why an organization is so good at what it does. Industry groups may also conduct this research, which is often provided to their members as part of membership or at a cost. For example, the Tennis Industry Association conducts research on trends in the sport and consumer behavior that would help those in the industry identify best practices in running a tennis facility or retail outlet.

HIGH FIVE is an example of a best practice that is being used in many leisure services organizations across Canada. HIGH FIVE supports quality assurance programming for recreation and sport programs for children aged 6 to 12 and provides a range of trainings, assessment tools, and resources to ensure that organizations

---

### Yukon Wellness

Yukon Wellness identified a best practice of using storytelling to promote health and well-being in their community:

> In the summer of 2013, we invited people from around the territory to tell us about "the great things in your community that support well-being." Most of these stories are featured in *Stories that Inspire: Working Together Towards Wellness*. We heard about community gardens and greenhouses, and connecting with culture through traditional dance, language, storytelling, and preservation of heritage sites. We learned about family nights and movie nights, breaking trails and breaking bread, and much more—25 stories in all!
>
> All these stories have many common features underlying their success. In December 2011, 40 people from around Yukon gathered to share their knowledge, experience, and ideas about how to achieve healthy weights for children and youth. We discovered that the best ideas and the greatest successes come when many people bring their talents and gifts to the table, think deeply and passionately about how to make a difference in their community, and roll up their sleeves to get the job done.

Reprinted by permission from Government of Yukon, Department of Health and Social Services. www.yukonwellness.ca.

---

can deliver the highest quality programs possible. HIGH FIVE ensures leaders, coaches, and instructors have the tools and knowledge to nurture a child's mental health and create positive experiences for children (HIGH FIVE 2018).

## Benchmarking

**Benchmarking** is a way to identify best practices. A benchmark is a standard of performance that allows an organization to compare its performance with others or an industry average. Internal benchmarking studies the practices and performance within a particular organization, whereas external benchmarking examines an outside organization. Benchmarking may sound like a quick and easy way to poach the best ideas from other companies, but seldom is that the case. Effective benchmarking is holistic—it involves understanding how a best practice fits into a particular organization. Each organization is unique and thus implementing a best practice in each organization is also unique. It is important to understand how making a change will affect not only the process being studied but also the organization as a whole.

For example, if an agency was considering a change from in-person registration to an online registration standard seen as a best practice, staff would want to look at a variety of its effects. What will it cost? How will it affect clients who do not have Internet access? Are the agency's programs similar to those where the best practice originated, or are they more complex and require human interaction to help clients? Does the agency have the technology support and infrastructure to use such a system? Is current staff trained or willing to be trained to use the new system?

> **benchmarking**—A standard of performance that allows an organization to compare its performance to others or to an industry average.

Because of these questions and the varying answers, benchmarking should be used with caution.

 Check out the web study guide for additional material, including learning activities, sample documents, interactive case studies, web links, CPRP exam connections, and more.

# Conclusion

Understanding how to conduct systematic evaluation is an integral part of a manager's job. This involves collecting information on what matters—the things that lead to effectiveness and success. The more effective managers are at collecting and using this information, the more likely they will be to accomplish organizational goals, provide the programs and services that clients desire, and create an environment where employees can help move an organization forward.

# Review Questions

1. Why is evaluation important?
2. Describe the steps in the evaluation process.
3. Compare and contrast probability sampling and nonprobability sampling.
4. How would you answer the question, "How many people do I need to sample?"
5. What is a sampling frame and how would you go about developing one?
6. What kinds of things might you evaluate as a director of aquatics at a municipal pool? As the general manager of a minor league baseball team? As the executive director of a local nonprofit organization such as the United Way?
7. Define performance measurement.
8. Describe ways to report evaluation results.

# Appendix A

## CERTIFIED PARK AND RECREATION PROFESSIONAL (CPRP) COMPETENCIES

The CPRP exam comprises 150 questions, 125 of which are scored and 25 that are unscored pretest items. You will not know which questions are scored. The questions come from five areas: communication, finance, human resources, operations, and programming. More information about the CPRP exam can be found at www.nrpa.org/certification/CPRP/.

### Communication

- Promote the benefits of specific programs and services to the community
- Provide education regarding the value and benefits of parks and recreation (e.g., for staff, the public, commissions, stakeholders, policy makers, etc.)
- Solicit public support for the mission and goals of the organization (e.g., formation/support of friends groups)
- Collect public input regarding policies (e.g., addressing constituent comments, public hearings, focus groups, surveys)
- Communicate organization's vision and mission to personnel and stakeholders
- Collaborate with external groups, committees, advisory boards, agencies, and councils
- Promote the organization through marketing and branding
- Formalize relationships with outside community organizations (e.g., leagues, associations, clubs, nonprofits, school districts, faith-based organizations)
- Advocate on behalf of the organization to public and media
- Follow the organization's internal chain of communication
- Foster internal and external departmental relationships
- Provide input for reports (e.g., annual, strategic plan, budget)
- Disseminate organization reports (e.g., annual report, financial reports, statistical data, project updates)
- Communicate financial policies, philosophies, and budget status to subordinates (e.g., cost recovery analysis philosophy, budget update reports)
- Convey to seasonal/part-time employees the importance of advocacy for the parks and recreation
- Develop marketing strategic plan (e.g., press releases, advertising, presentations)
- Provide input/updates for agency strategic/master plan (e.g., area specific work plan)

### Finance

- Collect financial and/or operating data (e.g., attendance, revenues, expenditures)
- Implement cash handling practices (e.g., retail sales, rentals, fee collection, deposits, petty cash)

- Purchase supplies, equipment, and services for program activities
- Prepare requests for alternative support (e.g., grants, donations, sponsorships, in-kind services, matching funds)
- Research sources of alternative support (e.g., grants, donations, sponsorships, in-kind services, matching funds)
- Conduct cost recovery analysis for a specific area in order to recommend fee schedules
- Manage area specific contracts
- Develop and implement fee collection procedures
- Recommend fee schedules and policies
- Communicate budget needs to supervisor
- Prepare budget for areas of responsibility
- Operate within an existing budget
- Initiate the bid process for commodities and capital acquisitions and improvements (e.g., obtain and approve specifications for RFPs and requisitions, comply with purchasing requirements)
- Prepare financial analyses and reports (e.g., reconciliation of revenues, cost recovery analysis, budget justification, trend analysis)

**Human Resources**

- Develop job descriptions
- Recruit candidates for seasonal/part-time employment and contracts
- Review candidate applications for seasonal/part-time employment and contracts
- Select and recommend candidates for seasonal/part-time employees and contractors
- Interview candidates for seasonal/part-time employment and contracts
- Conduct training for seasonal/part-time employees and contractors
- Design and conduct training for staff, board members, advocacy groups, sports officials, volunteers, etc.
- Develop work schedules for seasonal/part-time employees and contractors
- Supervise/manage seasonal/part-time employees and independent contractors
- Evaluate seasonal/part-time employee performance (e.g., develop goals, recommendations, work plans)
- Administer disciplinary action (other than termination) for seasonal/part-time employees and contractors
- Make recommendations for retention, renewal, dismissal, or termination of seasonal/part-time employees and contractors
- Manage volunteers (recruits, retention, schedules, evaluates, recognition)
- Conduct hiring process for new employees (recruit, review applications, interview, hire)
- Enforce the policies and procedures of the human resources department or union

- Evaluate personnel performance (e.g., develop goals, recommendations, work plans)
- Manage time cards, payroll, and/or employee records
- Perform personnel actions (e.g., disciplinary actions, coaching, recognitions, terminating, grievances)
- Supervise interns and employees

## Operations

- Manage contract agreements with independent contractors
- Conduct assessment of specific programs, areas, products, services
- Conduct inventories of assets, equipment, and supplies
- Conduct inventories of programs (internal and external) being offered
- Establish relationships with outside organizations (e.g., leagues, associations, clubs, nonprofits, school districts, faith-based organizations, advocacy/friends groups)
- Collaborate with related organizations (e.g., leagues, school districts, other districts/departments, state and federal environmental/natural resource agencies, state affiliates, professional associations)
- Follow energy efficient and environmentally friendly procedures (e.g., disposal methods, purchasing of efficient supplies, Green initiatives, LEED, recycling)
- Implement maintenance standards (e.g., perform or request troubleshooting, routine maintenance, preventative maintenance, repairs or replacement)
- Stay current with changes in applicable regulatory agency policies
- Maintain information systems (e.g., enter data, use permits, reservations, registrations, equipment use records)
- Provide direct supervision of specific facilities and areas (e.g., opening, routine, and closing inspections, monitor activities)
- Provide input for updating standard operating procedures/manuals
- Provide reasonable accessibility accommodations
- Analyze operating data (e.g., attendance, revenue, expenditures, maintenance, marketing)
- Develop standard operating procedures/manuals
- Compile information to defend agency in the event of accidents
- Enforce code of conduct for facility users and program participants, coaches, and staff
- Develop emergency management plan
- Respond to emergencies (incidents, first aid, CPR, etc.)
- Develop risk management, safety, security plans, policies and procedures
- Implement risk management, safety, security plan (e.g., addresses safety concerns, recognizes risk, identify hazards, pre- and post-opening inspections)
- Develop plan to accommodate participants with disabilities
- Provide customer service, both internal and external
- Manage customer relationships (e.g., service recovery, recognition, retention)

- Manage properties (e.g., parks, facilities, areas)
- Monitor capital improvements (e.g., renovations, building new facilities)
- Provide input regarding capital improvements based on operational needs
- Analyze trends and best practices
- Identify needs for new facilities, services, and capital improvements
- Develop and recommend agency specific policies, regulations, codes, laws, rules, etc.
- Ensure agency compliance with national, state, and local laws and regulations

## Programming

- Create recreation programming
- Supervise recreation programming
- Comply with reporting requirements for programs (statistics)
- Develop program purpose, goals, and objectives for a variety of age groups
- Develop schedules for leagues, programs, and facilities
- Evaluate participant satisfaction, program outcomes
- Identify resources available for programming
- Adjust programming as needed based on available resources (location, staffing, supplies, safety)
- Maintain customer relationships (e.g., respond to customer concerns, requests for information)
- Market programs (e.g., advertising, promotional pieces, news releases, brochures, web site content, social networking)
- Perform group and individual participant assessments
- Prepare programs and special events (e.g., content, lesson plans, activities, format)
- Provide direct leadership of recreation activities (facilitate programs)
- Recruit and retain customers/participants
- Develop comprehensive program plan

Courtesy of the National Recreation and Park Association.

# Appendix B

## ONE-PAGE STRATEGIC PLAN,
## CITY OF FAIRFAX, VIRGINIA

Reprinted by permission from City of Fairfax, VA.

# References and Resources

Adams, J.H. 2008. *Creating Community: An Action Plan for Parks and Recreation*. Champaign, IL: Human Kinetics.

Adams, J.S. 1963. "Towards an Understanding of Inequity." *The Journal of Abnormal and Social Psychology* 67, no. 5: 422–436.

Adams, J.S. 1965. "Inequity in Social Exchange." In *Advances in Experimental Social Psychology,* edited by L. Berkowitz, 267–299. New York: Academic Press.

Age Discrimination in Employment Act of 1967 (ADEA), 29 U.S.C. § 634 (1967).

Alberta Lottery Fund. 2017. http://albertalotteryfund.ca/aboutthealf/wherethemoneygoes.asp.

Alpert, R.T. 2015. "Cultural Diversity in the Workplace, Part 1." Diversity Resources. www.diversityresources.com/cultural-diversity-workplace/.

American Hospitality Academy. 2017. www.americanhospitalityacademy.com.

Americans with Disabilities Act of 1990 (ADA), 42 U.S.C. 126 §§ 12101–12117 (1990).

Andereck, K.L. 1997. "Case Study of a Multiagency Partnership: Effectiveness and Constraints." *Journal of Park and Recreation Administration* 15, no. 2: 44–60.

Arnold, M.L., L.A. Heyne, and J.A. Busser. 2005. *Problem Solving: Tools and Techniques for the Park and Recreation Administrator*. Champaign, IL: Sagamore.

Australian National Parks. http://www.australiannationalparks.com/.

Babbie, E. 2015. *The Practice of Social Research*, 15th ed. Boston: Cengage Learning.

Barcelona, B., and C.M. Ross. 2004. "An Analysis of Perceived Competencies of Recreational Sports Administrators." *Journal of Park and Recreation Administration* 22: 25–42.

Barcelona, R.J., M.S. Wells, and S.A. Arthur-Banning. 2016. *Recreational Sport*. Champaign, IL: Human Kinetics.

Barcelona, R.J., and S.J. Young. 2010. "The Role of Municipal Park and Recreation Agencies in Enacting Coach and Parent Training in a Loosely Coupled Youth Sports System." *Managing Leisure* 15, no. 3: 181–197.

BBC News. 2017. "British Columbia Ends High Heel Dress Code Requirements." www.bbc.com/news/world-us-canada-39536117.

Beggs, B.A., O. Butts, A.R. Hurd, and D.E. Elkins. 2018. "Differences in Employee Perceptions of Entry-Level Competencies of NIRSA Campus Recreation Professionals." *Recreational Sports Journal* 42, no. 1.

Ben and Jerry's Homemade Ice Cream. 2007. www.benjerry.com.

Bike and Roll Chicago. 2017. www.bikechicago.com.

Blake, R.R., and A. McCanse. 1991. *Leadership Dilemmas: Grid Solutions*. Houston: Gulf.

Blake, R.R., and J.S. Mouton. 1964. *The Managerial Grid*. Houston: Gulf.

Blinder, A.S., R.R.D. Caunetti, D.E. Labow, and J.B. Rudd. 1998. *Asking About Prices: A New Approach to Understanding Price Stickiness*. New York: Russell Sage Foundation.

Block, P. 2013. *Stewardship: Choosing Service over Self-Interest*, 2nd ed. San Francisco: Berrett-Koehler.

Blom, B., and S. Guajardo. 2000. "Multiyear Budgeting: A Primer for Finance Officers." *Government Finance Review* 16: 39–43.

BoardSource. 2012. Nonprofit Governance Index 2012. Washington, DC: BoardSource.

Bocarro, J.N., and R.J. Barcelona. 2003. "University and Community Park and Recreation Department Partnerships: Tips for Unlocking the Potential of Collaboration." *Parks and Recreation* 38, no. 10: 50–55.

Bolman, L.G., and T.P. Deal. 2013. *Reframing Organizations: Artistry, Choice, and Leadership*, 5th ed. San Francisco: Jossey-Bass.

Boyatzis, R.E. 1982. *The Competent Manager: A Model for Effective Performance*. New York: Wiley.

Boys & Girls Clubs of America. 2017. "Our Mission and Story." www.bgca.org/about-us/our-mission-story.

Brayley, R.E., and D.D. McLean. 2008. *Financial Resource Management*. Champaign, IL: Sagamore.

Bruton, C.M., M.F. Floyd, J.N. Bocarro, K.A. Henderson, J.M. Casper, and M.A. Kanters. 2011. "Physical Activity and Health Partnerships among Park and Recreation Departments in North Carolina." *Journal of Park and Recreation Administration* 29, no. 2: 55–68.

Bureau of Land Management. n.d. *Recreation and Visitors Service Planning*. https://www.blm.gov/sites/blm.gov/files/uploads/IM2013-027_att1.pdf.

Burke, M. 2017. "Consultant Estimates $90.75 Million in Arena TIF Costs for City, Millions More in Net Revenue." *The Norman Transcript*. October 15. http://www.normantranscript.com/news/consultant-estimates-million-in-arena-tif-costs-for-city-millions/article_bf2ef1c6-b164-11e7-b695-0be28731758c.html.

California Park and Recreation Society. n.d. *Creating Community in the 21st Century: Executive Summary VIP Action Plan*. Sacramento, CA: CPRS.

Cameron, K.S. 1994. "Strategies for Successful Organizational Downsizing." *Human Resource Management Journal* 33: 89–112.

Camp Fire USA. 2016. *2015–2016 Annual Report.* http://campfire.org/financials.

Canada Revenue Agency. 2017. *Excise Taxes.* www.canada.ca/en/revenue-agency/services/tax/businesses/small-businesses-self-employed-income/excise-taxes-excise-duties-softwood-lumber-products-export-charge-air-travellers-security-charge/excise-taxes.html.

Canadian Parks and Recreation Association. 2015. "A Framework for Recreation in Canada 2015: Pathways to Wellbeing." www.cpra.ca/about-the-framework/.

Central-Clemson Recreation Center. 2018. www.centralclemsonrec.com.

Certo, S.C. 2003. *Modern Management*, 9th ed. Upper Saddle River, NJ: Prentice Hall.

Chamberlain, C., and J. Wheeler. 2016. "Organizational Structure and Administrative Operations." In *Management of Park and Recreation Agencies*, edited by M. Moiseichik, 71–102. Champaign, IL: Sagamore.

Cherniak, C.T. 2017. "Canada's Sales Tax Rates as at July 1, 2017." *Canada-U.S.* Blog: Legal Developments Affecting Canada-U.S. cross border trade. www.canada-usblog.com/2017/07/12/canadas-sales-tax-rates-as-at-july-1-2017/.

City of Albuquerque, NM. 2017. "2017 G.O. Bond Summary." www.cabq.gov/municipaldevelopment/programs/2017-go-bond-program-2017-2026-decade-plan/approved-program/2017-g-o-bond-summary.

City of Austin, TX. 2017. "Annual Concession Report." www.austintexas.gov/edims/document.cfm?id=265251.

City of Brenham, TX. 2015. *Parks, Recreation and Open Spaces Master Plan 2015–2025.* http://cityofbrenham.org/parks/documents/rec-masterplan-2015.pdf.

City of Erie, CO. 2016. Vision Map. *Parks, Recreation, Open Space, and Trails Master Plan Update.* www.erieco.gov/DocumentCenter/View/8802.

City of Fairfax, VA. 2014. "Strategic Master Plan: Our Parks, Our Future." www.fairfaxva.gov/government/parks-recreation/general-information/advisory-board/strategic-master-plan.

City of Palo Alto, CA. 2013. "City IT Strategy." www.cityofpaloalto.org/gov/depts/it/city_it_strategy.asp.

City of Spokane, WA. 2010. *Roadmap to the Future.* https://static.spokanecity.org/documents/parksrec/aboutus/planning/spokane-parks-and-recreation-roadmap-to-the-future.pdf.

Clawson Freeo, S.K. 2007. *Crisis Communication Plan: A PR Blueprint.* www.niu.edu/newsplace/crisis.html.

Clear Creek Rafting Company. 2017. www.clearcreekrafting.com/choose-a-river.

Cole, K. 2001. *Supervision: The Theory and Practice of First-Line Management*, 2nd ed. Prentice Hall: Frenches Forest, NSW Australia.

Collins, J. 2001. *Good to Great.* New York: Harper Collins.

Collins, J. 2005. *Good to Great and the Social Sectors.* New York: HarperCollins.

Conger, J.A., and R.N. Kanungo. 1998. *Charismatic Leadership in Organizations.* Thousand Oaks, CA: Sage.

Corporation for National and Community Service. n.d. *Volunteering and Civic Life in America.* https://www.nationalservice.gov/vcla.

County of Franklin, NC. 2017. "Purchasing Policies." http://files.franklin.gethifi.com/services/finance/PurchasingPolicy.pdf.

Crainer, S. 2000. *The Management Century.* San Francisco: Jossey-Bass.

Crompton, J.L. 1999. *Financing and Acquiring Park and Recreation Resources.* Champaign, IL: Human Kinetics.

Crompton, J.L. 2015. "Reference Price Based Strategies: A Key to Raising Revenues without Alienating Users." *Managing Sport and Leisure* 28, no. 5: 275–292.

Crompton, J.L. 2016. "Implications of Prospect Theory for the Pricing of Leisure Services." *Leisure Sciences* 38, no. 4: 315–337.

Crompton, J.L., and C.H. Lamb. 1986. *Marketing Government and Social Services.* New York: John Wiley and Sons.

Crossley, J.C., L.M. Jamieson, and R.E. Brayley. 2018. *Introduction to Commercial Recreation and Tourism: An Entrepreneurial Approach*, 7th ed. Champaign, IL: Sagamore.

Dagger Kayaks. 2017. www.dagger.com/us/experience/kayaking-101/content/how-choose-whitewater-kayak.

Dallas Park and Recreation. 2017. www.dallasparks.org/facilities.

Dambach, C.F., M. Davis, and R.L. Gales. 2009. *Structures and Practices of Nonprofit Boards.* Washington, DC: BoardSource.

DeGraaf, D.D., D.J. Jordan, and K.H. DeGraaf. 2010. *Programming for Parks, Recreation and Leisure Services: A Servant Leadership Approach*, 3rd ed. State College, PA: Venture.

De Souza, M. 2013. "Visible Minorities in Canada: A Breakdown." *Postmedia News*, May 8, 2013. www .canada.com/Visible+minorities+Canada+breakd own/8354192/story.html.

Dessler, G., F. Starke, and D. Cyr. 2001. *Management: Leading People and Organizations in the 21st Century.* Toronto: Prentice Hall.

DiGrino, N., and S. Whitmore. 2005. "Recreation Program Planning." In *Management of Park and Recreation Agencies*, edited by B. van der Smissen, M. Moiseichik, and V.J. Hartenburg, 127–157. Arlington, VA: National Recreation and Park Association.

Dropinski, C. 2007. "Cost Recovery in Parks and Recreation." *Illinois Parks and Recreation* 38, no. 5: 12–17.

Drucker, P.F. 1954. *The Practice of Management.* New York: Harper.

Drucker, P.F. 2001. *The Essential Drucker.* New York: HarperBusiness.

Dumler, M.P., and S.J. Skinner. 2005. *A Primer for Management.* Mason, OH: Southwestern.

Eagles, P.F.J., and J.C. Hallo. 2016. "Parks and Protected Areas in Canada and the United States." In *Introduction to Recreation and Leisure*, 2nd ed., 93–126. Champaign, IL: Human Kinetics.

Edey-Nicoll, J. 2006. *Measuring Performance: A link between Resources and Results.* Master of Arts in Leadership and Training Thesis, Royal Roads University, Victoria, BC.

Edgar, W.B., and C.A. Lockwood. 2011. "Understanding, Finding, and Applying Core Competencies: A Framework, Guide, and Description for Corporate Managers and Research Professionals." *Academy of Strategic Management Journal* 10, no. 2: 61–82.

Elliot, T., and D. Mink. 1995. "Ethical Decision-Making." Workshop handout. Chicago: Redmink Resource Group.

Ewing, M.E., L.A. Gano-Overway, C.F. Branta, and V.D. Seefeldt. 2002. "The Role of Sports in Youth Development." In *Paradoxes of Youth and Sport*, edited by M. Gatz, M.A. Messner, and S. Ball-Rokeach, 31–48. Albany, NY: SUNY Press.

Fair Work Ombudsman. n.d. "Workplace Discrimination." https://www.fairwork.gov.au/how-we-will -help/templates-and-guides/fact-sheets/rights-and -obligations/workplace-discrimination.

Farris, S. 2005. "Ushering in the Future: Advice on Strategic Medical Technology Planning." *Health Facilities Management* 18, no. 5: 23–26.

Fayol, H. 1949. *General and Industrial Management.* London: Pitman.

Ferguson, R., and W.T. Dickens. 1999. *Urban Problems and Community Development.* Washington, DC: Brookings Institution Press.

Fiedler, F.E. 1971. *Leadership.* New York: General Learning Press.

Francis, C. 2016. "Capital Improvement Plans 101." OpenGov. https://opengov.com/article/capital -improvement-plans-101.

Fried, G., T.D. DeSchriver, and M. Mondello. 2013. *Sport Finance.* 3rd ed. Champaign, IL: Human Kinetics.

Gardner, J.W. 1993. *On Leadership.* New York: Free Press.

George, J.M., and G.R. Jones. 2011. *Organizational Behavior.* Upper Saddle River, NJ: Pearson.

Gilbreth, F.B., and L.M. Gilbreth. 1916. *Fatigue Study, the Elimination of Humanity's Greatest Unnecessary Waste.* New York: Sturgis & Walton.

Gittell, J.H. 2000. "Paradox of Coordination and Control." *California Management Review* 42, no. 3: 177–183.

Gladwell, N.J., C.M. Bruton, and G. Elder-White. 2016. "Financial Management." In *Management of Park and Recreation Agencies*, 4th ed., edited by M. Moiseichik, 525–575. Ashburn, VA: National Recreation and Park Association.

Gladwell, N.J., D.M. Anderson, and J.R. Sellers. 2003. "An Examination of Fiscal Trends in Public Parks and Recreation from 1986 to 2001: A Case Study of North Carolina." *Journal of Park and Recreation Administration* 21: 104–116.

Glossaire National Bank Financial. 2017. www .nbfinancial.com/webinfo/glossaire_an/outils _glossaire_bi.html.

Government of South Australia, Office of Recreation and Sport. n.d. "Funding." www.ors.sa.gov.au /funding.

Government of Yukon, Department of Health and Social Services. "Pathways to Wellness." www .yukonwellness.ca.

Gray, D.P., and C.D. McEvoy. 2005. "Sport Marketing: Strategies and Tactics." In *The Management of Sport: Its Foundation and Application* 4th ed., edited by B.L. Parkhouse, 228–255. New York: McGraw-Hill.

Greenloons. 2017. "Principles of Ecotourism." http:// greenloons.com/about-ecotourism.html.

Guba, E.G., and Y.S. Lincoln. 1989. *Fourth Generation Evaluation.* Newbury Park, CA: Sage.

Hammersley, C.H., and J.F. Tynon. 1998. "Job Competency Analyses of Entry-Level Resort and Commercial Recreation Professionals." *Journal of Applied Recreation Research* 23, no. 3: 225–241.

Hartman, N. 2014. "Seven Steps to Running the Most Effective Meeting Possible." *Forbes*, February 5, 2014. www.forbes.com/sites/forbesleadershipforum

/2014/02/05/seven-steps-to-running-the-most-effective-meeting-possible/.

Havitz, M.E., and T.D. Glover. 2001. *Financing and Acquiring Park and Recreation Resources: A Canadian Supplement.* Champaign, IL: Human Kinetics.

Henderson, K.A., M.D. Bialeschki, and L.P. Browne. 2017. *Evaluating Leisure Services: Making Enlightened Decisions,* 4th ed. Champaign, IL: Sagamore Venture.

Hersey, P., K. Blanchard, and D. Johnson. 2012. Management of Organizational Behavior, 10th ed. Upper Saddle River, NJ: Pearson.

Herzberg, F. 1966. *Work and the Nature of Man.* Oxford: World.

Herzberg, F., B. Mausner, and B.B. Snyderman. 1959. *The Motivation to Work.* New York: Wiley.

HIGH FIVE. 2018. www.highfive.org.

Howard County Museum. 2017. https://howardcounty museum.org/event-rentals.

Howard, D.R., and J.L. Crompton. 2005. *Financing Sport,* 2nd ed. Morgantown, WV: Fitness Information Technology.

Huebner, A.J., J.A. Walker, and M. McFarland. 2003. "Staff Development for the Youth Development Profession: A Critical Framework for Understanding the Work." *Youth and Society* 35, no. 2: 204–225.

Hult International Business School. 2017. "13 Benefits and Challenges of Cultural Diversity in the Workplace in 2017." www.hult.edu/news/benefits -challenges-cultural-diversity-workplace/.

Humphreys, J.M. 2004. "The Multicultural Economy 2004: America's Minority Buying Power." *Georgia Business and Economic Conditions* 64, no. 3: 1–28.

Hurd, A.R. 2004. "Competency Development for Board Members in Public Parks and Recreation Agencies." *Journal of Park and Recreation Administration* 22: 43–61.

Hurd, A.R. 2005. "Competency Development for Entry-Level Public Park and Recreation Professionals." *Journal of Park and Recreation Administration* 23: 45–62.

Hurd, A.R., and D.D. McLean. 2004. "An Analysis of Perceived Competencies of CEOs in Public Parks and Recreation Agencies." *Managing Leisure* 9: 96–110.

Indiana Fever. 2017. Indiana Fever ticket packages. http://fever.wnba.com/tickets.

Internal Revenue Service. 2016. "The Restriction of Political Campaign Intervention by Section 501c3 Tax-Exempt Organizations." www.irs.gov/charities -non-profits/charitable-organizations/the -restriction-of-political-campaign-intervention-by -section-501-c-3-tax-exempt-organizations.

Investopedia. 2017. "Petty Cash." www.investopedia .com/terms/p/pettycash.asp.

Jackson, A. 2002. "Taking the Plunge: The Conversion to Multi-year Budgeting." *Government Finance Review* 18, no. 4: 24–27.

Janes, P.C. 2006. *Marketing in Leisure and Tourism: Reaching New Heights for Profit and Nonprofit.* State College, PA: Venture.

Jensen, C.R., and S.P. Guthrie. 2006. *Outdoor Recreation in America,* 6th ed. Champaign, IL: Human Kinetics.

Jones, C., and N. Hellmich. 2006. "NYC Bans Trans Fats in Restaurants." *USA Today,* December 6, 2006. www.usatoday.com/news/health/2006-12-04 -trans-fat-ban_x.htm.

Jones, G. 2012. *Organizational Theory, Design, and Change,* 7th ed. Upper Saddle River, NJ: Pearson.

Jordan, D. 2016. "Needs Assessment, Evaluation and Action Research" In *Management of Park and Recreation Agencies,* 4th ed., edited by M. Moiseichik, 719–756. Ashburn, VA: National Recreation and Park Association.

Jordan, D.J. and R. Ramsing. 2017. *Leadership in Leisure Services: Making a Difference,* 4th ed. Urbana, IL: Sagamore Venture.

Kaczynski, A.T., and J.L. Crompton. 2004. "Development of a Multidimensional Scale for Implementing Positioning in Public Park and Recreation Agencies." *Journal of Park and Recreation Administration* 22, no. 2: 1–27.

Kaczynski, A.T., and J.L. Crompton. 2006. "Financing Priorities in Local Governments: Where Do Park and Recreation Services Rank?" *Journal of Park and Recreation Administration* 24, no. 1: 84–103.

Kelsey, C.W., H.R. Gray, and D.D. McLean. 1992. *The Budget Process in Parks and Recreation: A Case Study Manual.* Reston, VA: American Alliance for Health, Physical Education, Recreation and Dance.

Kirdahy, M. 2007. "Deconstructing Directors." *Forbes,* December 12, 2007. www.forbes.com/2007/12/21 /corporate-library-boardrooms-lead-governance -cx_mk_1221directors.html.

Kohm, A., D. LaPiana, and H. Gowdy. 2000. *Strategic Restructuring: Findings from a Study of Integrations and Alliances among Non-profit Social Services and Cultural Organizations in the United States.* Chicago, IL: Chapin Hall Center for Children, University of Chicago.

Kotler, P.T., and K.L. Keller. 2016. *Marketing Management,* 15th ed. Boston: Pearson.

Kouzes, J.M., and B.Z. Posner. 2017. *The Leadership Challenge: How to Make Extraordinary Things Happen in Organizations*, 6th ed. Hoboken, NJ: Wiley.

Lee, M.E. and B.L. Driver. 1992. *Benefits-Based Management: A New Paradigm for Managing Amenity Resources.* Paper presented at the Second Canada/U.S. Workshop on Visitor Management in Parks, Forest, and Protected Areas. Madison, WI.

LEED. 2017. "What Is LEED?" http://leed.usgbc.org/leed.html.

Locke, E.A. 1968. "Toward a Theory of Task Motivation and Incentives." *Organizational Behavior and Human Performance* 3, no. 2: 157–189.

Loehr, J. and T. Schwartz. 2001. "The Making of a Corporate Athlete." *Harvard Business Review* 79, no. 1: 120–128, 176.

Lovelock, C. 2001. *Services Marketing*, 4th ed. Upper Saddle River, NJ: Prentice Hall.

Lumadi, M.W. 2008. "Managing Diversity at Higher Education and Training Institutions: A Daunting Task." *Journal of Diversity Management* 3, no. 4: 1–10. DOI: 10.19030/jdm.v3i4.4996.

March of Dimes. 2007. "SMART" objectives. https://www.marchofdimes.org/chapterassets/files/SMART_objectives.pdf.

Maslow, A.H. 1954. *Motivation and Personality.* New York: Harper & Row.

Mayers, R.S. 2004. *Financial Management for Nonprofit Human Service Organizations*, 2nd ed. Springfield, IL: Charles C Thomas.

Mayo, E. 1933. *The Human Problems of Industrial Civilization.* New York: Macmillan.

McCarville, R. 2002. *Improving Leisure Services through Marketing Action.* Champaign, IL: Sagamore.

McClelland, D.C. 1961. *The Achieving Society.* Princeton, NJ: Van Nostrand.

McGregor, D. 1960. *The Human Side of Enterprise.* New York: McGraw-Hill.

McLean, D.D., and A. Hurd. 2015. *Kraus' Recreation and Leisure in Modern Society*, 10th ed. Boston: Jones and Bartlett.

McLean, D.D., A.R. Hurd, and D. Anderson. 2019. *Kraus' Recreation and Leisure in Modern Society*, 11th ed. Boston: Jones and Bartlett.

McLean, D.D., A.R. Hurd, and R.R. Jensen. 2005. Using Q-Methodology in Competency Development for CEOs in Public Parks and Recreation. *Managing Leisure* 10: 156–165.

McLean, D.D., J.J. Bannon, and H.R. Gray. 1999. *Leisure Resources: Its Comprehensive Planning*, 2nd ed. Champaign, IL: Sagamore.

Meadows, D. 2008. *Thinking in Systems: A Primer.* White River Junction, VT: Chelsea Green.

Ministry of Tourism, Culture and Sport. 2018. Ontario, Canada. www.ontario.ca/page/ministry-tourism-culture-and-sport.

Mintzberg, H. 1979. *The Structuring of Organizations.* Upper Saddle River, NJ: Prentice Hall.

Moiseichik, M. 2016. "Law and Jurisdiction." In *Management of Park and Recreation Agencies*, 4th ed., edited by M. Moiseichik, 27–53. Ashburn, VA: National Recreation and Park Association.

Moiseichik, M., and K. Bodey. 2005. "Legal Authority and Jurisdiction." In *Management of Park and Recreation Agencies*, 2nd ed., edited by B. van der Smissen, M. Moiseichik, and V.J. Hartenburg, 25–60. Ashburn, VA: National Recreation and Park Association.

Montgomery County Friends of Recreation. 2017. www.montgomeryparksfoundation.org.

Morris, P.V. 2010. "Building Cultural Competencies" In *Inclusive Recreation: Programs and Services for Diverse Populations*, edited by Human Kinetics, 39–60. Champaign, IL: Human Kinetics.

Mowen, A.J., L.L. Payne, E. Orsega-Smith, and G.C. Godbey. 2009. "Assessing the Health Partnership Practices of Park and Recreation Agencies: Findings and Implications from a National Survey." *Journal of Park and Recreation Administration* 27, no. 3: 116–131.

Mullin, B.J., S. Hardy, and W.A. Sutton. 2014. *Sport Marketing*, 4th ed. Champaign, IL: Human Kinetics.

Mulvaney, M.A., and A.R. Hurd. 2017. *Official Study Guide: Certified Park and Recreation Professional Examination*, 5th ed. Ashburn, VA: National Recreation and Park Association.

Myrtle Cottage Group. 2017. Values. http://myrtlecottage.org.au/about/.

National Advisory Council on State and Local Budgeting (NACSLB). 1999. *Recommended Budget Practices: A Framework for Improved State and Local Government Budgeting.* Chicago: Government Finance Officers Association.

National Archives. n.d. *Equality Act 2010.* https://www.legislation.gov.uk/ukpga/2010/15/contents.

National Association of State Park Directors. 2017. "2017 Annual Information Exchange." www.stateparks.org/about-us/state-park-facts/.

National Conference of State Legislatures. 2017. "Performance Based Budgeting: Fact Sheet." www.ncsl.org/research/fiscal-policy/performance-based-budgeting-fact-sheet.aspx.

National Environmental Policy Act (NEPA) of 1969, 42 U.S.C. § 4321 et seq. (1969).

National Park Service. 1972. Public Law 92-589, to establish the Golden Gate National Recreation Area. www.nps.gov/goga/learn/management/upload/ggnra_legislation.pdf.

National Park Service. 2017. "Federal Budget Process." www.nps.gov/training/essentials/html/federal_budget_topic.html.

National Recreation and Park Association. 2017. "2016 Annual Report." www.nrpa.org/contentassets/55d98e04a9fa4eaab1ba69cad5d0c663/annual-report-nrpa.pdf.

National Recreation and Park Association. 2018. Infographics Library. https://www.nrpa.org/our-work/Three-Pillars/health-wellness/ParksandHealth/infographics-library/.

Newfoundland and Labrador Canada, Department of Tourism, 2016. "Culture, Industry and Innovation, Tourism Division." http://www.tcii.gov.nl.ca/tourism/pdf/uncommonpotential-2016.pdf.

Niagara Parks Commission. n.d. Strategic Plan 2018–2028. https://www.niagaraparks.com/corporate/resources-reports/strategic-plan/.

North Carolina Department of Transportation. 2017. https://edmv.ncdot.gov/VehicleRegistration/SpecialPlate#term=.

North Carolina State Parks. 2017. www.ncparks.gov/more-about-us/parks-recreation-trust-fund/parks-and-recreation-trust-fund.

Northstar-at-Tahoe Resort. 2017. Northstar-at-Tahoe Golf Tee Times. https://www.northstarcalifornia.com/explore-the-resort/activities-and-events/golf.aspx.

Oakland County, MI. n.d. Creating a Multi-Year Budget Document: Technical Review." www.oakgov.com/exec/Documents/budgetsymposium/MultiYear_budget.pdf.

Opendorse. 2016. "Top 100 Highest-Paid Athlete Endorsers of 2016." http://opendorse.com/blog/2016-highest-paid-athlete-endorsers/.

Oss, M.E. 2004. "Eight Strategies for Human Resources Development." Behavioral Health Management, no. 2: 22–26.

O'Sullivan, E.L. 1991. Marketing for Parks, Recreation and Leisure. State College, PA: Venture Publishing.

Outward Bound Canada. 2017. "Impact Report 2017." http://www.outwardbound.ca/.

Park District of Oak Park. 2017a. "Values." www.pdop.org/about/mission-vision-values/.

Park District of Oak Park. 2017b. Capital Improvement Plan 2017–2021. www.pdop.org/file.aspx?DocumentId=8189.

Pascale, R.T., and A.G. Athos. 1981. The Art of Japanese Management: Applications for American Executives. New York: Simon & Schuster.

Patagonia. 2017a. "Patagonia's Mission Statement." www.patagonia.com/company-info.html.

Patagonia, 2017b. "Corporate Responsibility." www.patagonia.com/corporate-responsibility.html.

Patton, M.Q. 2001. Qualitative Research and Evaluation Methods. Newbury Park, CA: Sage.

Peretomode, O. 2012. "Situational and Contingency Theories of Leadership: Are They the Same?" Journal of Business and Management, no. 4: 3, 13–17.

Pew Charitable Trust. 2016. "State Parks Find New Ways to Save, Make Money." www.pewtrusts.org/en/research-and-analysis/blogs/stateline/2016/04/14/state-parks-find-new-ways-to-save-make-money.

Pew Research Center. 2017. "Social Media Fact Sheet." www.pewinternet.org/fact-sheet/social-media/.

PeyBack Foundation. 2017. www.peytonmanning.com.

Pink, D.H. 2009. Drive: The Surprising Truth about What Motivates Us. New York: Riverhead.

Pointer, D.D., and J.E. Orlikoff. 2002. The Higher Performance Board: Principles of Nonprofit Organization Governance. New York: Jossey-Bass.

Press, J. 2017. Visible Minorities May Comprise One-Third of Canadians by 2036. https://www.macleans.ca/news/visible-minorities-may-comprise-one-third-of-canadians-by-2036/.

Provo Shooting Sports Park. 2015. "Standard Operating Procedures." https://www.provo.org/home/showdocument?id=9720.

Queens Printer for Ontario. 2018. Ministry of Labour. https://www.ontario.ca/page/ministry-labour.

Recreation Nova Scotia. 2018. www.recreationns.ns.ca.

REI Stewardship. 2017. "Creating Access." www.rei.com/stewardship/creating-access.

Robbins, S.P., and M. Coulter. 2016. Managing, 13th ed. Boston: Pearson.

Robbins, S.P., D.A. Decenzo, and M. Coulter. 2013. Fundamentals of Management, 8th ed. Boston: Pearson.

Rossman, J.R., and B.E. Schlatter. 2015. Recreation Programming: Designing Leisure Experiences, 7th ed. Champaign, IL: Sagamore.

Saint Paul, MN. 2016. 2016–20 Strategic Implementation Plan. https://www.stpaul.gov/sites/default/files/Media%20Root/Parks%20%26%20Recreation/Parks%20Strategic%20Implementation%20Plan%202016-2020.pdf.

San Francisco Parks Alliance. 2017. www.sfparksalliance.org.

Saskatchewan Tourism, Parks, Culture, and Sport. 2017. www.pcs.gov.sk.ca/Recreation.

Sawyer, T.H., M.G. Hypes, and T.L. Gimbert. 2013. "Planning Facilities: Master Plan, Site Selection, and Development Phases." In *Facility Planning and Design for Health, Physical Activity, Recreation, and Sport*, 13th ed., edited by T.H. Sawyer, 3-20. Champaign, IL: Sagamore.

Schein, E.H., and P. Schein. 2017. *Organizational Culture and Leadership*, 5th ed. New York: Jossey-Bass.

Schlitterbahn Waterparks. 2017. www.schlitterbahn.com/community/mission.

Scholey, C., and K. Schobel. 2016. "Performance Measurement for Non-Profit Organizations: The Balanced Scorecard as an Approach." Chartered Professional Accountants Canada.

SCORE. 2017a. www.score.org.

SCORE. 2017b. "Business Plan Template for a Startup Business." www.score.org/resource/business-plan-template-startup-business.

Scott, M. 2014. "Steps to Complete a Parks and Recreation Master Plan." Delaware Complete Communities Planning Toolbox. Institute for Public Administration, University of Delaware. www.completecommunitiesde.org/planning/healthy-and-livable/steps-parks-rec-master-plan/.

Seidler, T.L. 2013. "Planning Facilities for Safety and Risk Management" In *Facility Planning and Design for Health, Physical Education, Recreation and Sport*, 13th ed., edited by Sawyer, T.H., 21–27. Urbana, IL: Sagamore Publishing.

Senge, P.M. 2006. *The Fifth Discipline: The Art and Practice of the Learning Organization*, 2nd ed. New York: Currency Doubleday.

Shaban, A. 2016. "Managing and Leading a Diverse Workforce: One of the Main Challenges in Management." *Procedia—Social and Behavioral Sciences* 230: 76–84.

Sinek, S. 2009. *Start with Why: How Great Leaders Inspire Everyone to Take Action*. New York: Penguin Group.

Smale, B.J.A., and W. Frisby. 1992. "Managerial Work Activities and Perceived Competencies of Municipal Recreation Managers." *Journal of Park and Recreation Administration* 10, no. 4: 81–108.

Small Business BC. 2017. www.smallbusinessbc.ca.

Solomon, S.A., S. Mason, and A. Scarbrough. 2012. "Moving to Multi-year Budgeting: The Time Is Now." Virginia Government Finance Officers Association Fall Conference. www.vgfoa.org/2012_Fall_Conference/PRESENTATIONS/10.18_Multi-Year%20Budgeting%20and%20Financial%20Forecasting%20-%20Why%20Now%20is%20the%20Time.pdf.

Sport and Recreation, Victoria, Australia. 2017. Goals. http://sport.vic.gov.au/about-us/what-we-do.

Stachura, M. 2015. "Number of Golfers Steady, More Beginners Coming from Millennials." *Golf Digest*, April 30, 2015. www.golfdigest.com/story/number-of-golfers-steady-more.

Stadiums of Pro Football. 2018. "Future Stadiums: Las Vegas Stadium." https://www.stadiumsofprofootball.com/stadiums/las-vegas-stadium/.

Stanton, T., S. Markham-Starr, and J. Hodgkinson. 2013. "Public Recreation." In *Introduction to Recreation and Leisure*, 2nd ed. 127–147. Champaign, IL: Human Kinetics.

State of Texas, Office of the Comptroller. 2017. "Bond Election Results." https://comptroller.texas.gov/transparency/local/bond-elections/bond-results-all.php.

Statistics Canada. 2012. "Internet and e-Commerce: Data from the 2012 Internet User Survey." www.statcan.gc.ca/eng/survey/household/4432b.

Statistics Canada. 2017. "Visible Minorities May Comprise One-Third of Canadians by 2036." www.macleans.ca/news/visible-minorities-may-comprise-one-third-of-canadians-by-2036/.

Stern, M. 2011. "Real or Rogue Charity? Private Health Clubs vs. the YMCA, 1970–2010." *Business and Economic History Online*. www.thebhc.org/sites/default/files/stern.pdf.

Steve Nash Foundation. 2017. www.stevenash.org.

Stogdill, R.M. 1974. *Handbook of Leadership: A Survey of the Literature*. New York: Free Press.

Storm Cares. 2017. www.seattlestormbasketball.com/stormcares/.

Strigas, A. 2006. "Making the Most of Volunteers." *Parks and Recreation* 41, no. 4: 26–29.

Taylor, F.W. 1911. *The Principles of Scientific Management*. New York: Harper.

Texas Parks and Wildlife Department. 2017a. "Mission." https://tpwd.texas.gov/about/mission-philosophy.

Texas Parks and Wildlife Department. 2017b. "Financial Overview." https://tpwd.texas.gov/publications/pwdpubs/media/pwd_rp_a0900_0679_01_17.pdf.

Tew, P.F., M.E. Havitz, and R.E. McCarville. 1999. "The Role of Marketing in Municipal Recreation Programming Decisions: A Challenge to Conventional Wisdom." *Journal of Park and Recreation Administration* 17, no. 1: 1–20.

Thomas, E.C. 2002. "The Challenge of Cutback Management." *Public Policy and Practice* 1, no. 2: 5–8.

Title VII of the Civil Rights Act of 1964, 42 U.S.C. §§ 2000e et seq. (1964).

Toosi, M. 2016. "A Look at the Future of the U.S. Labor Force to 2060." Bureau of Labor Statistics. www.bls .gov/spotlight/2016/a-look-at-the-future-of-the-us -labor-force-to-2060/home.htm.

Toronto Parks, Forestry and Recreation. 2018. "Parks, Gardens, and Beaches." www.toronto.ca/explore -enjoy/parks-gardens-beaches/.

Tuckman, B.W. 1965. "Developmental Sequence in Small Groups." *Psychological Bulletin* 63, no. 6: 384–399.

Tynan, K. 2005. "Budget and Performance Integration Innovation at Fish and Wildlife Service (FWS): FY 2007 Budget Planning Exercise for FWS Senior Managers." U.S. Fish and Wildlife Service. www .fws.gov/planning/Documents/FY07%20 Budget%20Exercise.pdf.

United Way of America. 1996. *Measuring Program Outcomes: A Practical Approach*. Alexandria, VA: United Way of America.

University of Georgia. 2014. "Minority Buying Power Rises, Hispanics Lead the Way." www.bizjournals .com/atlanta/news/2014/09/30/uga-minority -buying-power-rises-hispanics-lead-the.html.

University of North Florida, Center for Sustainable Business Practices. 2017. www.unf.edu/coggin /csbp/.

U.S. Bureau of Labor Statistics. 2016. *Volunteering in the United States*. Washington, DC: U.S. Government Printing Office.

U.S. Census Bureau. 2006. *Government Finance and Employment Classification Manual*. www2.census .gov/govs/pubs/classification/2006_classification _manual.pdf.

U.S. Census Bureau. 2012. "Most Children Younger than Age 1 Are Minorities, Census Bureau Reports." www.census.gov/newsroom/releases/archives /population/cb12-90.html.

U.S. Census Bureau. 2013. *Individual State Descriptions: 2012*. www2.census.gov/govs/cog/2012isd.pdf.

U.S. Census Bureau. 2015. "New Census Bureau Report Analyzes U.S. Population Projections." www .census.gov/newsroom/press-releases/2015/cb15 -tps16.html.

U.S. Census Bureau. 2016. "American Community Survey 1-Year Estimates: Computer and Internet Use in the United States: 2016." https://factfinder .census.gov/faces/tableservices/jsf/pages /productview.xhtml?pid=ACS_16_1YR _B28003&prodType=table.

U.S. Forest Service. 2017. *USDA Forest Service Strategic Plan: FY 2015–2020*. www.fs.fed.us/sites/default /files/strategic-plan%5B2%5D-6_17_15_revised .pdf.

Vancouver Parks and Recreation. 2017. "2015–2018 Final Capital Plan." http://parkboardmeetings .vancouver.ca/2014/140929/REPORT _CapitalPlan2015-2018_20140929.pdf.

Ventana Big Sur. 2018. www.ventanabigsur.com/resort /overview.

Vézina, M., and S. Crompton. 2012. "Volunteering in Canada." Statistics Canada. www.statcan.gc.ca /pub/11-008-x/2012001/article/11638-eng.pdf.

Virginia Beach Parks and Recreation Department. 2017. "Annual Report Fiscal Year 2017." www.vbgov .com/government/departments/parks-recreation /about-us/Documents/annual-report.pdf.

Volunteer Canada. 2015. https://volunteer.ca/.

Volunteering Australia. 2015. "Key Facts and Statistics about Volunteering in Australia." www .volunteeringaustralia.org/wp-content/uploads /VA-Key-statistics-about-Australian-volunteering -16-April-20151.pdf.

Volunteer Protection Act. 1997. Public Law No: 105-19.

Vroom, V.H. 1964. *Work and Motivation*. New York: Wiley.

Walczak, J., and S. Drenkard. 2017. "State and Local Sales Tax Rates in 2017. Tax Foundation Fiscal Fact, No. 539." www.taxfoundation.org.

Wayne County, PA. 2018. "Wayne County Room Rental Excise Tax." http://www.waynecountypa .gov/533/Wayne-County-Room-Rental-Excise -Tax.

We Are Social. 2017. "Digital in 2017: Global Review." https://wearesocial.com/us/special-reports /digital-in-2017-global-overview.

Wedel, M. 2001. "Is Segmentation History?" *Marketing Research* 13, no. 4: 27–29.

Westlaw Electronic Research. 1972. "Subchapter LXXVI—Golden Gate National Recreation Area." www.nps.gov/goga/learn/management/upload /ggnra_legislation.pdf.

Wilderness Act of 1964, 16 U.S.C. 23 §§ 1131–1136 (1964).

Wilson, L. 2016. "Social Media for Event Planners." *Business 2 Community*. www.business2community .com/brandviews/growing-social-media/social -media-event-planners-01676642.

Wirtz, J., and C. Lovelock. 2016. *Services Marketing: People, Technology, Strategy*. Hackensack, NJ: World Scientific Publishing.

Wolter, S.A. 1999. "Master Planning Leisure Resources." In *Leisure Resources: Its Comprehensive Planning,*

2nd ed., edited by D.D. McLean, J.J. Brannon, and H.R. Gray, 153–209. Champaign, IL: Sagamore.

Woodlands Township. 2017. *2018 Adopted Budget.* www.thewoodlandstownship-tx.gov/Archive Center/ViewFile/Item/7819.

YMCA of Austin. 2016. "Grow Good: 2016 Community Impact Report." www.austinymca.org/sites /default/files/YMCAofAustin_2016Annual ReportCover-WEB.compressed.pdf.

Zimmermann, J.M., and R. Davidson. 2016. "Budgeting." In *Management of Park and Recreation Agencies*, 4th ed., edited by M. Moiseichik, 577–629. Ashburn, VA: National Recreation and Park Association.

# Index

**A**

ABC (activity-based costing) 318-319
abilities, in job descriptions 224
absenteeism, in employees 258-259
accountability 114-116, 118
action planning 114-115
activity-based costing (ABC) 318-319
activity (efficiency) ratios 327
ADA (Americans with Disabilities Act) 70-71, 222
Adams, John Stacey 256-257
administrative consolidation 122
administrative support 216-217
admission fees 283
advertising 176-177
affective commitment 259
affirmative action 70
Age Discrimination in Employment Act of 1967 71, 222
AIDA approach to promotions 175-180
Alberta Lottery Fund 280
alliances 122
allocated funds 311
Americans with Disabilities Act (ADA) 70-71, 222
Anaya, Stacie 130
appreciation rewards 261
artifacts, in organizational culture 95
assault 61
assessment center interview 235-236
assumption of risk 58-59
atmosphere, in marketing mix 171
attitude scales 345
Australia 72-73, 83
authoritarian-compliance management 8
authority 33, 110-111
autocratic leadership 7

**B**

balanced scorecard 337-338
balance sheets 323-324
Bannon, J.J. 132
Barcelona, R.J. 125-126
Barnard, Chester 15
battery 61
behavioral characteristics, in marketing 162
behavioral theories
    leadership 6-8
    management 14-15

benchmarking 355-356
best practices 19, 354-355
bidding process 322
biennial budgets 319
Blanchard, K. 9
boards
    defined 96
    meetings 102-103
    members 98
    types 96-99
Bocarro, J.N. 125-126
bonds 288-289
branding 164
brand loyalty 162, 166
Brayley, R.E. 275
break-even analysis 322-323
broadcast communication 203
Brown, Jamie 332
budgets
    approaches to 316-319
    budget cycle 304-306
    budget statements 325-326
    cutback management 306-308
    defined 303
    implementation 319-322
    types 308-316
bureaucracies 13-14, 92
business plans 140-141
business structures 85-88
buying power 159
bylaws 100

**C**

Canada
    Alberta Lottery Fund 280
    demographic trends 219
    employment laws 73, 220, 222-223
    National Recreation Statement 81
    park and recreation agencies 82, 83
    Small Business BC 140
    taxes 275-279, 280
    voluntary sector 83
Canadian Charter of Rights and Freedoms 222
Canadian Human Rights Act 220, 223
Canadian Parks and Recreation Association (CPRA) 175
Canadian Wildlife Service 83
capital budgets 308-310
capital expenditures 287-289
capital improvement plans (CIPs) 308

careers
    competency-based advancement 24
    professional certifications 357-360
    progression of 38-39
case studies 347-348
cash-flow statements 324
C corporations 86-87
celebrity endorsements 178
centralization 90
Certified Park and Recreation Professional (CPRP) competencies 357-360
chain of command 89-90
change
    evaluation and 339
    planning and 131
    problem solving and 148-149
characteristics, defined 26
charismatic leadership 10
checklists 343
Chikuse, Joshua 274
CIPs (capital improvement plans) 308
city manager-council structure 81-82
civil law, defined 56
Civil Rights Act of 1964 68-69, 222
closed sessions 102
cohesiveness, in teams 119
collaborations 121-122
command, as job function 12
commercial sector 85-88
communication
    breakdowns in 189-190
    CPRP competencies 357
    crisis 195-196
    defined 187
    directions of 191-193
    external 196-205
    functions of 187
    informal 193
    internal 193-195
    positioning strategies 203-204
    process of 188
    repositioning strategies 204-205
    strategic approach 190-191
communication channels 188
communication mix 199-203
communication noise 189
community, in marketing mix 169-170
comparative negligence defense 59
compensatory model 170

competencies
  of board members 98
  CPRP 357-360
  defined 4
  elements of 4-5
  entry-level management 25-26
  in job descriptions 224
  organizational 133-134
  scorecard 26
  uses in organizations 24-25
competency-based management
  23-26
compulsory income 275-281
conceptual skills 35, 217-218
consideration (leader behavior) 7-8
contingency costs 291
contingency leadership theories
  8-9
contracts 62-64
contractual receipts 284-285
control
  adding personnel and 216
  communication and 194-195
  as job function 5, 13, 37
convenience sample 353
coordinating units 119
coordination
  adding personnel and 216
  communication and 194-195
  described 109
  external 120-126
  internal horizontal 116-120
  internal vertical 110-116
  as job function 13
corporate bonds 288-289
corporate communication 180
corporations 86-87
cost allocation 292
cost centers 298, 314, 317
cost-of-living adjustments 215
cost recovery 290, 297
counseling 180, 242
country club management 8
CPRA (Canadian Parks and Recreation Association) 175
CPRP (Certified Park and Recreation Professional) competencies 357-360
criminal law, defined 56
crisis communication 195-196
Crompton, John 173
cross-functional teams 94-95
cross-subsidization 296
cross-training of employees 214
cultural competence 48
cutback management 306-308

**D**
daily schedules, staggered
  262-263
debenture bonds 288

decision making 147-151
decoding 188
defamation 61
Deming, W. Edwards 18-19
democratic leadership 7
demographic trends
  marketing and 159, 160
  personnel planning and
    219-220
departmentalization 89
Derick, Sarah 210
deviant-case sample 354
Dickens, W.T. 125
differential pricing 297-298
direct costs 291
direct distribution 167-168
disabilities 70-71, 80, 222
discretionary income 159
discrimination in employment
  67-68, 71, 222-223
distribution channels 167-169
diversity
  target markets and 159
  of workforce 48-49, 219-220
Dombrowski, Jessica 78
Donnelly, Margaret 32
double taxation 296
Dover Kids Cabinet 123
downward communication
  191-192
dram shop laws 64
Drucker, Peter 19, 114, 115, 191
dynamic websites 202

**E**
earned income 283-284
EEOC (Equal Employment Opportunity Commission) 67-69
effectiveness
  continuum of 47
  defined 47
  human needs and 212
  model of 4-5
  planning and 131
efficiency 47, 131
efficiency (activity) ratios 327
electronic networks 120, 145
empirical research 16
employee benefits 238, 239
employee development 239-240,
  251
employee-oriented leaders 7
employee recognition 258-265
employees
  discipline and dismissal 242-
    243, 267-270
  diversity 48-49, 219-220
  engagement and motivation
    251-255
  evaluation 241-243
  health and safety 71-72

improvement plans 268-269
  protected classes 68-69, 70
  as resource 38
  retention 258
  suggestions from 266-267
  workforce reduction 306-307
employee training 239-240
Employment Equity Act (Canada)
  223
employment laws 67-72, 219-220,
  222-223
enabling legislation 64-65, 80-81
encoding 188
engagement, defined 251
entrance fees 283
entrepreneurial startup 91
EPA (Equal Pay Act of 1963) 70, 222
equal employment opportunity 70
Equal Employment Opportunity
  Commission (EEOC) 67-69
equal opportunity model 170
Equal Pay Act of 1963 (EPA) 70, 222
equal-share allocation 292
equity models 170
equity theory 256-257
espoused beliefs 95-96
ethics, in decision making
  150-151
evaluation (organizational)
  competencies in 24
  difficulties in 334-335
  informal 339
  performance measurement
    335-338
  process 339-349
  purposes 333-334, 354-355
  tools for 341-348
excise taxes 280-281
exemplary leadership (Kouzes
  and Posner) 10-11
expectancy theory 257-258
expenditures 287-289
expense budget 305
external communication 196-205
external-internal noise 189-190
external noise 189
extrinsic rewards 259

**F**
face-to-face communication 200
face-to-face interviews 234-236
Fairfax, Virginia strategic plan 361
fairness, and coordination 110,
  111-112
false imprisonment 62
Fayol, Henri 12-13, 35
federal park and recreation agencies 82-83
feedback 188
fees and charges 283-284. *See also*
  pricing

Ferguson, R. 125
Fiedler, F.E. 9
financial management
    CPRP competencies 357-358
    creative financing 298
    expenditures 287-289
    financial analysis 322-326
    financial indicators 327
    financial resources 37-38
    personnel management and 215
    pricing 289-296
    revenue sources 275-286
    risk financing 67
fiscal year 304
five practices of exemplary leadership 10-11
fixed costs 287, 291
flash mob evaluation 335
flextime 263
focus groups 136, 346-347
Follett, Mary Parker 15
formal bidding process 322
formalization 90-91
formative evaluation 342
Friesen, Allyson 253
functional resources 109

**G**
Gardner, John 111
general administrative management 11, 12-14
general obligation bonds 288
Gentry, David 156
geography, in marketing 160
Gilbreth, Frank and Lillian 12
goals 35
Good Samaritan statutes 64
goods vs. services 165
grants 281
grapevines 193
gratuitous income 281-282
Gravink, Jill 108
Gray, H.R. 132
gross negligence 64
group interviews 234-235

**H**
harassment 67, 69-70
hardware 144-145
Hawthorne studies 14-15
health and safety, of employees 71-72
Hersey, P. 9
Herzberg, Frederick 16-17, 255
HIGH FIVE 354-355
high-threshold training 240
home rule legislation 81
horizontal communication 192-193
horizontal coordination 116-120
human capital 111

human relations era 15-18
human relations skills 35, 217-218, 254-255
human resources 211-213
human resources capacity 213

**I**
ideas contest 266-267
IFB (invitation for bid) 322
impact objectives 46
impoverished management 8
improvement plans 268-269
income statements 324
incremental budgeting 318
indirect (overhead) costs 291-292
indirect distribution 167-168
infographics 205
informal communication 193
information richness 200
inherent risks 58, 64
initiating structure (leader behavior) 7-8
intensity of distribution 168-169
intentional torts 60-62
intermediate goals 44
internal communication 193-195
internal noise 189
intersectoral partnerships 120-124
interviews, in evaluation 346
intrinsic motivation 253-254
intrinsic rewards 259-260
investment income 284
invitation for bid (IFB) 322
invoices 322

**J**
job announcements 224-229
job-based rewards 264
job demands 5
job descriptions 24, 223-224
job interviews
    competency-based questions 24
    legal, illegal questions 237
    order of questions 235
    types 231-236
job offers 236
job titles 225
joint and several liability 60
joint facility use 122
joint programming 122
joint ventures 123-124
judgmental (purposive) sample 353

**K**
knowledge, in job descriptions 224
Kouzes, J.M. 10-11

**L**
laissez-faire leadership 7
language use, in communication 190

law of diminishing returns 213
leadership
    defined 6
    as job function 5, 37
    leader values 40
    role in management 5-6
    styles of (Lewin) 7
    in teams 117-118
    theories of 6-11
Leadership Grid 8
learning organizations 20-21, 252
LEED (Leadership in Energy and Environmental Design) 50
legal issues
    civil vs. criminal law 56
    contracts 62-64
    employment laws 67-72, 219-220, 222-223
    importance of understanding 55
    job interview questions 237
    legislation 64-65, 79-81
    potential litigation 55-56
    risk management 65-67
    torts 57-62
leisure services (term) 4
leisure services managers
    career progression 38-39
    cultural competency 48-49
    functions 34-37
    legal foundations. See legal issues
    levels of 33-34
    resources managed by 37-38
    sustainability and 49-50
Lewin, Kurt 7
libel 61
license and permit fees 284
Likert scale 345
limited liability 86
limited liability companies (LLCs) 87-88
limited liability partnerships (LLPs) 87-88
line-item budgets 310
liquidity ratios 327
lobbying 180
location, in marketing mix 170-171
Loehr, Jim 267
long-term goals 35, 44
loss exposures 65-66
low-threshold training 240

**M**
management. See also leisure services managers
    behavioral theories 14-15
    classical theories (machine models) 11-14
    competency-based 23-26
    defined 3

management *(continued)*
   effective 4-5
   leadership in 5-6
   legal foundations. *See* legal
     issues
   modern theories 18-20
   multisector approach 4
   people-oriented approach 15-18
   self-care in 265-267
   trends in 20-25
   universality of 4
management by objectives (MBO)
   115-116
management drivers
   defined 39
   goals 43-44
   mission 42-43
   objectives 44-46
   values 40-41
   vision 42
market, defined 159
market equity model 170
marketing
   defined 157
   demographics and 159, 160
   external communication in
     196-203
   grassroots 161
   history 157-158
   market segmentation 159-162
   planning 141-142
   social media for 181-183, 199
   target market 163
marketing mix
   defined 164
   place 167-171
   pricing 171-175
   product 164-167
   promotion 175-180
market position 164, 203-204
Maslow, Abraham 16, 252, 255
mass marketing 159
master plans 138-140
master-servant rule 60
matching grants 281
matrix structure 94-95
Mayo, Elton 14-15
mayor-council structure 81
MBO (management by objectives)
   115-116
McAfee, Kate 186
McBride, Dave 266-267
McClelland, David 255-256
McGregor, Douglas 16, 255
McIntyre, Sue 340
McLean, D.D. 132, 275
media communications 196
media relations 179
meetings
   board 102-103
   staff 116-117

membership-based rewards
   261-262
member values 40
mental models 21
mentorship 39
mergers 124
middle-of-the-road management 8
minority populations 159
Mintzberg, H. 114-115
monetary rewards 260
Moreno, Alexis 2
motivation
   defined 255
   employee engagement and
     252-255
   theories of 255-258
motivation-hygiene theory 16-17
multiyear budgeting 319
municipal organizations 79, 81

**N**
National Recreation and Park
   Association (NRPA) 175, 205
needs assessments 333
needs hierarchy (Maslow) 16, 252
negligence 57-60
negligence per se 60
negligent entrustment 60
networks (organizations) 122
Nivison, Heather 250
nongovernmental organizations
   83-85
nonmonetary rewards 260-261
nonprobability sampling 352-354
nonprofit sector 83-85
nonprogrammed decisions 147
nontraditional rewards 262-263
NRPA (National Recreation and
   Park Association) 175, 205
Nunes, Chris 302

**O**
object classification budgets
   310-311
observation 345-346
Occupational Health and Safety
   Act 71
Ohio State studies 7-8
Open Meetings Act 102, 103
operating budgets
   line-item 310
     object classification 310-311
     performance budgets 314-316
     program budgets 311-317
operating expenditures 287
operations competencies (CPRP)
   359-360
organization (job function) 5, 12,
   35-37
organizational culture 95-96
organizational design 91-95
organizational environment 5

organizational hierarchies
   110-111
organizational resources 109
organizational structure
   commercial sector 85-88
   defined 88
   elements of 89-91
   in employee orientation 238
   factors influencing 103-104
organization charts 93
outcome objectives 46
outcomes-based management
   21-23
overhead (indirect) costs 291-292

**P**
parks and recreation
   commercial sector 85-88
   professional certifications
     357-360
   term usage 4
Parks Canada 83
parliamentary procedure 102-103
partnership integration 123-124
partnerships (between
   organizations)
   benefits 124-125
   defined 121
   as exchange 124
   successful 125-126
   types 120-124
partnerships (business entity)
   85-86
Patagonia, Inc. 40, 50, 95
people-oriented management 15-18
percentage of budget allocation 292
performance analysis 133-134
performance appraisals (employees) 241-243
performance-based rewards 261-
   262, 264-265
performance control 115
performance measurement (organizations) 335-338
personal mastery 21
personal property taxes 278-279
personal selling 178
personnel, defined 211
personnel management
   capacity for 213-217
   CPRP competencies 358-359
   employee diversity and 48-49,
     219-220
   employee orientation 238-239
   human resource perspectives
     211-213
   job announcements 224-229
   job descriptions 223-224
   performance appraisals
     241-243
   personnel needs and 217-218

progressive discipline 242-243, 268-270
recruitment 229-230
training and development 24, 239-240, 251-255
volunteers 243-245
persuasion 198
petty cash 320
phone interviews 233
physical resources 38, 216-217
Pink, Daniel 252-253
place, in marketing mix 167-171
planned giving 282
planning
  business plans 140-141
  as job function 5, 12, 35
  marketing plans 141-142
  master plans 138-140
  personnel needs 220
  purposes of 131
  recreation program 142-143
  strategic plans 23, 132-138
  technology 143-147
policies 111-112
policy making 112-113
politics, and budgets 307-308
positioning strategies 164, 203-204
Posner, B.Z. 10-11
PR (public relations) 178-180
Pregnancy Discrimination Act 222
pricing
  approaches to 290
  differential 297-298
  issues in 296-298
  in marketing mix 171-175
  objectives of 289-290
  program pricing 290-296
probability sampling 351-352
problem solving 147. *See also* decision making
problem-solving teams 93, 117
procedures, defined 113
process objectives 46
product, in marketing mix 164-167
production-oriented leaders 7
product life cycle 165-167
product publicity 179
profit, and sustainability 50
profitability ratios 327
program budgets 311-317
program fees 283
programmed decisions 147
programming competencies (CPRP) 360
progressive discipline 242-243, 268-270
promotion 175
promotions mix 175-180
property taxes

personal property 278-279
  real property 275-278
provincial park and recreation agencies 82
psychographics 160-162
public sector 79-83
public relations (PR) 178-180
purchase orders 320
purchase requisitions 320
purchasing procedures 320-322
purpose, in employee motivation 253-254
purposive (judgmental) sample 353

**Q**
qualitative research 342
quantitative research 342
questionnaires 343
quorum 102
quota sample 353

**R**
raters 346
rating scales 343
real property taxes 275-278
recreational user statues 59
recreation program plans 142-143
recruitment strategies 229-230, 243-244
reduced workweek 262
Rehabilitation Act of 1973 222
REI Co-op 281
releases and waivers 59
rental fees 283
repositioning strategies 204-205
request for proposal (RFP) 322
request for quotation (RFQ) 322
*Res ipsa loquitur* 60
resources
  adding personnel and 215-217
  team performance and 118
  types to manage 37-38
respondeat superior doctrine 60
responsibility, defined 33
retaliation, and employment laws 67
revenue bonds 288
revenue budget 305
revenue facilities 140
revenues, defined 275
revenue sources
  compulsory income 275-281
  contractual receipts 284-285
  earned income 283-284
  gratuitous income 281-282
  investment income 284
rewards, defined 259
RFP (request for proposal) 322
RFQ (request for quotation) 322
risk management 65-67
Robert's Rules of Order 102-103

rules, defined 113
rumors 191

**S**
sales promotions and incentives 177-178
sales revenue 284
sales tax 279-280
sampling 349-354
Schein, E.H. 95
Schein, P. 95
Schwartz, Tony 267
scientific management 11-13, 211
SCORE 140
S Corporations 87
screening interviews 231-233
secondary data 347
self-care 265-267
self-managed teams 93
self-perpetuating board 99
Senge, Peter 20-21, 191-192, 252
seniority-based rewards 264
services vs. goods 165
sexual harassment 67, 69-70
shared values, defined 40. *See also* values
shared vision 21, 42
shareholders 86
short-term goals 35, 44
simple structure 91
situational leadership theories 8-9
skill-based rewards 264
skills, in job descriptions 224
slander 61
Small Business BC 140
SMART objectives 45-46
snowball sample 353-354
social media
  as marketing tool 181-183, 199
  trends in 199
social networks 193
societal values 40-41
sociocultural noise 190
software 145
sole proprietorships 85
SOPs (standard operating procedures) 113
Southwest Airlines 111
sovereign immunity 59
span of control 90
special districts 80, 278
special fees 284
special recreation and park laws 79-80
sport safety statutes 59
staffing levels 213-214
staff meetings 116-117
staff relations 244-255
stage-based screening process 231
staggered daily schedules 262-263

standard operating procedures (SOPs) 113
standards 113-114
statement of financial position 323-324
state park and recreation agencies 82
states rights amendment 82
statute of limitations 59
strategic management 23
strategic planning
    defined 132
    Fairfax, Virginia example 361
    questions to answer 132
    six-step model 133-138
stratified sampling 351
strict liability 62
structural differentiation 109
suboptimization 110
subsidy rate 294-296
summative evaluation 342
supervisors
    adding personnel and 215-216
    in organizational structure 89-90
suspension of employees 242
sustainability 49-50
SWOT analysis 134-136
synergy 118-119
systematic changes 307
systematic sampling 352
systems theory 17-18
systems thinking 20-21

**T**
target marketing 159, 163
task forces 93, 117
tax abatements 276
tax-increment financing (TIF) 279
tax revenue 275-281
Taylor, Frederick 12
Taylorism 211
team leaders 8

team learning 21
teams
    defined 117
    in organizational design 92-94
    performance challenges 117-119
technical skills 34-35, 217-218
technology. *See also* social media
    in communication 199, 202
    in horizontal coordination 120
    resource management 38
technology planning 143-147
termination procedures 242, 270-271
three needs theory 255-256
TIF (tax-increment financing) 279
time-budget study 292
Title VII (Civil Rights Act) 68-69, 222
torts
    intentional 60-62
    negligence 57-60
total quality management (TQM) 18-19
traditional management 11-14
trait theories of leadership 6
transactional leadership 10
transformational leadership 10
transportation, and location 170-171
triple bottom line 49
Truesdale, Alyssa 54
Tuckman, B.W. 118-119

**U**
underlying assumptions 95
United Kingdom 72
unity of command principle 94
University of Michigan studies 7-8
unlimited liability 86
upward communication 192
user fees 283

**V**
values
    in employee orientation 238
    in internal communications 194
    sample value statements 41
    in teams 118
variable costs 287, 291
verbal communication 200-202
vertical coordination 110-116
vicarious liability 60
vision 21, 42, 131
voluntary sector 83-85
Volunteer Protection Act of 1997 65
volunteers
    defined 243
    discipline and dismissal 270-271
    immunity 65
    management of 243-245, 251
    rewards for 265
Vroom, Victor 257-258

**W**
waivers 59
Weber, Max 13-14
websites, dynamic 202
work allocation 214
workforce. *See* employees
work groups 92-93
working from home 263
work plans 304
work redesign 307
work schedules, as rewards 262-263
work specialization 89
written communication 202-203
written warnings 242, 268

**Y**
Yukon Wellness 355

**Z**
zero-based budgeting 317-318

# About the Authors

**Amy Hurd, PhD, CPRE,** is the director of the Illinois State University Graduate School and a professor of recreation and park administration within the School of Kinesiology and Recreation. While at Illinois State University, Hurd has taught undergraduate and graduate courses in management with an emphasis on marketing, human resources, and finance. Prior to coming to Illinois State University, she was a visiting lecturer in management at Indiana University, where she received her PhD.

As a practitioner, Hurd worked as the special events coordinator and as the marketing director for the park district in Champaign, Illinois. She has presented on and written extensively about management, competencies, and succession planning in public parks and recreation, including authoring four textbooks. Hurd was a visiting scholar at Srinakharinwirot University (Bangkok, Thailand) in the subject area of sustainable tourism, and she traveled to Opole University of Technology (Opole, Poland) and the Universidad de Cuyo and Universidad de Mendoza in Mendoza, Argentina, for a student and faculty cultural immersion experience. She is a regular instructor for Indiana University's executive development program, and she was elected to the American Academy for Park and Recreation Administration in 2014.

**Robert J. Barcelona, PhD,** serves as the department chair and as an associate professor in the department of recreation management and policy at the University of New Hampshire (UNH). Barcelona's research and writing interests focus on the intersection of sport and physical activity, positive youth development, and community recreation management, with a focus on improving access to active recreation and sport opportunities. He is also interested in training and professional development in the recreation and sport fields, particularly in community and campus recreation organizations.

Barcelona teaches both undergraduate and graduate courses focusing on management and leadership, research methods, strategic and master planning, program evaluation, youth development, and recreational sport management. He also works closely with community recreation and sport organizations on issues pertaining to master planning, strategic planning, and program evaluation. Barcelona worked as a practitioner in intercollegiate athletics and campus recreation. He has been on the faculty at Indiana University, Clemson University, and UNH, and he frequently teaches online courses in the distance education program at North Carolina State University.

**Jo An M. Zimmermann, PhD, CPRP,** is an associate professor and the undergraduate coordinator in the recreation administration program at Texas State University within the department of health and human performance. Zimmermann teaches undergraduate and graduate courses related to administration, finance, and marketing as well as the senior capstone course. Prior to coming to Texas State University, she was a senior lecturer in recreation management at Victoria University in Melbourne, Australia, as well as a visiting assistant professor in recreation administration at Clemson University, where she earned her PhD.

As a practitioner, Zimmermann worked as a recreation manager for the park district of Oak Park, Illinois, and as a recreation supervisor for the park district of Morton Grove, Illinois. She has presented and written on management and administrative roles in parks and recreation, including authoring chapters in textbooks. Zimmermann is a visiting professor at Beijing Sport University in Beijing, China, and has led students on study-abroad experiences in Australia. She is a regular presenter at the Texas Recreation and Park Society Annual Institute and is a co-convener of the Leisure Management Special Interest Group (SIG) for the World Leisure Organization.

**Janet Ready, MA,** received her master's degree in leisure studies from the University of Victoria and teaches in the recreation studies department of Angara College in Vancouver, British Columbia. Ready started her recreation career with the City of Burnaby parks, recreation, and cultural services department and worked in public recreation for over a decade prior to teaching. She has also guided hiking programs with Metro Vancouver and was a snowshoe guide at Mt. Seymour.

Ready is a past member of the Boys and Girls Club program committee and served as a director on the British Columbia Recreation and Parks Association board. She is passionate about connecting recreation theory to practice and works on applied research projects that support people working in the recreation field. She has presented at recreation conferences locally and nationally. In her free time, she mountain bikes, hikes, trail runs, does stand-up paddle boarding (with her dog Murphy), and volunteers on the Royal Canadian Marine Search and Rescue team.